SHAKESPEARE IN PRODUCTION

THE TAMING OF THE SHREW

The story of Katherina Minola and her marriage to Petruchio has been popular in the theatre for four centuries. The ongoing appeal of *The Taming of the Shrew* is easy to understand – it offers almost production-proof farce, plus the perennially popular joke of the battle of the sexes – but Katherina's story, and the joke of taming an unruly woman, have become increasingly controversial. This edition of *The Taming of the Shrew* examines how theatre directors and performers have explored the complexities of Katherina's story and that of Christopher Sly, the poor man whose story frames that of Katherina. The edition surveys a wide variety of theatrical interpretations of the play in the English-speaking world, particularly in the UK, North America, and Australia and New Zealand. It informs readers about precise details of the stage action in the context of contemporary theatrical, social and political conditions.

SHAKESPEARE IN PRODUCTION

SERIES EDITORS: J. S. BRATTON AND JULIE HANKEY

This series offers students and researchers the fullest possible staging of individual Shakespearean texts. In each volume a substantial introduction presents a conceptual overview of the play, marking out the major stages of its representation and reception. The commentary, presented alongside the New Cambridge Shakespeare edition of the text itself, offers detailed, line-by-line evidence for the overview presented in the Introduction, making the volume a flexible tool for further research. The editors have selected interesting and vivid evocations of settings, acting and stage presentation, and range widely in time and space.

ALREADY PUBLISHED
A Midsummer Night's Dream, edited by Trevor R. Griffiths
Much Ado About Nothing, edited by John F. Cox
Antony and Cleopatra, edited by Richard Madelaine
Hamlet, edited by Robert Hapgood
The Tempest, edited by Christine Dymkowski
King Henry V, edited by Emma Smith
The Merchant of Venice, edited by Charles Edelman
Romeo and Juliet, edited by James N. Loehlin

FORTHCOMING VOLUMES
Macbeth, edited by John Wilders
As You Like It, edited by Cynthia Marshall
Troilus and Cressida, edited by Frances Shirley
Twelfth Night, edited by Elizabeth Schafer

THE TAMING OF
THE SHREW

EDITED BY
ELIZABETH SCHAFER

Reader in Drama and Theatre Studies,
Royal Holloway, London University

CAMBRIDGE
UNIVERSITY PRESS

PUBLISHED BY THE PRESS SYNDICATE OF THE UNIVERSITY OF CAMBRIDGE
The Pitt Building, Trumpington Street, Cambridge, United Kingdom

CAMBRIDGE UNIVERSITY PRESS
The Edinburgh Building, Cambridge CB2 2RU, UK
40 West 20th Street, New York, NY 10011-4211, USA
477 Williamstown Road, Port Melbourne, VIC 3207, Australia
Ruiz de Alarcón 13, 28014 Madrid, Spain
Dock House, The Waterfront, Cape Town 8001, South Africa

http://www.cambridge.org

First published 2002

Printed in the United Kingdom at the University Press, Cambridge

Typeface Ehrhardt 10/12.5 pt.   *System* QuarkXPress [BTS]

A catalogue record for this book is available from the British Library.

Library of Congress Cataloguing in Publication Data

Shakespeare, William, 1564–1616
The Taming of the Shrew / edited by Elizabeth Schafer
p.   cm. – (Shakespeare in Production)
Includes bibliographical references and index
ISBN 0 521 66137 4 (hdbk) – ISBN 0 521 66741 0 (pbk)
1. Married people – Drama.   2. Padua (Italy) – Drama.   3. Shakespeare, William,
1564–1616. Taming of the Shrew.   4. Shakespeare, William, 1564–1616 – Dramatic
production.   5. Shakespeare, William, 1564–1616 – Stage history.   I. Schafer, Elizabeth.
II. Title.
PR2832.A2 S33 2002
822.3'3–dc21   2002067264

ISBN 0 521 66137 4 hardback
ISBN 0 521 66741 0 paperback

For my mother, Rosemary Schafer, who brought me up
to know better than ever to fall for a Petruchio

CONTENTS

ILLUSTRATIONS

SERIES EDITORS' PREFACE

It is no longer necessary to stress that the text of a play is only its starting-point, and that only in production is its potential realised and capable of being appreciated fully. Since the coming-of-age of Theatre Studies as an academic discipline, we now understand that even Shakespeare is only one collaborator in the creation and infinite recreation of his play upon the stage. And just as we now agree that no play is complete until it is produced, so we have become interested in the way in which plays often produced – and pre-eminently the plays of the national Bard, William Shakespeare – acquire a life history of their own, after they leave the hands of their first maker.

Since the eighteenth century Shakespeare has become a cultural construct: sometimes the guarantor of nationhood, heritage and the status quo, sometimes seized and transformed to be its critic and antidote. This latter role has been particularly evident in countries where Shakespeare has to be translated. The irony is that while his status as national icon grows in the English-speaking world, his language is both lost and renewed, so that for good or ill, Shakespeare can be made to seem more urgently 'relevant' than in England or America, and may become the one dissenting voice that the censors mistake as harmless.

'Shakespeare in Production' gives the reader, the student and the scholar a comprehensive dossier of materials – eye-witness accounts, contemporary criticism, promptbook marginalia, stage business, cuts, additions and rewritings – from which to construct an understanding of the many meanings that the plays have carried down the ages and across the world. These materials are organised alongside the New Cambridge Shakespeare text of the play, line by line and scene by scene, while a substantial introduction in each volume offers a guide to their interpretation. One may trace an argument about, for example, the many ways of playing Queen Gertrude, or the political transmutations of the text of *Henry V*; or take a scene, an act or a whole play, and work out how it has succeeded or failed in presentation over four hundred years.

For, despite our insistence that the plays are endlessly made and remade by history, Shakespeare is not a blank, scribbled upon by the age. Theatre history charts changes, but also registers something in spite of those changes. Some productions work and others do not. Two interpretations may be entirely different, and yet both will bring the play to life. Why? Without setting out to give absolute answers, the history of a play in the theatre can often show where the energy and shape of it lie, what has made it tick, through many permutations. In this way theatre history can find common ground with literary criticism. Both will find suggestive directions in the introductions to these volumes, while the commentaries provide raw material for readers to recreate the living experience of theatre, and become their own eye-witnesses.

J. S. Bratton
Julie Hankey

This series was originated by Jeremy Treglown and published by Junction Books, and later by Bristol Classical Press, as 'Plays in Performance'. Four titles were published; all are now out of print.

ACKNOWLEDGEMENTS

I would like to thank the Arts and Humanities Research Board (AHRB) for funding research trips to Australia and New Zealand, as well as to North America. Even more crucially, an AHRB teaching-relief grant enabled me to process the results of my research trips. I would also like to thank Royal Holloway, London University, for granting me sabbatical leave in autumn 2000.

I have incurred debts of gratitude at theatre archives in many countries. Special thanks go to: Jane Edmonds at the Stratford, Ontario Festival archive; Tom Gutteridge at the Queensland Theatre Company; Elizabeth Bernard at the Performing Arts Museum, Melbourne; Rachel Vowles at the Northcott Theatre, Exeter; Frances Carlyon at the Bristol Theatre Collection; Herbert Poetzl at the Reinhardt archive, Binghampton, New York State; Annette Fern at the Harvard Theatre Collection; David Ward and Helen Haynes at Royal Holloway; all the staff at the Shakespeare Centre, Stratford, Warwickshire; staff at the Toronto Metro Reference library, at the Billy Rose Collection, New York Public Library, at the Folger Library, Washington, and at the London Theatre Museum (especially at Blythe House). I would like to thank Pamela King and the Doomsday project archive at Lancaster University and St Martin's College for allowing me access to the Mediaeval Players' archive. Thanks also go to Pat Hawthorn at Downstage Theatre, Wellington, and to the press offices at the West Yorkshire Playhouse, the English Touring Company, and the Manchester Royal Exchange theatre. *Shrew*-hunting in general was also made easier thanks to help provided by Claire Cochrane, David Carnegie, Helen Ostovich, Jan McDonald, Julie Hankey and Barbara Hodgdon. Margaret Berrill was an excellent copy-editor; Maren Urschel and Caroline Steinbeis helped me with translations from German.

Shrew-spotting round the world was more fun because of the generosity of many people but special thanks go to: Ken and Rose Schafer; Anne Shells; Louise Woodford and Dave Foodey; Joanne Tompkins and Alan Lawson; Sally Jones and Mark Webb; Alan Filewod; Edwina and Neil Carson; Sue and Steve Stroud; Colin and Patti Lazzerini; Jenny and John Davies.

Special thanks also to Jacky Bratton, Richard Proudfoot and Vincent Jones, who all in different ways kept me up to scratch, read various drafts of this work with scrupulous attention to detail, and continued to challenge my thinking about this play.

EDITOR'S NOTE

Unless specified otherwise all notes on cuts and stage business are derived from promptbooks, printed acting editions or my own observations of video recordings and live performances. Precise source details can be found in the promptbook bibliography and Shattuck numbers (e.g. s34) are used to distinguish specific promptbooks where several exist.

Books listed in the Bibliography are referred to in the notes and commentary by author and page number; where an author has more than one entry in the Bibliography the date of publication is also given. Productions are referred to by name of director and date.

The play text used is *The Taming of the Shrew*, edited by Ann Thompson for the New Cambridge Shakespeare, Cambridge University Press, 1984. All references to and excerpts from *The Taming of A Shrew* are to the text edited by Stephen Roy Miller, for the New Cambridge Shakespeare, Cambridge University Press, 1998.

ABBREVIATIONS

AS	*The Taming of A Shrew*
BM	*Birmingham Mail*
BP	*Birmingham Post*
C&P	*Catharine and Petruchio* by David Garrick
DE	*Daily Express*
DM	*Daily Mail*
DS	*Daily Sketch*
DT	*Daily Telegraph*
ES	*Evening Standard* (earlier *Evening Standard and St James's Gazette*)
G	*Manchester Guardian*
G&M	*Toronto Globe and Mail*
I	*Independent*
ILN	*Illustrated London News*
IS	*Independent on Sunday*
K&P	*Katharine and Petruchio* by John Philip Kemble
KMK	*Kiss Me, Kate* music by Cole Porter, book by Bella and Samuel Spewack
NYT	*New York Times*
O	*Observer*
pbk	promptbook
RSC	Royal Shakespeare Company
s	Shattuck promptbook reference
s.d.	stage direction
SAG	*Shakespeare Around the Globe*, ed. Samuel Leiter
SMH	*Sydney Morning Herald*
ST	*Sunday Times*
STel	*Sunday Telegraph*
SUAH	*Stratford–Upon–Avon Herald*
T	*The Times*
TC	Theatre Company

PRODUCTIONS

This is a select chronology of English-language productions: unless otherwise stated, their location is London. Dates refer to first performance in the majority of cases; occasionally dates may refer to the earliest review located. When casting is known, the list of actors gives the performer of Katherina and then Petruchio. Some productions survived over decades but when the overall conception of the play remained stable, despite changes in production details and personnel, only the opening production is listed. Such revived productions are indicated by 'rev.'.

A survey of spin-offs and adaptations appears in Appendix 2, pp. 238–40.

Date	Director	Actors	Theatre
11 June 1594 (may be *A Shrew*)		Chamberlain's Men	Newington Butts
26 November 1633		King's Men	St James's Palace
9 April 1667	*Sauny the Scot*, by John Lacy	(1698 rev.) Susanna Verbruggen George Powell	(1698 rev.) Drury Lane
24 January 1716	*The Cobler of Preston*, by Christopher Bullock	n/a	Lincoln's Inn Fields
3 February 1716	*The Cobler of Preston*, by Charles Johnson	n/a	Drury Lane
25 February 1735	*Cure for a Scold*, by James Worsdale	Kitty Clive Charles Macklin	Drury Lane
18 March 1754	*Catharine and Petruchio*, by David Garrick	Hannah Pritchard Henry Woodward	Drury Lane
10 January 1789	*Katharine and Petruchio*, by J. P. Kemble	Sarah Siddons J. P. Kemble	Drury Lane
16 March 1844	Benjamin Webster (rev. 1847)	Louisa Nisbett Benjamin Webster	Haymarket

Date	Director	Actors	Theatre
15 November 1856	Samuel Phelps	Miss Atkinson Henry Marston	Sadler's Wells
18 January 1887	Augustin Daly (rev.)	Ada Rehan John Drew	Daly's, New York
23 January 1890	Frank Benson (rev.)	Constance Benson Frank Benson	Touring, then Globe, and Stratford-upon-Avon
30 May 1899	Oscar Asche (rev.)	Lily Brayton Oscar Asche	Theatre Royal, Wigan, then tour
2 October 1902	J. R. Pitman (rev. by the John Craig company)	Lillian Lawrence John Craig	Castle Square Theatre, Boston, Massachusetts
26 September 1903	Charles B. Hanford (rev.)	Marie Drofnah Charles B. Hanford	Lyceum, New York and touring
18 September 1905	Julia Marlowe, E. H. Sothern (rev.)	Julia Marlowe E. H. Sothern	Cleveland, then tour
12 August 1907	Clive Currie	Emil Leslie Clive Currie	West London
1908	D. W. Griffith	Florence Lawrence Arthur Johnson	Silent film – Biograph
26 September 1908	Margaret Anglin (rev.)	Margaret Anglin Henry Kolker (later Eric Blind)	Her Majesty's, Melbourne, later touring USA
15 December 1909	Max Reinhardt	Lucie Höflich Albert Basserman	Deutsches Theatre, Berlin (in German)
13 May 1911	Eade Montefiore	Alice Crawford Frederic Worlock	Robert Arthur's Company, Coronet Theatre
4 March 1913	Martin Harvey, William Poel as coadjutor	Nina de Silva Martin Harvey	Grand Theatre, Hull, then London and tour
5 October 1914	Hutin Britton, Matheson Lang	Hutin Britton William Stack	Old Vic
22 February 1915	Henry Jewett	Irby Marshal Leonard Willey	Boston Opera House, Massachusetts
25 June 1915	Clive Currie	Helena Millais Clive Currie	Tottenham Palace
28 February 1916	Philip Ben Greet (rev.)	Sybil Thorndike William Stack	Old Vic

Date	Director	Actors	Theatre
6 November 1916	Allan Wilkie (rev.)	Frediswyde Hunter-Watts Allan Wilkie	Touring, mainly Australia
15 June 1918	John Drinkwater	Margaret Chatwin William J. Rea	Birmingham Repertory Theatre
13 January 1919	George R. Foss	Catherine Willard Charles Warburton	Old Vic
12 January 1920	Charles Warburton and Russell Thorndike	Catherine Willard Charles Warburton	Old Vic
21 April 1920	W. Bridges-Adams (rev.)	Ethel Warwick Edmund Willard	Stratford-upon-Avon
13 December 1920	Robert Atkins (rev.)	Mary Sumner Rupert Harvey	Old Vic
29 December 1920	Walter Hampden	Mary Hall Walter Hampden	Arlington, Boston, Massachusetts, and touring
31 May 1921	Henry Baynton (rev.)	Gertrude Gilbert Henry Baynton	Touring UK
28 December 1921	Fritz Leiber (rev.)	Virginia Bronson Fritz Leiber	Lexington Theatre, New York
28 April 1922	Father Geoffrey Heald	Laurence Olivier as Katherina	All Saints Choir School, Stratford-upon-Avon
16 October 1922	Robert Atkins (rev.)	Florence Buckton Rupert Harvey	Old Vic
1923	Edwin J. Collins	Mlle Dacia Lauderdale Maitland	Silent film – Walturdaw, Gems of Literature
26 October 1925	Andrew Leigh	Edith Evans Balliol Holloway	Old Vic
18 December 1925	Richard Boleslavsky (rev.)	Estelle Winwood Rollo Peters	Klaw Theatre, New York
4 May 1927	Edward Massey	Miss Small K. A. Perry	Harvard Dramatic Club, Massachusetts
12 September 1927	Andrew Leigh	Sybil Thorndike Lewis Casson	Old Vic at the Lyric, Hammersmith
25 October 1927	H. K. Ayliff	Mary Ellis Basil Sidney	Garrick Theatre, New York

Date	Director	Actors	Theatre
14 December 1927	Anew McMaster	Esme Biddle Anew McMaster	Abbey Theatre, Dublin, touring
30 April 1928	H. K. Ayliff (rev.)	Eileen Beldon Scott Sunderland	Court Theatre
May 1928	J. Beresford Fowler	Sylvia Archer J. Beresford Fowler	Little Art Theatre Group, Playhouse, Melbourne
2 October 1928	Edward Dunstan (rev.)	May Fairclough Edward Dunstan	Dunstan Company, touring UK
1929, re-released 1966	Sam Taylor	Mary Pickford Douglas Fairbanks Snr	United Artists feature film
27 March 1930	Fritz Leiber	Virginia Bronson Fritz Leiber	Shubert, New York, (touring earlier)
13 October 1931	Harcourt Williams	Phyllis Thomas Ralph Richardson	Old Vic at Sadler's Wells
29 and 30 January 1932	Howard Rose, text cut by Dulcima Glasby	Barbara Couper Francis James	BBC radio
20 April 1932	Peter Dearing	Eileen Thorndike Russell Thorndike	Kingsway
27 January 1933	Percival Vivian	Mary Hone Curtis Cooksey	Shakespeare Theatre, New York
23 May 1933	W. Bridges-Adams	Madge Compton Anew McMaster	Stratford-upon-Avon
2 November 1933	Anew McMaster	Diana Wilson Anew McMaster	Chiswick Empire
7 March 1934	Michael Martin-Harvey	Elizabeth Addyman Henry Baynton	Oxford Playhouse
26 May 1934	Thomas Wood Stevens (40-minute version)	Jackson Perkins Carl Benton Reid	Globe, World's Fair, Chicago
1 January 1935	Henry Cass	Cathleen Nesbitt Maurice Evans	Old Vic at Sadler's Wells
10 March 1935	Peter Creswell	Mary Hinton Godfrey Tearle	BBC radio
22 April 1935	Harry Wagstaff Gribble	Lynn Fontanne Alfred Lunt	Theatre Guild, New York, touring
5 August 1935 (rev.)	Iden Payne	Catherine Lacey Neil Porter	Stratford-upon-Avon

Date	Director	Actors	Theatre
29 October 1935	Hilton Edwards	Coralie Carmichael Hilton Edwards	Gate Theatre, Dublin
February 1936	Kenneth Wicksteed (stage director)	Peggy Livesey Duncan Yarrow	Harold V. Neilson Co., touring
23 March 1937	Claud Gurney	Edith Evans Leslie Banks	New Theatre
26 July 1937		Elaine Barrie John Barrymore	NBC radio
2 August 1937	Angus Bowmer (rev. 1938)	Roberta Nourse Robert Stedman	Ashland, Oregon
2 August 1937	Brewster Morgan (adaptation by Gilbert Seldes)	Frieda Inescort Edward G. Robinson	CBS radio, USA
11 October 1937	Andrew Leigh	Phyllis Neilson-Terry Donald Wolfit	Malvern
28 March 1939	Tyrone Guthrie	Ursula Jeans Roger Livesey	Old Vic
3 April 1939	Theodore Komisarjevsky	Vivienne Bennett Alec Clunes	Stratford-upon-Avon
30 April 1939	Margaret Webster (cutdown version)	Grace Coppin Erford Gage	Globe, World's Fair, New York
12 May 1939	Thomas R. Ireland	Sara Luce K. Elmo Lowe	Cleveland Playhouse
28 May 1939	Margo Jones	Alice Krahl Reigh Walston	Houston Playhouse
9 August 1939	William Cottrell	LaVelle White Robert Stedman	Ashland, Oregon
8 November 1939	Donald Wolfit, Andrew Leigh	Rosalinde Fuller Donald Wolfit	Touring (extracts broadcast 11 July 1950, BBC radio)
1 October 1940	Phyllis Carver	Lorraine Stuart Ronald Sherman	Majestic Theatre, Brooklyn
16 February 1941	Peter Creswell	Fay Compton Godfrey Tearle	BBC radio
1 July 1941	Robert Atkins (rev.)	Claire Luce Patrick Kinsella	Open Air, Southwark Park

Date	Director	Actors	Theatre
12 October 1943	H. K. Ayliff	Margaret Leighton Scott Sunderland	Birmingham Repertory Theatre
26 April 1944	Clare Harris	Phyllis Barker Richard Matthews	Wilson Barrett Co., in Edinburgh, then Glasgow. Extracts broadcast on radio in 1946
2 August 1946	George Roche	Diana Stewart Michael Ingham	Grand Theatre, Wolverhampton
22 August 1946	Richard Taylor	Anne Deans Philip Morant	Grand Theatre, Halifax
2 March 1947	Eugene S. Bryden	Kristofa Simms John Ireland	El Patio, Hollywood
26 August 1947	John Burrell	Patricia Burke Trevor Howard	Old Vic at the Lyceum, Edinburgh, then New Theatre, London (extracts broadcast 2 September 1947, BBC radio)
15 December 1947	Margo Jones	Katherine Squire Tod Andrews	Gulf Oil Playhouse, Dallas
7 May 1948	Michael Benthall	Diana Wynyard Anthony Quayle	Stratford-upon-Avon
8 October 1948	Robert T. Eley	Beatrice Arthur Jack Burkhart	Cherry Lane, New York
6 August 1949	Allen Fletcher	Alta Wilson Richard Graham	Ashland, Oregon
23 January 1950	André Van Gyseghem	Ursula O'Leary George Hagan	Nottingham Playhouse (extracts broadcast 2 February 1950, BBC radio)
10 April 1950		Joyce Redman Meredith Burgess	ABC Theatre Guild US television
5 June 1950	Paul Nickell, adaptation by Worthington Miner	Lisa Kirk Charlton Heston	Studio One, CBS-TV
17 July 1950	Robert Atkins	Ruth Lodge Anthony Eustrel	Open Air, Regent's Park

Date	Director	Actors	Theatre
30 January 1951	Denis Carey	Yvonne Coulette John Phillips	Arts Theatre Salisbury, touring
25 April 1951	Margaret Webster	Claire Luce Ralph Clanton	City Center, New York (previously touring with Louisa Horton and Kendall Clark)
21 May 1951	Denis Carey	Pamela Alan Peter Coke	Bristol Old Vic, Theatre Royal
21 January 1952	Geoffrey Ost	Benedicta Leigh Patrick McGoohan	Playhouse, Sheffield
20 April 1952	Desmond Davis (adaptation by Barbara Nixon)	Margaret Johnston Stanley Baker	British TV
20 October 1952	Peter Potter	Iris Russell Andrew Keir	Glasgow Citizens'
16 February 1953	Douglas Emery	Elizabeth James John Boulter	Marlowe Repertory, Canterbury UK
2 March 1953	Paul Lee	Antonia Pemberton Patrick McGoohan	Midland TC, Coventry then touring
27 April 1953	Donald Wolfit	Rosalind Iden Donald Wolfitt	King's, Hammersmith
5 May 1953	Harry Lomax	Madeleine Newbury Maxwell Jackson	Oldham Repertory Theatre
9 June 1953	George Devine	Yvonne Mitchell Marius Goring	Stratford-upon-Avon
9 July 1953	Bobker ben Ali	Sonia Sorel Henry Brandon	Pasadena Playhouse
10 July 1953	Warren Jenkins	Margaret Drysdale Neil Landor	Arena TC, touring UK
4 August 1953	Philip Hanson	Patricia Saunders Howard Miller	Ashland, Oregon
2 March 1954	Val May	Catherine Campbell Paul Eddington	Ipswich Theatre
28 May 1954	Stuart Burge	Brenda Saunders Lee Montague	Hornchurch Theatre

Date	Director	Actors	Theatre
1 June 1954	George Devine (rev. of Devine 1953)	Barbara Jefford Keith Michell	Stratford-upon-Avon
29 June 1954	Tyrone Guthrie	Barbara Chilcott William Needles	Stratford, Ontario
9 August 1954	Peter Watts	Mary Wimbush Joseph O'Conor	BBC radio
18 October 1954	Hilton Edwards	Peggy Marshall Anew McMaster	Gaiety, Dublin
30 November 1954	Denis Carey	Ann Todd Paul Rogers	Old Vic
23 May 1955	Michael Benthall	Katharine Hepburn Robert Helpmann	Old Vic tour, Australia
29 October 1955	Ray Taylor	June Purdie Anthony Haigh	Bradford Civic Playhouse
18 March 1956	George Schaefer	Lilli Palmer Maurice Evans	NBC television, USA
23 July 1956	Paul Hebert	Andrée St Laurent Jean Coctu	Ste Adèle-en-Haut, Canada
3 August 1956	Stuart Vaughan	Colleen Dewhurst Jack Cannon	East River Park Amphitheatre, New York
5 August 1956	Norman Lloyd 1956 (rev. New York 1957)	Nina Foch Pernell Roberts	Stratford, Connecticut
7 May 1957	Willard Stoker	Mona Bruce William Roderick	Liverpool Playhouse
23 June 1958	Leslie French	Cecilia Sonnenberg Bernard Brown	Open Air, Regent's Park
21 August 1958	Robert Sheaf	Sheila Conner Keith Buckley	Garden Theatre, Stratford-upon-Avon
24 February 1959	Frank Dunlop	Joan Heal Peter Wyngarde	Bristol Old Vic, (televised 25 March 1959, ITV)
22 October 1959	Denis Carey (rev.)	Kate Reid Max Helpmann	Orillia Opera House, Canada
1960	Howard Sackler	Margaret Leighton Trevor Howard	HarperCollins audio books
26 April 1960	Frank Hauser	Sian Phillips Brewster Mason	Oxford Playhouse

Date	Director	Actors	Theatre
21 June 1960	John Barton	Peggy Ashcroft Peter O'Toole	Stratford-upon-Avon
25 July 1960	Robert Loper	Ann Hackney Gerard Larson	Ashland, Oregon
18 August 1960	Gerald Freedman	Jane White J. D. Cannon	Belvedere Lake, Central Park, New York
22 September 1960	David Turnbull	Margaret Robertson Peter Henchie	Gateway, Edinburgh
3 October 1960	David Paul	Julie Paul Michael Ellison	Guildford Repertory
13 September 1961	Maurice Daniels, redirecting Barton 1960	Vanessa Redgrave Derek Godfrey	RSC, Aldwych
6 February 1962	Frank Dunlop	Joan Heal John Neville	Nottingham Playhouse
14 May 1962	Derrick Goodwin	Jill Gascoine Peter Blythe	Living Theatre, Leicester
19 June 1962	Michael Langham	Kate Reid John Colicos	Stratford, Ontario
6 July 1962	Craig Noel	Diana Frothingham Michael Forrest	Old Globe, San Diego
6 March 1963	Stuart Vaughan	Nan Martin Robert Gerringer	Phyllis Anderson Theatre, New York
13 March 1963	John Wylie	Kay Chevalier Len Wayland	Alley Theatre, Houston
23 March 1963	William Glennon	Margaret Andrews Jonathan Frid	Playhouse, Pittsburgh
25 March 1964	Mel Shapiro	Bella Jarrett Jonathan Farwell	Arena Stage, Washington
16 July 1964	Chris Parr	Maria Aitken Andrew Snell	Oxford Stage Company, touring
15 July 1964	Vladek Sheybal	Sheila Ballantine Dinsdale Lansden	Open Air, Regent's Park and tour
9 November 1964	John Brockington	Jaqueline Brooks Lee Taylor	Vancouver Playhouse
30 December 1964	John Hirsch	Pat Galloway Len Cariou	Manitoba TC, Winnipeg

Date	Director	Actors	Theatre
10 March 1965	Robert Cartland	Lisa Daniely Donald Douglas	Belgrade, Coventry
22 June 1965	Joseph Anthony	Ruby Dee John Cunningham	Stratford, Connecticut
28 June 1965	Joseph Papp	Ellen Holly Roy Shuman	Delacorte Mobile Theatre, New York
5 October 1965	Ann Stutfield	Bronwen Williams Roger Heathcott	Marlowe Theatre, Canterbury
11 October 1966	Michael Ashton	Gemma Jones Philip Voss	Colchester, Essex
29 November 1966	Clive Perry	Patricia Heneghan Kenneth Farrington	Phoenix Theatre, Leicester
1967	Franco Zeffirelli	Elizabeth Taylor Richard Burton	Columbia Pictures feature film
5 April 1967	Trevor Nunn and Mike Leigh	Janet Suzman Michael Williams	Stratford-upon-Avon
5 April 1967	Christopher Denys	Fionnula Flanagan Frederick Jaeger	Old Vic at the Little Theatre, Bristol
24 July 1967	Richard D. Risso	Ann Kinsolving Tom Donaldson	Ashland, Oregon
29 January 1968	Eugene Gallant	Karen Austin Anthony Jenkins	Bastion TC, Victoria, Canada
7 August 1969	J. Morton Walker	Robin Humphrey Alvah Stanley	Missouri Repertory Theatre
26 November 1969	John Ulmer	Lucy Martin Eric Tavaris	West Springfield, Massachusetts
31 March 1970	John Going	Cleo Holladay David Frazier	Cleveland Playhouse, Ohio
28 October 1970	Anton Rodgers	Elizabeth Bennett David Suchet	Northcott, Exeter
18 November 1970	Frank Dunlop	Jane Lapotaire Jim Dale	Young Vic
1970–1	Antony Tuckey	Jenny Austen Paul Shelly	Liverpool Playhouse
31 March 1971	Val May	Barbara Jefford John Turner	Theatre Royal, Bath, Bristol Old Vic company

Date	Director	Actors	Theatre
8 June 1971	Nagle Jackson	Elizabeth Huddle Laurence Guittard	Old Globe, San Diego
20 July 1971	Anthony Wiles	Jeanne DeBaer David Darlow	Champlain Shakespeare Festival
20 September 1971	Michael Langham	Michele Shay Len Cariou	Guthrie Theatre, Minneapolis
14 October 1971	Dorothy Dryden	Annette Campbell Robert Wolberg	Stagelights Two, New York
29 October 1971	Richard Eyre	Kika Markham Antony Webb	Lyceum, Edinburgh
23 January 1972	Gene Feist, Gui Andrisano	Joan Bassie Michael Wager	Roundabout Theatre, New York
30 January 1972	R. Edward Leonard	Lillian Evans Woody Eney	Alley Theatre, Dallas
7 March 1972	Richard Simpson	Joanna van Gyseghem Richard Moore	Everyman, Cheltenham
10 March 1972	Robin Lovejoy	Lyndell Rowe John Bell	Old Tote TC, Parade Theatre, Sydney (later broadcast by the ABC)
23 March 1972	Kenneth Parrott	Alexandra Browning Victor Winding	Orbit TC, Nuffield Studio, Lancaster and tour
18 June 1972	Robert Benedetti	Elizabeth Cole James Edmondson	Ashland, Oregon
27 June 1972	Paul Barry	Catherine Byers Peter MacLean	New Jersey Shakespeare Festival, Madison
5 July 1972	Jonathan Miller	Joan Plowright Anthony Hopkins	Festival Theatre, Chichester
5 October 1972	Douglas Campbell	Jane Casson Paul Angelis	Crucible, Sheffield
15 January 1973	Jean Gascon	Pat Galloway/ Anni Lee Taylor Alan Scarfe	Stratford, Ontario, and European and Canadian tour

Date	Director	Actors	Theatre
13 February 1973	Val May	Elizabeth Power Stephen Moore	Old Vic, Bristol, Little Theatre, and tour
1 March 1973	Warren Enters	Linda Carlson Richard Greene	Studio Arena Theatre, Buffalo
7 April 1973	Tina Packer	Susan Cardwell Kingsley Terry Hinz	Shakespeare and Company, Stratford-upon-Avon, later New York
11 June 1973	Ian Cottrell	Fenella Fielding Paul Daneman	BBC Radio 4 broadcast, repeated 2 August 1976
14 September 1973	Richard Eyre	Prunella Scales Bryan Marshall	Nottingham Playhouse
25 September 1973	Clifford Williams	Susan Fleetwood Alan Bates	Stratford-upon-Avon
3 October 1973	Joan Knight	Angela Barlow Philip Guard	Perth, Scotland
1 November 1973	Charles Marowitz (adaptation)	Thelma Holt Nikolas Simmonds	Open Space Theatre
December 1973	William Ball (rev.)	Fredi Olster Marc Singer	American Conservatory Theatre, San Francisco, (TV broadcast, 10 November 1976)
1974	Peter Seabourne	Madeline Blakeney David Suchet	The Shakespeare Series video
January 1974	Malcolm Black	Tammy Grimes Ron O'Neal	Walnut St Theatre, Philadelphia
22 February 1974	Giles Havergal	Angela Chadfield David Hayman	Glasgow Citizens'
6 March 1974	Malcolm McKay	Stephanie Fayerman David Sibley	Gateway Theatre, Chester
29 March 1974	Hilton Edwards	Kate Flynn Paddy Bedford	Gate, Dublin
6 July 1974	Frank Dwyer	Jacqueline Yancey Patrick Egan	Monmouth, USA

Date	Director	Actors	Theatre
28 September 1974	Mervyn Thompson	Alannah O'Sullivan Stewart Ross	James Hay Theatre, Christchurch, New Zealand
2 October 1974	Jonathan Pryce	Katherine Fahy Del Henney	Liverpool Everyman
7 October 1974	James Roose-Evans	Susan Hampshire Nicky Henson	Shaw Theatre, London
7 October 1974	Christopher Newton	Denise Fergusson Michael Ball	Playhouse Theatre Centre, Vancouver
18 October 1974	Caroline Eves	Yvonne Edgell Robert McIntosh	Theatre Royal, Stratford East
23 January 1975	Garland Wright	Linda Carlson Michael Parish	Indiana Repertory Theatre
13 February 1975	Jan Sargent	Mary McCusker John Livesey	Tyneside TC
14 March 1975	James Cellan Jones	Penelope Wilton Daniel Massey	Lyceum, Edinburgh
2 April 1975	Alan Edwards	Diane Cilento Robin Ramsay	Queensland TC, Brisbane
7 May 1975	Mervyn Willis	Zoe Wanamaker Jeremy Irons	New Shakespeare Company, touring
16 September 1976	Bill Cain	Sandy Proctor Gray Sterling Swann	Boston Shakespeare Company, Massachusetts
6 October 1976	Ian Mullins	Charlotte Cornwell Christopher Timothy	Redgrave Theatre, Farnham
10 November 1976	William Ball (revival of 1973 production)	Fredi Olster Marc Singer	WNET-TV, US
19 November 1976	Chris Hayes	Heather Ramsay Jonathan Burn	Marlowe Theatre, Canterbury
18 February 1977	Frank Hauser	Wendy Craig Joss Ackland	Billingham Forum Theatre, touring
5 March 1977	William Davis	Lally Cadeau Dan MacDonald	Theatre New Brunswick, Fredericton, Canada
31 May 1977	Laird Williamson	Maureen Anderman Daniel J. Travanti	Old Globe, San Diego

Date	Director	Actors	Theatre
14 June 1977	Peter Bell	Shirin Taylor Clive Wood	Jolliffe Studio Theatre, Swindon
July 1977	Barnet Kellman	Susannah Halston John Woodson	North Carolina Shakespeare Company
3 August 1977	R. Lev Mailer	Leigh Kavanaugh Pierrino Mascarino	Globe Playhouse, Los Angeles
18 August 1977	Daniel Sullivan	Sara Woods Dennis Lipscomb	Great Lakes Shakespeare Festival
15 September 1977	Bill Cain	S. Proctor-Gray Sterling Swann	Boston Shakespeare Company, Massachusetts
22 September 1977	John North	Joanna Zorsian Trevor Allen Davis	Derby Playhouse
10 February 1978	Robert Robertson	Miranda Bell Boyd Nelson	Dundee Repertory Theatre
10 March 1978	J. P. Duffy	Terry Mazer Peter Duffy	RML Theatre, New York
6 April 1978	John Henry Davis	Stephanie Cotsirilos Eric Booth	Equity Library Theatre, New York
19 April 1978	Michael Bogdanov	Paola Dionisotti Jonathan Pryce	Stratford-upon-Avon
29 April 1978	Martin S. Platt	Greta Lambert Daniel Kern	Alabama Shakespeare Festival
16 June 1978	Judd Parkin	Fredi Olster Rick Hamilton	Ashland, Oregon
26 June 1978	Frederick Proud	Kate O'Mara Henry Knowles	Ludlow Festival
4 July 1978	Michael Bishop	Rosalind Barker Peter Cluer	Cotswold Playhouse, Stroud
16 August 1978	Wilford Leach	Meryl Streep Raúl Juliá	Delacorte, New York
8 February 1979	Martin L. Platt	Shannon Eubanks John-Frederick Jones	Alaska Repertory Theatre

Date	Director	Actors	Theatre
15 May 1979	Bob Carlton	Sarah Beck Russell Henderson	Theatre Royal, York, and touring
30 May 1979	James Dunn (rev. of 1970 College of Marin production)	Alice Rorvik Mark Rasmussen	Cannery Theatre, San Francisco
1 July 1979	Pamela Hawthorn	Margot Dionne Graeme Campbell	Stratford, Ontario, Third Stage
19 July 1979	Hal Passoth	Lynne Kadish Mircha Carven	Theatre Ensemble, New York
14 August 1979	Graham Dixon, Graham Corry	Rikki McDonald Paul Mason	Bondi Pavilion, Sydney
30 October 1979	John Dillon	Rose Pickering James Pickering	Milwaukee Repertory Theatre
14 December 1979	Denise Coffey (rev. 1980)	Susan Wright John Neville	Neptune Theatre, Halifax, Canada
6 February 1980	Daniel Sullivan	Katherine Ferrand J. Kenneth Campbell	Seattle Repertory Theatre
13 February 1980	Richard McElvain	Janet Rodgers Henry Woronicz	Boston Shakespeare Company, Massachusetts
1 April 1980	Roger Hendricks Simon	Ellen Newman John Neville- Andrews	Folger, Washington
27 June 1980	Gillette A. Elvgren	Lisa Bansavage Ken Stirbl	Stephen Foster Memorial Theatre, Pittsburgh
11 July 1980	Nagle Jackson	Leslie Geraci John S. Mansfield	Shakespeare Festival of Dallas
22 July 1980	Ted Davis	Cecile Mann Paul Haggard	Cumston Hall, Monmouth, USA
September 1980	Douglas C. Sprigg	Jennifer Savidge Al Alu	Theatre 40, Beverly Hills
8 October 1980	Keith Digby	Sharry Flett John Peters	Theatre Three, Edmonton, Alberta
8 October 1980	Felicity Taylor	Lesley E. Bennett Robert Duncan	Octagon, Bolton
23 October 1980	Jonathan Miller	Sarah Badel John Cleese	BBC TV

Date	Director	Actors	Theatre
5 November 1980	Nicolas Young	Nyree Dawn Porter Christopher Neame	Connaught, Worthing
4 February 1981	Antony Tuckey	Geraldine Wright Brian Ralph	Wolsey, Ipswich
11 February 1981	Pamela Brighton	Susan Hogan Michael Hogan	Toronto Young People's Theatre
14 February 1981	Lane Davies	Karen Austin Steve Stuart	Globe Playhouse, Los Angeles
21 May 1981	Lyall Watson	June Abbott David Purcell	Finborough Arms, then Court Theatre
15 June 1981	Peter Dews	Sharry Flett Len Cariou	Stratford, Ontario (CBC broadcast 1982)
23 June 1981	William Foeller	Terry Fimiano Brian Morgan	Villanova Festival, Philadelphia
4 July 1981	Mary Rae Thewlis	Lura Dolas Tony Amendola	Berkeley Shakespeare Festival
17 July 1981	Tom Markus	Margaret Reed David O. Harum	Colorado Shakespeare Festival
17 September 1981	Anne McNaughton	Kandis Chappell John Callahan	San Jose Repertory
11 February 1982	Richard Ouzounian	Leueen Willoughby Michael Ball	Manitoba Theatre Centre, Winnipeg
21 January 1982	Richard Cottrell	June Ritchie Terence Wilton	Cambridge Arts Theatre, touring
1982 (taped December)	John Allison	Karen Austin Franklin Seales	Shakespeare Video Society, Century, USA
1 May 1982	Kenneth Kramer	Nancy Palk Tom McBearth	Globe Theatre, Regina
7 June 1982	Richard Digby Day	Kate O'Mara Christopher Neame	Open Air, Regent's Park
8 July 1982	Bob Carlton	Karen Mann Richard Blain	Bubble TC, Cheam Park

Date	Director	Actors	Theatre
22 July 1982	Joseph Hardy	Amanda McBroom Tony Musante	Old Globe, San Diego
3 August 1982	Frank Condon	Laurie O'Brien Ralph Steadman	San Francisco Actors' Craft Repertory
14 September 1982	Paul Chamberlain	Nina Holloway Greg Crutwell	Orchard TC, Barnstaple, touring
7 October 1982	Barry Kyle	Sinead Cusack Alun Armstrong	Stratford-upon-Avon
7 February 1983	Roy Surrette	Kim Seary Colm Feore	Carousel Theatre, Vancouver
28 May 1983	Toby Robertson	Margot Dionne David Purdham	Huntington TC, Boston, Massachusetts
8 June 1983 rev. 1984	Fred Ollerman et al.	Marie Mathay David Cecsarini	American Players, Spring Green, Wisconsin
1 July 1983	William James Kelly	Susanne Egli Julian Bailey	Camden Shakespeare Company, Maine
1 August 1983	Allen Belknap	Lilene Mansell John-Frederick Jones	Alabama Shakespeare Festival
5 August 1983	Ron Palmer	Elizabeth Charrot Christopher Birch	Kent Repertory
10 November 1983	John Briggs	Judith Townsend Traber Burns	Texas Shakespeare Theatre, Dallas
14 January 1984	Gary Gisselman	Penny Metropulos Don West	Arizona TC
15 March 1984	Pamela Hawthorne	Laura Ann Worthen Jack Stehlin	Missouri Repertory Theatre
9 May 1984	Gordon M. Smith	Jane Davidson Richard Hammond	Drama Centre, Glasgow
10 May 1984	Adrian Brown	Elvi Hale George Murcell	St George's
5 June 1984	Pat Patton	Joan Stuart-Morris Joe Vincent	Ashland, Oregon

Date	Director	Actors	Theatre
12 July 1984	Sanford Robins	Joyce Harris Stephen Pelinski	Cedar City, Utah
9 August 1984	David Hammond	Taylor Young John Hertzler	Lake Tahoe, USA
10 January 1985	Janet Farrow	Julann Rosa Douglas Overtoom	American Shakespeare Repertory Theatre, New York
7 March 1985	David Ultz	Susan Cox Fiona Victory	Theatre Royal, Stratford East
1 May 1985	Zoe Caldwell	Frances Conroy David Rasche	Stratford, Connecticut
1 May 1985	Bruce Cornwell	Judith Reagan Dugg Smith	Pearl TC, Nameless Theatre, New York
8 July 1985	Michael Fawkes	Gabrielle Rose Leon Pownall	Nanaimo, Vancouver Island
12 July 1985	Carl Heap	Mark Heap Mark Saban	Mediaeval Players, touring UK and Australia
26 July 1985	Maureen Clarke	Sonja Lanzener David Adamson	Riverside Shakespeare Company, New York
27 August 1985	Di Trevis	Sian Thomas Alfred Molina	RSC tour
1986	John Hale	Sian Phillips Peter O'Toole	Living Shakespeare, New York (56-minute cassette)
29 January 1986	Ron Ulrich	Marcia Kash James Haworth	St Catharine's Press Theatre, Canada
22 April 1986	Toby Robertson and Christopher Selbie	Vanessa Redgrave Timothy Dalton	Theatr Clwyd, then Theatre Royal, Haymarket
27 October 1986	Jean-Luc Bastien	Nathalie Gascon Guy Nadon	Théâtre Denise Pelletier, Montreal
5 February 1987	Glen Walford	Eithne Hannigan Bob Hewis	Everyman, Liverpool
7 February 1987	Elizabeth Ball	Barbara E. Russell David Ley	Carousel Theatre, Vancouver

Date	Director	Actors	Theatre
10 August 1987	Lesley Hill	Karen Gluck Gary Merry	Carlton Centre, Edinburgh
3 September 1987	Jonathan Miller	Fiona Shaw Brian Cox	Stratford-upon-Avon
September– October 1987	David Kershaw	Jo Mossman-Ellis Andrew Sheldon	Red Bull TC, Lincs.
26 October 1987	Peter Woodward ('play manager')	Kate O'Mara Tim Woodward	British Actors' TC, touring
9 October 1987	Keith Digby	Colleen Winton Eric Schneider	Bastion TC, Victoria, Canada
22 January 1988	Jeremy Mortimer	Cheryl Campbell Bob Peck	BBC sound archive
27 January 1988	Charles Nowosielski	Emma Currie Robin Begg	Brunton Theatre, Musselburgh
16 February 1988	Julie Taymor	Sheila Dabney Sam Tsoutsouvas	Triplex Theatre, New York
1 June 1988	Richard Monette	Goldie Semple Colm Feore	Stratford, Ontario
1 July 1988	Gordon McCall	Pamela Haig David Beairsto	Shakespeare on the Saskatchewan
7 July 1988	Richard Palmer	Elaine Hallam Peter Sowerbutts	Kent Repertory
13 October 1988	Michael Winter	Belinda Davison Richard Bonneville	Mercury Theatre, Colchester
26 January 1989	John Ramster	Claire Davies Scott Handy	European Theatre Group, Cambridge
31 May 1989	Spiro Veloridos	Stephanie Clayman Dan Gately	Publick Theatre, Boston, Massachusetts
31 May 1989	Tony Rust	Tim Zary Denise Dalfo (reverse gender production)	Quinapulus TC, Village Theatre New York
17 August 1989	Aubrey Mellor	Victoria Longley John Wood	Royal Queensland TC
26 October 1989	Pat Trueman	Tesa Wojtczak Lennox Greaves	Swan Theatre, Worcester

Date	Director	Actors	Theatre
22 June 1990	A. J. Antoon	Tracey Ullman Morgan Freeman	Delacorte Theatre, New York
10 July 1990	Robin Midgley	Toyah Willcox John Labanowski	Cambridge TC, touring
25 September 1990	Bill Alexander	Naomi Wirthner Gerard Murphy	RSC touring
10 October 1990	Alison Sutcliffe	Kate Nicholls Ian Gelder	Leicester Haymarket
7 November 1990	Virginia Boyle	Leigh Gleeson Mathew Stewart	Darned Sock TC, Sydney
8 November 1990	Mark Brickman	Maureen Beattie Bruce White	Crucible, Sheffield
29 May 1991	David Beaton	Caroline Lawrie Robin Brockman	Rose Theatre
14 June 1991	Sandy McCallum	Sheryl Taub Henry Woronicz	Ashland, Oregon
21 June 1991	Murray Lynch	Judith Gibson Jim Moriarty	Hannah Playhouse, Downstage Theatre, Wellington, New Zealand
22 June 1991	Roger Hodgman	Pamela Rabe Hugo Weaving	Melbourne TC
28 October 1991	Dee Hart	Debbie Radcliffe John Hug	New End Theatre, London
29 February 1992	Hallum and Clark	Sandra Rasmussen K. C. Kelly	Arts Centre, Christchurch, New Zealand
26 March 1992	Bill Alexander	Amanda Harris Anton Lesser	Stratford-upon-Avon
25 April 1992	Janet Farrow	Carol Dearman Kevin Keating	Classic TC, Dallas
12 June 1992	Jon Pope	Lucy Tregear Chris Wright	Dukes Theatre, Lancaster
16 July 1992	John Hadden	Melinda Lopez Malcolm Ingram	Shakespeare and Co., Lenox, Massachusetts
25 September 1992	Greg Miron	Christina Collins Nigel Hamer	Bathurst Street Theatre, Toronto

Date	Director	Actors	Theatre
23 October 1992	Ian Wooldridge	Kathryn Howden Kenny Bryans	Royal Lyceum, Edinburgh
19 April 1993	Jude Kelly	Nichola McAuliffe Brian Protheroe	West Yorkshire Playhouse
22 April 1993	Patrick Sandford	Louise Gold Jason Connery	Nuffield, Southampton
May 1993 tour	Freda Kelsall	Janet George John Spooner	Hebden Bridge
1 June 1993	Toby Robertson	Cathy Tyson Geordie Johnson	Open Air, Regent's Park
3 July 1993	Kenneth Albers	Sarah Day Jonathan Adams	American Players Spring Green, Wisconsin
22 July 1993	John Bourgeois	Maria Ricossa John Evans	Skylight Theatre, Toronto
2 November 1993	John Durnin	Jacqueline Dutoit Alan Cody	Northcott, Exeter
23 November 1993	Barbara Gaines	Kristine Thatcher Scott Wentworth	Shakespeare Repertory, Chicago
March 1994	Robin Midgley	Paula McFetridge Ian Beattie	Lyric Theatre, Belfast
17 March 1994 rev. 1996	Sue Rider	Deborah Mailman Andrew Buchanan	La Boite, Brisbane
24 April 1994	John Bell	Essie Davis Christopher Stollery	Bell Shakespeare Company, touring Australia, ABC radio broadcast and audio-cassette
25 June 1994	Val May	Prunella Gee Michael Simkins	Ludlow Castle
7 July 1994	Jeremiah Kissel	Chloe Leamon Michael O'Brien	Cumston Hall, Monmouth, Massachusetts
15 July 1994	Peter Hinton	Eleanor Crowder Greg Kramer	Ottawa Shakespeare Festival
1994 tour	Mary Hartman	Margaret McGirr Steve Cardamore	Shenandoah Express
21 April 1995	Mihai Maniutiu	Josette Simon James Macpherson	Leicester Haymarket

Date	Director	Actors	Theatre
21 April 1995	Gale Edwards	Josie Lawrence Michael Siberry	Stratford-upon-Avon
8 July 1995	Alison Quigan	Rachel Nash Ross Gumble	Centrepoint Theatre, Palmerston, New Zealand
5 January 1996	Jackson Phippin	Kate Skinner James McDonnell	Center Stage, Baltimore
28 February 1996	Alan Holy	Veronica Housen Peter Green	Lightning Strike Theatre Experience, Adelaide Zoo
25 April 1996	Patrick Tucker	Lucy Peacock Geraint Wyn-Davies	Original Shakespeare Company, Toronto
30 June 1996	James Dunn	Colleen Quinn Mark Harelik	Old Globe, San Diego
1 August 1996	Gregory Thompson	Katherine Grice Danny Scheinmann	aandbc TC, Lincoln's Inn
13 April 1997	Denise Coffey	Michelle Fisk Andrew Gillies	Citadel Theatre and NAC Ottawa
13 May 1997	Richard Rose	Lucy Peacock Peter Donaldson	Stratford, Ontario
1998	Clive Brill	Frances Barber Roger Allam	Arkangel audio-cassettes
12 February 1998	Andrei Serban	Kristin Flanders Don Reilly	Boston Phoenix, Massachusetts
27 May 1998	Nick Cohen and David Bridel	Vanessa Earl Christopher Brand	Bloomsbury Theatre, London
20 June 1998	Eleanor Holdridge	Mark Woollett Celia Madeoy	Shakespeare and Co., Lenox, Massachusetts
2 July 1998	Kevin Sheard	Alex Johnston Victor Correia	Queere Shakespeare Company, Toronto
5 October 1998	Stephen Unwin	Kacey Ainsworth David Cardy	English Touring Theatre
27 October 1998	Andrei Serban	Sophia Skiles Charles Anthony Burks	La Mama, New York

Date	Director	Actors	Theatre
1998 tour	Ralph Alan Coren and Peggy O'Brien	Kate Norris Carl Martin	Shenandoah Express
17 June 1999	Mel Shapiro	Allison Janney Jay O. Sanders	Delacorte Theatre, New York
23 June 1999	Peter Hamilton	Rachel Vowles Tim Knight	Crediton, Devon
20 July 1999	Ben Crocker	Anna Northam Mark Healey	Northcott, Exeter
27 August 1999	Guy Roberts	Andrea Osborn Steve Shearer	State TC, Austin, Texas
20 October 1999	Lindsay Posner	Monica Dolan Stuart McQuarrie	RSC, the Pit, then tour
10 September 2000	Melanie Harris	Ruth Mitchell Gerard McSorley	BBC Radio 3 and audio-cassette
28 February 2001	Helena Kaut-Howson	Tanya Ronder Lloyd Hutchinson	Manchester Royal Exchange

INTRODUCTION

The story of Katherina Minola and her marriage to Petruchio has been popular in the theatre for over four centuries. While the ongoing appeal of *The Taming of the Shrew* is easy to understand – it offers almost production-proof farce plus the perennially popular joke of the battle of the sexes – Katherina's story has nevertheless gone through some startling permutations over the years. So while for two hundred years Katherina's taming was unambiguously applauded, and it was standard practice for Petruchio to crack a whip around the stage like a lion tamer, more recent Katherinas and Petruchios tend to be complex, sometimes even tragic; performances of Katherina's notorious last speech often suggest signs of resistance or irony, and *The Shrew* now routinely attracts controversy. However, controversy is nothing new in relation to this play: controversies of various kinds – theatrical, bibliographical and political – have dogged it from the very beginning.

A TALE OF TWO SHREWS

The Taming of the Shrew was first published in the 1623 Folio of Shakespeare's plays, a collection put together by Shakespeare's colleagues John Heminges and Henry Condell. The Folio text of the play is unsatisfactory in several ways, the most obvious problem being poor continuity.[1] *The Taming of the Shrew* is also clearly related to, but very different from, a quarto text published in 1594, *The Taming of A Shrew*, and while there is still disagreement about the precise nature of the quarto, the most popular arguments are:[2]

1 It is a memorial reconstruction of Shakespeare's play, based on memories of performances, by persons unknown, for reasons unknown, with substantial changes and additions.
2 It is a first draft which Shakespeare revised.
3 It is an adaptation by someone (possibly Shakespeare himself) who was not unduly concerned about preserving Shakespeare's original words.
4 It is a source for Shakespeare's play.
5 It is a play which uses the same source (an Ur-*Shrew*) as Shakespeare.
6 It is a combination of any of the above.

---

1 For a list of problems with the Folio text, see e.g. Thompson (160–4), Wells and Taylor.
2 See Miller 1998 for a recent, detailed discussion of these arguments.

Personally, I am most persuaded by the argument that *A Shrew* originates from a deliberate adaptation of *The Shrew*, possibly an adaptation made for touring, where a smaller group of performers would be playing in found spaces rather than in playhouses equipped, for example, with the means for placing Christopher Sly 'aloft', as in the Folio (Induction 2.0 s.d.), instead of more simply in a chair, as in the quarto.

A Shrew is important to the stage history of *The Shrew* for three reasons: it helps to date the play; it may reveal details of early modern staging (see commentary, e.g. 4.3.35); and it is the only extant source of the full Christopher Sly framework. While *The Shrew* opens with two Sly scenes but then drops him after he starts falling asleep at the end of 1.1, *A Shrew* keeps Sly onstage commenting on, and occasionally interacting with, the characters in the inner play until he finally falls asleep at the end of what would be 5.1 in the Folio. Sly is then returned to the alehouse where the Lord first found him, and wakes up to find he is no longer a lord, but convinced that he now knows how to tame a shrew, a naïve confidence which is not shared by the audience.[3]

A Shrew also condenses the taming story, relocates to Athens, gives Katherina (now Kate) two sisters instead of one, adds some Marlovian poetry (which could be read as plagiarism, *hommage* or parody) and, like the Folio, gets into some continuity tangles. While Kate differs from the Folio's Katherina in several ways, perhaps the most striking difference is that Kate reveals in an aside why she is taking on Petruchio, renamed Ferando, as a husband:

> But yet I will consent and marry him,
> For I methinks have lived too long a maid,
> And match him too, or else his manhood's good   (3.169–71)

This contrasts with the Folio's Katherina, who never articulates why, after stating in 2.1 that she will not marry Petruchio, she shortly afterwards becomes upset in 3.2 when it appears Petruchio is not going to turn up to the wedding. Kate's aside, which may be making explicit what the boy actor playing Katherina enacted between the lines of the original performance of *The Shrew*, also anticipates what many actresses have tried to indicate: that Katherina does choose to marry Petruchio, whether this is because she has

---

3 That the original reception of the play included this reading is suggested by Sir John Harington, who in 1596 noted in *The Metamorphosis of Ajax*: 'For the shrewd wife, read the book of Taming a Shrew, which hath made a number of us so perfect, that now every one can rule a shrew in our country, save he that hath her.' Although Miller (1993, 66) suggests that Harington's comments are proverbial, they fit very well with the post-play action implied by *A Shrew*.

decided she has lived too long a maid, or because she relishes the battle to come, or even because she has, in the favourite modern interpretation, fallen in love or lust with him at first sight.

A Shrew was clearly popular – there were three printings of the text – and it was the only form of Katherina's story in print during Shakespeare's lifetime; the Folio superseded *A Shrew* only in 1623, seven years after Shakespeare's death. The quarto text used to be denigrated as a 'bad' quarto but recently Graham Holderness and Bryan Loughrey (13) have argued that it is rather a 'brilliantly inventive popular Elizabethan play', Mychelle Hopkins directed a production (Shakespeare Institute, Birmingham University, 24–6 March 1999) which demonstrated that the text is playable, and Leah Marcus has put the case that *A Shrew* has been undervalued and misread by many critics. The title page of *A Shrew* also tells us that the play was 'sundry times acted by the Right Honourable the Earl of Pembroke his servants'.[4] In a letter of 1593, Philip Henslowe, whose knowledge of the financial perils of theatre management was second to none, reported that Pembroke's Men were in such economic dire straits that they were having to pawn their possessions. Several plays belonging to Pembroke's Men appeared in print around this time and although we do not know for certain that they sold their play texts to a publisher in a bid to raise funds, it is a plausible theory.

A Shrew appears in the Stationers' Register for 2 May 1594 and Henslowe's Diary records a performance on 11 June, when the combined Lord Chamberlain's and Lord Admiral's Men were playing in Newington Butts.[5] This large company would have had ample personnel to cope with the full Sly framework, and it is plausible that this framework was subsequently cut, as too expensive in terms of manpower, when the companies divided. Stephen Miller (1998, 37–9) argues against this theory because he considers the savings in terms of absolutely required acting personnel to be insignificant, but while the Sly framework *can* be done, as Miller suggests, with just Sly, the Lord and Sly's 'wife', several modern productions (e.g. Barton 1960, Dews 1981, Alexander 1990, 1992) have shown how lively the Sly framework can be when it includes a very large onstage audience pretending to be attendants solicitously waiting on the fake lord. If this is how the framework was played originally, cutting Sly after 1.1 would have made significant personnel savings.

---

4 While *A Shrew* identifies the theatre company that performed it, Shakespeare's name does not appear, presumably as there was little to be gained in terms of marketing from mentioning it. The first play to be published and actually identified as by Shakespeare was *Love's Labour's Lost* in 1598.

5 See Foakes and Rickert (22).

The early stage history of *The Taming of the Shrew* is also illuminated by John Smethwick's 1631 quarto of the play. As several editors point out, Smethwick's connection with the play demonstrates that Shakespeare's contemporaries didn't necessarily distinguish between *The Shrew* and *A Shrew*: Smethwick owned the right to publish *A Shrew* but he was part of the group who published the Folio, a group which did not register *The Shrew* for printing, presumably because Smethwick was deemed already to own the printing rights to Katherina's story. Certainly Miller (1998, 33) argues that the 'treatment of the publishing rights to *A Shrew* and *The Shrew* by the consortium who published the Folio suggests that they regarded *A Shrew* as a version of Shakespeare's play'. As the title page of Smethwick's quarto states that *The Shrew* was performed at both the Blackfriars and the Globe playhouses, and the King's Men only acquired the indoor playhouse at Blackfriars in August 1608, this suggests that *The Shrew* was still being staged many years after it was first performed. The question of when exactly the play was first performed, however, remains contentious: probably before the 1594 publication of *A Shrew*, and the performance noted by Henslowe in the same year. Richard Proudfoot demonstrates that both *The Shrew* and *A Shrew* must have existed in some form when fragments of *both* texts appeared embedded in the text of *A Knack to Know a Knave* (published in 1594) and possibly before a 1592 performance of that play, if what was performed was the text which was subsequently published. *A Shrew* has to postdate all the Marlowe plays it borrows lines from, but dates for Marlowe's plays are difficult to establish. William H. Moore suggests that an allusion to the action of *The Taming of the Shrew* exists in a text of 1593, *Beautie Dishonoured* by Anthony Chute, but the earliest date for *The Taming of the Shrew* is proposed by Brian Morris: Morris dates it 1589 and argues that *The Shrew* is Shakespeare's first play, and that the fact that the Induction is located in Warwickshire reflects Shakespeare's recent departure from Stratford. As there is no conclusive evidence, the precise dates of the premiere(s) of *The* and *A Shrew* remain unproven.

The three playhouses that we know *The Shrew* and *A Shrew* were staged in – Blackfriars, the Globe and Newington Butts – were in some ways quite different but shared the features of an unlocalised platform stage and upstage entry points. The Folio's stage action and stage directions also reveal something about expected playing conditions: the text requires enough space for characters to *stand by* while other action is going on (1.1.47 s.d.), for Tranio and Hortensio to observe Lucentio and Bianca in 4.2, and for Gremio to be *out before* at the beginning of 5.1; an *aloft* (Induction 2.0 s.d.) and an *above* (1.1.238 s.d.) large enough for Sly and company to *sit and mark* (1.1.243 s.d.) and possibly a *window* for the Pedant (Merchant) (5.1.13 s.d.). As noted above, *A Shrew* does not place Sly 'aloft' but merely on a chair, which may reflect a simplified staging for touring. Properties required by the Folio include trumpets, a *basin and ewer, and other appurtenances* (Induction 2.0 s.d.), *a lute and books* (2.1.38 s.d.), *supper* (4.1.113 s.d.), *meat* (4.3.35 s.d.), and a *banquet* (5.2.0 s.d.). In addition, the Folio specifies several costumes: Lucentio is disguised *in the habit of a mean man* (2.1.38 s.d.); the Pedant (Merchant) is *booted and bare headed* (4.4.0 s.d.); Biondello describes Petruchio's wedding clothes in detail (3.2.41–5). Stage directions in *A Shrew* may also reveal details of early staging practice: for example, *A Shrew* indicates in no uncertain terms that, after her submission speech, Kate *lays her hand under her husband's feet* (*AS* 14.142 s.d.). While these details are noted in the commentary, their authority is entirely contingent on the individual reader's belief in the authority, or otherwise, of *A Shrew*.

EARLY RESPONSES

Around 1611 John Fletcher wrote a sequel to *The Shrew*, *The Woman's Prize or the Tamer Tamed*.[6] *The Woman's Prize* subjects the newly widowed Petruchio to the kind of medicine he gave Katherina in *The Taming of the Shrew*; Petruchio's new wife Maria delays consummation of the marriage, dresses up in strange clothes and acts outrageously. *The Woman's Prize* remembers Katherina (who is never named but is always Petruchio's 'other wife' or 'first wife') as untamed, as having 'abundant stubbornesse' and as subjecting Petruchio to 'daily huy and cries' (1.1.17, 18). Although Petruchio is 'famous for a woman tamer' and 'wife-breaker' (1.3.268, 269), he still wakes in the night dreaming of Katherina, crying 'out for Cudgels, Colstaves, any thing; / Hiding his Breeches, out of fear her Ghost / Should walk' (1.1.34–6) and he reminisces:

> Had I not ev'ry morning a rare breakfast,
> Mixt with a learned Lecture of ill language,
> Louder then *Tom* o'Lincoln; and at dinner,
> A dyet of the same dish? Was there evening
> That ere past over us, without thou knave,
> Or thou whore, for digestion?   (3.3.157–62)

---

6 This is the date which most scholars favour, a date immediately before Fletcher's collaborations with Shakespeare (*Henry VIII*, *The Two Noble Kinsmen* and *Cardenio*). The fact that the two dramatists went on to work together suggests that Shakespeare was unperturbed by *The Woman's Prize*. Sandra Clark (176–7 note 30) argues for 1604 as the date of *The Woman's Prize*.

As Fran Dolan (37) observes, 'This play suggests that not all Shakespeare's contemporaries assumed that Petruchio had triumphed decisively.'

The stage histories of *The Taming of the Shrew* and *The Woman's Prize* converge in 1633 when they were performed on 26 and 28 November respectively for Charles I and Henrietta Maria at St James's.[7] Sir Henry Herbert noted that *The Taming of the Shrew* was 'Likt' but *Tamer Tamed* was 'Very well likt' (Bawcutt 185). The extant Prologue and Epilogue for *The Woman's Prize*, two speeches which duck and weave on gender issues, were probably written for this performance. First they say that *The Woman's Prize* is a riposte to *The Shrew*, then that the play is just 'sport' (Prologue 15); finally they hope that *The Woman's Prize* teaches 'both Sexes due equality' (Epilogue 7) and 'to love mutually' (8). The 'Very well likt' *Woman's Prize* may have helped *The Shrew* remain in theatrical circulation, and certainly Michael Dobson (23) argues that during the Restoration period *The Woman's Prize* 'took precedence over its source'. Indeed, John Lacy's Restoration adaptation of *The Shrew*, *Sauny the Scot*, functions so much as a 'companion piece for Fletcher's spin-off' (Dobson 23) that the Epilogue closes stating, 'I've *Tam'd the Shrew*, but will not be asham'd / If next you see the very *Tamer Tam'd*.'

It is not clear precisely when *Sauny* superseded Shakespeare's play. Sir Henry Herbert recorded fees paid or due for licensing a 'Re[vived] Play Taminge ye shrew' some time after 3 November 1663 (Bawcutt 284) for Killigrew's King's Company at the Theatre Royal, Drury Lane (283–5). Pepys saw Lacy play Sauny on 9 April 1667 and 1 November 1667, although Dobson (23) suggests that the adaptation may have been ready 'considerably earlier'. *Sauny* radically truncates the action of *The Shrew*, and creates a vehicle for Lacy's own comic talents in the role of Sauny. As the Grumio character is called Sander in *A Shrew*, this may be where the name 'Sauny' originates, as both names are diminutives of Alexander (Summers xxix). Other echoes of *A Shrew* also appear (see Miller 1998, 41–3) such as Margaret's (Katherina's) speech '*I* have a good mind to marry him to try if he can *Tame* me' (2.2.252–4), which is reminiscent of *A Shrew* 3.169–71.

Sauny has a joke Scottish accent, he specialises in crass jokes (e.g. 3.2.136–8) and constantly upstages the taming narrative. Lacy also plays overtly to Restoration theatrical taste by making the characters more aristocratic in rank, relocating the action to London, and adding a bedroom scene, with a threatened onstage disrobing of Margaret, and an attempted ravishment of Biancha, who is recognised as a shrew in the making, having 'a Little Spice of *Peg*' in her (3.1.315). In 1698, Susanna Verbruggen played Margaret

---

7 Herbert (Bawcutt 182) records on 21 October 1633 that *Tamer Tamed* had been 'purgd of oaths, prophaness, and ribaldrye'.

alongside a Petruchio, William Powell, who was 'seldom sober, and frequently imperfect' according to Genest (I, 560).

In *Sauny* Margaret is tormented more brutally than Katherina, but Margaret does stage a final rebellion at the end of the play: she refuses to speak, Petruchio threatens to have her teeth pulled out and then, in a borrowing from Maria's treatment of Petruchio in *The Woman's Prize*, he declares her dead and makes preparations for her burial. Margaret recants, passes the obedience test, and makes a very brief speech on the duty that wives owe husbands.

Sauny also inspired an extended and detailed piece of comparative literary criticism in Arthur Bedford's *Serious Remonstrance* of 1719 which fulminates: 'he who will compare this Performance with the Original, will find it ten times more the Child of Hell than the first. But the *Moral* in either is good for nothing' (371–3). Bedford mainly objected to the increased swearing and blasphemy in *Sauny* and in Sauny's impertinence 'to both *Master* and *Mistress*, and indeed upon all occasions' (372).

Lacy's text was published in 1698, with no acknowledgement of Shakespeare's contribution, and until Garrick's *Catharine and Petruchio* displaced it in 1754, *Sauny* was the nearest thing to *The Taming of the Shrew* that London audiences saw. After Lacy's death William Bullock played Sauny, and one particularly noteworthy performance of the play was for the entertainment of two Native American princes on 21 December 1719 (Van Lennep II, 560–1).[8]

There is evidence that Sly was still in circulation during this period. Several allusions to Sly are extant but, intriguingly, two allusions cited by G. Thorn-Drury indubitably refer to the full Sly framework. A reference to a speech by Henry Cromwell in 1659 (Thorn-Drury 11) certainly invokes Sly's full story: 'The Players have a Play, where they bring in a Tinker, and make him believe himself a Lord, and when they have satisfied their humour, they made him a plain Tinker again.' Over twenty years later the Prologue to Edward Ravenscroft's popular play, *The London Cuckolds*, printed in 1682, comments:

> Then waking (like the Tinker in the Play)
> She finds the golden Vision fled away   (Thorn-Drury 27)

Montague Summers (xxix) suggests that a recent staging of *A Shrew* may have inspired the latter reference, and H. W. Crundell argues that *The Shrew* was sometimes performed with the Epilogue from *A Shrew* and sometimes not.

---

8 For a list of revivals of *Sauny* see Haring-Smith 174–7.

In 1716 two farces by the same name, *The Cobler of Preston*, were staged in London, both making use of the full Christopher Sly story: that is, including his awakening as well as his deception. While the Sly scenes from *A Shrew* resurfaced in print in Alexander Pope's edition of Shakespeare (1723–5), with Pope printing the additional Sly scenes from a 1607 reprint of *A Shrew* in his possession, both of the *Cobler of Preston* rewrites suggest that the full framework was still known well before Pope revived it in print.

Christopher Bullock's *Cobler of Preston* (first performance 24 January 1716) is a lively farce which Bullock claims was written in two days, and then produced only three days later at Lincoln's Inn Fields. Bullock had heard that Charles Johnson was writing a play for Drury Lane, relocating the Sly story to Preston, which was at that time associated with the Young Pretender's initially successful foray into England. Bullock stole Johnson's title and produced his own play. Although Bullock concentrates on Sly, renamed Guzzle, he does retain some traces of the taming story in that Guzzle, while he is in the role of a lord, acts as a justice of the peace in a dispute between his own wife and the innkeeper Dame Hacket (both played by men). Guzzle orders both of the women to be whipped or ducked in the river Ribble, stating, 'I'll try if I can tame you' (Bullock 14). When Guzzle awakes and is confronted by the women, 'Wet and Dirty' from their ducking (17), they fight. They eventually agree to peace and Dorcas Guzzle, once she understands the trick that has been played on her husband, reflects ''tis a plaguy thing that poor Folks Bones must pay for rich Folks Frolicks and Whims' (17). Bullock is very open about his borrowings from *The Taming of the Shrew* and claims in his preface that all lines directly borrowed from Shakespeare are prefaced with quotation marks (vi).

By contrast, Charles Johnson's *The Cobler of Preston* (first performance Drury Lane, 3 February 1716) does not acknowledge its many borrowings from Shakespeare, merely commenting that its source material is 'the worst Plot that ever was' (Prologue). Johnson's focus first and foremost is to comment on contemporary politics, as is evident when the baffled Kit Sly, who cannot work out whether or not he is really a lord, makes the politically loaded comment: '*I am devilishly afraid I am but a Pretender*' (Johnson 36). Sly is seen to deserve his treatment by the significantly named Sir Charles Briton and his friend Captain Jolly, partly because of Sly's Jacobite sympathies and partly because the Lord knows Sly to be a drunkard and trouble-maker (4). There are some vestiges of the source's taming story in a song which enacts a quarrel between a cobbler and his wife, which is performed to entertain Sly while he is installed as a lord. The production went to some trouble to establish a realistic appearance of a cobbler's shop, hiring a 'Cobler's Bench and Tools', as well as a pair of 'Fine Holland sheets and

Pillowbiers', a rug and a blanket (Van Lennep II, cv) for the deception of Sly. Johnson's play was later turned into a musical farce, and performed at Drury Lane (29 September 1817).

Both texts of *The Cobler of Preston* are slight farces, designed to fill only one half of a double bill (Van Lennep II, cxviii–ix), but they pre-empt some late twentieth-century productions by bringing Mrs Sly (or Mrs Guzzle) onstage. James Worsdale's *Cure for a Scold*, which first appeared on 25 February 1735, also created more space for women by giving the actress playing Margaret (Katherina) an epilogue in which she disowns the 'mean' part she has just played: 'Thank Heav'n! I'm not the Thing I represented' (Epilogue 2, 4). Worsdale's two-act ballad farce generally portrays marriage as a fate worse than death for both men and women but although his preface talks of the 'Great Author' Shakespeare, whose work he has 'attempted to abbreviate', *Cure for a Scold* actually owes more to *Sauny*: not only is the heroine named Margaret, but the Grumio character, Archer, is onstage for the wooing scene and the bedroom scene, and Petruchio threatens to have Margaret's teeth pulled out during her final revolt as in *Sauny*.

The most enduring adaptation of *The Shrew*, David Garrick's *Catharine and Petruchio*, was devised in 1754 as an afterpiece. Garrick himself never acted in *Catharine and Petruchio*: the original cast had Henry Woodward as Petruchio (see illustration 1) and Hannah Pritchard as Catharine, but it was when Kitty Clive played Catharine in 1756 that the afterpiece became popular, partly because Clive and Woodward were known to dislike each other and stories circulated suggesting that they used onstage fights to settle offstage scores. Thomas Davies (I, 312) judged Woodward's Petruchio 'more wild, extravagant, and fantastical than the author designed it should be' and carried 'to an almost ridiculous excess', while Clive was 'perfect mistress of Catherine's humour' but 'overborne by the extravagant and triumphant grotesque of Woodward'.

Garrick's text focuses entirely on Catharine's taming. The Bianca subplot is radically cut, with Bianca already married to Hortensio at the beginning of the play, which opens with Petruchio and Baptista negotiating terms. The play then moves straight into Petruchio's first scene with Catharine. Shakespeare's cruder jokes are cut or made dignified: for example, the jokes in 2.1 about wasps' stings are transformed into badinage about honey and kissing. Motivation is also changed: on first viewing Petruchio, Catharine observes approvingly 'the man's a man' (1.139) and she decides to marry and 'tame this haggard' (1.285), that is, Petruchio. Catharine also has another reason for marrying Petruchio: Baptista is threatening to turn her out of doors if she doesn't agree to the marriage, and Bianca is calling her 'poor abandoned Cath'rine' (1.279).

1 Henry Woodward as Petruchio in David Garrick's *Catharine and Petruchio.*

Catharine and Petruchio's marriage follows immediately after the wooing, which then leads directly into the arrival at Petruchio's house, and the disrupted dinner. The final scene of the play combines the fight between the Tailor, Grumio and Petruchio, the sudden arrival of Baptista, and Catharine's submission speech (without the indecorous wager to prompt it), which is interrupted by encouraging remarks from Petruchio and discouragement from Bianca. The final lines of the speech are given to Petruchio, who *Goes forward with* Catharine *in his hand* (3.276 s.d.) and from downstage addresses the audience, with Catharine 'as an exhibit' (Dobson 197), calling on wives to be as obedient as subjects should be loyal. Haring-Smith (16) stresses that Catharine 'no longer receives our individual attention, and she loses the spotlight' when her final speech is thus broken up. Sentiment also reigns as Petruchio says he will 'doff' the 'mask' he has assumed of 'lordly husband' (3.269–70), promises Catharine a life 'Of mutual love, compliance, and regard' (3.273) and refuses the second dowry offered by Baptista because 'My fortune is sufficient. Her(e)'s my wealth: / Kiss me, my Kate' (3.266–7).

By contemporary standards *Catharine and Petruchio* put a significant amount of Shakespeare's text onstage, but the overall effect of the adaptation was to produce a simple, farcical battle of the sexes, which proclaims the duty wives have to submit and makes *The Taming of the Shrew* seem a masterpiece of ambiguity and complexity by comparison. Dobson (190) describes *Catharine and Petruchio* as 'family entertainment for the 1750s'; Haring-Smith (17) sees it as a 'moral farce'.

Garrick's adaptation was designed to be only an afterpiece, not the main theatrical event of the evening, but it, and variations on Garrick's text, replaced *The Taming of the Shrew* on the English-speaking stage during much of the nineteenth century.[9] When John Philip Kemble adapted Garrick's adaptation, the whip-cracking Petruchio also entered stage history, despite Kemble's Petruchio being a rather gentlemanly creation.[10] Kemble only played Petruchio 'some half a dozen times' and this was 'usually, *mirabile dictu*, with Mrs Siddons as his Kate' (Shattuck 1974, i) but variations on the Kemble adaptation, a version of which was published in 1810 as *Katharine and Petruchio*, were used by most leading nineteenth-century performers such as Edwin Booth or Charlotte Cushman, while Ellen Terry and Henry Irving actually made their first appearance onstage together in *Katharine and Petruchio* in 1867, over ten years before their Lyceum partnership began. The published text of *Katharine and Petruchio* does not demand whip-cracking but A. C. Sprague (1945, 57) records that it is in 'Kemble's own marked copy of *Catharine and Petruchio*' that there first appears 'the ominous words "whip for Petruchio" . . . written opposite the Tamer's entrance in the wedding scene', although Sprague considers that Kemble's 'stately' stage persona makes him an unlikely comic innovator, and the fact that *Catharine and Petruchio* explicitly invites whip-cracking, in Pedro's speech describing how Petruchio 'shook his whip in token of his love'

9 Haring-Smith provides a list of revivals of *Catharine and Petruchio* (177–87 and 194–204). The Annual bibliography in *Shakespeare Quarterly* records a production as recently as 1993.
10 Petruchio was still cracking his whip in Kyle (1982).

(2.120–1) at his wedding, certainly suggests that whip-cracking went back
further than Kemble.

Garrick's adaptation, or versions of it, not only took over from
Shakespeare, but it also furnished much stage business which carried on
being popular even after *The Taming of the Shrew* had returned to the stage:
for example, Garrick inaugurated the enduring tradition of Curtis being a
woman, usually old, garrulous, sometimes drunk, sometimes a nurse, always
ridiculous. *Catharine and Petruchio* only started to decline in popularity
towards the end of the nineteenth century, in a period when, as Haring-
Smith (15) points out, afterpieces were becoming less fashionable.

NINETEENTH TO EARLY TWENTIETH CENTURY

The first return to Shakespeare's play took place in 1844 when Benjamin
Webster, in collaboration with J. R. Planché staged *The Taming of the Shrew*
in what was declared to be the Elizabethan manner (see illustration 2).
Webster restored the Induction and Sly was 'ejected from a scenic alehouse'

2 Benjamin Webster's 1844 *Taming of the Shrew*, designed by J. R. Planché.

before being 'installed in the "lord's" chamber' and treated to a play performed, as it were, with no scenery, before a couple of screens and a tapestry curtain (*Athenaeum*, 23 March 1844). A view of Elizabethan London formed the backdrop, placards identified scene location, and Henry Howe, who played Hortensio, remembered that 'At the beginning of each scene, one of the troupe of actors removed the old placard, and hung a fresh one denoting the place in which the action was to be represented.'[11] The *Examiner* (23 March 1844) commented that this 'absence of scenery, in an age when scenes are every-day things' became 'in its turn a scenic effect' and 'More persons came to see how a stage was fitted up in the sixteenth century, than for any other purpose whatsoever.' Of the 1847 revival the *Spectator* (30 October 1847) also commented that the lack of scenery 'becomes a quasi-spectâcle itself'. Reviews which mention the 'speed and vivacity' of playing (McDonald 163) may reflect the fact that prolonged scenery changes, customary in the theatre of the time, were not slowing the play down. Meanwhile, the strolling players who performed for Sly were dressed in Elizabethan costumes and made up to look like Shakespeare, Ben Jonson and Richard Tarleton. Interact music of madrigals and 'traditional English airs' was played (McDonald 162). *Bell's Weekly Messenger* (23 March 1844) had some fun pointing out inconsistencies: for example, that to be really authentic the audience should arrive by boat, boys should play the female roles, and so on.

Webster's Petruchio was not liked: he was not the 'gay, high-mettled gallant' pretending 'a peremptory manner and tyrannically capricious humour' (*Spectator*, 23 March 1844) that many reviewers wanted and in addition he had imperfectly mastered the lines. He overused his whip, applying it to both his servants and to Baptista's as well (*Morning Chronicle*, 18 March 1844). Haring-Smith argues that 'Webster's acting probably was inadequate, but he suffered as well from the critical assumption that a truly Shakespearean hero / lover should be genteel. Because he violated the public's expectations (however ill-founded), he was censured' (48). In addition, Webster's impersonation of Shakespeare in the Induction was felt to be impertinent: it made his 'subsequent misconception and undignified personation of *Petruchio* more glaring' (*Athenaeum*, 23 March 1844) and constituted a 'very equivocal compliment to the Great Immortal!' (*Examiner*, 23 March 1844). Webster was also attacked for retaining Shakespeare's indecent jokes (e.g. *Morning Post*, 18 March 1844), although he seems to have cut them

11 Quoted in Child (185). McDonald (1971, 166) reproduces a cartoon from *Punch* which ridicules the placards and suggests they might be used in future to abolish all scenery – placards could stand in stead of 'clouds', etc.

later, as the *Morning Advertiser* (27 October 1847) commented on 'various improvements and judicious alterations' in the 1847 revival.[12] Despite his poor notices Webster seems to have been proud of his achievement (McDonald 168) and played excerpts of the production at a gala at Covent Garden to raise money for Shakespeare's birthplace (7 December 1847).

Webster envisaged the production of *The Taming of the Shrew* partly as a vehicle for Louisa Nisbett, a popular comedy actress who was recently widowed and wished to return to the stage. Nisbett was almost universally applauded as Katherina, especially for her delivery of her final speech. The *Athenaeum* (30 October 1847) commented of the revival that Nisbett offered 'a practical proof that woman's ascendancy is never more absolute than when she seems to relinquish it'. Katherina's transformation was not smooth; 'now and then' she 'broke out into short ebullitions of the hasty temper she was wont to indulge in', although, reassuringly for the reviewer, always 'through the veil of the termigant [sic] the lady was still visible' (*ILN* 23 March 1844). Contemporary sentiment was also to the fore when Nisbett's Katherina was described as 'fierce, yet feminine at first, and afterwards fluttering as a dove, trembling under the hand even of its feeder' (*Bell's Weekly Messenger*, 23 March 1844).

Overall, critical opinion was very divided; reviewers either loved the production or hated it. Meanwhile, the theatre was 'crowded to suffocation' (*Era*, 24 March 1844) and the vast majority of reviewers gave credit to Webster at least for the boldness of the staging ideas. In his memoirs Planché contests Webster's claims here: he asserts that the entire credit for the revival belonged to him, declares that the 'restoration of this "gem"' (that is, the Induction) 'is one of the events in my theatrical career on which I look back with the greatest pride and gratification' (Planché 298) and he used a memorable sketch of Charles Strickland as Sly as the frontispiece to his book. *The Times* (18 March 1844) felt that the German Shakespeare scholar, Ludwig Tieck, should also be given credit for his ideas on Elizabethan staging.

No one followed Webster's lead in restoring Shakespeare until 1856 when Samuel Phelps played most of the Folio text of *The Shrew*. Phelps staged almost all of Shakespeare's plays during his management of Sadler's Wells, but *The Taming of the Shrew* had to wait until Phelps's thirteenth season before being revived and it was twenty-ninth in the list of Shakespeare plays that he produced (Phelps had already presented *Katharine and Petruchio* earlier in his career). Phelps chose the role of Sly for himself, turned in a star

---

12 This suggests that the promptbooks s9 and s10, where risqué jokes are cut, are from the revised production.

performance and provided the first recorded example of Sly completely upstaging Katherina. In addition, the final scene was much trimmed and Katherina's submission so reduced that Katherina became a minor role. Phelps also cut bawdy jokes, classical allusions and anything indelicate. Reviewers applauded Phelps's Sly enthusiastically (see p. 60) but some found the restoration of Bianca's narrative a mixed blessing: the *Spectator* (22 November 1856) thought the subplot a 'dull tangled tale'. Most, however, recorded an enthusiastic audience response.

The landmark production in terms of establishing *The Taming of the Shrew* as a popular play was Augustin Daly's 1887 New York staging. In the US until then *Catharine and Petruchio* 'had held the stage . . . since 1768, when it was first given at the John Street Theatre by Lewis Hallam's company' (Felheim 238). Daly's production was a great commercial success, which toured internationally and revealed Katherina as potentially a star part, and Joseph Daly claims his brother's production as 'the first performance of a Shakespearian comedy by an American company in Europe' (461), as well as 'the first performance of "The Taming of the Shrew" given in Stratford' (463). Its extraordinary success encouraged imitators, and the repeated publication of the playing text allowed Daly's staging and cuts to become very influential; however, it also reveals that Daly's claims to be restoring Shakespeare were overstated, and that the production cut the text deeply as well as retaining several Garrickisms.[13]

Ada Rehan's Katherina was to haunt her successors, who were always found wanting alongside the fiery, imperious character she created. Rehan was praised for her 'grand air', 'natural refinement' and the fact that she was 'tall and stately', 'proud', 'no vulgar scold' and that Petruchio's 'very cruelty seems fascinating to her strange capricious nature' (*DT* 30 May 1888). Her 'movements had something of the rage of a captured animal' and her 'outcries' were beyond most actresses (*Athenaeum*, 2 June 1888). Rehan was 'tall, lithe, supple, with queenly demeanour, flashing eyes, scornful countenance, an impetuosity that seemed invincible' (*SUAH* 2 May 1902) but 'Under all her splendid pride of bearing and freakish outburst of passion the innate womanliness of her nature was apparent' (*Saturday Review*, 2 June 1888). Daly's apologist, William Winter, also insisted that one could always sense the 'loving and lovable woman, latent beneath the shrew' (1898, 54) and Rehan's Katherina for Harold Child, writing in 1928, remained 'in the memory of playgoers as a work of genius' (Child 186). The production made Katherina the star but as Shattuck (1987, 66) comments 'Daly was no

---

13 Daly had previously produced the Garrick text on many occasions. The published acting texts were prepared with the help of the critic William Winter.

3   Ada Rehan as Katherina in Augustin Daly's 1887 *Taming of the Shrew*.

feminist' and the focus on Katherina came about because Daly 'was sentimental about women, and he could not bear to see his heroine defeated'.

Major text manipulation, however, was needed to sustain Rehan's dignified brand of shrewishness. Most importantly Rehan's famous first entry,
when she stormed onto the stage, achieved much of its impact because
Katherina was omitted from 1.1. Hence Katherina's first scene was not a
crowded, unfocused street scene, with her jostling for attention and enduring the humiliation of hearing herself openly discussed in public. Instead
Katherina first entered in 2.1, with the theatrical focus entirely on her, and
importantly, she was followed on by Bianca, meekly trailing behind.[14] This
explosion of energy left Rehan little room to manoeuvre; after entering at full
throttle, she could only lower the energy levels or at most maintain her rage.
Katherina's subsequent development was also something of an anticlimax as
the text ran 4.1 straight on into both 4.3 and 4.5, saving on scenery changes,
but also radically condensing the process of Katherina's taming.

While much in this production was still heavily indebted to Garrick, Daly
did restore Sly and the Induction.[15] The trick on Sly was good-humoured,
but London reviewers, who missed the sottish simpleton that Phelps had
provided in the role, were less keen than the Americans on William Gilbert's
Sly, who was felt to be too quick-witted to be fooled by the Lord's trick.
Joseph Daly suggests that 'with the Induction restored, we find a comedy of
manners' (426) and this element was emphasised. Rehan and her first
Petruchio, John Drew, were previously known mainly for drawing-room
drama; Drew applied 'polish' to Petruchio (Daly 428) and was always a gentlemanly tamer, although he wielded 'his long whip with the dexterity of a
cowboy' (*T* 31 May 1888). James Lewis even made Grumio 'an intellectual'
(*Athenaeum*, 2 June 1888) while comic violence was played down, and crude
language cut or rendered polite.

The settings and costumes were expensive and very elaborate. *Queen* (14
July 1888) devoted an entire article to detailed descriptions and assessments
of the costumes but the *Daily News* (30 May 1888) considered Baptista's
house to be 'marred' by 'some preposterously huge and showy articles
of gilded furniture' and the cumbersome if lavishly decorative settings
necessitated running scenes together, out of sequence, in order to reduce
the number of scene changes. Daly's decoration of the text included the
introduction of Henry Bishop's song 'Should He Upbraid', which was sung

---

14 Winter (1915, 521) also records Bianca being driven on first.
15 Winter, Daly's dramaturg, gives the statistics as: Shakespeare's text is 2,671 lines,
    Daly's around 2,000 including 200 from Garrick or somewhere else (Winter 1915,
    513).

at the opening of the final scene, and became a standard feature of performances of *The Taming of the Shrew* for some time (see commentary 5.2).

Daly's production of *The Taming of the Shrew* was revived many times – Ada Rehan's last performance as Katherina was in 1905 – and it set new standards for gentrification of the play. Other popular, early twentieth-century productions, however, adopted a less dignified approach. Those of Frank and Constance (Fetherstonhaugh) Benson, Oscar Asche and Lily Brayton, E. H. Sothern and Julia Marlowe were all robustly comic rather than dignified. The Bensons played *The Shrew* so frequently that their company joked about performing *The Merry Shrews of Venice* everywhere they went.[16] Although she was criticised for her early attempts at Katherina, Constance Benson remembered *The Shrew* as 'one of our most successful plays, and invariably a favourite, especially with the men' (86), and she continued to perform the role even late in life during the First World War, when she toured a 'potted' version of the play (301). The Bensons' production offered robust, broad comedy, which included demonstrations of athletic table-leaping in 4.1 from Frank Benson. They cut the subplot deeply, and produced a durable, tourable, physical comedy. Excerpts of this production were filmed in 1911, directed by Will Barker, but the film is lost.

Although in many ways the Bensons' production stayed the same over the decades, performances inevitably changed, if nothing else because the Bensons were aging. Its reception also changed: Susan Carlson demonstrates that several reviewers became uncomfortable in response to the Bensons' 1909 production, and she attributes this partly to the recent Stratford by-election, in which suffrage protest had loomed large. Later in the year when suffrage activist Violet Vanbrugh played Katherina to Frank Benson's acrobatic tamer, Vanbrugh made Benson's Petruchio 'look threateningly excessive' (Carlson 95). In 1912 the *Birmingham Gazette and Express* (23 April 1912) thought Vanbrugh 'gentle in voice and gesture' and while 'it is true that she flared up, and threw cushions about, and even pulled Petruchio's hair' yet her 'soft womanly heart' was apparent. This Katherina displayed only 'mild suburban drawing-room tantrums', was 'shivering with fear' and, at Petruchio's house, a 'frightened prisoner, longing to escape rather than the fire-eating wife that needed breaking in' (*Birmingham Daily Post*, 23 April 1912). However, the *Daily Telegraph* thought this Katherina masochistic and that she 'visibly liked being beaten' (23 April 1912).

The Bensons' production was very busy: as Constance Benson admits (86) 'the prompt-book is crammed with directions'. One set piece was the

16 Trewin, 1964, 16. The first performance of the Benson production was in 1890 and Benson was still playing Petruchio in old age in 1932.

appearance of a donkey during the return to Padua (4.5) and as, on tour, a local, untrained donkey would be used, Constance Benson (87), who had to ride the donkey, often suffered bruising. Despite their commitment to broad comedy, the Bensons did not perform the Induction, even though the reviewer for the *Stratford-Upon-Avon Herald* kept arguing over the years (e.g. 1 May 1902) that the local references would be appreciated at the Stratford festival. The same paper (6 May 1904) also called for 'a toning down of exuberance' in the playing.

Old Bensonian Oscar Asche offers a revealing comment on the Benson company ethos: 'Women did not count with us in those days. We were too fond of athletics to think of anything else' (Asche 75). Significantly 'Mrs Benson was always looked upon as one of the boys. She was a good sport' (96). Given this prevailing mood, little other than a jolly rough and tumble could really be expected from the Bensons, and when Asche mounted his own production of *The Taming of the Shrew*, he drew on his experience with the Bensons and used many of the same cuts and business.[17] Asche's biggest divergence from the Bensons' production appeared in his restoration of the Induction, which enabled him to become probably the first actor to double Sly and Petruchio (a doubling impossible in Shakespeare's time, as immediately after Sly and his wife *sit and mark* (1.1.243 s.d.) Petruchio enters). Asche presented the Sly episodes as a curtain-raiser, completely separate from the rest of the play; his Sly was Falstaffian in appearance, and 'highly delighted with his big bed and the tassel of his nightcap and the prospect of a play presented entirely for himself' (*London Budget*, 11 May 1913).

Asche considered that he and Lily Brayton made their names in *The Shrew* (Asche 113), such was their commercial success with the play. Asche chose *The Shrew* for the opening performance of his first tour of his homeland of Australia, and he estimated 'My wife and I have played [*The Shrew*] something like fifteen hundred times, in many parts of the world' (112). Almost inevitably, Brayton's Katherina was compared unfavourably with Ada Rehan's, but most adverse critical reaction focused on Asche's rough-diamond Petruchio. Asche was a big man, who in later life topped twenty stone; he was very sporting, loved boxing and often played heavy villains with

17 Technically Otho Stuart was responsible for the 1904 Asche/Brayton production at the Adelphi, London. However, Asche and Brayton had performed *The Taming of the Shrew* as early as 1899 in Wigan, Brayton's home town, and their performances dominated the production. Although some changes did take place over the years – sometimes Curtis was a woman and sometimes not, and the Induction was not always played – much comic business survived over the twenty years of the production's life and as late as 1944 Wilson Barrett (118) records that his company's production, directed by Clare Harris, was indebted to Lily Brayton for advice.

great apparent violence onstage. Physically he towered over Brayton's spit-fire Katherina and the *Times* felt he ran 'the risk of being taken for a bully in earnest' and then 'Kate's taming would be a tragedy' (30 November 1904). The *Sydney Morning Herald* (2 June 1913) also risked introducing a serious element into the play when it compared Katherina with the 'hunger-strikers in London' and wondered if 'Baptista's daughter could boast the same grim tenacity of purpose as the modern suffragist'.

In his autobiography Asche states that he aimed to present the characters of *The Shrew* realistically, 'as human beings' (Asche 118). Consequently 'the characters walked, ate and drank like living people. And they ate real food and drank real wine, not property-made cakes and fruit and coloured water' (119). After she submitted, Katherina was allowed to sit 'with a bowl of milk eagerly drinking spoonful after spoonful, while her husband tossed into the bowl pieces of bread' (*Brisbane Courier*, 2 April 1913) and a great deal of real onstage drinking is documented by the promptbook. J. C. Trewin suggests (1964, 33) that Asche's notion of real life was actually 'larger than life' but 'he had always worked on this scale himself and expected it in others'.

In 1905, the United States again saw a production of the play which was a box-office success, this time starring E. H. Sothern and Julia Marlowe. A very large number of promptbooks survives from this production, and the text used, and the interpretation of that text, changed substantially over the many years of the production's lifetime (1905–23).[18] For example, the production evolved from using a five-act text with a pictorial set, full of furniture, into a comparatively bare-boards presentation of a four-act text. Katherina's first entry was in 1.1 in earlier versions (e.g. S47) but in later versions it was in 2.1 (S48). As Bianca's first entrance then also became 2.1 (S48), the story of how Lucentio fell in love with her became confusingly condensed and their courtship was reduced to a sequence of tossing white roses lovingly at each other.

Most of the Sothern and Marlowe promptbooks are packed with interpolated business – flower girls drift around Padua, Petruchio pantomimes his love for Katherina at every opportunity by touching her hair, her discarded stockings, her shoes (see commentary 4.1) while Katherina pantomimes her continuing resistance to Petruchio (see commentary at the end of 4.3). Several reviewers thought the production too farcical, although they found Marlowe tame compared with Ada Rehan, and 'too attractive and lovable' like 'some normal American girl, full of the joy of living and feigning an incontinently shrewish disposition as an expedient to protect herself against

18 Two records were also made according to the 1922 catalogue of Victor Records –
74704 recorded the wooing scene and 74705 Katherina's advice to women.

fortune-hunting husbands' (*Washington Post*, 12 February 1912). However, the promptbooks suggest a Katherina who carried on resisting: as late as 5.2.131 she 'protestingly falls on stool' (S49) at Petruchio's demand that she make a speech on wifely duty. Ranald (215) also records that Marlowe's Katherina wielded a whip, but her violence generally consisted of biting and throwing things: 'She grinds her heels into Petruchio's toes, she scratches, she threatens his head with a wooden shoe, she bites – but, somehow, you feel that her bark is really very much worse than her bite' (*NYT* 17 October 1905). Meanwhile, the taming process was sentimentalised, and indeed became almost saccharine, as Sothern's Petruchio semaphored to the audience that he adored Katherina.

The production retained some Garrickisms but Marlowe herself, who often carefully prepared promptbooks in advance of productions (Russell viii), certainly saw the production as a counterblast to Daly. Her extended defence of her work (reprinted in Russell 342–5) argues that *The Taming of the Shrew* is a farce, and not to be played in a 'subdued, dignified, restrained' way (343).[19] She explicitly attacks Booth's edition (*Katharine and Petruchio*), Daly's production for being full of 'interpolated and transposed' text, and Winter's published version, based on Daly, 'which is heavily interlarded with long passages foreign to Shakespeare's original text' (Russell 343). Marlowe claims to be relying on the Folio, although she dismisses the Induction as 'commonly admitted to be spurious and certainly wholly unrelated' (343) to the body of the play. She argues that Katherina is 'tamed not so much by physical overbearance as by the arousing of her sense of humour and of the ridiculous' (344) and Russell reports Marlowe's opinion that Katherina's shrewishness was mostly brought about because Bianca 'was a nasty little cat' and yet 'was surrounded with suitors' (334). Reviewers pining for Rehan were told by Marlowe: 'we have given the text absolutely without interpolating a line; and we have acted it plainly in accordance with the author's stage directions, and with its indubitably farcical nature – but so ingrained is the impression left by former misconceptions, perversions and un-Shakespearean 'Shrews,' that we do not look for its universal acceptance and appreciation' (344). This seems disingenuous when placed alongside the evidence of cuts and 'business' recorded in the promptbooks, but box office was good over the many years of the production's run.

E. H. Sothern and Julia Marlowe worked together as a team on *The Taming of the Shrew*, but the first woman to take total artistic responsibility for a production of the play, Margaret Anglin, played Katherina far more in the tradition of Julia Marlowe than Ada Rehan. Anglin included the Induc-

---

19 Marlowe wrote this defence for the *Evening Telegram* (Russell 342).

tion in her opening performances in Melbourne, and it is marked up in her promptbook, but she had dropped it by the time she got to Adelaide (see *Adelaide Advertiser*, 13 November 1908) and this is symptomatic of how Anglin's production grew more decorous with time. Anglin also set the record for the lateness of Katherina's first entry by delaying it until her first meeting with Petruchio (see e.g. *NYT* 20 March 1914). Despite the fact that she omitted Katherina's early less dignified scenes, Anglin was attacked in print by William Winter, Daly's apologist, who vilified her production as presenting a Katherina who was 'ponderous, mature, and frumpishly without distinction, charm, vivacity, or even a suggestion of latent sweetness of womanhood' (Winter 1915, 537); Winter was particularly offended by Anglin's delivery of Katherina's last speech 'as if it were mere mockery, – implying that it is hypocritical, a jest, secretly understood between Petruchio and his wife' (538).

After years in the wilderness, in the sense of being replaced by Garrick, *The Taming of the Shrew* was by the early twentieth century beginning to become one of the most performed of Shakespeare's plays in either the dignified Daly mode or the broadly farcical tradition (the Bensons, Asche, Sothern and Marlowe). A significantly new approach to *The Taming of the Shrew* appeared in Max Reinhardt's 1909 Berlin production, which emphasised commedia dell'arte, harlequinade, gambolling and singing.[20] Huntly Carter (259) reports that Reinhardt wanted to 'preserve the "play within the play" illusion throughout', and so seated 'the intoxicated Sly where the orchestra well usually is, and from where, partly seen, he can witness the play', while making 'all the changes of scene by the use of properties, which appear to be actual properties, either brought on by the players in their waggon or extemporised out of the furniture and effects of the Lord's house'. Robert Speaight (204) remembers the production as:

> a rumbustious farce, played entirely for the benefit of Sly – for this alone, [Reinhardt] thought, would excuse Petruchio's intolerable behaviour. The actors appeared in the costumes of the clowns, harlequins, columbines, and pantaloons of the Commedia dell'Arte, inspired by the engravings of Callot. They wheeled their cart into the hall of the great house, used its staircase as it suited their convenience, and made packing-cases serve as furniture.

Nevertheless the production was not without its complex moments: for example, Petruchio was occasionally nervous or spoke lines surprisingly gently.

20 The production was in the repertoire for over a year – Else Bassermann sometimes played Katherina instead of Lucie Höflich – and Reinhardt returned to the *Shrew* in 1922 with Elisabeth Bergner as Katherina and Eugen Klöpfer as Petruchio. See Huesmann for details.

4 Victor Arnold as Baptista, and Hans Wassman as Schlau in Max Reinhardt's 1909 *Taming of the Shrew* in Berlin.

Reinhardt's influence on the 1913 production of *The Taming of the Shrew* by Martin Harvey (later Sir John Martin-Harvey) was also crucial. Harvey was in correspondence with William Poel about the possibility of producing the play as early as September 1912, the year that Reinhardt directed Harvey as Oedipus, in an open stage production of Sophocles' play. Several aspects of Harvey's production echo Reinhardt's, especially the ongoing use of Sly and the emphasis on the travelling-player motif: for example, the entry of the players 'in a waggon which was . . . painted scarlet and yellow, in harmony with the motley of the players' (Carter 262) sounds reminiscent of Reinhardt's use of a players' waggon. Harvey's production was perhaps most significant for beginning the rehabilitation of the scenes from *A Shrew*, and here he went further than Reinhardt, performing several interludes from *A Shrew* although, in the end, he omitted the Epilogue (see p. 53).

Harvey claimed to be producing *The Shrew* in 'the new way' and reviewers welcomed this approach, although many commented that it was actually the 'old way', that is, Elizabethan.[21] They detected various influences on Harvey besides Reinhardt: William Poel, Gordon Craig, Granville Barker. Poel, who was famous for his promotion of 'Elizabethan'-style stagings, was actually a 'coadjutor' (programme) although Harvey, a visual artist himself, claimed in his autobiography that the décor was his doing and Poel had only concerned himself with cutting the text. Correspondence between the two men reveals that Poel spent some time trying to persuade Harvey not to do the play at all (he particularly disliked the traditional horseplay, and felt that after Oscar Asche's production 'there is not very much more to get out of [the play]'); however, if Harvey were determined to do *The Shrew*, Poel suggested the 'underplot' should be cut 'altogether' (letter of 20 September 1912).[22] The promptbook which Poel marked up, most of which was followed by Harvey, certainly cut the subplot heavily.

Given Harvey's attempt to evoke Elizabethan staging, every theatre where Harvey's production appeared had to be modified; the proscenium arch had to be adapted, a platform erected out over the orchestra pit, and a 'carved stone seat' of 'about four feet in width' constructed to seat Sly and Bartholomew with their backs to the audience and 'commanding a view of the stage' (Carter 260). During the performance of the inner play, changes of scenery were indicated by curtains or screens and costumes were elaborate and opulent (cinquecento and slightly oriental) to compensate for the plainness of the set, which consisted mainly of arches and steps.

Disher, in his biography of Harvey (213–14) claims that the enthusiastic use of the Sly frame 'removed' the play 'from reality' so that 'whatever Petruchio might do would be excusable. Even the most ardent suffragettes of 1913 could hardly have objected even to a wife-beating in what made little more pretence to verisimilitude than a harlequinade.' Other reviewers, however, read Harvey's production as backlash: the *Sunderland Echo* (11 March 1913) commented that 'In these days of feminine emancipation women of the shrew type are not scared into either love or obedience'; the

21 The phrase 'the new way' comes from the production programme. Provincial reviewers commented that it was the first time these 'modern' methods had been seen outside London. The *Eastern Morning News* (3 March 1913) carried an article for the audiences of Hull (where the production premiered) entitled 'Mr Martin Harvey's Methods Explained'. Reviewers also characterised these methods as the 'only way', a phrase which played on Harvey's smash hit *The Only Way* based on *A Tale of Two Cities*. Information on Harvey's production is taken from the Sir John Martin-Harvey scrapbooks, London Theatre Museum (Blythe House).

22 Letters in the possession of Jan McDonald. For more discussion of this production and its use of *A Shrew* see pp. 53–4.

Weekly Budget (4 May 1913) thought the end of the play 'not quite in tune with the modern woman's idea of wifely duty'. One reviewer anticipated trouble from 'ardent feminists' in the audience (*Star*, 9 May 1913) and the *Morning Post* (12 May 1913) noted 'stray signs of dissent' in the audience, and 'protest against the militant methods of Petruchio and the final capitulation of Kate'. The *News of the World* (11 May 1913) decided that 'Katherine was obviously a suffragette'; the *People* (11 May 1913) saw her as an 'old-time "militant"'. The *East Anglian Daily Times* (12 May 1913) consoled 'the male sex, now sadly beset by shrews' that 'Petruchio, at any rate, succeeded in dealing with a mediaeval suffragette'.[23] The *Referee* (11 May 1913) was very specific: 'Katharines (and Christabels) are more violent and virulent than ever' and the *Daily Mail* (12 May 1913) characterised Katherina's sufferings in revealing terms: 'the reverse of a hunger strike'. The *Evening News* (12 May 1913) queried 'Whether this is precisely the most tactful moment for the revival of so truculently anti-feminist a play' and *Vanity Fair* (14 May 1913) felt the production was pitched at 'a sadly reactionary public'. If so the production sometimes missed its target as *Vanity Fair* also reported booing and hissing from women in all parts of the house. H. Jennie Baker wrote in to the *Daily Citizen* (20 May 1913) to state: 'I can only regard the play as an incomplete tragedy. Katherine could not have acted the hypocrite so completely if she had not had a dagger in her possession and the confident assurance that she was going to stab her tyrant that night.'

Harvey may, pragmatically, have been trying to capitalise on contemporary debates in order to generate a good box office. However, a month after the production opened in London, its meanings changed irrevocably when Emily Wilding Davison died, trampled to death by the King's racehorse, as she protested in the suffragette cause. In the massive publicity succeeding this event, Harvey's staging of *The Taming of the Shrew* became unavoidably and overtly political. Nevertheless, Harvey continued to tour his production through the UK during the rest of the year; indeed the play continued to be in his repertory well into the 1920s. Martin-Harvey (416) actually records disappointing box office for his first London run with *The Shrew* and closed it to open a production of *The Faun* by Edward Knoblauch. This play shows the successful diversion of a suffragette away from politics and into married life.[24]

23 This comment also appeared in other syndicated papers, e.g. *The Cork Constitution*, 12 May 1913.
24 Harvey's political activism was often enthusiastic and was really in evidence during the First World War when he ran a vigorous recruitment campaign. Nicholas Butler (95) speculates that later on Harvey didn't give Reinhardt sufficient credit for his influence on Harvey's production because of Harvey's anti-German feelings during and after the war.

Harvey himself was an improbable Petruchio, as he was best known for tragic and reflective roles, although he and his Katherina, his wife Nina de Silva, had in earlier years done Lyceum summer tours starring in *Catharine and Petruchio*. Harvey argued that Petruchio was 'one of the greatest gentlemen Shakespeare ever drew', the traditional 'whip-cracking' is 'maddening', and Katherina's surrender is 'whimsical', a gesture implying 'Let the man have his way, it saves a lot of trouble and seems to keep him happy' (Martin-Harvey 414). Harvey cut back on lines which stress Petruchio's interest in Katherina's money, thus making the character far more romantic than the text suggests, and Katherina's submission speech was cut by 27 lines with 'little feeling for either the verse, the message or the comedy of the play' (Macdonald 68).

In some ways it is not surprising that the actor-manager Harvey did not restore the Sly Epilogue: he ended the play with Petruchio's 'God give you good night' (5.2.187), that is giving himself the curtain. When the *Times* (12 October 1922) announced that 'an unusual feature' that is 'the playing of the epilogue' was about to take place, the company concerned was one that was determinedly ensemble, poverty-stricken and opposed to the star ethos: the Old Vic. This underfunded, bare-boards production was directed by a graduate from Philip Ben Greet's shoestring touring company, Robert Atkins (see also p. 54). While documentation on this production is scarce (the pre-Second World War Old Vic archives were bombed in 1941), some success is indicated by the fact that 1920s Old Vic productions of *The Taming of the Shrew* frequently staged the Epilogue, and when Atkins came to prepare an acting edition of the play for Samuel French, he provided expansive stage directions encouraging aspirant directors to stage the play in Elizabethan costume on a pseudo-Elizabethan stage and with the full framework.[25] Atkins's text (iii) states unequivocally that 'The audience is intended to view the play through the bemused eyes of Sly', and it gives new emphasis to the 'Induction', labelling this sequence scenes 1 and 2, while what is conventionally labelled 1.1 becomes scene 3. In addition, at the end of the Folio text, Atkins's edition ploughs straight on, with only an aside to indicate the source of the text, into the Epilogue from *A Shrew*, pressuring directors to include this scene. So at a time when professional mainstream theatre was still nervous of the full Sly framework, amateur theatre and schools, Samuel French's target market, were getting accustomed to the Epilogue.[26]

25 The edition does not credit Atkins but the Samuel French archive at the London Theatre Museum (Blythe House, Box 26) records that Atkins was paid 25 guineas for the preparation of this text.
26 The full framework was also being played in the amateur productions overseen by Nugent Monck at the Maddermarket, Norwich, at least from 26 September 1927 on.

The 1920s is also the period when *The Shrew* went into twentieth-century dress. Garrick's *Catharine and Petruchio* had of course been dressed in eighteenth-century modern dress (see illustration 1) but Daly had made lavish period costume fashionable. Twentieth-century dress proved a mixed blessing – it made the play contemporary, but it also evoked contemporary gender debates. Nevertheless H. K. Ayliff had very considerable success with modern-dress productions of *The Taming of the Shrew* in New York in

5 Mary Ellis as Katherina and Basil Sydney as Petruchio in H. K. Ayliff's 1927 modern-dress *Taming of the Shrew* in New York (revived in London in 1928).

1927 and then in 1928, with a Birmingham Repertory Theatre production, produced by Barry Jackson as part of his controversial, experimental series of modern-dress Shakespeares (see illustration 5).[27] In New York the production ran for 175 performances, and was located socially as taking place amongst New York high society. However, Ayliff was partly anticipated by a Harvard Dramatic Club musical adaptation directed by Edward Massey which brought *The Shrew* into the jazz age, featured a Petruchio who turned up to his wedding dressed as a cowboy and had Katherina and Petruchio travelling to Padua by means of a flivver, or cheap motor car (*Boston Evening Transcript*, 4 May 1927). Subsequently a dispute took place (*NYT* 13 November 1927) as to who exactly first put *The Taming of the Shrew* into twentieth-century dress but Sly and the Induction went into twentieth-century dress as early as Firmin Gémier's production of de la Fouchardière's 1918 adaptation of the play.[28]

When Ayliff reprised his New York production in London in 1928, some reviewers were still reacting with knee-jerk outrage to modern-dress Shakespeare *per se*, but Ayliff's production also disturbed some British reviewers because it evoked contemporary gender issues, something 'made more acute by the granting, at long last in 1928, of the vote to all women over twenty-one' (Cochrane 136), and the topical debate as to whether to keep the vow 'to obey' in the marriage service (e.g. *O* 6 May 1928). The *Weekly Scotsman* (12 May 1928) was moved to suggest that, post-Ibsen, *The Taming of the Shrew* 'becomes a problem play'; the *Birmingham Post* argued that when a modern Katherina performs her last speech without irony, 'she becomes positively Victorian' (19 May 1928). The majority of reviewers, however, insisted that the production was so full of high jinks that feminism was never an issue (e.g. *T* 1 May 1928; *G* 1 May 1928).

Ayliff used the Sly framework and the Induction was set in Warwickshire outside 'The Swan' alehouse in winter. The Lord (Laurence Olivier) and his party wore hunting pink, and Sly was washed, dressed in evening dress and then positioned in a theatre box. From there Sly watched most of the play, accompanied by both his 'wife', a man 'tastefully attired as a modern flapper with an Eton-cropped wig, flimsy sleeveless frock and matching heeled shoes' (Cochrane 131–2), and the Lord. Soliloquies were spoken to Sly, who often 'interpolated snorts and grunts' when he had no lines (*Town Crier*, 14 December 1928). *A Shrew* was ransacked for lines well into the second half of

---

27 Ayliff (1927) was very similar to Ayliff (1928); the former is described in detail in Margarida.

28 Although when the production opened in Lyons in 1918 Gémier did not use Sly, by the time he opened in Paris he had reinstated the Prologue. He discusses this in Gsell 130–3.

the play but although producer Barry Jackson was keen to use the final scenes from *A Shrew*, 'it was actually rehearsed, but finally omitted, because the actual words in the old edition are so corrupt as to be illiterate' (*BP* 19 May 1928).

Eileen Beldon's flapper Katherina was quickly tamed, and essentially the fight was over at the end of 2.1. Although Katherina struggled valiantly during this scene, she collapsed into tears by the end, after a wrestling sequence which 'left the lovers as breathless as any pair of professional wrestlers' (*Outlook*, 12 May 1928). Petruchio wielded a whip and was presented as a tweedy, country gentleman with a liking for horseplay, with elements of 'the pet of the modern novelist of the more popular type, the heman, the cave-man' (*BP* 2 May 1928), while the *Scotsman* (1 May 1928) characterised the by-play as 'Shakespeare's comic sheik business'. More sinisterly, with historical hindsight, at Katherina's and Petruchio's wedding, Grumio was dressed as 'a black-shirted Fascist' (*Era*, 9 May 1928), and later the tailor appeared as 'an obsequious Jew from Whitechapel' (Speaight 162).

As her shrewishness had already evaporated, Katherina's suffering at Petruchio's house seemed like overkill. However, some reviewers were confident that politics would be forgotten by 'feminine members of the audience' as the production provided a 'golden opportunity for débutantes to decide what they will wear at Ascot, Lord's, and the season's dances' (*DT* 1 May 1928). In pre-publicity articles fashions designed by Elspeth Fox Pitt were much discussed, especially the daring 'trousered gown' (*DS* 30 April 1928) worn by the Widow at Katherina's wedding.

One advantage of the frock parade was that class issues were to the fore because of the evocation of contemporary high society. Norman Marshall felt the outrage of Petruchio's wedding attire was far clearer when seen 'against a crowd dressed with the formal correctitude of the guests at a fashionable wedding at St George's, Hanover Square' (172). However, as the superlatives heaped on Ralph Richardson's Tranio reveal, the class commentary was conservative: Richardson's Cockney chauffeur Tranio, was full of 'plebeian cheerfulness' (*T* 1 May 1928) and equipped with 'the accent and the overweening self-confidence that seem to grow naturally in garages' (*NYT* 27 May 1928).[29]

Ayliff cut the text of the subplot heavily and transposed some sections in order to establish a clearer narrative. Hortensio gave up his pursuit of Bianca at the end of 3.1, so Hortensio's contributions to the rest of the Bianca plot

---

29 Richardson had already at this stage in his career played the Pedant (Merchant), Vincentio and Lucentio in various revivals for the touring Charles Doran Company, but he had also played Tranio as early as 1921 for the St Nicholas Players.

were all cut and the Pedant (Merchant)'s scenes (4.2, 4.4) were reduced and run together into one scene. The production, like Ayliff's in 1927, got a lot of laughs from its anachronisms: the presence of a car (4.5), an electric fire (4.1), a flash photographer and cine cameraman (3.2), a Kodak (1.1) as well as gramophones, wirelesses, carpet-sweepers, speaking-tubes and so on. The attention reviewers paid to the modern paraphernalia suggests that their primary impact was distracting, and did not challenge audiences with the question of whether gender politics had moved on since the 1590s.

Nineteenth and early twentieth-century productions were crucial in establishing the patterns that were to dominate the subsequent stage history of *The Taming of the Shrew*: Webster's *faux* Elizabethanism; Daly's dignity; Sothern and Marlowe ladling on the sentiment; acrobatics with the Bensons and Asche; commedia with Reinhardt; and the increasing use of Sly with Harvey and Atkins. Perhaps in spite of their directors, some of these productions also prepared the ground for tragic Katherinas (e.g. Violet Vanbrugh's performance for Benson) and certainly feminist politics was beginning to affect reception of the play.

MID- AND LATE TWENTIETH CENTURY

While *The Shrew* continued to be popular in the UK, particularly at the Old Vic and Stratford, the big success of the mid-twentieth century was the 1935 *Taming of the Shrew* featuring Lynne Fontanne and Alfred Lunt, a production which was revived many times and which toured all over the US.[30] Although Harry Wagstaff Gribble was technically the director, Fontanne and Lunt had their significant creative input acknowledged in the programme, which stated that the 'scheme of production' was by them. The text was full of transpositions and adjustments, it included substantial cutting and featured 'a band with drums, a troupe of tumblers, a cluster of midgets, a pair of comic horses and some fine songs set to good beer-garden music by Frank Tours' (*NYT* 1 October 1935). Comic business abounded: 'Alfred Lunt skipped rope in a scene with the tailor using a string of sausages' and the famished Katherina 'surreptitiously stuffed pineapples in her bustle and sausages and oranges into her bodice' (Cocroft 207–8). Any opportunity to clown was seized upon, latecomers were heckled, particularly by Sly, and the play sometimes stopped while the actors explained to the latecomers what had happened so far. Loud coughing from anyone in the audience also risked

---

30 The final revival was in 1940 as a fundraiser for the Finnish Relief Fund. Support for the Fund generally indicated an anti-communist stance; however, Lunt was partly brought up in Finland and felt particularly strongly about the country's plight.

6 Lynn Fontanne and Alfred Lunt in the 1935 *Taming of the Shrew* (which inspired *Kiss Me, Kate*) directed by Harry Wagstaff Gribble.

bringing on an attack of coughing from the actors. An excessive, even camp quality in the production is suggested by the final moments which featured Fontanne and Lunt in a golden chariot, ascending to the heavens in a sunburst, and accompanied by a grand chorus (*San Franciso News*, 14 November 1939).

Fontanne found Katherina difficult as "she's supposed to be fiery but her actual lines are not really at all hot" (quoted in Zolotow 204). One way the production coped with this was to make Katherina a terrifying offstage presence and to delay her actual arrival onstage. Katherina kept most of her lines in her opening scene (1.1) but they were shouted from her offstage lair, behind the stage balcony, and they were underscored by her hurling objects – such as a boot or a shoe – onto the stage. In addition, Fontanne's Katherina 'before being seen, was heard off stage smashing crockery and shouting defiance' (*San Franciso Examiner* 14 November 1939) and her entrance was 'heralded by a noisy blunderbuss, which brings down a goose from the theater's rafters' (*San Franciso Chronicle* 14 November 1939). Katherina broke the lute over Hortensio's head onstage, she fought Petruchio ferociously, and her submission was 'tongue-in-cheek' as she was in love but 'she considered herself his equal' (Zolotow 204).

The fact that Katherina and Petruchio were played by the most famous theatrical married couple in the US at the time meant that the production was also read as Lynn Fontanne skirmishing with Alfred Lunt, a double vision which helped to inspire the 1948 musical based on Fontanne's and Lunt's production, and their backstage quarrels, *Kiss Me, Kate*, with music by Cole Porter and book by Bella and Sam Spewack. The protagonists of *Kiss Me, Kate* Lilli and Fred are even named for Fontanne, who was christened Lillie Louise Fontanne (Zolotow 10), and Al/fred Lunt. While it is generally recognised that the Fontanne/Lunt production of *The Taming of the Shrew* inspired *Kiss Me, Kate*, the extent to which it in some ways still lives on in stagings of *Kiss Me, Kate* has not been sufficiently acknowledged. Some of the stage directions for *Kiss Me, Kate* very precisely recall features unique to the Fontanne/Lunt production. For example, in the equivalent of 1.1 Kate/Lilli Vanessi lurks in her own balcony area, from which she hurls objects onstage after hearing Bianca's suitors discussing her (*KMK* 40–1); a bird is shot and falls from the skies (used for Katherina's first entrance by Fontanne, brought about by a trigger-happy gangster in *Kiss Me, Kate* (47)); Lilli's Kate stuffs a string of sausages down the front of her dress, as Fontanne did when playing Katherina (*KMK* 49); Fontanne as Katherina got spanked by Lunt's Petruchio on their first meeting and the spanking of Lilli in *Kiss Me, Kate* is crucial to the plot.[31] Of course the performance of *The Taming of the Shrew* in *Kiss Me, Kate* is chaotic: it reassigns lines and changes characters even *before* the gangsters arrive on the scene and confuse matters; however, when Baptista offers a dowry of 20,000 crowns, and Petruchio demands 30,000, the book of *Kiss Me, Kate* is echoing a joke recorded in

---

31 There were even continuities in personnel: the first producer of *Kiss Me, Kate*, Arnold Saint-Subber, had worked backstage on the Fontanne/Lunt production and John C. Wilson co-produced *The Taming of the Shrew* and directed *Kiss Me, Kate*.

the promptbook for the Fontanne/Lunt production at 2.1.118, and when Kate wields a bouquet like 'a stiletto' (*KMK* 40), this echoes a stage direction which appears in 3.2 in the Fontanne/Lunt promptbook. While the Fontanne/Lunt production thus still lives on in *Kiss Me, Kate*, the success of the musical has also impacted on subsequent productions of *The Taming of the Shrew*. Ranald comments that 'almost every post-1948 review of [*The Taming of the Shrew*] laments the absence of the Cole Porter music' (220), and certainly some lines in the play – 'I come to wive it wealthily in Padua' (1.2.72), 'Where is the life that late I led?' (4.1.111) as well as 'kiss me, Kate' (2.1.313, 5.1.116 and 5.2.180) – resonate for audiences because of their prominence in the musical.

The camping up of *The Shrew* which occurred in both the Fontanne/Lunt production and in *Kiss Me, Kate* can also be found in work of Michael Benthall and his partner Robert Helpmann. Benthall first made the unsuitable suggestion (in the opinion of the Stratford theatre governors) that he should direct Helpmann as Katherina in a production of *The Taming of the Shrew* during the 1948 season.[32] *Variety* (5 November 1947) reported that the proposed all-male production had been called off after being criticised as 'decadent', and instead Benthall directed Diana Wynyard and Anthony Quayle in the lead roles. Sally Beauman (189) claims that Barry Jackson's departure from his post of Artistic Director at Stratford was hastened by his failure to dismiss quickly enough the proposal that Helpmann play a transvestite Katherina. However, Benthall went on to direct Helpmann as Petruchio in 1955 for an Old Vic tour of Australia, with Katharine Hepburn playing Katherina. The production was one of great excess: Hepburn was tipped upside down so that her bloomers showed, spanked with a slipper and made obediently to trot 'around the stage jumping over furniture' while Helpmann 'cracked his whip' (*Bulletin*, 1 June 1955). The word 'biz' occurs frequently in the promptbook, and the production was stuffed with excessive, gymnastic violence, whip–cracking and all the old, well-worn, popular gags. Meanwhile the Australian press were extremely distracted by Hepburn's insistence on wearing trousers offstage, and by her reputation for shrewish behaviour towards journalists.

Another important development in the mainstream stage history of *The Taming of the Shrew* occurred in 1954, when Tyrone Guthrie directed the play at Stratford, Ontario.[33] Guthrie had directed the play previously for

32 Helpman's most celebrated venture into transvestite performance was in the ballet of *Cinderella*, in which Helpmann and Frederick Ashton danced the Ugly Sisters.

33 *The Shrew* is one of the most-performed plays at Stratford, Ontario, being produced six times in forty-six years. It was the first play to get a second production (Langham 1962), and the first to get a third production (Gascon 1973).

the Old Vic in 1939 where he had stressed slapstick and custard pies. He was more restrained at Stratford, but he made the decision to relocate the play to a very specifically Canadian setting. All the characters except for Baptista had Canadian accents, and the Induction presented a shooting party coming back from Canada's northern woods (Robertson Davies 32). Localised settings are now common: Wild West cowboy productions are popular in the US (e.g. Antoon 1990); Robin Lovejoy directed the first in a long line of Australianised stagings in 1972. However, it was Guthrie's Canadianised production which really started the trend for finding a localised and meaningful context for the 'problem' of the unruly woman, Katherina.

The middle of the twentieth century saw the beginning of a massive increase in the number of documented stagings of *The Taming of the Shrew*, and instead of attempting an exhaustive, and exhausting, account, I will concentrate on what seem to me the biggest challenges associated with these productions: playing Katherina, playing Petruchio, and what to do about Sly.

PLAYING KATHERINA

Katherina has been played as anything from stock comic joke to full-blown tragic heroine. Details on how individual moments in Katherina's journey have been played can be found in the commentary but a useful focus is provided by five particularly crucial aspects of the role: Katherina's notorious last speech; the impact of feminism on Katherina's story; the attempt to present her as a tragic heroine; the kind of violence or shrewish behaviour she has displayed; and the importance of period setting in establishing the meanings of her revolt and submission.

Katherina's last speech

The challenge of Katherina's long last speech, where she speaks in favour of the submission of wives to their husbands, is essentially that of tone. Performers have a wide range of choices here: is Katherina ironic, sincere, angry, exhibitionist, lobotomised, in love, masochistic, feminist, indulgent, threatening, or does she just have her eyes on the cash, which 5.2.128 draws to her attention? Historically Katherinas have moved from unambiguous submission (particularly when the final Sly scenes weren't played), to a whole range of subversive and complex readings. In a production which began its long life in 1905, Julia Marlowe gave the speech 'with chosen emphases by which she showed that in her heart she despised the gossamer things to whom she was speaking and . . . she was merely biding her time until she could reassert her dominion . . . one would not care to be in *Petruchio*'s shoes' (Russell 337).

Nina de Silva, in her husband Martin Harvey's 1913 production, rattled through the speech 'as a sort of jesting formula' (*Daily Chronicle*, 12 May 1913), and twenty-seven lines of the speech were cut. By the late twentieth century the speech was often critiqued in the playing: Michael Bogdanov's 1978 production had Katherina spit 'out her famous speech of submission with such indomitable scorn that [Petruchio] flinches and turns away' (*ES* 5 May 1978). In 1988 Goldie Semple delivered the speech with flamboyance, and with laughter in her voice. Although Petruchio went for a kiss mid-speech, Semple's Katherina carried on, as she had more to say, and the speech gradually became 'a kind of verbal sexual foreplay with Petruchio' (*Hamilton Spectator*, 2 June 1988). Perhaps Kevin Sheard's production for Queere Shakespeare Company (Toronto 1998) gives an indication of how difficult this speech can be. This subversive, high-camp production had Katherina, a drag queen, take 'her' wig off to deliver 'her' submission speech but had this speech neutered: 'women' became 'people' or 'a person'; 'husbands' became 'partners'. The original speech was too extreme even for high-camp.

The question of tone is complicated further by the range of individual responses generated by any one production's performance choices. For example, the *Canberra Times* (30 July 1994) reported that, in Sydney, 'most evenings' women booed and hissed Katherina's last speech in John Bell's 1994 production, but this did not happen every night. Reviewers witnessing the speech on the same night also frequently disagree on the tone of its delivery: for example, in Jean Gascon's 1973 production, *Plays and Players* (April 1973) thought the speech was delivered with the 'perfect light touch of cynicism'; the *Detroit News* (5 June 1973), disturbingly, thought this Katherina 'remembers to make Kate's eyes say yes while her lips say no' and the *Windsor Star* (5 June 1973) felt that the whole production degraded women almost as much as the then recent film, *Last Tango in Paris*.

Subversion of Katherina's final speech became increasingly popular after Mary Pickford's famous knowing wink in the 1929 film of *The Taming of the Shrew*, although reviewers had complained about hints of something less than complete docility in earlier performances by, for example, Julia Marlowe or Margaret Anglin. Some Katherinas have subverted the speech by sending it up and performing it in an exaggerated, over-enthusiastic, melodramatic or self-consciously rhetorical style (for example, Josie Lawrence in 1995). Some Katherinas are seen to realise that there is money to be won and subvert the sentiments of the speech by clearly going along with Petruchio's demands solely in order to rake in the cash: for example, Stephen Unwin's 1998 production had Grumio whispering in Katherina's ear, before she entered in response to Petruchio's summons, priming her about what was happening. In 1997 Richard Rose also emphasised the importance of cash and ended with a vision of Katherina and Petruchio in bed on the upper stage, joyfully dividing the money they had won together. Katherinas have even subverted the gesture of placing their hands below their husband's foot: for example, Tracey Ullman did this only then to tip her Petruchio, Morgan Freeman over (*Daily News*, 20 July 1990). These ingenious responses can also be argued to have some kind of historical legitimacy in that *A Shrew* clearly did, if not subvert, then at least undercut the speech by returning to Sly and his foolish idea that the inner play indubitably demonstrates how to tame a shrew.

Feminism

Feminist critiques of *The Taming of the Shrew* have had a particular impact on late twentieth-century productions of the play, although nervousness about the play's gender politics was prominent much earlier, for example in the reviews of Harvey's 1913 production (see above, pp. 24–5) and even the popular 1887 Daly production must, the *Boston Advertiser* (31 October 1895) felt, 'give serious offence to the new woman'. The feminist movements of the 1960s made productions marketing themselves as apolitical sound disingenuous, but as the play continued to be popular in the theatre, feminist theatre-workers began to find a variety of strategies for dealing with Katherina. While an obvious riposte to such strategies is to suggest that rather than injecting feminism into a recalcitrant text it might be easier simply to do another play, nevertheless feminist spin on Katherina has produced a series of inventive, entertaining and comic versions of her story.

Rescue is one feminist option, particularly rescuing Katherina from the ending the Folio text gives her, and importing subtext, or play between the lines, to indicate that Katherina remains at the end untamed. A more complex outcome was achieved by the first woman to direct *The Taming of the Shrew* for the RSC, Di Trevis, who achieved an impressive balancing act by keeping both gender and class politics in focus. Although Trevis argued that *The Taming of the Shrew* was 'not so much about the position of women as about wealth and class, about people being treated as objects by others in more powerful positions' (*Northamptonshire Evening Telegraph*, 24 August 1985) gender was never sidelined. The production programme quoted Germaine Greer, J. S. Mill and George Bernard Shaw on feminism, and included photographs of a women's protest march. Trevis's production was also unusual in going against the dominant trend of playing Bianca as a scheming, manipulative, sometimes promiscuous, minx. Trevis had Sîan Thomas as Katherina playing alongside her real-life sister Sara Mair-Thomas as a

Bianca who thought 'Kate is the sister Bianca would like to become' (*FT* 3 October 1985).[34]

Later, again for the RSC, in 1995 Gale Edwards used the Sly framework (see pp. 59–60) to contextualise Katherina's story because Katherina was also Mrs Sly. Josie Lawrence as Katherina delivered her last speech in over the top mode and yet also ambiguously, alternating from loud and angry, almost growling at the other women, to a breathy, parody Marilyn Monroe style. While the *Independent on Sunday* (14 April 1996) could only find 'something like a confession at a show-trial', this virtuoso performance was unexpected, confrontational, and segued straight back into the Slys' marital problems. Edwards then deliberately left the final moments of the play ambiguous, leaving open the question of whether Katherina and Petruchio, or the Slys, would ever be able to work through Petruchio's/Sly's dreams of supremacy. The production closed with a challenge to the audience to think through their own fantasies and experiences of domination and submission.

Edwards was taken to task by many reviewers for her interventionist, feminist approach but other directors have been rebuked precisely for not providing a feminist riposte to the play. Pamela Hawthorn experienced this in 1979 when she became the only woman so far to direct the play at Stratford, Ontario.[35] The high-energy, no frills, no fuss, no props production disappointed Gina Mallet in the *Toronto Star* (2 July 1979), who complained: 'For a woman to direct this play more or less the way it's been written seems an act of sado-masochism . . . Hawthorn has apparently perceived the shrew as a form of Harlequin romance.' On similar lines two years later the Toronto *Globe and Mail* (12 February 1981) also complained of Pamela Brighton's 1981 production that 'There is nothing overtly feminist in the treatment, apart from the fact that [Brighton] could not bear to leave Kate's final cringing speech in a woman's mouth and gave it to Petruchio instead.'[36] After he delivered the speech Katherina handed him a drink and Petruchio tossed it in his own face.

Periods of active feminism have also, unsurprisingly, inspired backlash productions of *The Taming of the Shrew*, often productions claiming to be 'straight' or honouring what they identify as Shakespeare's intentions. For

34 Eyre (1971) also had real-life sisters playing the Minola sisters: Kika and Petra Markham played Katherina and Bianca respectively.
35 Hawthorn's production of the play was also the only one to take place on the Third Stage, the smallest theatre space at Stratford, the first time a Shakespeare play had been done in the smallest venue. In addition the production didn't receive the usual very extensive press coverage.
36 Handing most of the speech over to Petruchio first appeared in Garrick's *C&P*.

example, in 1960 John Barton directed a politically conservative *The Taming of the Shrew*, nostalgic in its loving recreation of an Elizabethan Golden Age, a production far more in tune with gender politics of the 1590s than those of the 1960s. The production inspired blatant sexism in reviewers (see McCullough 669), even, notoriously, Kenneth Tynan, who usually situated himself in terms of liberal politics, but who claimed that, as Katherina, Peggy Ashcroft rendered her last speech 'with an eager, sensible radiance that almost prompts one to regret the triumph of the suffragette movement' (*O* 26 June 1960). Barton's production was 'a complete and uncompromising anti-feminist version' where there is no doubt that 'women's suffrage suffers a considerable beating in the completeness of [Katherina's] capitulation' (*ES* 22 June 1960). Even when the role of Katherina was taken over by the politically radical Vanessa Redgrave, who was then active in the 'Ban the Bomb' sit-down protests and facing arrest on a daily basis, one reviewer found Katherina was 'a woman discovering that the delivery of a grovelling and submissive speech can actually give her a special new sensual kick' (*Sunday Express* 17 September 1961). However, for another reviewer Redgrave's sit-down protest 'in the middle of the stage in one of the shrewish scenes' also evoked Redgrave's real life sit-down protests in Parliament and Trafalgar Squares (*BP* 14 September 1961). Unfortunately, when Redgrave returned to Katherina in 1986 the production was so sentimental that even the conservative *Daily Mail* (11 June 1986) thought the romantic novelist 'Barbara Cartland . . . could not have put it better.' The *Observer* (15 June 1986) felt that 'This is the way the play used to be given at Stratford in the Fifties and early Sixties' and the production's anti-feminist line seemed well suited to Thatcher's Britain.

Tragic Katherinas

For many the logical extension of a seriously feminist approach to Katherina is to present her story as a tragedy and tragic Katherinas became increasingly popular after Charles Marowitz's entirely tragic Kate in his 1973 adaptation, *The Shrew*. Marowitz rejigged the play to confront and expand on its worst aspects, and had Kate held down and anally raped onstage. She delivered her final speech as a lobotomised broken woman wearing an institutional gown, stuttering her words. Kate's tragedy was 'that she underestimates the magnitude of Petruchio's bestiality' (Marowitz 18) and Marowitz (21) hoped that women in the audience would feel 'fury'. The mission to infuriate women rather than men is suggestive. Although Marowitz often positioned himself as a leftish radical, his text is available to an intensely conservative reading in terms of gender politics, that is, that uppity women get anally raped and brainwashed, so women should think twice before creating trouble. Barbara Hodgdon (4) also suggests that 'at worst, by emphasizing brainwashing and concentration-camp brutality, [Marowitz]'s overreading deprives sexual relations of any humanity or intersubjectivity and thus questions, if not erases, their association with pleasure'. However, while the depressing Marowitz collage became a box office hit around the world (Marowitz 17), and started a fashion for thuggish Petruchios and tragic Katherinas, Katherina as tragic heroine had certainly appeared much earlier: for example, the *Stage* (29 April 1920) was concerned that Ethel Warwick 'made people feel sorry for Katherina, which is fatal to the complete enjoyment of the farce', and this performance appeared in Bridges-Adams's extremely conventional production at Stratford.

After Marowitz tragic Katherinas were on the increase. Paola Dionisotti, in Michael Bogdanov's 1978 RSC production, certainly played Katherina's last moments as desolate. Dionisotti felt that Katherina's submission speech is 'full of affection for women' (Rutter 23), pointing out the horror of the women's situation but encouraging them to play with it. The production's ending, however, was bleak: 'The last image was of two very lonely people. The lights went down as we left – I following him, the others hardly noticing we'd gone. They'd got down to some hard gambling. They just closed ranks around the green baize table' (Dionisotti in Rutter 23).

An even more tragic Katherina appeared in Keith Digby's 1980 and 1987 productions. The 1980 modern-dress production evoked 'the politics of terrorism' (*SAG* 678) and while the first part of the play was genial, with Petruchio as a 'game-playing little boy' who arrived at his wedding 'riding a broomstick toy horse with a stuffed head', the closing moment before the interval evoked 'a more foreboding note with Kate's throat at sword's edge' (*SAG* 678). This set the tone for the second half where Sharry Flett's Katherina was 'Deprived of food and sleep for days', 'physically weak and ill . . . vacant-eyed and in rags' and Petruchio and two servants 'wore sacklike hoods with eye holes. Moving about, tormenting her, they barked commands and countercommands until, with a final scream, Kate disintegrated' and her final speech was delivered 'as a ranting sermon' by a broken and brainwashed wreck (*SAG* 678). Digby upset 'feminists, chauvinists, and Shakespeare purists alike' (*SAG* 678). In 1981, when Sharry Flett returned to the role of Katherina in the broadly comic Stratford, Ontario, production directed by Peter Dews, traces of the tragic Katherina still remained and in that production's riotously comic play world, Flett's Katherina was set apart, and because Flett is so slightly built, there was a real sense of her vulnerability alongside her Petruchio, Len Cariou, a huge, pirate-king figure. In Keith Digby's 1987 production Katherina was again a torture victim but there was enough energy left in her to slap Bianca during her last speech (*Times-Colonist*, 10 October 1987).

There was no relief from tragedy at all in David Ultz's 1985 production of *The Taming of the Shrew*; humour was suppressed, diction was deliberately anti-realistic, monotonous, and accompanied by the beating out of a rhythm, a 'steady monotonous thump' (*Time Out*, 14 March 1985). Katherina went mad as she gave her final speech and was bundled off in a blanket serving as a straitjacket. The production was advertised as 'The Women's Version' of the play and the action was placed 'within a feminist theatre group meeting', starting as the cast entered in 'blue boiler suits and luminous orange workmen's vests and pick up their scripts' (*FT* 12 March 1985). Fiona Victory was praised for her vicious Petruchio, who was a torturer, encasing 'Kate in a muzzle labelled "Scold"' and subjecting 'her to a barrage of flashing lights' while 'studying a book on falconry' (*G* 12 March 1985). As Carole Woddis maintained, however (*City Limits*, 15 March 1985), this 'Women's Version' was still circumscribed by male artistic vision as the director, technical crew and movement director were all male.

Another tragic view appeared in Peter Hinton's 1994 staging, which set the play in a sixteenth-century brothel and had all the roles, except for Petruchio, played by female 'prostitutes' in their underwear.[37] In order to perform, the women donned costumes of 'farthingales, pantaloons, two-foot high wigs' and makeup which was 'a ghastly take on the sickly decadence of the brothel, white faces and grotesque red lips masking the bruises of the profession', which helped Hinton stress that *The Shrew* was a 'brutal, brutal play' (*Ottawa Citizen*, 16 July 1994).

Tragic Katherinas are sometimes rescued or released from their tragedies by their Petruchios. Nichola McAuliffe's 1993 Katherina was initially vulnerable, because she wore a surgical boot, she was old, sullen, unloved and defensive. McAuliffe communicated 'the accumulated pain of (Katherina's) endurance in a world so fixated upon an ideal of female beauty that she – unlike her delectable sister – has never been able to match' (*I* 24 April 1993). McAuliffe herself stressed Katherina's situation as 'an older daughter not as loved or cherished as the younger daughter' (*Northern Echo*, 15 April 1993). Her bohemian Petruchio released her into an exciting, unconventional world but Jude Kelly's production succumbed to romance at the end when the 'tamed Kate and reformed Petruchio strike the advert pose of loving honeymooners on an ocean liner. Across the water an elderly couple wave benignly,

---

37 This played alongside a bilingual English/French version of the play entitled *The Return of the Shrew/ Le Retour de la Mégère* directed by Danielle Grégoire and set in a World Wrestling Federation-style ring.

a mirror of their future' (*Yorkshire Evening Post*, 24 April 1993). As Katherina, Nichola McAuliffe felt that 'if you really love somebody you can say "If you want me to I will do these things" ' (*Northern Echo*, 15 April 1993) and her Petruchio's response to her last speech was gratitude, close to tears. By contrast romance was on the wane in Aubrey Mellor's 1989 production, where Petruchio's demands meant that Katherina's final speech was delivered 'as a speech in which love dies' (Gay 1998, 174).

Some tragic Katherinas are presented as needing therapy and the director who has done most to proselytise on this subject is Jonathan Miller. His third production of *The Taming of the Shrew* in 1987 diagnosed Katherina initially as an isolated, self-harming, unshrewish, depressed woman in breakdown. Katherina was 'hideously deranged' (*STel* 11 September 1988), 'clearly borders on the psychotic' (*ES* 7 September 1988) and cultivated 'a bent posture that expresses agonies of self-contempt' (*T* 10 September 1987). Miller's shrew, Fiona Shaw, describes her director as 'complicatedly conservative' (Rutter 5) and eventually she became 'persuaded' that Miller's analysis, that Katherina was a 'disturbed child was misconceived' (6).[38] This was dressing up 'modern neuroses' in 'Renaissance costume' (Gay 1994, 116), something which depended on acting 'between the lines' (*T* 10 September 1987). Shaw herself stresses that Katherina 'doesn't have the language, she doesn't have the lines. So you have to hear Kate's silence and to interpret the clues of the silence' (Rutter 8). Shaw spoke her final speech as 'a statement, not on behalf of how great men are, but on behalf of our inability to change things' (21) and she felt Katherina was saying ' "I acknowledge the system. I don't think we can change this" – which is a terrible indictment of a system of patriarchy that is so strong it is unchangeable *even for its own good*' (24).

Rendering Katherina a tragic heroine in this way may gain sympathy for her cause; however, clinically diagnosing her condition as an illness carries with it the risk of suggesting that Katherina really does need Petruchio's abusive therapy.

Violence

How tragic or comic Katherina's story becomes is often related to her demonstrated ability to be violent. Really ferocious Katherinas might always choose to pick up the boxing gloves again, Annie-get-your-gun Katherinas might reload their rifles. Less violent Katherinas, although they make the

---

38 The production's emphasis on Baptista's poor parenting skills was also evident in Bianca's incipient alcoholism.

7 Tanya Ronder as a twenty-first-century Katherina in Helena Kaut-Howson's
production for the Manchester Royal Exchange.

point that society is constructing Katherina unfairly, seem more victimised. What kind of violence actresses can enact onstage also varies: shrewish violence in nineteenth-century promptbooks tends to centre around pulling hair, biting, throwing pillows, cushions and books. More recent shrews are more likely to throw right hooks and dole out half Nelsons.[39] However, in 1988 Goldie Semple's Katherina, a complex creation described as 'Hedda Gabler before the revolver was invented' with shades of Stella Kowalski (*G&M* 3 June 1988), created an absolute sensation, to judge from the archival video, when in a moment of comic violence she slowly and deliberately pulled the limbs off Bianca's teddy bear.

A more robust approach to comic violence appeared in Lynch (1991). Astonishing physical prowess was displayed by all Lynch's cast but Judy Gibson as Katherina excelled, and executed several judo-style throws on other characters. At the beginning of 4.3 Gibson threw the large, burly Grumio – played 'like a demented Hunchback of Notre Dame' (Wellington

39 For practical reasons films of *The Taming of the Shrew* are able to exhibit Katherina's
destructive tendencies more extravagantly and have often featured her wrecking
Baptista's house.

Evening Post, 25 June 1991) – around the room several times, suggesting she was well capable of looking after herself. Similarly capable Katherinas include Kate Reid's 1962 virago, remembered twenty years later by the *Ottawa Citizen* (18 June 1981) for displaying 'wrath' which was 'truly enough to make strong men tremble', punk Katherinas such as Tanya Ronder who played the role as 'a disaffected, deeply unhappy punk wild-child with a snake tattooed on her cheek' (*DT* 8 March 2001) and the 1990 sharp-shooting Katherina of Tracey Ullman, whose skills were memorably displayed in 2.1 when Katherina used Bianca for target practice.

Katherina as 'rottweiler' (*What's On*, 8 April 1992) appeared in Bill Alexander's 1992 RSC production, a Katherina who was 'glaring, snarling, stomping', and 'looks almost psychotic as she circles her sister, Bianca, with a vast pair of scissors' (*T* 3 April 1992). The *Observer* (5 April 1992) described Amanda Harris's Katherina as 'a marvellously full-throated roaring girl', and the *Sunday Telegraph* (5 April 1992) saw her as 'a termagant who steams about like the mad woman in the attic, her face set in a perpetual lockjawed scowl'. The taming of this Katherina was somewhat sidelined because the production focused on class rather than gender analysis and in 4.1, Katherina's first major taming lesson, the characters really suffering were the Lord's party, who were being forced to play Petruchio's servants. By comparison Katherina didn't suffer much, indeed as an actress who knew her lines and knew what was going on 'Katherina' was better off than the aristocrats who were standing awkwardly embarrassed, with scripts in their hands and being assaulted by both Petruchio and Grumio.

Another variation on the play's violence was achieved in Carl Heap's 1985 production for the Mediaeval Players, where both Katherina and Bianca were played by men. Because Mark Heap, complete with five o'clock shadow, played a Katherina who was very much bulkier than Petruchio, there was little sense that Petruchio could ever really do Katherina damage. The *Times* commented (29 November 1985) 'Knowing Kate to be, beneath her farthingale, a six-foot male eases the conscience when the taming begins' although the production's constant reaffirmation of the 'play within a play' scenario also helped here, as did the fact that, very unusually, not only was Sly doubling with Petruchio but the caricature, upper-class Lord was doubling with Katherina, a framing which always suggested a reversal of the inner play's power narrative. Producer Dick McCaw maintained, 'If Kate is played by a man, then it's like a knowing wink to the audience, it's tongue-in-cheek', it 'frees the play from reality, from being straight, serious drama with a straight and serious solution to the conflicts portrayed on stage' and the play becomes 'more of a witty debate on role playing rather than a full-on costume drama between a sex object and a sexist' (*Age*, 27 May 1986). For the *Scotsman* this production was able to focus on the absurdity of male/female relations in the play and *The Taming of the Shrew* then became 'a savage satire on masculinity' (12 September 1985).

The performance of violence can also invoke alternative sexualities. In Roger Hodgman's 1991 production, Pamela Rabe as Katherina elaborated the submissive/masochistic gesture of placing her hand under Petruchio's foot in 5.2. Rabe describes herself as trying 'to be as *seductive* as possible doing it, to be as *sexy* as possible' (Devlin-Glass 28) and when Petruchio raised his booted foot, as if demanding that Katherina place her hand there, Katherina prostrated herself on the floor, face down, but because she then turned over on her back, moving sexually and appearing to enjoy herself hugely, an intrigued and turned-on Petruchio couldn't resist joining Katherina on the floor. The submission then became one more item in Katherina's and Petruchio's repertoire of sex games. Flirting with hints of S&M may be appropriate given that, as Barbara Hodgdon (3) argues, *The Taming of the Shrew* aligns with 'the image repertory of classic pornography' and 'shares affinities with pornographic films'.[40] Mihai Maniutiu also played on related associations in his 1995 Leicester Haymarket production starring black actress Josette Simon as a highly sexed Katherina who performed 'a funky chicken striptease with sensual abandon' (*G* 3 May 1995). The production 'interestingly incorporates sexual sado-masochism' and this Katherina's sleepless wedding night was a result of 'thrashing around in bed' with Petruchio (*O* 30 April 1995). More recently in Lindsay Posner's 1999 RSC production, S&M was very much to the fore: the inner play was produced as Sly was refused access to a porn website and instead got *The Taming of the Shrew*. Petruchio was brutally violent and Katherina a dominatrix, and the *Times* (29 October 1999) asked 'Is the dominatrix agreeing to be dominated for the sexual fun of it?' The Epilogue concluded with Prodigy's 'Smack My Bitch Up' blaring out as the ladettes Katherina and Bianca entered a rave club, making the point that violence against women is still extremely marketable. Indeed, it may be that the ongoing popularity of *The Taming of the Shrew* is very much connected to its sado-masochistic subtext.

Period

Period costuming contextualises Katherina's struggle and can suggest Katherina is not alone as, for example, when debates over women's suffrage were deliberately evoked in the early twentieth-century costuming of Lovejoy (1972). Reviewers detected shades of Shaw's New Woman (*SMH* 13

---

40 See Burt for a discussion of pornographic versions of the play.

March 1972) and Ibsen (*Australian*, 1 April 1972) while the *Entertainer* (27
March 1972) was sure Katherina 'had a copy of *The Female Eunuch* concealed
in her luggage, or, to be nearer the period, a portrait of Mrs Pankhurst'. The
play was still problematic: the *Sunday Australian* (26 March 1972) felt 'sexual
domination' was endorsed, with Katherina suffering a 'physical and mental
beating by a cool sadist'. The *Australian* (1 April 1972) also reported 'shouted
vociferous approval' by some of the audience in relation to sexism in the play.
Katherina appeared as a more modern feminist in Barry (1972) where she
had 'sharp bangs, sports hip boots, a slit skirt and a T-shirt with a women's lib
sign on it' (*NYT* 29 June 1972) but the problem with modern versions of the
feminist Katherina is working out why on earth she turns up to her own
wedding. In Pope (1992), with a 1940s setting, Katherina actually tried to
'end it all by leaping from the bridge' over the park lake to avoid marrying
Petruchio (*I* 17 June 1992).

A thoughtful use of historical period appeared in Sue Rider's 1994
Brisbane production, when casting Katherina (Deborah Mailman) as
Aboriginal added an important dimension to the undervaluing of her.
Simply because the production was set immediately after the Second World
War, that is before Aboriginal people had the vote, Katherina became doubly
oppressed as a woman in a period of backlash, when women workers were
having to make way for returning soldiers, and also as a disenfranchised Aboriginal person. Petruchio was taking on a wife who was not only a shrew but
who would also be discriminated against. Penny Gay has argued that the
taming narrative of *The Shrew* has extra nuances in a culture 'tamed' or sub-
jugated by colonisers, where the colonised are feminised by their defeat and
political impotence, and 'the categories of women and indigenous people'
can be 'conveniently conflated' (1998, 170). Her arguments apply doubly
when Katherina is Aboriginal.[41] Mailman's Katherina, however, subverted
gender stereotypes of masculine strength and feminine weakness, impress-
ing the *Courier Mail* (19 March 1994) with her 'awesome half-nelson', while
Theatre Australasia (May 1994) reported Mailman's 'formidable physical
presence', particularly in 'wrestling matches' with Petruchio.

The supposedly reactionary 1950s provided a useful contextualisation for
Katherina's rebellion in Roger Hodgman's 1991 staging and the programme
reproduced several paternalistic 1950s magazine articles on how to be a good
wife. Cultural contexts as well as period contexts for the shrewish woman can
also be very suggestive. In 1997 Richard Rose situated the play in late 1950s

---

41 Rider's commitment to this reading of Katherina was confirmed when the
production was revived in 1996 and she cast another Aboriginal actress, Roxanne
McDonald, as Katherina.

Little Italy, New York, and included a *Seven Year Itch* Marilyn Monroe model for the tailor scene (4.3). Rose argued that Katherina does not cave in and that in her last speech she is joking but deadpan; he also approvingly cited the advice of his artistic director Richard Monette: 'Do not set this play after the Pill' (*Stratford for Students*, Summer 1997). While this production fell in love with its setting and paraded too many scene-stealing effects, Rose found 'in the fossilized machismo of an immigrant culture' 'a place where women are treated as goods for barter' (*G&M* 5 June 1997). This meant that stereotypes of Italian culture were in circulation and the production flirted with racism, an accusation which could also be levelled against Glen Walford's Liverpool Everyman production, which located *The Taming of the Shrew* in North Africa. For the *Liverpool Echo* (6 February 1987) this 'remains a world where fathers still decide the fates of their daughters and husbands the destiny of their wives', but the *Stage* (26 February 1987) seems complacent in its assertion that 'Nowhere in the modern world would any woman give vent to such sentiments except perhaps under Moslem law, where the wife is still a chattel.' Walford certainly played with stereotypes in her setting: Katherina and Bianca, 'yashmaked beauties', were accompanied onstage by such clichés as palm trees, a belly dancer, a snake charmer, 'the traditional scrofulous beggar and several curly-toed youths' (*Stage*, 26 February 1987).

PLAYING PETRUCHIO

Ironically, *The Taming of the Shrew* gives far more lines to Petruchio than it does to the shrewish, supposedly talkative woman Katherina, and Petruchio can easily become the star role. While whip-cracking machismo was for a time almost compulsory for Petruchios, more recently Petruchios tend to fall into the following categories: brutes; therapists or in therapy; mavericks or bohemians.[42]

The brute

Brutish Petruchios are often playing opposite tragic Katherinas and Marowitz established new benchmarks here, anthologising the most potentially unpleasant elements in Shakespeare's text, making them worse and, according to Marowitz, showing that while 'in the good old days, the man could brutalise the woman using physical means, today the woman could tyrannise the man using the more subtle weapons of psychology and social exploitation' (Marowitz 16–17). The modern demonstration of this moral

---

42 Some Katherinas, such as Mary Pickford, have also cracked whips.

8 The final scene in Michael Bogdanov's 1978 RSC *Taming of the Shrew*.

was communicated via a narrative of a particularly ill-suited modern couple's journey towards marriage.

Following the lead of Marowitz, Michael Bogdanov in 1978 directed Jonathan Pryce as a brutish Petruchio/Sly, both of whom used violence crudely. That brutishness in men was socially acceptable under the veneer of conventional behaviour was indicated in the final scene, set in a traditionally male club-like setting with a large green baize table, with men smoking, drinking port or brandy, and casually gambling, a society 'in which well-fed men slouch indolently over their port, baying 'hear, hear' when one of their number extracts a particularly ignominious confession of inferiority from his woman' (*New Statesman*, 12 May 1978) (see illustration 8).

Michael Billington has been much quoted for reporting that this production's 'sheer brutality' was 'almost unbearable' and for calling for *The Taming of the Shrew* to 'be put back firmly and squarely on the shelf' (*G* 5 May 1978). The following year, reviewing the London revival, however, Billington felt differently and argued that the production was actually 'entirely about the taming of Petruchio', his humiliation by 'a mature, witty and ironic Kate', although he had to admit that this was 'far more complex and interesting than Shakespeare's ending' (*G* 30 April 1979). For Penny Gay, by contrast, the production simply lost its edge and 'a radical experiment collapsed before the old theatrical urge to entertain the punters, and . . . Pryce's "star" qualities insisted that – whatever the enlightened reading of the play – it was about Petruchio, not Kate' (1994, 109).

For real nastiness the Petruchio of Keith Digby's 1987 *The Taming of the Shrew* was particularly memorable. Following very similar lines to his 1980 production, Digby emphasised Petruchio's brainwashing of Katherina, and Petruchio took 'cruel, drawn-out pleasure' in 'whipping the shrew out of Kate', a process which included her tormentors donning Ku Klux Klan hoods, as well as the usual starvation and sleep deprivation (*Times-Colonist*, 10 October 1987). Lindsay Posner's 1999 RSC production also featured a Petruchio who repelled with his violence. This Petruchio was seen aiming heavy kicks and blows at his servants, and there was the suggestion of off-stage violence against Katherina, who appeared with a large red weal on her arm after her marriage.

Bill Alexander produced two versions of Petruchio the brute in his closely related RSC productions of 1990 and 1992. The *Jewish Chronicle* (10 April 1992) saw the 1992 Petruchio as a psychiatrist 'whose course of food and sleep deprivation and humiliation is the equivalent of modern electric-shock treatment', although this Petruchio's brutish behaviour was also directed against the Lord's party, who were made to play his servants in 4.1 and who got hit and slapped. The original production in 1990 had Gerard Murphy, a physically imposing, tough actor playing Petruchio. In 1992 the Petruchio of Anton Lesser was more slightly built but capable of injecting bitter anger into the sunniest of lines.

The romantic form of brutishness, swashbuckling, still has adherents although it was probably epitomised in Douglas Fairbanks Snr's thigh-slapping performance in Sam Taylor's 1929 film. More recent swashbucklers include Peter O'Toole in John Barton's 1960 staging, 'the most aggressive, virile, dominating Petruchio in years' (*Evening Standard*, 22 June 1960), and Derek Godfrey, who succeeded O'Toole in the role, and who combined swashbuckling with playing 'Master Petruchio of Wimpole Street, consultant in nervous disorders' (*SUAH* 22 September 1961). Picking up on the recent *Lady Chatterley* censorship trial, the *Sunday Telegraph* (17 September 1961) also discerned in this Petruchio 'a touch of the devil and the tenderness of Mellors'. Much earlier, reviewers of H. K. Ayliff's 1928 production saw Petruchio as he-man lover, a sexy sheikh or a Valentino (e.g. *BP* 2 May 1928,

Scotsman, 1 May 1928). The great swashbuckling moment, when Petruchio bundles Katherina over his shoulder and abducts her from the wedding feast in 3.2, is still popular and Petruchios are often even now applauded by the audience for this feat.

The therapist

This reading is central to all of Jonathan Miller's productions of the play (1972, 1980, 1987), and John Cleese's 1980 Petruchio exemplified the approach. His Petruchio's therapy consisted of imitating and mocking Sarah Badel's Katherina, treating her like a small child in need of behaviour therapy, and making chicken-like noises at her. Petruchio has also played social worker in order to rescue Katherina from herself, and in Peter Dews's 1981 production the programme explicitly stated that Petruchio 'frees' Katherina from the role she is 'trapped' in.

Petruchio is also occasionally in therapy himself during the taming process: for example in Zeffirelli (1967) Richard Burton's Petruchio clearly begins to reform and is less of a drunkard and boor by the end of the film. Tyrone Guthrie also saw Petruchio as maturing during the taming process and in his best-documented *Taming of the Shrew*, his 1954 production at Stratford, Ontario (which had many continuities with his 1939 custard pie production at the Old Vic), Guthrie played against audience expectations and mobilised a timid, bespectacled Petruchio (William Needles) who looked like Harold Lloyd, was terrified of Katherina, and had to screw up his courage before meeting her. Guthrie turned the play into 'a psychological study of shyness' (Robertson Davies 38), and Katherina seemed as afraid of Petruchio as he was of her. Robertson Davies (39) thought this was 'playing against the lines', but the key for Guthrie came in the Lord's lines, 'This fellow I remember / Since once he played a farmer's eldest son' (Induction 1. 79–80), and Petruchio became a farmer's son in town for the fair (Davies 34). By the end of the play he had become a Zorro (*Los Angeles Times*, 4 July 1954), and had 'doffed his gait, glasses and Western attire' and become 'romantic gaucho' (*G&M* 1 July 1954).

The maverick

Petruchio sometimes offers Katherina the chance of an escape to an alternative lifestyle, an escape from the stifling conventionality of her bourgeois, rage-inducing social environment. The most popular modern version of this is Petruchio as Easy Rider, arriving onstage on a motorcycle. While Greg Miron in 1992 and Helena Kaut-Howson in 2001 both employed this motif,

9   Pamela Rabe's Katherina about to kick Hugo Weaving's Petruchio in the testicles in
Roger Hodgman's 1991 production for the Melbourne Theatre Company.
Photograph by Jeff Busby.

other directors have sent it up: Barnet Kellman in 1977 and Roger Hodgman
in 1991 reduced Petruchio to a moped.[43] When Jonathan Pryce made his first
entrance as Petruchio in 1.2 on a motorbike, in Michael Bogdanov's 1978
production, he fulfilled a longstanding ambition: when Pryce directed the
play at the Liverpool Everyman in 1974, he could only afford 'Leader of the
Pack' motorcycle noises-off. Hugo Weaving as a 1950s Petruchio in Roger
Hodgman's 1991 staging exuded 'a swaggering confidence and a smoulder-
ing sexuality' (*Age*, 24 June 1991), which evoked Marlon Brando and James
Dean but also brought gay dynamics provocatively into play because of
Weaving's androgynous charisma and his leather gear. Barry (1972) had
a Petruchio who wore 'a Hell's Angels motorcycle jacket with "Losers"
printed on the back and a Kaiser Wilhelm helmet' (*NYT* 29 June 1972), but
this Petruchio's home was a hippie commune, something which points to

43   The earliest motorcycling Petruchios I have found are both in 1928. Katherina
travelled in a sidecar in Beresford Fowler's production and Petruchio rode a
motorcycle in one of Fritz Leiber's many revivals of *The Shrew*.

another popular modern reading: Petruchio the dropout. Thus, in 1993, when Jude Kelly had Katherina trapped in a 1920s cruise ship play-world of rich, claustrophobic conformity, she was rescued by Brian Protheroe's Petruchio, a Bohemian artist, who arrived for 'the wedding on stilts wearing green King of the May gear', and whose studio home, 'like the fabled studio of the late Francis Bacon', was 'spattered beyond belief' (*Plays and Players*, June 1993). This Petruchio offered a real escape for Katherina from a life of dull cocktail parties.

Similarly, in John Bell's 1994 *The Taming of the Shrew* Petruchio was a dropout from the world of the Australian Gold Coast 'spivs, the indolent rich and shark-speculators', a 'brash, colourful . . . bad taste paradise' (*Sun-Herald*, 3 July 1994) where Baptista tapped 'out a marriage settlement on a color-coordinated computer' (*Age*, 26 May 1994). Petruchio, 'a scrungy-looking bloke from up in the hills' took Katherina 'the daughter of a wealthy golfing type in a posh urban district' (*Newcastle Herald*, 2 May 1994) to live among northern New South Wales Nimbin dropouts, hippies, surfers and skate-boarders, in a home that was a commune full of junk, centred around a pink and purple VW Beetle which *Theatre Australasia* (June 1994) records had its bonnet 'used as an entrance'. This Petruchio inhabited a production where the focus was always on 'the superficiality of judging people by their position', and less on Katherina's story (*Bulletin*, 7 June 1994).

Dropout Petruchios who reject bourgeois materialism, however, have problems with Petruchio's statement that he comes 'to wive it wealthily in Padua' (1.2.72). Another problem is that if Katherina is subjected to a class education (and her speech at the beginning of 4.3 suggests she might benefit from class consciousness raising), Katherina's oppression as a woman can become secondary to her status as upper-middle-class, spoilt, rich girl.

The maverick Petruchio can also fit well with cowboy stagings of *The Shrew* such as Antoon (1990), where grizzled, older, African American Morgan Freeman played a Petruchio who tamed the frisky, gun-toting filly that was Tracey Ullman's Katherina. The earliest cowboy Petruchio I have located was in Edward Massey's 1927 Harvard production, although Petruchio only donned 'the sombrero, red shirt and silvered leathers of a he-man from the great out-doors adjoining Hollywood' (*Boston Evening Transcript*, 4 May 1997) for his wedding.

THE THEATRICAL ADVENTURES OF CHRISTOPHER SLY

Although Sly may have carried on his career during the Restoration (see above p. 7) and he actually starred in the two texts of *The Cobler of Preston*, the success of Garrick's *Catharine and Petruchio* banished him from the stage for nearly a century. Sly staged his comeback in Benjamin Webster's 1844 production and he is now back with a vengeance: Ellen Dowling (88) in her survey of sixty-five major productions of *The Taming of the Shrew* from 1844 to 1978 found that 75 per cent of the productions surveyed used Sly, many using the full framework from *A Shrew*, rather than just the three scenes supplied by the Folio. When this happens, and Sly is spotlighted, the result is that sometimes Katherina is upstaged.

The spirit of Sly's full story reappeared in Webster's 1844 staging, which kept Sly onstage after the Induction, but gave him no lines. Martin Harvey used several Sly Interludes from *A Shrew* (see Appendix 1, pp. 236–7) in 1913 but not the Epilogue. Robert Atkins was the first director who indubitably reinstated the Epilogue, at the Old Vic in 1922, something which started a tradition of playing the full frame in Old Vic productions, usually with D. Hay Petrie as a scene-stealing Sly.

Approaches to Sly have varied widely and for convenience the four most popular will be discussed here: 'ersatz Elizabethanism'; Sly's dream; working-class hero; and Sly equivalents.

'Ersatz Elizabethanism'

The phrase is Jan McDonald's, describing Martin Harvey's staging, and it vividly evokes what several directors have tried to do with Sly: that is, to use him to help create a sense of Elizabethan staging. The inner play then becomes a jolly, unsophisticated romp, played for a drunken tinker in olde Merry England. This has the advantage of granting modern audiences permission to laugh at Katherina's taming, because it is seen to be the sort of story that only drunken Elizabethan tinkers enjoyed or believed in.

The first example of Sly-led ersatz Elizabethanism appeared in Benjamin Webster's 1844 production. J. R. Planché's Elizabethan stage design allowed Sly and the Lord to sit downstage left and right (see illustration 2) through most of the play. The *Spectator* (23 March 1844) records that Sly, 'being clothed in his own dirty rags', was 'brought on in the last scene as though being carried out to wallow in the mire' and 'The Lord bestows a purse upon the actors after all is done.'[44] Charles Strickland as Sly was much praised for his 'embodiment of all the poetry of drunkenness', his 'stolid asinine bewilderment' and he was carried out at the end of Act 4 'amidst a parting cheer of sympathy from the audience' (*Morning Chronicle*, 18 March 1844).

---

44 Planché (297) claims that Sly was carried out at the end of Act 5 but this is contradicted by the promptbooks and by contemporary reviews which state Sly was carried out at the end of Act 4.

Anticipating many later, more sympathetic, attitudes towards Sly, this reviewer also recorded an 'unpleasant feeling' when Sly was 'carried out' to be put 'out of doors', although most reviewers were so confident that the Lord's trick was great fun that the production's Lord was castigated as being too solemn and 'too grave to suit the madcap humour of a lord who would fancy such a jest' (*Spectator*, 23 March 1844). The *Daily News* (27 October 1847), which did not like the production at all, felt the Lord and Sly became 'perfect eyesores', looking 'as dull and inanimate as a set of wax figures'. Others record the Lord and his attendants performing 'a dumb show of merriment and courtesy to the tinker, who sits in a state of drunken stupor; the servants plying him with wine, until he becomes insensible' (*Spectator*, 23 March 1844).

Martin Harvey's 1913 production provided the next major dose of ersatz Elizabethanism and restored several of the Interludes from *A Shrew* (see Appendix 1, pp. 236–7). Harvey's Sly, Bartholomew and the Lord sat in front of the stalls in an ornamental seat roughly in the space normally occupied by the orchestra conductor.[45] Sly had the freedom to react strongly to the inner play: he tried to obtain an introduction to Katherina (Martin-Harvey 415), Petruchio shook his hand (Macdonald 70) and occasionally Sly attempted to get onstage and join in the fun. After being carried out asleep, Sly reappeared to 'stagger on to the stage and shake hands with the "stars" ' (*ST* 11 May 1913) and to join in as 'The play ended with a gay chain dance of all the performers across the stage and back again' (*Standard*, 12 May 1913). Harvey and his 'coadjutor' Poel had discussed restoring even more of *A Shrew*: in a letter of 20 September 1912 Poel offered to provide Harvey with a facsimile of the quarto text, at a cost of 10 shillings.[46] Sections from this text appear in the promptbook marked up by Poel (S58), including a slightly cut version of the Sly Epilogue but this is accompanied by the comment, 'NB The waking of Sly was not played.' In reinstating the Sly Interludes, Harvey and Poel were leading the way towards the return to the theatre of the framework from *A Shrew*.

Charles Glenny, who played Sly for Harvey in London, was praised for making Sly inoffensive, for his 'realistic . . . stupidity and semi-bestiality' (*Pall Mall Gazette*, 12 May 1913) and his sheer bulkiness![47] In an interview (*ES* 21 May 1913), Glenny explained that, as Sly, he responded differently to the action every night, that he led the audience, and provided a focus for his

---

45 Sly's wife was played by a boy in London but by Mary Gray at the premiere in Hull.
46 Letter in the possession of Jan McDonald.
47 This was featured in publicity material, e.g. the cartoon in *Hearth and Home* (5 June 1913) and a photograph in the *Daily Sketch* (22 May 1913).

fellow players so that 'they are absolutely sure of a certain response, and can establish a rapport at once'.

Harvey's views on Sly were also much reported (e.g. *Standard*, 2 May 1913) and are reproduced in his autobiography: his theory was that the low comedian playing the original Sly had got out of hand, and so the part had been cut back and the full frame reduced to a remnant. Harvey approved of this cut although, paradoxically, he thought that Charles Glenny's ad libbing in the role was wonderful (Martin-Harvey 413). Sly's potential for letting the audience relax about the politics of the play was evident to the *Daily Chronicle* (12 May 1913), which argued that Glenny's performance released the audience 'from the eternal temptation to take things too seriously'.

In Robert Atkins's 1922 production D. Hay Petrie as Sly played the full framework from *A Shrew* at the Old Vic, where ersatz Elizabethanism was in full flow partly because the theatre couldn't afford anything other than bare boards productions. The Vic's enthusiastic use of the full framework over the next decade was very much associated with Petrie, who played Sly in many productions, most using the full frame. The different balance this produced in the play is suggested by the *Times* (17 October 1922), which headed its review 'Mr Hay Petrie's Sly', commented on his double role of Sly and Pedant (Merchant) and reported that Katherina and Petruchio did not 'overwhelm the play' as they 'are accustomed to do', even though Florence Buckton's Katherina was played 'with an unexpected seriousness'. The *Sunday Times* (22 October 1922) also felt 'On the whole, it was Mr Petrie's evening' and the *Era* (19 October 1922) confirmed that Petrie's performance was 'the outstanding feature' of the production.

Sly's first full-framework appearance at Stratford had to wait until 1935, where under the direction of Ben Iden Payne much ersatz Elizabethanism was on display. Sly dominates reviews of this production, particularly when, after 1940, Sly was played by music hall comedian Jay Laurier, although reviewers also enjoyed Payne's first Sly, Roy Byford, a huge man who, like Oscar Asche, played Sly as a lower-class version of Falstaff. Sly's status as a tinker was signalled by the pots and pans he wore around his neck, he sat at the edge of the stage 'audibly crunching sweetmeats and drinking pots of small ale' (*T* 6 August 1935) and the *Birmingham Gazette* (6 August 1935) noted Sly's effectiveness as a 'magnificent claque' and that he 'guffawed his delight' at 'every joke', encouraging the paying audience to do likewise. Meanwhile C. Rivers Gadsby started carving out a career for himself with his *Charley's Aunt* version of Bartholomew as Sly's wife, a role he reprised frequently over the next decade at Stratford. Once again reviewers felt that the use of the full frame enabled 'the flavour of brutality which clings to the piece' to be 'considerably mitigated when we are constantly reminded that

Petruchio's wooing is an entertainment devised for the amusement of a drunken tinker' (*T* 6 August 1935).

George Devine (1953, 1954) again used the full Sly frame at Stratford, and his very scholarly approach to the play was followed by John Barton, whose 1960 production went even further in playing 'Elizabethan' and using Sly. Barton often privileged *A Shrew* over *The Shrew*, and Folio lines in the Induction were cut to make room for the equivalents from *A Shrew*. Despite the fact that this production nearly fell to pieces before opening night because the leading performers had insufficient confidence in their director, it became a hit and was revived twice in the next two years, thus really entrenching Sly in the consciousness of the reviewers and making the use of all the Sly scenes *de rigueur* at the RSC for a while.[48] Reservations about the framework were still expressed, however, and Harold Hobson disliked the casting of a young boy as Bartholomew, which made Induction 2.112–23 uncomfortable, as a boy talked 'of sharing the pleasures of bed with a man' (*ST* 26 June 1960).

Barton's engaging, Irish Sly, Jack MacGowran, became 'the inevitable hero of the play' (*SUAH* 27 April 1962) in an enthusiastically evoked Elizabethan tavern and improvised playhouse setting: the touring company who were performing the inner play were seen 'offstage' as well as on, changing costumes, drinking ale, checking their lines, being prompted and 'the actress who is to play Kate' was 'nursing a baby' (*Evening News*, 14 September 1961).

Ersatz Elizabethanism fits well with the main stage at Stratford, Ontario, which evokes an Elizabethan playhouse feel, and Michael Langham's 1962 production of *The Taming of the Shrew* certainly exploited this. Langham, like Barton, used *A Shrew* extensively and was willing to rewrite lines for clarity. As Sly, Hugh Webster was 'afraid he is not dreaming and more afraid that he may be' (*Chicago Tribune*, 20 June 1962), and he remained visible on a couch bed with Bartholomew, at the front of the audience area, for the entire play. The Lord and his huntsmen sat separately, above on the upper stage, watching Sly as well as the inner play. The *New York Herald Tribune* (21 June 1962) particularly enjoyed Sly's 'various and dogged attempts to slip into one of the parties the principal characters are always giving'.

At Stratford-upon-Avon in 1967 Trevor Nunn (who first directed the play in 1961 for Cambridge University's Marlowe Society) again created an Elizabethan play-world accompanied by a full Sly framework, which meant

---

48 For the inexperienced Barton's problems and his rescue by Peter Hall, see e.g. *BM* 22 June 1960; *John O'London* (30 June 1960); O'Connor (130). The revivals of this production were directed by Maurice Daniels but Daniels changed very little, although reviewers did complain of an increase in the clowning.

that the audience were 'never allowed for one moment to think of the main play's characters as real people' (*DT* 6 April 1967). This was probably a wise decision as the production was in competition with the full-blown, realistic evocation of sunny Renaissance Padua in Zeffirelli's film of *The Taming of the Shrew*. Nunn's production countered with snow and 'a dark-timbered Warwickshire alehouse, late 16th century, with hares hanging from the roof' and 'old snow melting with a thaw' (*DT* 1 April 1967). The pub then opened up and the inner play was performed inside: 'The players trudge out of the snow, huddled in cloaks and balaclavas. They clear a space before a fire which flickers over a chimney-breast hung with smoking hams, rafters dripping gutted hares' (*O* 9 April 1967). These strolling players tumbled, sang, juggled and passed the hat around their onstage audience.

There is a risk of getting lost in the golden glow of Merry England, something suggested by Alan Edwards's 1975 Brisbane staging, which had Sly thrown out of a very carefully realised alehouse, specified by the programme as existing in Warwickshire in 1623. The action moved into a candlelit Lord's house for the inner play, and costumes were extravagantly beautiful period dress. Reviews of this lovingly nostalgic production lie alongside reports of the rather grimmer reality of Australia's participation in the Vietnam War. By contrast, in Clifford Williams's 1973 RSC production, Merry England was held at bay by slides informing the audience that the players were being forced to tour while the playhouses were closed due to plague in London in 1592.

Again in 'Elizabethan' mode, with placards for scene changes, onstage audience and lots of Merry England bonhomie, Peter Dews at Stratford, Ontario, in 1981 used the whole Sly framework with great comic effect, even in the television recording of the production, where, perhaps inevitably, Sly seems over the top on the small screen. The overall impact was Brechtian without ever being too solemn. Sly, Bartholomew and the Lord occupied the upper stage to watch the play, and the joke of Sly's enthusiasm for having sex with a tall, over-rouged Bartholomew in unconvincing drag got lots of laughs.

Sly's dream

Several Slys, particularly in the latter half of the twentieth century, have dreamt the inner play, an approach that picks up on the Lord's prediction (Induction 1.40) that Sly will believe his experiences to be 'a flatt'ring dream', and Sly's Bottom-like pronouncements at the end of *A Shrew* that 'I have had the bravest dream tonight / That ever thou heardest in all thy life', and 'thou hast waked me out of the best dream / That ever I had in my life'

(15.12–13, 18–19). The 'Sly's dream' approach has often included doubling Sly and Petruchio, although the first production to use this doubling, Oscar Asche's in 1905, did not explore the dream theme, but presented Asche's Falstaffian Sly in an Induction performed separately, as a curtain raiser. When the inner play becomes Sly's Dream, the Epilogue from *A Shrew* works particularly well, but the risk is that if Sly and Petruchio are doubled, Sly and his *alter ego* then completely dominate the play.[49]

In Donald Wolfit's 1953 production the programme explained that the idea was 'to present the play as if it were the Dream of Christopher Sly, the drunken tinker. The Lord of the Induction has been imagined as the God of Dreams and, as is common in all dreams, Sly finds himself involved in the action of the play itself and appears as a Servant and a Pedant.' Unfortunately this Lord, in his manifestation as God of Dreams, appeared to be 'flitting about like Peter Pan on the end of a wire' (*DT* 28 April 1935) and had trouble making his landings on some nights (*Glasgow Herald*, 4 May 1935).

An Australian version of Sly's dream appeared in Robin Lovejoy's 1972 production where Sly, a 'freely ad-libbing drunken swagman', was chased up onto the stage by 'stockmen with whips cracking' and 'two kelpie sheepdogs', where he experienced 'a version of the legendary drover's dream' (*SAG* 673). Sly was persuaded that he was a judge (*The Review*, 18–24 March 1972) and a band of touring players caught in a thunderstorm performed to him at the request of a wealthy squatter. Sly was very active throughout, constantly ad libbing, intervening, and taking bets with Petruchio on whether or not he would manage to tame Katherina.

At the RSC Michael Bogdanov (1978) entirely recast the play as Sly's vicious, supremacist dream. The Induction was modified, Sly's lines were largely modernised, and began with a brawl between a drunk (Jonathan Pryce) and an usherette (Paola Dionisotti) at the front of the stalls. Sly then climbed onto the stage, wrecking the old-fashioned set of balconies and pillars and became Petruchio, while the usherette became Katherina.

Jonathan Pryce's Sly was extremely violent in his dream of power, maltreating not only Katherina but also his newly acquired servants (see Induction 2.67) as a way of testing out his new upper-class status: for him status meant the ability to assault others with impunity. Although Bogdanov was confident that Shakespeare's 'sympathy is with the women' (Holderness 1988, 90) and saw the play as 'A wish-fulfilment dream of a male for revenge on a female' he also stressed that 'the "Induction" . . . is the key to the whole play. Sly . . . dreams a dream of revenge and power; not only power over

---

49 Less frequently the performer playing Katherina doubles the Hostess (e.g. Bogdanov 1978), or Mrs Sly (e.g. Mellor 1989).

10   Scene from the 1988 Stratford Ontario Festival production, directed by Richard
Monette and designed by Debra Hanson with, from left to right: Keith Dinicol as
Grumio, Colm Feore as Petruchio, David Lloyd-Evans as a Servant, Juan Chioran
as a Servant and Goldie Semple as Katherina.

women, but class power through wealth' (Holderness 1988, 90). At the end
of the production, the sound of hunting horns reminded the audience of
the dream framework, and an actor dressed as Sly appeared onstage, and
watched the final moments of his dream.

At Stratford, Ontario, in 1988, Richard Monette had a Sly who was
young, good-looking, and out on the town. Sly was so drunk he couldn't light
a cigarette on his own, and his dream began as he collapsed, mouthing some
lines from the Induction, without any prompting from a Lord or travelling
players. Colm Feore as Sly became Petruchio, while Goldie Semple, the
Hostess, became Katherina; at the end, an outbreak of romantic waltzing and
music on the crowded stage covered Feore's quick change back to Sly, still
unsteady with drink, speechless, dazed, confused and suddenly revealed as
the crowd parted.

In Brisbane, Aubrey Mellor's 1989 *The Taming of the Shrew* offered a different twist when Sly's dream became a nightmare. Sly was a drunk up from the country, visiting the 1988 Brisbane Expo with his wife. At the Italian pavilion 'The sophisticated, arrogant Europeans pull him inside in order to have some fun at his expense' (*Bulletin*, 5 September 1989) and 'a plain Expo pavilion exterior divides to reveal an open Italian piazza surrounded by colonnaded and balconied houses' where the main action took place (*Financial Review*, 1 September 1989). Mellor's interest in the Australian myth of mateship produced a staging that was more focused on the bloky Sly/ Petruchio, and constructions of masculinity, than on Mrs Sly/Katherina, and the *Courier Mail* (19 August 1989) noted that the production 'is so much the boys' own club that the women barely get a look in'. Despite the extreme self-abasement of Katherina, there was some hope at the end: 'When Kate moves to place her head beneath the foot of her husband, a shamed Petruchio avoids it. At the same time, Sly awakes from his dream, the piazza disappears and the battle is re-invoked on a wittier footing' (*Financial Review*, 1 September 1989). Penny Gay (1998, 173–5) describes how as Petruchio fell asleep, reawoke as Sly and Katherina reappeared as Mrs Sly, the production used a collage of lines from *A Shrew*, pure invention and lines from elsewhere in the play. Importantly it was Mrs Sly's anger with her husband's drunkenness that prompted the line, 'Why there's a wench. Come on and kiss me, Kate' and Sly was relieved he wasn't still married to the tamed creature of his nightmare. Mellor's adaptation here was partly driven by a belief that 'the original [ending] can only be tragic, unless Kate is a masochist' (Gay 1998, 174).

Mrs Sly also appeared in Gale Edwards's 1995 RSC production, which featured a feminist rewriting of Sly's dream, producing a gender parable for the 1990s. Edwards opened with an argument between Sly/Petruchio (Michael Siberry) and Mrs Sly/Katherina (Josie Lawrence) against the background of a huge storm. Sly drove his wife away from him, fell asleep and dreamt the main play action. Sly began to re-emerge from this dream while Katherina delivered her submission speech, a moment the programme glossed for the audience: 'Petruchio slowly realizes what he has been attempting to do to Katherina in the name of love. By the end of the speech his dream has become a nightmare.' Michael Siberry recalls his Petruchio became 'sobered and then shamed' as he listened to the speech, realising that he has 'pushed Kate too far; he has abused her trust' and humiliated her (Siberry 57). Sly was beginning to acknowledge 'that his behaviour has been unacceptable' (58) but the relationship between Petruchio/Sly and Katherina/Mrs Sly was in deep trouble: 'He fell to his knees, trying to make some sense of what had happened, understanding that he has made an awful mistake and trying to come to terms with it' (58–9). Petruchio went into shock, completely forgot about the wager money and as Mrs Sly reappeared, kneeled and 'clasped his wife's waist like a small child needing comfort; Mrs Sly didn't respond but stared into the distance, leaving the state of the relationship and the amount of damage done, ambiguous' (Schafer 68). The music accompanying the moment was melancholic but for some reviewers this 'was a final image of hope, for others of inevitable suffering for her' (Siberry 59).

A more straightforward rewriting of Sly's dream appeared in Sue Rider's 1994 *The Taming of the Shrew*, which abandoned the Lord and simply had the drunken Sly disrupting the players' attempts to begin their performance. As Sly collapsed, the actors decided to play the trick on him, and turned Sly into Petruchio. On suddenly becoming Sly again, and realising that the main story was a drunken fantasy or dream, Sly's disappointment found expression in a one-word epilogue: 'shit'.

Working-class hero

Until the late twentieth century, Sly's working-class status was deemed primarily a joke and the oppressive nature of what the Lord does to Sly was downplayed. For example, Samuel Phelps's 1856 bravura Sly was applauded for presenting Sly as a gross, repellent being full of 'brutal sottishness' (*Morning Advertiser*, 17 November 1856), a man 'purely sensual and animal, brutish in appetite' with a 'stupid stare' and eyelids 'drooped in the heavy slumberousness of a stupid nature' (*Examiner*, 6 December 1856). Phelps's Sly was 'little better than a machine' and turned 'his head mechanically from one to another when spoken to, like a clairvoyant under the influence of mesmerism' (*ILN* 22 November 1856). This was an 'exhibition of a thoroughly low and grovelling nature, still further debased by the least poetical form of drunkenness' (*T* 17 November 1856). Phelps's Sly was a specimen of the undeserving poor, hardly evolved beyond Darwin's apes.

Sly's promotion to working-class hero initially came via comic appeal. For example, in Komisarjevsky's madcap 1939 Stratford production, Sly became a contemporary tramp 'corduroys and all' (*BM* 4 April 1939), while the Lords were Restoration fops. Sly, the music hall comedian Jay Laurier, not only had the full framework from *A Shrew* to work with but he also took reaction lines from the main play, and became 'the central figure of the production' (*DT* 4 April 1939) while Katherina and Petruchio became 'puppets in a side-show' (*Birmingham Evening Despatch*, 4 April 1939). Like Laurier's Sly, Donald Wolfit's performance of the role in John Burrell's 1947 production upstaged the inner play; the red-nosed Sly 'dominates this production' (*Reynolds*, 9 November 1947) and was accompanied by a throng of attendants who took up at least a quarter of the stage playing space. Sly emitted 'satisfied animal noises as the fun waxes hotter, pointing excitedly as the scenes are moved and exchanging signs and even congratulatory handshakes with the clown of his fancy' (*BM* 23 September 1947). The *Times* (5 November 1947) felt that Sly's 'childlike, if flamingly bibulous appreciation' of the inner play assuaged the brutality of the proceedings and the *Telegraph* (8 November 1947) concurred: modern audiences can laugh at the taming 'since it is not designed to appeal to us but to a drunken tinker'.

As patronising attitudes towards the working class as objects of mirth *per se* began to go out of fashion, Sly's career as working-class hero took off. In Frank Dunlop's long-lived 1970 production for the Young Vic, which was revived internationally for over eight years, Sly was 'a contemporary drunken dustman' (*DT* 20 November 1970), a 'drunken layabout (in jeans)' (*Lady*, 24 November 1977) or, across the Atlantic, 'a freaked-out Greenwich Village type who lurches out of the onstage bleachers that hold part of the audience' (*Newsweek*, 25 March 1974).[50] In 1977 Sly is described, before the play started, as 'arguing at the door about taking a bottle in with him' (*FT* 14 November 1977), then 'demanding a seat belligerently while the audience assembled, and interrupting the first scene until we realised what the noise was all about' (*BP* 14 November 1977). Sly objected 'to the poverty of costumes and props' but was 'given enough drink to convert him into an actor' and to play the Pedant (Merchant), commenting 'A pedant? You can get locked up for that, can't you?' (*T* 12 November 1977).[51] Dunlop's vision of Sly developed further in the work of Denise Coffey, originally Dunlop's Associate Director at the Young Vic, who has directed *The Taming of the Shrew* many times and has continued to stress the framework, and the robustness of the comedy.

As Sly's class identity became more heroic, the Lord's trick turned into an outrageous and callous assault on one of the unwaged (although this interpretation, to get full sympathy for Sly, has to play down the evidence from the Epilogue to *A Shrew* of his ambitions as a wife beater). Di Trevis, who directed a very class-conscious staging for the RSC in 1985, emphasised this aspect by playing Brechtian: the production included a *Mother Courage*-style cart dragged by Katherina, a chalk circle on the floor to focus the acting (further defined by footlights), chalked place names to indicate locations, a

---

50 In New York Sly was played by Richard Gere. Dunlop's longstanding relation with *The Taming of the Shrew* actually began in 1959 with a Slyless production for the Bristol Old Vic.

51 Sly quite often ends up acting in the inner play, and the Pedant (Merchant) is his most frequent role: e.g. Coffey (1979).

banner proclaiming 'The Taming of the Shrew – a Kind of History', frequent use of music to break up the action, plus the pairing of the production on tour with *Happy End* by Brecht and Elisabeth Hauptmann. Sly was a kindly, working-class man treated appallingly by the Lord, and Sly's victim status was equated with that of Katherina. So, for example, at the end of the play Sly generously offered the travelling actress playing Katherina some of the money the Lord had thrown at him, the Lord's contempt contrasting vividly with Sly's act of solidarity with a poverty-stricken fellow (Cousin 281). Holderness and Loughrey (33) felt this showed 'The poor man and the poor woman have both been victimised: and in a mutual recognition of that they find both a shared experience and a common cause.' Trevis's production emphasised the imposition of the pretence, its cruelty and 'the Lord's caprice' (Holderness and Loughrey 33), but when Sly responded to Petruchio's discomfort at the end of Katherina's submission speech by acting tenderly towards his 'wife', Bartholomew immediately mocked Sly's gentleness by taking off his wig and revealing the trick that had been played. This gained sympathy for Sly, but it also kept the audience's mind on the question of what we accept as representing 'woman', as well as looking back to the Induction when Bartholomew was made to stand on a stool in order to be dressed up as Sly's 'wife', to be reconstructed as a 'woman', before sitting down to watch the taming of Katherina.

The sympathetic Sly was taken even further in Bill Alexander's RSC productions (1990, 1992) but here gender became marginalised by the production's attention to class war. The production located the action in the present, and updated the language of the Induction and the Sly Interludes of *A Shrew*. The frame showed a nasty trick played on a Brummie Sly by a gang of Hooray Henry and Henriettas, who also victimised the Lord's younger brother, 'Rupert Llewellyn', who was the quarry in the opening hunt, and who was made to dress up as Sly's 'wife'. Alexander cut very little indeed and he explained that modernising the language of the Induction plus the use of the full framework enabled him to make 'the play modern' as well as 'setting it in its period context' at the same time (Gilbey 11). Reviewers, however, worried about the updated dialogue and several disapprovingly quoted the moment (from Induction 1) when the toffs decided Sly was 'working class' and that they should 'mess with his mind' (e.g. *IS* 5 April 1992; *Jewish Chronicle*, 10 April 1992).

The Lord had commissioned the performance of the inner play for a Valentine's celebration (1990 pbk) and once the actors had turned up 'bejeaned and anoraked' (*Manchester Evening News*, 16 October 1990), the action moved to the Lord's Jacobean Warwickshire stately home: 'grandly furnished with tapestry and oak caryatids', even in the touring version of the production (*T* 4 October 1990). The Lord's party watched the inner play from upstage, while the players, now in Elizabethan costume, performed downstage, in between the Lord's party and the paying audience. The Lord's party became unwillingly incorporated into the action, when they were forced to play Petruchio's servants in 4.1, and were cuffed and beaten by Petruchio. This shock turned into therapy for some of the women, and by the end of the play the Lord's girlfriend, 'Lady Sarah Ormsby', had seen enough of Petruchio in 'Lord Simon Llewellyn' to begin distancing herself from him.

Despite an energetic Katherina and a complex Petruchio, the frame story often took over and this imbalance was much commented upon in 1992: *The Taming of the Shrew* was turned from 'a comedy of sexual supremacy into an act of class vengeance' (*IS* 5 April 1992); 'such weight' was given to the frame that 'the play itself has sunk almost without trace' (*G* 23 July 1993); the frame was 'intriguing, but it removes attention from Katherine' and turned play into 'social warfare' (*IS* 25 July 1993). The *Times* (3 April 1992) suggested, but then dismissed, the idea that the inner play was presented as 'a sexist entertainment for drunks and upper-crust louts'. Peter Holland comments that the production 'nearly convinced me that the play is . . . about class and that male subjugation of women is only an example of masters' oppression of servants' (129). This tension between the competing claims of gender and class analysis can perhaps be seen as early as *A Shrew*, where in the text's use of a male tapster rather than the female hostess of *The Shrew*, Holderness and Loughrey argue, there is a shift in political focus: 'the conflict is more class- than gender-based, and is resolved in the play's conclusion by the establishing of a masculine freemasonry between Tapster and Slie' (90).

Sly equivalents

Many directors have radically rewritten the Sly frame. For example, Eugen Gallant in 1968 had 'an intriguing mixture of commedia dell'arte and Brighton Pier slapstick, as pierrots, cute and coy, replace the induction scene' (*Vancouver Province*, 29 January 1968). Jean Gascon in 1973 had the Induction 'telescoped into a brief introductory speech' (*Ottawa Citizen*, 15 January 1973) and deployed a crowd of harlequins who watched the action and helped to create stage and sound effects. A more robust Sly substitute was provided in Australia, by John Bell in 1994. The *Newcastle Herald* (2 May 1994) advised readers to get to the show early enough to catch the pre-show entertainment, which stood in for the Induction, and included a chicken raffle, a Wurlitzer organ and variety acts, setting up a working-men's 'club context' (*Age*, 26 May 1994). The *Australian* (3 May 1994) found the 'Friday night at the local club' frame effective as 'Bell has translated high culture, the theatre of the Bard, back into popular entertainment without pandering to prejudices in the process.' Helena Kaut-Howson's 2001 production origi-nally included a specially commissioned rewrite of the Induction by Snoo Wilson 'set in a present-day Manchester wine-bar during a raucous hen-night' (*DT* 8 March 2001), but this was abandoned before opening night.

Even when directors choose to retain Sly's Induction, the circumstances they are placing him in get more and more varied. Lindsay Posner in 1999 had Sly view the taming of Katherina via the internet, after trying to access a porn site, when left alone to play with the Lord's PC. Jon Pope in 1992 had Sly as 'a tipsy ARP warden', while the play-world was Second World War, and the inner play was performed 'by a troupe of ENSA performers', with lots of 1940s songs (*I* 17 June 1992). In 1993 Jude Kelly made Sly a drunk, downing duty free booze on a cruise ship, and the ship's captain, in the tradition of crossing-the-equator jokes, arranged the trick that was played on him. Sly's 'wife' was 'an uncomfortable sailor in a pastel dress and Doc Marten boots' (*Heckmondwyke Reporter*, 6 May 1993). In 1970 Anton Rodgers had Sly as 'a Victorian drunk found alcoholically asleep beneath a gas lamp outside a tavern' (*Western Morning News*, 30 October 1970). In 1993 John Durnin set *The Taming of the Shrew* in a 1950s Italian film studio, 'a massive scaffold construction depicting a multitude of scenes from a bar to a laundry-filled back alley' (*Express and Echo*, 3 November 1993) and Sly was allowed to watch the movie actors 'poised ready to assume their roles when the lights snap on and the clapper board announces the scene – and take-number' (*Plymouth Evening Herald*, 4 November 1993).

Sly also encounters a wide variety of theatrical events in the guise of the inner play: Michael Benthall's 1948 production, which cut the Lord, had the taming narrative semi-improvised by rehearsing actors, pulling what costume took their fancy from the costume baskets. At the end of this show Sly was bundled into the stage property basket (*Evesham Journal*, 14 May 1948). Sly was treated to an expensive, elegantly performed show in Augustin Daly's 1888 production, but a poverty-stricken, strolling player piece in Di Trevis's 1985 staging. Emphasis on the 'play within a play' dynamic in *The Taming of the Shrew* almost inevitably helps to suggest a proto-Brechtian alienation, which is likely to problematise the play's gender- and class-politics, even in a production using Sly primarily for high jinks.

In the theatre Sly is now extremely popular, and is more often used than not. The one area of performance where Sly has been least successful in making a comeback is film, where opportunities for filmic realism are almost inevitably in tension with the anti-realistic style invited by the Sly framework.

RECORDINGS OF THE PLAY

Although recorded productions are not necessarily the most exciting, their availability makes them disproportionately important in the stage history of *The Taming of the Shrew*; many can be easily accessed, and even moderately successful films are seen by far more people than even very popular theatrical productions. Many different readings are possible in relation to these recorded productions, but those offered here are in sympathy with Diana Henderson's suggestion (151) that despite the fact that all the films of *The Taming of the Shrew* ultimately 'are works of ideological containment' they can 'work otherwise, and could be employed and extended in ways that might lead away from a co-opted and conservative gender politics'.[52]

Henderson establishes that *The Taming of the Shrew* is a much-filmed play: she refers to 'More than eighteen screen versions of the play . . . in Europe and North America' (148) and argues that films of *The Shrew* tend to surface particularly in times of feminist backlash. The first extant film of *The Shrew* was made by D. W. Griffith in 1908 for Biograph. Ball (62) describes this film as one of Griffiths's 'fumbling experiments to express himself artistically in a new form'. Rothwell and Melzer (270) praise Florence Lawrence as Katherina but feel that overall Griffith 'privileged the crowd-pleasing slapstick over the play's more serious concern with gender politics'. Griffiths's film has no Sly, and is full of Garrickisms: the Bianca narrative is minimised, and at the end of the film Baptista witnesses Katherina's transformation when visiting her and Petruchio at home. Petruchio cracks his whip, Katherina hits him with a pillow and the wedding procession scene is very elaborate.

Many of the silent films of *The Shrew* listed by Ball have not survived, but those that have suggest that several directors identified film potential in the same offstage scenes, such as the journey to Petruchio's house; or the wrecking of the marital bedroom. A scenario for a silent film prepared by Mrs C. H. Jones (S60) also includes these two set pieces but is unusual in its sympathy for Katherina. The scenario shows Katherina 'terrified to death' at her wedding and 'very frightened' and 'trembling' during her stay at Petruchio's house. In the final scene, once the wager is set up among the men, the film would cut to a room in Baptista's house where 'Discovered. Katherine

---

52 Foreign-language recordings are not discussed here but include an Italian silent film from 1908 and films directed by: Henri Desfontaines (France 1911); Arrigo Frusta (Italy 1913); Ferdinando Poggioli (Italy 1942); Roman Antonio (France and Spain 1955); Sergei Kolosov (Soviet Union 1961); Ludwig Bergers (Germany 1961). Information taken from Ball, and Rothwell and Melzer. *Japan News* (21 December 1954) records that Nippon Television network broadcast a production that year.

reading. Bianca sewing, and Widow playing the lute'. The scenario has Biondello enter and deliver his message to each of the women. Bianca 'points to work' and refuses, the Widow 'rises, then seats herself coquettishly shaking her head'. When Katherina obeys, Bianca and the Widow 'laugh and jeer and point their fingers at her' before she exits. This depiction of the final scene from the offstage women's point of view is unique.

Several of the early film-makers anticipate later feature film-makers and present, for example, Katherina's and Petruchio's wedding at length rather than describing it. Cuts compensating for such expansions can be staggering: Edwin J. Collins's 1923 film has an extraordinarily truncated ending, which takes place in the equivalent of 4.3, where once Katherina has thanked Petruchio for the food he has prepared, all they have left to do is kiss and live happily ever afterwards. Ball (286) dismisses this film as stagey, and featuring a Petruchio who looked 'both fat and old' but Collins is not unoriginal and includes an unusual amount of sisterly support from Bianca, when it looks as if Katherina has been deserted at the altar.

Sam Taylor's 1929 film of *The Taming of the Shrew*, starring Mary Pickford and Douglas Fairbanks Snr, was the first full-length film of the play and also the first feature-length, talking Shakespeare film. As not all cinemas then had facilities for talkies, a silent version was also filmed, and this explains some of the film's radical cutting. Other cutting was part of the film's large debt to Garrick, especially in the Bianca narrative.[53]

Fairbanks is the ultimate swashbuckling Petruchio, although the film also sends him up: Katherina does a good imitation of his gratingly jolly laugh at their wedding, and Gremio and Hortensio laugh at Petruchio behind his back when he is boasting of hearing lions roar (1.2). The film was made at a time when Pickford's and Fairbanks's marriage was crumbling, and Pickford maintained: 'The making of that film was my finish. My confidence was completely shattered, and I was never again at ease before the camera or microphone' (Pickford, 312). Pickford felt Katherina was 'one of my worst performances', a mere 'spitting little kitten' when she should have been 'a forceful tiger cat' (311).

Despite Pickford's bleak memories, her Katherina is lively, untamed and, although her lines are comparatively few, her speaking face acts eloquently in her silences. Sam Taylor, like Zeffirelli after him, allows extra textual space for Katherina by exploiting the actress's ability to communicate with her face, or, as Diana Henderson points out, 'adding gestures, glances, and private speech

---

53 Garrick's text was still attractive to film-makers as late as 1939 when the text was broadcast (12 April) in a production directed by Dallas Bower starring Austin Trevor and Margaretta Scott.

to the script's most notorious silences' (148) and using the camera 'to gesture at female subjectivity' (149). In addition film could render Katherina's shrewish violence much more realistically than theatre, and Pickford has an extended sequence of wrecking Baptista's home, terrorising his servants, and then glowering, whip in hand, at the camera and the audience.

Although the Induction was cut, a sense of framing still exists. Russell Jackson (110) suggests that this film, like Zeffirelli's, had a 'ready-made "frame" of the audience's expectation of the stars' but in addition Taylor chose to open with a Punch and Judy show, with the Judy sinking into Punch's arms after being bashed. This is in marked contrast with Pickford's Katherina, who never sinks. In the huge wedding scene, for example, a sequence which includes 'a series of silent film gags' (Rothwell 32), Katherina is resistant throughout. The wedding only goes ahead after Petruchio stamps on Katherina's foot and her cry of pain is taken as assent. Katherina refuses help from Petruchio when she falls in the mud on arriving at his house, and she actually sets off home again, only to be put off by the stormy weather. Katherina chooses to refuse meat at dinner, but most importantly of all, she overhears Petruchio's hawk-taming speech (4.1), which is normally a soliloquy but here is addressed to an extremely large dog, presumably Troilus. Katherina then proceeds to compete with, and surpass, Petruchio in his shrewish behaviour. When Petruchio finds a spot on the bedclothes and messes up the sheets, Katherina finds a worse spot and completely upturns the mattress. This competition only terminates when a stool thrown by Katherina knocks Petruchio out. As Katherina checks Petruchio is not too seriously wounded, the argument over the sun and moon, from 4.5, takes place and Katherina agrees it is the sun, reassuring the dazed Petruchio. The film then cuts to the final banquet and Katherina's submission speech, which Pickford's famous wink subverts. Unlike Shakespeare's Katherina, Pickford's Katherina knows what Petruchio is trying to do in taming her, and she responds to this tactically and successfully. Her surpassing of Petruchio's outrageous behaviour leaves him both nonplussed and concussed.

The last scene is little more than Katherina's final speech, which is delivered standing, while Petruchio lolls in a chair, grinning inanely, his bandaged head a reminder of Katherina's blow with the stool. The Pickford wink, directed at Bianca on line 164's 'obey' exploits the filmic, non-theatrical facilities for close-up, and became much copied. Henderson (154) also points out that 'Uniquely among screen *Shrew*s, Katherine's final assertion of voice does not require the disappearing or rejection of Bianca.'

In a sophisticated reading of this film Hodgdon (15) finds a 'regressive fantasy that depends on occupying – and performing – infantile roles', and the containment of Katherina in the closure of the film, when the entire wedding party sing in harmony.[54] However, Pickford's whip-cracking, cunning and still shrewish Katherina also offers a powerful image of female insubordination, which could, and can, be read empoweringly.

Sly entered the lists of recorded productions in 1935 although the *Times* (11 March 1935) thought Peter Creswell's radio production unsubtle. The script reveals a sensible use of Sly, whose confusion as to what is happening allows Bartholomew to inform both Sly and the listeners who is who, and what they are up to. The full Sly framework was used and when Creswell returned to the play in 1941 with 'an excellent drunken Sly' (*Listener*, 20 February 1941), a script very similar to his 1931 version was used, although Creswell had ironed out some of the glaring inconsistencies introduced by his deep cutting of the Bianca narrative. Peter Watts's 1954 radio production also deployed a very active Sly, and in this production the Lord was Sly's guide to the action. In the US Brewster Morgan's 1937 one-hour radio production starring Edward G. Robinson and Frieda Inescort depended heavily on Conway Tearle as narrator to make the story clear, and the promptbook details the narrator's descriptions of Bianca in light blue silk, Katherina in dark red, and Petruchio dressed as a scarecrow for his wedding.[55] The narrator also commented at the end of 4.5: 'We know that Katharina obeys her husband, but has her spirit been really tamed I wonder?' Another 1930s radio production was performed amidst a flurry of elopements, divorces, very public quarrels and reconciliations, when John Barrymore and his young wife Elaine Barrie presented scenes from *The Shrew* on 26 July 1937 for NBC-CBS radio.[56]

Paul Nickell's television production of *The Taming of the Shrew* was broadcast in black and white on 5 June 1950 on CBS-TV in under an hour, accompanied by three advertisements for the sponsors, Westinghouse.[57] Cutting was very deep, particularly in the Bianca narrative, Tranio becomes Baptista's neighbour and Grumio doesn't speak until 4.1. The setting is the present, men wear suits and drink beer in cafés, while Katherina sports riding jodhpurs and a riding crop and Petruchio turns up to his wedding

54 Jonathan Miller closed the BBC production with a similar insistence on harmony, trumpeted via group singing.

55 The ABC Theatre Guild radio production broadcast in 1950 helped listeners with 'a special continuity' which was 'narrated in song by Tom Glazer to bridge gaps between scenes' (Rothwell and Melzer entry 588).

56 Morrison (378) notes that a copy of this production is held in the Museum of Television and Radio, New York.

57 See Hodgdon (23–4) for a discussion of the interplay between *The Shrew* and the adverts.

dressed as a cowboy. Charlton Heston's laughing Petruchio plays his two soliloquies directly to the camera and is frequently seen, in close-up, trying to hide laughter at the mayhem he is causing. By contrast, Lisa Kirk's Katherina has *silent* close-ups, conveying meaning solely by her expression, and her quasi soliloquy at the beginning of 4.3 is played with the actress silent and the speech delivered in voice-over.[58] The male lead thus has far more direct contact with the audience and the production is overwhelmingly Petruchio's, even though Katherina, in the middle of her final 'Kiss me, Kate' embrace with Petruchio, turns to the camera and winks. Diana Henderson (154) suggests that this production 'relentlessly reiterates conventional postwar ideals of gender difference'.

On 20 April 1952 Desmond Davis's *Taming of the Shrew* was broadcast on British television with 'frankly fantastic' sets from the 'art-ballet stable', although the production 'moved briskly' along (*Listener*, 24 April 1952). *The Shrew* then moved into colour television with Maurice Evans and Lilli Palmer starring in George Schaefer's 1956 television production. Sly nearly made his television debut here as the preliminary script by Michael Hogan included the Induction, kept Sly throughout the play and finally showed him triumphantly beating his wife, encouraged by the travelling players who have just entertained him. Hogan's script was extensively revised by William Nichols, 'normally the production idea man for "Your Hit Parade" ' (*NYT* 19 March 1956), Sly disappeared and the Induction was replaced with a carnival, commedia opening. The production cut deeply into the Bianca plot, Gremio and the Widow completely disappeared, but there was still room for a ballet version of Katherina's and Petruchio's power struggle, performed at their wedding. The pair's first encounter was seen as a boxing bout: the sequence started with them 'talking in close-up and then, as the argument grew more bitter, their seconds appeared from the wings. When the camera finally backed off, there was a full ring, with Mr Evans doing a pugilist's unlimbering squat' while Palmer had her face towelled (*NYT* 19 March 1956).

Franco Zeffirelli's first major feature film project was a *Taming of the Shrew*, a remake of Taylor's 1929 film, and a joint production with the stars Elizabeth Taylor and Richard Burton. Holderness comments that 'The Burtons, as a highly public and publicity-conscious screen couple, were in the habit of presenting to the media an image of domestic life not altogether unlike the relationship of Katherina and Petruchio' (1989, 67), nor unlike the relationship featured in their film of the previous year, *Who's Afraid of*

---

58 Kirk was best known as a musical actress and had played Bianca/Lois Lane in the original production of *Kiss Me, Kate*.

Virginia Woolf? Unsurprisingly Burton, as the classical actor experienced in Shakespeare, had far more lines than Taylor;[59] however, Taylor's Katherina is given far more agency than in the Shakespearian text.

This Katherina's violence is exhilarating: she really goes on the rampage, smashing windows, and ransacking her father's house. However, Zeffirelli, who believed the ultra-professional 'one-shot Liz' 'truly understood the camera' and whose 'great skill is the ability to achieve the maximum effect doing almost nothing except raise an eyebrow or highlight a moment with a slight nod' (Zeffirelli 215) also gives Taylor several moments of silent soliloquy using her face to convey motivation, explanation and desire for Petruchio. One of these 'silent soliloquies' signals Katherina's decision to stay with Petruchio after the wedding. This huge set piece verges on 'Carry On' comedy (*ST* 5 March 1967) and shows Katherina's attempt to reply 'I will *not*' to the priest's question as to whether she will marry Petruchio. Katherina's rebellion is then thwarted by Petruchio who kisses her and stifles the '*not*'. After Petruchio has carried Katherina off from the wedding, however, he gallops off with Grumio, calling to Katherina to follow them on a donkey. At this moment Katherina could easily abandon the marriage. Instead Taylor's Katherina looks thoughtfully at two wretched creatures left over from the opening sequence of the film, a Christopher Sly-type drunkard in a cage, and a wife-stealer, and she decides to leave Padua behind.

Jack Jorgens (68) points out that 'Twice Kate chooses Petruchio over the collection of fops and old men in Padua: by maintaining silence behind the stained glass window when Petruchio announces their wedding on Sunday, and by following him in the rain when he leaves her at Padua's gates.' Barbara Hodgdon's analysis emphasises the film's presentation of Katherina's desire even further, although much of this desire is played between the lines not on them: for example, Katherina, who in the play is offstage, is seen to be gazing on and desiring Petruchio even when he is bargaining with Baptista, that is, at one of his most mercenary moments. Taylor's Katherina did not, however, entirely succumb to her desire: in another extra-textual scene, the wedding-night bedroom scene, an intensely nervous Katherina knocks the lecherous Petruchio out with a warming pan, cries herself to sleep, and gets up the next morning to start renovating Petruchio's house.

Although Taylor's Katherina submits to Petruchio enthusiastically, there is some reciprocity: Petruchio has begun to reduce his alcohol intake. There is no humiliating cap-trampling incident and it is Katherina herself who

---

59 Ace Pilkington provides the following statistics for the film overall: Zeffirelli 'kept only 773.5 lines of *The Taming of the Shrew*' constituting 'approximately thirty per cent' of the text (165).

decides to drag in and shrewishly bully the other women, on her own initiative. The submission speech is entirely Katherina's own idea, not a command performance, and the submission is then turned around as, while Petruchio's attention is momentarily elsewhere, Katherina slips away and Petruchio then has to chase after her. By delaying the consummation of the marriage, Katherina is not being submissive and her disappearance 'problematizes' the ending (Rothwell 133).

Zeffirelli's autobiography (215–16) suggests the director was not entirely in control of his star actress here as he was expecting 'one-shot Liz' to deliver the submission speech ironically. Knowing the chase was to follow, Taylor could afford to say the words of the speech 'straight' because it is impossible to read Katherina as an embodiment of obedience when the film's memorable closing sequence shows her disappearing, that is, not being obedient.[60] And if Taylor's Katherina included extra-textual associations with Liz Taylor's lifestyle, obedience towards any of her husbands was not what Taylor was famous for.

Barbara Hodgdon's reading of Zeffirelli's film acknowledges the power of Taylor's presence, and Hodgdon's emphasis on Taylor's performing body also suggests a presence that is not only visually extraordinary but uncontainable. It is not only the costumes, designed by Taylor's own chosen designer, that scarcely contain her:[61] Burton's Petruchio, Zeffirelli's directing and the text itself fail to contain that body, acting in the silences between the lines that Shakespeare wrote.

Overall the film is intensely conservative. The advertising campaign even described *The Taming of the Shrew* as: 'A motion picture for every man who ever gave the back of his hand to his beloved . . . and to every woman who deserved it. *Which takes in a lot of people!' (ST* 19 February 1967). As Russell Jackson (116) suggests, in foregrounding Katherina's desire the film offers 'a 1960s liberation more likely to appeal to Lawrentians than present-day feminists'. Yet in offering a gutsy Katherina who chooses her own punishment, tames her tamer, domesticates his household and still has to be pursued at the end of the film, the film does more for Katherina than many contemporary stage productions (e.g. Barton 1960, Nunn 1967, Dunlop 1970). Because of the sheer power of Taylor's presence, Katherina also occupies far more memorable filmic space than the dramatic space she has in the original play.

60 My reading differs from that of Henderson (160) who discerns a power struggle between director and actress which the director won because his ironic vision prevailed.

61 Zeffirelli (214) and Taylor skirmished over costume. Taylor's designer Irene Sharaff designed costumes for Burton which Zeffirelli disliked. The compromise was that Burton wore designs Zeffirelli approved of and Taylor wore Sharraff creations.

The film is also less sympathetic towards Petruchio than many theatre productions of the time. Kenneth Rothwell points out that '[e]lements of the oafish Sly surface in Burton's boorish portrayal' (130) and the film stresses Petruchio's mercenary motives: he checks the silverware when he first visits Baptista and 'only the camera sees this, so his interest in wealth seems real' (Jackson 114). Katherina sees her father handing over a chest of coins to Petruchio on her wedding day, and when Katherina rushes out onto a roof in the wooing scene, Petruchio gasps in horror at the risk to 'my twenty thousand crowns'. Petruchio's materialism plays alongside another form of material obsession: Zeffirelli's sentimental materialism as director. One of the most important presences in the film is materialised Renaissance Italy, and Zeffirelli's loving, sensuous and realistic evocation of the fabric of his vision of Renaissance Italy dominates the production.

In 1976 US television broadcast William Ball's production of *The Taming of the Shrew*, an immensely popular theatre production, first staged in 1973. The production was grounded in commedia, acrobatic clowning, tumbling, pantomime violence and stylised, choreographed jumping and bouncing around. The television broadcast was filmed with an audience, and included cuts to audience reactions, but there was also a large onstage audience, the commedia troupe who provided comic sound effects – drums for fisticuffs, tings for good ideas, romantic music for the besotted Lucentio. Consequently, even though the Induction was cut completely, a meta-theatrical effect was achieved although many lines were cut to make room for comic activity, and some of the gags were extraneous: for example, a time-consuming, running gag about Gremio having bad breath.

Marc Singer's Petruchio is a macho, bare-chested and absurd man in tights who swings onto the stage for his wedding like a Renaissance Tarzan.[62] Fredi Olster's dignified, deep-voiced Katherina is very much in charge of the proceedings, never in danger of real pain in this world of pantomime violence, and she winks clearly at the audience after her final speech as *she* holds Petruchio in a clinch on 'Kiss me, Kate.'

Although Diana Henderson (150) aptly describes Jonathan Miller's 1980 BBC recording as 'the perfect production to usher in the neo-conservative 1980s', in fact Miller was largely reprising his 1972 Chichester Festival production of the play, starring Anthony Hopkins as Petruchio and Joan Plowright as Katherina. Continuities between these two productions include a puritanical Petruchio, a spoilt rich girl Katherina in need of doctor

---

62 Henderson (161) discusses the celebration of 'the male body as erotic object' in Singer's performance and the representation of a 'charismatic, slyly self-parodic' figure.

Petruchio, and a belief that the play should be staged in terms of realism. The Chichester production 'expunged all the fun and laughter', had a Petruchio verging on the 'ferocious, mad fanatic' (*STel* 9 July 1972), a Katherina in 'severe psychosis' (*O* 9 July 1972) and it foisted 'gravity' on the play (*DT* 7 July 1972). It also, like the BBC production, cut Sly.

Whereas at Chichester this was simply another directorial decision, with the BBC production it was something more. As Stanley Wells (1980, 1229) fulminated: 'In a series announcing itself as "The complete Dramatic Works of William Shakespeare", this leaves a serious gap.' The BBC productions were intended to last 'in consumer-durable (video-cassette) form' (Holderness 1989, 96), to target the educational market and present traditional productions of the plays. Given this mission, it seems extraordinary that *The Taming of the Shrew* should have its first two scenes cut out. The justification for the decision offered by David Snodin in the BBC text of the play edited by John Wilders (30) is that Sly might

> confuse the viewer coming to the play for the first time, very possibly to the detriment of his [sic] enjoyment of the play as a whole; secondly . . . it is an essentially theatrical device which . . . .would not come across successfully in the very different medium of television; and lastly . . . it is a device which presents the play's characters as 'actors', and we felt that this would hinder the attempt . . . to present them as real people in a real, and ultimately quite serious situation.

Quite apart from the smug paternalism here identified by Holderness (1989, 98), the aspiration to reactionary realism and seriousness seems bizarre in dealing with a play which clearly labels one of its characters, Gremio, as a commedia stereotype, a 'pantaloon'. Snodin's argument that Sly does not suit television, however, is undercut by the fact that Miller has ducked the challenge of Sly in the theatre (twice) as well as on television; when he returned for the third time to the play, for the RSC in 1987, Miller deployed a band playing ancient instruments instead of Sly's Induction.

Miller is belligerent on the question of the play's gender politics: 'What we think now is really quite beside the point. If everything is done in the light of what we think it's a sort of historical egocentricity which is quite intolerable, I think: what T. S. Eliot calls "historical provincialism"' (Fenwick, BBC text, 18). Elsewhere Miller characterised the same tendency as 'historical suburbanism' (Hallinan 140). How precisely Miller expected to transcend his own cultural specificity, accessing *The Shrew* with no interference whatsoever from 'what we think now' is not explained.

John Cleese's Petruchio was generally admired by reviewers, and 'Basil Fawlty was sternly excluded . . . although the possibility that he might at any point erupt into it gave the show a fine, dangerous edge' (*T* 24 October 1980). Some also felt that the shrewish Sybil Fawlty was lurking in the wings (*DT* 24 October 1980). There was a 'terrible kind of manic seriousness' about Cleese's 'steely, authentically puritanical – almost Cromwellian – character' (*O* 26 October 1980). That the Cromwell comparison was intended by Miller is confirmed by an interview in the *Radio Times* (18–24 October 1980, p. 97), an interview which also characterises Miller as happiest working 'with actors who are either university graduates or, at least, highly intelligent'.

Sarah Badel's Katherina did not receive much attention from reviewers and Badel's small stature made the outcome of a physical struggle with the towering Cleese a foregone conclusion. Quotations from Vermeer dominated visually and the play concluded with the entire assembled company singing 'a Puritan hymn, a paraphrase of one of the psalms' (Wilders, BBC text, 16) celebrating marriage. The thought of what Christopher Sly would have made of all this, had he been forced to watch it, is irresistible.

The argument that Sly is unsuitable for television was completely disproved a year later when Peter Dews's 1981 *Taming of the Shrew* at Stratford, Ontario, was televised, retaining Sly in all his glory.[63] Dews presented an anti-illusionistic, Elizabethan staging, full of big, very theatrical jokes, filmed with a live, and appreciative, audience. The video demonstrates that Sly could be funny on screen, and the use of filmic close-up helps Sharry Flett as Katherina carefully chart a move from despair to laughter: for example, at the end of 4.3 the television audience can 'see' thoughts crossing Katherina's mind, as she stands alone onstage, thinking hard, gradually beginning to see the joke. In 5.2, when Katherina hesitates before throwing her cap to the floor, again Flett's face signals that Katherina is thinking hard, trying to work out what is really going on.

The televising of William Ball's production in 1976 made it a very influential staging and in 1982, when John Allison directed a video production of *The Taming of the Shrew*, he followed Ball very closely in cutting and comic business. Although the video jacket ambitiously claims that the play is 'staged as seen in the 16th Century', what this means is that for most, but not all, scenes there is a strong sense of an Elizabethan playhouse setting, although, rather surprisingly, there is also a fountain in the middle of the stage.[64]

63 The production was directed and produced for television (CBC) by Norman Campbell. It cut more than Dews's stage production, although Dews had already cut many obscure jokes and classical references and paraphrased unclear phrases.

64 This video comes complete with suggestions for further work with students. Although *The Taming of the Shrew* doesn't have the standing in educational curricula enjoyed by, for example, *Hamlet*, the education market was also the target of Peter Seabourne's video production of 1974, as part of 'The Shakespeare Series' of videos (Rothwell and Melzer entry 601).

The production opens with the Globe-like stage space filled with washing, straw bales, carts, livestock, nuns and priests. The Renaissance folk bustling about their business replace the Induction, and this crowd business, which lasts right through until Katherina and Petruchio's first meeting, is used to generate an atmosphere of laughter as the onstage townsfolk laugh, clap noisily and run away when Katherina appears. The sense of hearty comedy is energetically maintained until the very end, when Petruchio and Katherina tip each other into the water-fountain, and the production successfully avoided all the potentially darker elements of the play.

BBC Radio has broadcast *The Taming of the Shrew* many times in the last fifty years, including a 1973 Radio 4 production directed by Ian Cottrell, starring a breathy Fenella Fielding as Katherina and Paul Daneman as Petruchio. More recently a much-cut text, minus the Induction and minus Biondello, was directed by Melanie Harris in 2000, relocating Padua to the north of England, giving Petruchio an Ulster accent and chopping the play into very short scenes, interspersed with a percussive and vocal chorus. The information booklet accompanying the audio-cassette of this production dates the first BBC broadcast of extracts from this play to 18 November 1924.

All recorded productions of *The Taming of the Shrew* I have located, with the exception of the audio-cassette, full Folio text, received-pronunciation recording directed by Howard Sackler in 1960, cut and remake the play radically to conform to the director's vision of the play. These recorded productions may not be the most compelling in terms of artistry or politics, but their influence, simply because they were broadcast so widely and because they continue to be accessible, is often disproportionately great; Zeffirelli's film has to be taken seriously simply because it has probably been seen by more people than any other production of the play ever.

CONCLUSION

The popularity of *The Taming of the Shrew* is indisputable: quite apart from the productions discussed here and in the commentary, the play has another vast stage history of productions performed by amateur and student groups, summer festival companies, Shakespeare in the Park companies and so on, some of whom, away from the pressures of commercial theatre, have been far braver than the mainstream in experimenting with the play. *The Taming of the Shrew* has also been phenomenally popular outside English-speaking countries, presumably at least partly because the physical comedy is almost guaranteed to survive translation, and the play has been particularly popular in Europe, especially in Germany, where productions have ranged from Reinhardt's seminal commedia production to Peter Zadek's freakish assault on the play (3 September 1981, Berlin). While the play continues to do such

good box office theatre companies are unlikely to banish it from the repertory, but a stage history like this one provides reassuring evidence that while
the taming of Katherina has been played out so very many times, in so many
different periods and cultures, at least some Katherinas have fought back,
subverted their taming, and sometimes even (the best possible outcome in my
view) had a laugh at Petruchio's expense.

THE TAMING OF THE SHREW

✛ ✛
✛

LIST OF CHARACTERS

The Induction

CHRISTOPHER SLY, *a tinker*
HOSTESS *of an alehouse*
LORD
BARTHOLOMEW, *the Lord's page*
HUNTSMEN *and* SERVANTS *attending on the Lord*
PLAYERS

The Taming Plot

BAPTISTA MINOLA, *a rich citizen of Padua*
KATHERINA, *the Shrew, elder daughter of Baptista*
PETRUCHIO, *a gentleman of Verona, suitor to Katherina*
GRUMIO, *Petruchio's personal servant*
CURTIS, *Petruchio's chief servant at his country house*
TAILOR
HABERDASHER
SERVANTS *attending on Petruchio*

The Subplot

BIANCA, *younger daughter of Baptista*
GREMIO, *a rich old citizen of Padua, suitor to Bianca*
HORTENSIO, *a gentlemen of Padua, suitor to Bianca, pretends to be Litio*
LUCENTIO, *a gentleman of Pisa, suitor to Bianca, pretends to be Cambio*
TRANIO, *Lucentio's personal servant, pretends to be Lucentio*
BIONDELLO, *Lucentio's second servant (a boy)*
VINCENTIO, *a rich old citizen of Pisa, father of Lucentio*
MERCHANT *of Mantua, pretends to be Vincentio*
WIDOW, *in love with Hortensio*
SERVANTS *attending on Baptista and Lucentio*

CHRISTOPHER SLY For a range of Sly's manifestations, see Introduction pp. 51–64. Holderness and Loughrey (35) point out that although the Folio s.d.s and speech headings refer to Sly as a 'beggar', editors normally promote Sly to the status of tinker. Sly sometimes also plays roles in the inner play, including Petruchio (e.g. Bogdanov 1978), the Pedant (Merchant) (e.g. Dunlop 1970), Vincentio (Sullivan 1980), and in Harris (1944) Wilson Barrett's Sly took on the role of Grumio. In Hamilton (1999) Sly changed sex and became Chrissie Sly, a young, drunk, female student.

HOSTESS In *AS* she changed sex and became a Tapster. Sometimes doubled with Katherina, e.g. Bogdanov (1978).

LORD Often now seen as a class oppressor, and made completely obnoxious in e.g. Alexander (1990, 1992). Earlier on the Lord was seen as a madcap role, e.g. Webster (1844). In *AS* the Lord takes the name 'Simon' or 'Sim' when in disguise. In Wolfit (1953) he became the God of Dreams. In Taylor (1980) he played Petruchio in the inner play, in Heap (1985) he played Katherina.

BARTHOLOMEW The age of the actor playing Bartholomew can be crucial in determining the impact of this role. A fully adult Bartholomew playing Sly's wife in the style of *Charley's Aunt*, such as that played during the 1930s and 1940s by C. Rivers Gadsby in every production at Stratford, is unproblematically funny but Harold Hobson was disturbed when a young boy page in Barton (1960) discussed going to bed with Sly (*ST* 26 June 1960). Earlier the *Athenaeum* (3 December 1904), reviewing Asche (1904), felt that 'while the page-boy is permitted such proceedings as those in which he indulges we do not regard the restitution of the scenes as an unmixed good'.

BAPTISTA MINOLA Was socially elevated and became Lord Beaufoy in *Sauny the Scot*. Became a star role in Nunn (1967) when played by Roy Kinnear. Has occasionally become mother of Katherina and Bianca (e.g. Hallum and Clark 1992) and in Miron (1992) Baptista was 'a domineering Italian yenta with a beehive hairdo and a desperate need to find her girls the right man' (*Toronto Star*, 25 September 1992) who also flirted with Petruchio.

KATHERINA Katherine is her own expressed preference, Petruchio calls her Kate, which is her name in *AS*. Garrick made her 'Catharine', Kemble 'Katharine'. Different productions spell her name differently but here 'Katherina' is always used for the Folio text character, except within quotations using variants. For performance traditions, see Introduction pp. 34–46. The character was renamed Margaret in *Sauny the Scot*.

PETRUCHIO Pronounced soft but Petrookios often occur, e.g. Asche (1904), and, more understandably, given the director's Italian nationality, in Zeffirelli's film. For performance history, see Introduction (pp. 46–51). Renamed Ferando in *AS*.

GRUMIO Usually played as likeable but Quigan (1995) deployed a Grumio described by the *Dominion* (26 July 1995) as 'shave-headed, splay-kneed, gap-toothed grotesque, ape-like and dangerous'. Hodgman (1991) had a lugubrious Grumio, who was jealous of Katherina displacing him in Petruchio's affections. An early modern-dress production, Massey (1927), turned Grumio into a racist stereotype with a 'black-skinned, red-lipped Jolsonian mask' (*Boston Evening Transcript*, 4 May 1927). The Grumio character is named Sander in *AS*, and became the star role, Sauny, in *Sauny the Scot*, where he became Scottish and specialised in crude jokes.

CURTIS Often played as a woman after Garrick (e.g. Daly 1887) and the practice occasionally continues today (e.g. Quigan 1995). At the height of this tradition's popularity, Curtis was an old woman, a gossip and occasionally tipsy.

TAILOR It was traditional for the tailor to be effeminate, and he sometimes acquired a stutter, but the Tailor's effeminacy in many productions would have been read as gay (e.g. Robert Helpmann's performance in Guthrie 1939) and the character thus became, in the theatre, homosexual, at a time when overt representations of homosexuality were not legal in Britain. Productions have also flirted with racism with this character: Speaight (162) remembers Ayliff (1928) presenting 'the tailor as an obsequious Jew from Whitechapel' and in the Wild West staging of Antoon (1990) the Chinese tailor was 'alternately servile and contentious, blending two Asian stereotypes from old movies in a way that might anger some humourless Asian-American media watchdogs' (*Wall Street Journal*, 16 July 1990).

HABERDASHER Often conflated with the Tailor.

SERVANTS Attending on Petruchio. Their names often change with relocations of the action: e.g. Antoon (1990) had Wild West names like 'Joe Bob'. Italianising productions (e.g. Rose 1997) sometimes do away with the very English names in the text and use Italian names. The speech headings in the Folio, plus all the names mentioned in the text, add up to a lot of servants and productions often economise (see commentary 4.1).

BIANCA Now often played as the real shrew of the family, e.g. Alexander (1992). Biancas behaving badly include Hammond (1984) where she was 'sexually impatient' with Lucentio, indulged in a 'roll in the hay with him', was 'overly fond of chianti' and in the final scene 'was so drunk she fell down on the stage and had to be helped to stagger up' (Babula 1985, 360). Trevis (1985) was unusual in having a Bianca who actually admired Katherina and in having real-life sisters play the roles. Bianca is often a blonde, as suggested by her name, in contrast to a dark- or red-haired Katherina, e.g. Nunn (1967). The pun on 'white' (see 5.2.186) as the centre of the target that everyone strives to hit was translated into modern terms in Kaut-Howson (2001) where Bianca was dressed in gold, signalling her status as the golden girl. Unwin (1998) had Bianca as a serious student, wanting to learn in the lesson scene, and by the end of the play she was troubled and drinking to drown her sorrows.

GREMIO Identified as a commedia character, 'a pantaloon' in 1.1.45 s.d. In *Sauny the Scot* he becomes Woodall, who attempts to kidnap Biancha and force her into marriage.

LUCENTIO Became Winlove in *Sauny the Scot* but was cut in Garrick and Garrick derivatives (e.g. Taylor 1929). In 1954 Tyrone Guthrie's production, William Shatner, the future Captain James T. Kirk, played Lucentio as a fresh-faced college boy.

TRANIO This can be a scene-stealing role, e.g. Ralph Richardson's performance in Ayliff (1928). In Burrell (1947) Tranio was a great hit as a version of 'Flying Officer Kite', a contemporary radio comic character, a 'chocks away', handlebar-moustached, RAF type. In Williams (1931) Tranio was Harlequin with 'mask, parti-coloured dress, and lath sword' (Crosse 96). Alexander (1992) made Tranio a real contender for Bianca's love, and he became jealous of Lucentio, although Bianca clearly preferred him to his master. This Tranio was also 'deeply reluctant to go back to his identity as servant' (*T* 22 July 1993). In Posner (1999) Tranio was also disgruntled at his return to servant status, 'standing on ceremony behind the banquet – scowling' (*IS* 31 October 1999). Kyle (1982) made Tranio a camp and outrageous squanderer of money whilst in disguise.

BIONDELLO In Komisarjevsky (1939) Biondello became a compere, announcing the scene locations, but he lost his big comic routine speeches in 3.2.

VINCENTIO Usually genial, but Dews (1981) had a very irascible Vincentio who was angry at being mocked.

MERCHANT In *AS* the disguise plot involves a merchant figure and the Folio lines at 4.2.89–90 suggest that this character is indeed a merchant; however he is nearly always played in the theatre as a caricature pedant/schoolteacher and appears in cast lists as 'Pedant'. Consequently he is designated in the commentary here as Pedant (Merchant). The only merchant I have discovered is in Pope (1992) where the Bianca doubled as 'a salesman of Mantua' (*I* 17 June 1992). The character became a 'tipsy, itinerant ham actor made up to resemble W. C. Fields at his most pink-cheeked and Dickensian' (*NYT* 13 July 1990) in Antoon (1990), a Wild West staging, and Massey (1927) made him 'a red-nosed gentleman with a trick-cane, trick-cigar and experience of the burlesque-theaters' (*Boston Evening Transcript*, 4 May 1927). In *Sauny the Scot*, the character becomes Snatchpenny, a petty crook and professional liar. The Pedant is often played as drunk (see commentary).

THE TAMING OF THE SHREW

INDUCTION 1

Enter CHRISTOPHER SLY *and the* HOSTESS.

SLY I'll feeze you, in faith.

HOSTESS A pair of stocks, you rogue!

SLY Y'are a baggage, the Slys are no rogues. Look in the Chronicles;
we came in with Richard Conqueror. Therefore *paucas pallabris*,
let the world slide. Sessa!   5

Despite their unimpeachable authority, Induction scenes 1 and 2 are still sometimes cut
by directors with an antipathy for their robust and Brechtian theatricality (e.g. Miller 1972,
1980, 1987). Pope's decision to label these scenes the 'Induction' possibly contributed to the
scenes' vulnerability to cutting and it is hard to imagine any other play by Shakespeare so
frequently stripped of what the Folio labels 'Actus Primus. Scæna Prima'. Substitutions for,
updatings, and reworkings of the Induction have been legion (see Introduction pp. 51–64)
and many directors have felt free to rewrite the Induction far more overtly than they have
rewritten the inner play. For example, Alexander, in 1990 and 1992, controversially
reconfigured the scenes, adhering to the literal meaning of the speeches but updating
the language, while the Lord's party became a 1990s party of hooray Henrys and Henriettas
named Hugo Daley-Young, Lady Sarah Ormsby and Mrs Ruth Banks-Ellis and so on.

The scene often opens with a crash of breaking glass offstage (e.g. Devine 1953) followed
by horseplay. The hefty Oscar Asche (1899) as Sly was hustled on by two ostlers and then
thrown down over a trough. Harvey (1913): the Hostess beat Sly with a broom. Devine
(1953): the Hostess swiped at Sly with a warming pan. Dews (1981) had a chase sequence
with much swinging and ducking. Unwin (1998): the modern-dress Sly was thrown out of
an Indian restaurant. Trevis (1985) opened with the sound of a baby belonging to one of the
travelling players wailing, followed by wild gypsy music (*O* 22 September 1985) and a
'Trudge' of the players across the stage (Howard 184) before the eruption of Sly onstage.

Although this scene is clearly set close to Stratford-upon-Avon, the Hostess's tavern has
been relocated all over the world. Brighton (1981) had a 'rowdy Klondike pub' where the
Hostess clutched 'a pipe between her teeth like Mammy Yokum' (*Toronto Sun*, 6 March
1981). Guthrie (1954) translated the play to Canada with the Lord's shooting party coming
back from the northern woods (Robertson Davies 32). *AS* opens with a more specific s.d.
than the Folio: *Enter a* TAPSTER *beating out of his doors* SLY, *drunken.* Payne (1935) opened
with *AS* 1–6, Barton (1960) with *AS* 1–3.

1 Dews (1981) changed 'feeze' to 'fix'. Sly has had a variety of working-class accents, e.g. a
Birmingham accent in Kyle (1982), Alexander (1992).

HOSTESS You will not pay for the glasses you have burst?

SLY No, not a denier. Go by, Saint Jeronimy, go to thy cold bed and
warm thee.

[He lies down.]

HOSTESS I know my remedy; I must go fetch the thirdborough.
[Exit]

SLY Third, or fourth, or fifth borough, I'll answer him by law. I'll not   10
budge an inch, boy. Let him come, and kindly.

He falls asleep.

Wind horns. Enter a LORD *from hunting, with his train [of* HUNTSMEN
and SERVINGMEN*].*

LORD Huntsman, I charge thee, tender well my hounds.
Breathe Merriman – the poor cur is embossed –
And couple Clowder with the deep-mouthed brach.

3–4 Mellor (1989) relocated the action to Brisbane, and instead of claiming descent from the
Norman Conquest, Sly stated 'we came with the First Fleet', which suggests descent from
transported convicts (Gay 1998, 173).

4 *'paucas pallabris'* is sometimes cut e.g. Kelly (1993).

7 'denier' was changed into 'penny' in e.g. Langham (1962).

9 'thirdborough' was changed into 'constable' in e.g. Langham (1962).

11 s.d. Trevis (1985): Sly appeared to vomit and urinate here, before falling asleep (*FT* 30 October
1985). Some Lords enter with a huge entourage and the hunters sometimes have animals
with them. Cass (1935) had a hunting horse 'lent by the Duke of Westminster' (*Stage*, 3
January 1935). Langham (1962) had two scene-stealing golden retrievers onstage. Dews
(1981) had dogs and a hawk. Sullivan (1980) had 'beagles on leashes' (Frey 1981, 274). Daly
(1887): the hunters carried 'Boar spears' (s34). Ayliff (1928): the Lord (Laurence Olivier) lost
several of his lines to a party of Ladies, especially those lines which suggested a more gentle
approach to the trick (e.g. 62, 64). Williams (1973) cut the Lord entirely and had the trick
proposed and performed by the travelling players, who were on tour in 1592 while the
plague was raging in London, information that was conveyed to the audience by slides. Kyle
(1982) opened in midwinter snow, and had a chorus of 'Good King Wenceslas' here, the
carol's 'poor man' perhaps linking with Sly. Alexander (1992): the object of the hunt, the
Lord's younger brother 'Rupert Llewellyn', who was clearly badly bullied by his elder
brother, appeared onstage first. Sutcliffe (1990) modernised the Induction and Sly was
discovered sleeping in a cardboard box by yuppie Lords (*DT* 18 October 1990).

13–24 The detailed discussion of the hunting dogs is vulnerable to cutting, e.g. Payne (1935).

14 'brach' was changed into 'bitch' in e.g. Langham (1962).

Saw'st thou not, boy, how Silver made it good 15
At the hedge corner, in the coldest fault?
I would not lose the dog for twenty pound.

1 HUNTSMAN Why, Belman is as good as he, my lord;
He cried upon it at the merest loss,
And twice today picked out the dullest scent. 20
Trust me, I take him for the better dog.

LORD Thou art a fool. If Echo were as fleet
I would esteem him worth a dozen such.
But sup them well, and look unto them all:
Tomorrow I intend to hunt again. 25

1 HUNTSMAN I will, my lord.

LORD What's here? One dead, or drunk? See, doth he breathe?

2 HUNTSMAN He breathes, my lord. Were he not warmed with ale,
This were a bed but cold to sleep so soundly.

LORD O monstrous beast, how like a swine he lies! 30
Grim death, how foul and loathsome is thine image!
Sirs, I will practise on this drunken man.
What think you, if he were conveyed to bed,
Wrapped in sweet clothes, rings put upon his fingers,
A most delicious banquet by his bed, 35

---

15 Langham (1962) changed 'Silver' into 'Ginger' to fit the golden retrievers then onstage.

17 Bogdanov (1978) interpolated 5.2.72–3 here to emphasise the notion of the wager and the Lord then threw a fox skin on Sly.

27 Ayliff (1928): Sly was discovered as the Hostess, who had returned to serve drinks to the hunting party, stumbled over him.

28 Daly (1887): Sly snored loudly to cue this line (s34). Leiber (1921, 1930): the investigating huntsman 'receives Sly's hickup' (pbk). Barton (1961) semaphored here that Sly had bad breath.

30 Ayliff (1928): Sly interpolated a denial here and drowsily repeated his claim to be descended from Richard Conqueror.

31 Sometimes cut by sunnier productions e.g. Daly (1887) (s34). Reinhardt (1909) had a sobering pause at the end of the line. Leach (1978): the Lord delivered the line in over-the-top, tragic style and took a round of applause from his attendants.

32 Daly (1887): the Lord was 'struck with a sudden thought and turns to train' (s31).

33 Nunn (1967) performed the inner play in the tavern and so changed 'to bed' into 'within', line 35 'his bed' to 'close at hand', cut the details of the Lord's house, and wrote new lines for the Lord to welcome the players.

And brave attendants near him when he wakes –
Would not the beggar then forget himself?
1 HUNTSMAN Believe me, lord, I think he cannot choose.
2 HUNTSMAN It would seem strange unto him when he waked –
LORD Even as a flatt'ring dream or worthless fancy.   40
Then take him up, and manage well the jest.
Carry him gently to my fairest chamber
And hang it round with all my wanton pictures;
Balm his foul head in warm distillèd waters
And burn sweet wood to make the lodging sweet;   45
Procure me music ready when he wakes
To make a dulcet and a heavenly sound;
And if he chance to speak, be ready straight
And with a low submissive reverence
Say, 'What is it your honour will command?'   50
Let one attend him with a silver basin
Full of rose-water and bestrewed with flowers;
Another bear the ewer, the third a diaper,
And say, 'Will't please your lordship cool your hands?'
Some one be ready with a costly suit   55
And ask him what apparel he will wear;
Another tell him of his hounds and horse,
And that his lady mourns at his disease.
Persuade him that he hath been lunatic,
And when he says he is, say that he dreams,   60
For he is nothing but a mighty lord.
This do, and do it kindly, gentle sirs.
It will be pastime passing excellent,
If it be husbanded with modesty.

40 ff. The elaboration of this speech is often substantially trimmed, e.g. Trevis (1985).

43 The 'wanton' reference was cut in e.g. Asche (1899). The line was taken very literally in Harvey (1913) which played the next scene in front of a 'nude women' curtain (McDonald pbk).

45 Dews (1981): Sly's bad breath was indicated as the reason why the lodging needed to be made 'sweet'.

47 Payne (1935): a 'sound' was provided as Sly snored loudly.

51 ff. Burrell (1947) built up the character of the Hostess and gave her most of this speech, and all the lines dealing with the organisation of the show, which was being performed in her tavern, not the Lord's hall.

53 'diaper' was changed to 'napkin' in e.g. Guthrie (1954).

1 HUNTSMAN My lord, I warrant you we will play our part   65
        As he shall think by our true diligence
        He is no less than what we say he is.
LORD Take him up gently and to bed with him,
        And each one to his office when he wakes.

                                            [*Sly is carried off*]
                    Sound trumpets.
        Sirrah, go see what trumpet 'tis that sounds.   70

                                            [*Exit Servingman*]
        Belike some noble gentleman that means,
        Travelling some journey, to repose him here.

                    Enter Servingman.

        How now? Who is it?
SERVINGMAN   An't please your honour, players
        That offer service to your lordship.
LORD Bid them come near.

                    Enter PLAYERS.

                    Now, fellows, you are welcome.   75

65 In Asche (1899) three huntsmen began to pick up the burly Oscar Asche as Sly. When they
    dropped him Sly didn't wake up.

67 Barton (1960) used a version of *AS* 1.35–6, 47–8 here.

69 s.d. *trumpets* became Glenn Miller in Rider (1994), a production set immediately after the
    Second World War. Productions adopting the 'Sly's dream' approach can make the Players
    redundant: e.g. Bogdanov (1978) cut heavily from around here.

75 s.d. The Players have inhabited various centuries and degrees of prosperity. Webster (1844)
    dressed three players recognisably as Shakespeare, Jonson and Tarleton (*T* 18 March 1844).
    The 'travelling players' element was next emphasised sixty-five years later by Reinhardt
    (1909), who had a commedia troupe, and by Harvey (1913), who had the players visiting the
    mansion of a great Elizabethan lord. Ayliff (1928) had modern-dress actors and 'a porter
    staggered across the stage bearing a basket labelled "Birmingham Repertory Company"'
    (*BP* 2 May 1928). Gribble (1935): the players all had capes over their costumes, large black
    hats and white domino masks. They were accompanied by music, tumbling acrobats, one of
    whom was walking on a large ball, plus a 'Lady Harpist' playing 'furiously' who was 'drawn
    in on a small decorated wagon' (s65 CS). A more *Mother Courage*-style cart was used in
    Langham (1962) and Trevis (1985): Trevis chose a very Brechtian style, stressing the realities
    of 'an early-Victorian fit-up company' (*G* 9 October 1985) with two of the 'actresses' in
    the inner play nursing babies when not acting. The actors were camped at one end of the
    traverse stage, watching the Lord with Sly and 'hopeful for work, seize their chance to

PLAYERS We thank your honour.

LORD Do you intend to stay with me tonight?

1 PLAYER So please your lordship to accept our duty.

LORD With all my heart. This fellow I remember
        Since once he played a farmer's eldest son –   80
        'Twas where you wooed the gentlewoman so well –
        I have forgot your name, but sure that part
        Was aptly fitted and naturally performed.

2 PLAYER I think 'twas Soto that your honour means.

LORD 'Tis very true; thou didst it excellent.   85
        Well, you are come to me in happy time,
        The rather for I have some sport in hand
        Wherein your cunning can assist me much.
        There is a lord will hear you play tonight –

offer a play' (Howard 184). Lovejoy (1972): the players were a J. C. Williamson's touring company, part of the organisation that almost monopolised Australian theatre in the early twentieth century, stranded at an Australian outback train station in a tropical storm. They then performed for a wealthy landowner who was tricking a swagman Sly. The players were also waiting for train connections in Newton (1974) which was set 'on a railway station in Padua, Italy in 1860' (Vancouver Playhouse Newsheet, October 1974). The Mediaeval Players (Heap 1985), who self-consciously modelled their theatre practice upon the idea of travelling players, also stressed this aspect. Production photographs of Edwards (1975) show the travelling player Diane Cilento (later Katherina), demonstrating her fire-eating skills.

    Marcus (112) argues that the Players in *AS* are of a lower status than their counterparts in the Folio: the Quarto players are not announced by trumpets, Sander is not secure in his use of the word 'comedy' (although his malapropism 'commodity' (1.57) may be a deliberate joke), the two players who enter have *packs at their backs* (1.55 s.d.), which suggests limited means, and the players seem to be trying to get the Lord to provide property food partly so that the players can actually eat it.

79a Gribble (1935): Petruchio proceeded to distribute costumes in bundles to all the players. The acrobats then formed a human ladder in order to hang a backdrop of 'elaborate baroque pictures of Padua. The name Padua appearing in large letters' (s65).

79b is often addressed to the player who will later play Petruchio, who then replies as Second Player at line 84, e.g. Dews (1981). Gribble (1935) had 'This fellow . . .' addressed to Tranio as the Lord 'lifts his domino to see his face' (s65).

85 Leiber (1921, 1930): the Lord was seen to get his big idea at this moment.

86 Ayliff (1928) used a version of *AS* 1.56–62, as did Barton (1960).

But I am doubtful of your modesties,   90
Lest over-eyeing of his odd behaviour
(For yet his honour never heard a play)
You break into some merry passion
And so offend him; for I tell you, sirs,
If you should smile, he grows impatient.   95
1 PLAYER Fear not, my lord, we can contain ourselves
Were he the veriest antic in the world.
LORD Go, sirrah, take them to the buttery
And give them friendly welcome every one.
Let them want nothing that my house affords.   100
Exit one with the Players
Sirrah, go you to Barthol'mew my page
And see him dressed in all suits like a lady.
That done, conduct him to the drunkard's chamber,
And call him 'madam', do him obeisance.
Tell him from me – as he will win my love –   105
He bear himself with honourable action
Such as he hath observed in noble ladies
Unto their lords, by them accomplishèd.
Such duty to the drunkard let him do
With soft low tongue and lowly courtesy,   110
And say, 'What is't your honour will command
Wherein your lady and your humble wife
May show her duty and make known her love?'
And then with kind embracements, tempting kisses,
And with declining head into his bosom,   115

98 Leach (1978) substituted 'public house' for 'buttery'. Barton (1960) used *AS* 1.79–80, and most of Sander's subsequent speech, divided among Baptista, the prompter and boy. The production then privileged *AS* over the Folio text for the rest of the scene. Nunn (1967) used a version of *AS* 79–85 around line 108 and also transposed several sections of the Folio.

100 s.d. Harvey (1913): the jollity of the players was stressed as the Lord's 'Major Domo waves them with dignity to follow him – Petruchio imitates him – all copy him and exit laughing' (McDonald pbk). Daly (1887): the thought of using Bartholomew was seen to be suddenly striking the Lord (s31).

102 Occasionally pointed in modern productions by having an actress playing a boy player about to play Katherina, e.g. Devine (1953), Robertson and Selbie (1986).

114–26 Cut in Phelps (1856), possibly as risqué.

Bid him shed tears, as being overjoyed
To see her noble lord restored to health,
Who for this seven years hath esteemèd him
No better than a poor and loathsome beggar.
And if the boy have not a woman's gift   120
To rain a shower of commanded tears,
An onion will do well for such a shift,
Which in a napkin being close conveyed
Shall in despite enforce a watery eye.
See this dispatched with all the haste thou canst;   125
Anon I'll give thee more instructions.

                                                        Exit a Servingman

I know the boy will well usurp the grace,
Voice, gait and action of a gentlewoman.
I long to hear him call the drunkard 'husband',
And how my men will stay themselves from laughter   130
When they do homage to this simple peasant.
I'll in to counsel them. Haply my presence
May well abate the over-merry spleen
Which otherwise would grow into extremes.

                                                        [*Exeunt*]

122 Heap (1985): the Lord actually produced an onion.

INDUCTION 2

Enter aloft [SLY] *with* ATTENDANTS – *some with apparel, basin and ewer, and other appurtenances* – *and* LORD.

SLY For God's sake, a pot of small ale!

1 SERVINGMAN Will't please your lordship drink a cup of sack?

2 SERVINGMAN Will't please your honour taste of these conserves?

3 SERVINGMAN What raiment will your honour wear today?

SLY I am Christophero Sly – call not me 'honour' nor 'lordship'. I   5
ne'er drank sack in my life, and if you give me any conserves,
give me conserves of beef. Ne'er ask me what raiment I'll wear,
for I have no more doublets than backs, no more stockings than
legs, nor no more shoes than feet – nay, sometime more feet than
shoes, or such shoes as my toes look through the overleather.   10

LORD Heaven cease this idle humour in your honour!
O that a mighty man of such descent,

os.d. Slys are rarely placed 'aloft' although Dews (1981) had Sly on the Elizabethan-style balcony at Stratford, Ontario, from here until the end of the play and Gribble (1935) usually had Sly 'aloft' in a stage box. Burrell (1947) had Sly semi 'aloft', placed, along with a large retinue, on a bed on a raised platform upstage right. *AS* does not specify 'aloft' but *Enter two with a table and a banquet on it and two other with* SLY *asleep in a chair, richly apparelled, and the music playing.*

Bogdanov (1978), Posner (1999): Sly was bathed onstage as this scene opened. Phelps (1856): Sly was discovered in 'a magnificent bed, surrounded by all the appliances of luxury' (*ST* 23 November 1856), and attended by servants who were having difficulty in 'repressing their laughter' (pbk). Asche (1899) had prolonged business with ringing of bells, shouts of 'My Lord!' and ad libbing to wake Sly up (pbk). J. Beresford Fowler (24) admired Asche's 'business with the tassel of his nightcap and his inability to comprehend the elaborate four-poster bed as the muddy-minded rascal comes out of his sottish stupor to the glory of palatial surroundings'. Barton (1960) used a medley from *AS* 2.11-15.

Some productions do not make the move to the Lord's house but stay at the inn, e.g. Burrell (1947); Williams (1973) also cut the Lord entirely (see Induction 1.11).

1 'God' became 'Heavens' in Webster (1844 s9).

5 Dews (1981) had a long pause before Sly started this speech as he considered the situation.

9 Gribble (1935): Sly wept and showed his feet.

11 Bridges-Adams (1920): Sly drew his legs up under the coverlet, shaking with fright.

             Of such possessions and so high esteem,
             Should be infusèd with so foul a spirit!

SLY What, would you make me mad? Am not I Christopher Sly, old   15
Sly's son of Burton-heath, by birth a pedlar, by education a
cardmaker, by transmutation a bear-herd, and now by present
profession a tinker? Ask Marian Hacket, the fat ale-wife of
Wincot, if she know me not. If she say I am not fourteen pence
on the score for sheer ale, score me up for the lying'st knave in   20
Christendom. What, I am not bestraught! Here's –

3 SERVINGMAN O, this it is that makes your lady mourn.

2 SERVINGMAN O, this is it that makes your servants droop.

LORD Hence comes it that your kindred shuns your house
             As beaten hence by your strange lunacy.   25
             O noble lord, bethink thee of thy birth.
             Call home thy ancient thoughts from banishment,
             And banish hence these abject lowly dreams.
             Look how thy servants do attend on thee,
             Each in his office ready at thy beck.   30
             Wilt thou have music? Hark, Apollo plays, *Music*
             And twenty cagèd nightingales do sing.
             Or wilt thou sleep? We'll have thee to a couch
             Softer and sweeter than the lustful bed
             On purpose trimmed up for Semiramis.   35
             Say thou wilt walk, we will bestrow the ground.
             Or wilt thou ride? Thy horses shall be trapped,
             Their harness studded all with gold and pearl.
             Dost thou love hawking? Thou hast hawks will soar
             Above the morning lark. Or wilt thou hunt?   40
             Thy hounds shall make the welkin answer them
             And fetch shrill echoes from the hollow earth.

1 SERVINGMAN Say thou wilt course, thy greyhounds are as swift
             As breathèd stags, ay, fleeter than the roe.

15–16 Dews (1981): all the servants shook their heads repeatedly.

   21 Trevis (1985) changed the broken off 'Here's' into 'Cheers'. Daly (1887) cut 'Here's' (534).

31 s.d. Ayliff (1928): the music was played on a wireless. Leiber (1921, 1930): the music was awful
       (pbk).

31–63 Often slimmed down and cut back, particularly the classical references, e.g. Ayliff (1928).
       Asche (1899) cut the lustful 33–5, as did e.g. Anglin (1908).

   35 Harvey (1913): 'Sly on floor, buries himself in the cushions in fear' (McDonald pbk).

2 SERVINGMAN Dost thou love pictures? We will fetch thee straight   45
    Adonis painted by a running brook,
    And Cytherea all in sedges hid,
    Which seem to move and wanton with her breath
    Even as the waving sedges play wi'th'wind.
LORD We'll show thee Io as she was a maid,   50
    And how she was beguilèd and surprised,
    As lively painted as the deed was done.
3 SERVINGMAN Or Daphne roaming through a thorny wood,
    Scratching her legs that one shall swear she bleeds,
    And at that sight shall sad Apollo weep,   55
    So workmanly the blood and tears are drawn.
LORD Thou art a lord, and nothing but a lord.
    Thou hast a lady far more beautiful
    Than any woman in this waning age.
1 SERVINGMAN And till the tears that she hath shed for thee   60
    Like envious floods o'er-run her lovely face,
    She was the fairest creature in the world –
    And yet she is inferior to none.
SLY Am I a lord, and have I such a lady?
    Or do I dream? Or have I dreamed till now?   65
    I do not sleep: I see, I hear, I speak,
    I smell sweet savours and I feel soft things.

45–56 Harvey (1913) played this scene in front of what the McDonald promptbook always refers to as 'nude women' curtains, actually classical figures on tapestry, as suggested by these lines. Ayliff (1928) had a portfolio of smutty photographs, as did Bogdanov (1978). Payne (1935): Sly tried to drink from a washbowl and wash in a goblet. Kyle (1982): the Lord and his attendants mimed some of the action described, e.g. swaying as 'the waving sedges'.

53 Elvgren (1980) had a huge wooden picture frame onstage which Sly stepped through 'to signify belief in his supposed transformation from ruffian to nobleman'; this edifice also framed dramatic renditions of the actions described here such as 'Daphne's travel through the woods' (Labriola 205).

64 Sly's shift to verse signals his growing belief in the trick. Webster (1844) had everyone upstage except for Sly, thus marking out this speech as a moment of discovery for him. Reinhardt (1909) had a very long pause before Sly capitulated and began this line. Leach (1978): Sly gazed into a hand mirror and his failure to recognise himself helped convince him of the truth of what he was being told.

67 'soft things' Gribble (1935): Sly was feeling Bartholomew. Bogdanov (1978): Sly tested out whether he was a lord by maltreating his servants, pushing one to the ground, slapping

Upon my life, I am a lord indeed,
And not a tinker, nor Christopher Sly.
Well, bring our lady hither to our sight,   70
And once again a pot o'th'smallest ale.

                                      [Exit a Servingman]

2 SERVINGMAN Will't please your mightiness to wash your hands?
O, how we joy to see your wit restored!
O, that once more you knew but what you are!
These fifteen years you have been in a dream,   75
Or when you waked, so waked as if you slept.

SLY These fifteen years! By my fay, a goodly nap.
But did I never speak of all that time?

1 SERVINGMAN O yes, my lord, but very idle words,
For though you lay here in this goodly chamber,   80
Yet would you say ye were beaten out of door,
And rail upon the hostess of the house,
And say you would present her at the leet
Because she brought stone jugs and no sealed quarts.
Sometimes you would call out for Cicely Hacket.   85

SLY Ay, the woman's maid of the house.

3 SERVINGMAN Why, sir, you know no house, nor no such maid,
Nor no such men as you have reckoned up,
As Stephen Sly and old John Naps of Greece,
And Peter Turph and Henry Pimpernell,   90
And twenty more such names and men as these,
Which never were, nor no man ever saw.

one in the face, kicking one in the testicles, spraying foam at another and then, finally, threatening to spray the front row of the stalls with foam. Harvey (1913): Sly 'falls forward on hands and knees' at his realisation (McDonald pbk). Reinhardt (1909): Sly jumped out of bed.

69 Benthall (1948): the perpetrators of the trick on Sly all cheered at this. A version of *AS* 2.27 ff. is sometimes inserted here, e.g. Devine (1953), Nunn (1967), Kyle (1982) pbk.

72 In Leiber (1921, 1930) this line was a response to Sly messily wiping his nose. Phelps (1856): Sly 'when he has grasped the fact that a basin is being held before him in which he must wash, enters upon such a wash as sooty hands of tinkers only can require, and having made an end of washing and bespattering, lifts up instinctively the corner of his velvet robe to dry his hands upon' (*Examiner*, 6 December 1856). Harvey (1913): Sly drank the water after smelling it (McDonald pbk). 72 ff. is sometimes split between several speakers e.g. Guthrie (1954), Burrell (1947). Benthall (1948): Bartholomew was prepared behind a screen to play Sly's wife.

SLY Now Lord be thankèd for my good amends!
ALL Amen.

> *Enter* [BARTHOLOMEW, *a page, dressed as a*] *lady, with*
> ATTENDANTS, [*one of whom gives Sly a pot of ale*].

SLY I thank thee, thou shalt not lose by it.   95
BARTHOLOMEW How fares my noble lord?
SLY Marry, I fare well, for here is cheer enough. [*He drinks.*] Where
    is my wife?
BARTHOLOMEW Here, noble lord, what is thy will with her?
SLY Are you my wife, and will not call me 'husband'?   100
    My men should call me 'lord'; I am your goodman.
BARTHOLOMEW My husband and my lord, my lord and husband,
    I am your wife in all obedience.
SLY I know it well – What must I call her?

---

93 Daly (1887) had this line as 'pivotal' to the Induction and Sly's 'gradual assumption of lordly state – his complacency, his comic gravity' was praised (*New York Tribune*, 19 January 1887). Barton (1960) played *AS* 2.26–35 here instead of the Folio text.

94 s.d. The original Bartholomew would have been a boy actor, and his presence onstage could have served to remind the audience, in proto-Brechtian style, that boys originally presented all the women's parts. This metatheatrical effect cannot be achieved in the modern theatre. Bartholomews have varied in their credibility as women and have ranged from convincingly attired, demure boy pages, to a hefty sailor (Kelly 1993), or in Ayliff (1928) a strapping man 'tastefully attired as a modern flapper' (Cochrane 131). In Leach (1978) Bartholomew towered above a diminutive Sly, and Dews (1981) had Bartholomew as an over-rouged young man, who paraded brazenly on the mainstage for the delectation of Sly on the balcony. Later on whenever Sly became too amorous, this Bartholomew simply put him in an arm-lock. Some Bartholomews enter the scene gamely and then, once they see Sly, try to escape, e.g. Bridges-Adams (1920). Daly (s34): Bartholomew tripped on his dress as he entered, striding like a man. Anglin (1908): Bartholomew 'carries onion tied to fan' (pbk.)

95 Ayliff (1928): Sly felt in his pocket for a tip but found that the pocket was empty. Harvey (1913) inserted *AS* 2.27–33 here (McDonald pbk) and delayed Bartholomew's entry until afterwards. Nunn (1967) used *AS* 2.44–9.

100 Reinhardt (1909): this line is marked as spoken gently.

102–3 Anglin (1908): Bartholomew tried to curtsey but the Lord was standing on his train. Bartholomew kicked out and then seeing it was his master became frightened.

104a Harvey (1913): suggested business here is that Sly kisses his wife with a 'sounding smack' (s58).

LORD 'Madam.'   105
SLY 'Al'ce madam' or 'Joan madam'?
LORD 'Madam' and nothing else. So lords call ladies.
SLY Madam wife, they say that I have dreamed
   And slept above some fifteen year or more.
BARTHOLOMEW Ay, and the time seems thirty unto me,   110
   Being all this time abandoned from your bed.
SLY 'Tis much. Servants, leave me and her alone.
           [*Exeunt Servingmen*]
   Madam, undress you and come now to bed.
BARTHOLOMEW Thrice noble lord, let me entreat of you
   To pardon me yet for a night or two,   115
   Or, if not so, until the sun be set.
   For your physicians have expressly charged,
   In peril to incur your former malady,
   That I should yet absent me from your bed.
   I hope this reason stands for my excuse.   120
SLY Ay, it stands so that I may hardly tarry so long, but I would be

107 Barton (1960) cut the Folio text and substituted *AS* 2.41–3.

108 Burrell (1947), which presented the joke on Sly very genially, had Sly kiss his wife's hand
  here.

110 Dews (1981): Bartholomew here used an onion (as recommended by the Lord, Induction
  1.122) to generate tears. Daly (s34): Bartholomew embraced Sly and cried loudly, but the
  next 13 lines were cut so the joke did not become too risqué.

111 Bogdanov (1978): Bartholomew (David Suchet, who went on to play Grumio) immediately
  realised the mention of 'bed' was dangerous, and swore under his breath. Sly instantly
  dropped his trousers and Bartholomew then had to prevent Sly from 'raping' him (pbk),
  only just stopping himself from flooring Sly as he did so. By contrast Ayliff (1928) had
  Bartholomew snuggling up to Sly. Komisarjevsky (1939) had Sly drag Bartholomew across
  to the bed.

111–23 Indecorous lines cut in Webster (1844), Anglin (1908), Harvey (1913). Asche (1899)
  substituted Sly chasing the Page 'who evades him and gets behind servants' but who
  then mocked the befuddled Sly and 'attracts his attention by calling cuckoo' (pbk).

114–20 Dews (1981): Sly became amorous so Bartholomew pinned him to his seat. In Marowitz
  (1973) these lines became a desperate plea by Kate to Petruchio at the end of the play;
  his response was to rape her anally while his gang of thugs held her down.

121 Sly's reference to his erection was often cut (e.g. Phelps 1856, Ayliff 1928) until recently.
  However, in Heap (1985) Sly had to cover his groin with a jacket because he was so aroused.
  Reinhardt (1909) had Sly chasing after Bartholomew here.

loath to fall into my dreams again. I will therefore tarry in despite of the flesh and the blood.

Enter a MESSENGER.

MESSENGER Your honour's players, hearing your amendment,
　　　Are come to play a pleasant comedy;　　　　　　　　　　125
　　　For so your doctors hold it very meet,
　　　Seeing too much sadness hath congealed your blood
　　　And melancholy is the nurse of frenzy –
　　　Therefore they thought it good you hear a play
　　　And frame your mind to mirth and merriment,　　　　　　130
　　　Which bars a thousand harms and lengthens life.
SLY Marry, I will. Let them play it. Is not a comonty a Christmas gambold or a tumbling trick?
BARTHOLOMEW No, my good lord, it is more pleasing stuff.
SLY What, household stuff?　　　　　　　　　　　　　　　　135
BARTHOLOMEW It is a kind of history.
SLY Well, we'll see't.

[Exit Messenger]

121–2 Alexander (1992) modernised 'I would be loath' into 'I would hate', and the line was stressed.

123 Ayliff (1928): Sly asked 'What pastime's toward', was offered the play and was then pushed into a theatre box. The Messenger's speech was then designated 'Prologue' (pbk). Trevis (1985): a Brechtian chalk circle was drawn to mark out the playing area, the Lord's antique furniture was piled up at one end of the 25-metre traverse and a huge banner, with 'The Taming of the Shrew – a Kind of History' written on it, was thrown over the furniture. Barton (1960) substituted *AS* 2.44–55 for the Folio text.

124–31 Burrell (1947): the Hostess, who had become mistress of ceremonies, delivered this speech. Komisarjevsky (1939) had Biondello as master of ceremonies and so he took on 124–5 as well as 134 and 136, explaining the nature of the piece to Sly. Harvey (1913) gave the lines to the Lord's major domo (McDonald pbk), Daly (1887) gave them to the disguised Lord himself (534). Anthony (1965) had this speech as a prologue spoken to the paying audience by Petruchio (Beckerman 332). Nunn (1967) had a mime as a prelude to the inner play with a collage of *AS* lines. Kyle (1982) used *AS* 1.62 (pbk) ''Tis a good lesson for us, my lord, for us that are married men.'

132 Kelly (1993) inserted *AS* 2.47.

136 Williams (1973) here played a version of *AS* 1.60–2. From here on in Creswell (1935, 1941) Bartholomew became Sly's guide to the play, introducing characters, explaining what was going on and at the same time helping the radio audience to follow the plot. Watts (1954) did something very similar with the Lord as Sly's guide.

> Come, madam wife, sit by my side,
> And let the world slip. We shall ne'er be younger.
> [*They sit down.*]
> [*A flourish of trumpets to announce the play.*]

139 Webster (1844) had music to accompany the players rearranging the Lord's chamber. Trumpets then sounded three times in Elizabethan style to signal the commencement of the inner play. Phelps (1856): the Lord and servants were now 'almost bursting with suppressed laughter' (pbk). Harvey (1913): Sly sat in the front of the stalls. Guthrie (1954) placed Sly downstage left to watch the play. Langham (1962): Sly settled down with Bartholomew, attended by two maids who brought 'great trays of fruits' and 'sack in silver tankards' (*Chicago Tribune* 21 June 1962). Dews (1981) had Sly, who was still amorous but cowed by his strapping 'wife', sit down along with a very large crowd of onstage audience. The *Oxford Mail* (27 April 1960) was impressed with Hauser (1960) where the actors brought their 'tiny stage' on with them, and pieced it together 'in a twinkling before the amazed Sly's couch, its curtains doing stout work as backcloths. Their props – a light-weight tree, a cardboard fire – are similarly serviceable; their parts, with the aid of masks, various.' Bogdanov (1978) made the transformation to the main play via a train station sequence with lots of people toing and froing. 'Sly takes programme from someone in front row, reads it, then returns it' as if to check which play he's in (pbk). A band came through the set and Sly tried to talk to them, but they couldn't see him. He then remained onstage in a café watching the entire first scene, ensuring he saw Katherina in action before he returned as Petruchio to woo her. Posner (1999) had Sly attempt to access a porn website, fail, and instead *The Taming of the Shrew* appeared on his computer screen. Asche (1899), which took Sly off here, concluded 'in a pillow fight' (*T* 30 November 1904). Bridges-Adams (1920) ended the Sly narrative with a slow curtain as Lucentio began to perform his first lines to Sly, lines which were then repeated when the curtain was raised again. Harvey (1913) drew off the 'nude' women curtain (McDonald pbk) and revealed the full set for the inner play behind it.

ACT I   SCENE I

Enter LUCENTIO *and his man* TRANIO.

LUCENTIO   Tranio, since for the great desire I had
　　To see fair Padua, nursery of arts,

For productions which cut the Induction (e.g. Miller 1972, 1980, 1987) this becomes the opening scene. Excessively Italianised versions of Padua often play with Italian stereotypes and accents, e.g. Dillon (1979) where Baptista owned a trattoria in post-Second World War Italy and Petruchio was an occupying GI. Italian cafés also featured in e.g. Hawthorne (1984), Coffey (1979). Monette (1988) used clichéd Italian music, *La Dolce Vita* street scenes and lots of Italian spoken and sung by the characters. Mellor (1989) was set in the Italian pavilion at the 1988 Brisbane Expo with running gags about the leaning tower of Pisa and a wedding cake ornamented 'with the figures of the Venus de Milo and Michelangelo's David as the bride and groom' (*Courier Mail*, 19 August 1989). Rose (1997) moved between early 1960s Italy and Little Italy, New York (New Padua), via Alitalia airlines and was full of Mafia stereotypes. The latter also appeared in Bogdanov (1978) and Kaut-Howson (2001) although Kaut-Howson lightened the mood by also mobilising vendors of pizza and gelati. Lovejoy (1972) had fake Italian accents adopted by several characters at the insistence of Sly, who objected to the actors' 'Pommie' accents. A less extravagant vision of Padua appeared in Gascon (1973), which was set in 1820s Italy, the era of early Rossini or Donizetti operas. Hammond (1984) was set during the Italian unification movement of 1853 and included a funeral for one of those fallen in the conflict. The most realistically Italian production of all perhaps was Zeffirelli (1967), where Renaissance Italy was lovingly recreated in the film studios. Zeffirelli's deliberately fake pastoral opening was pastiched in Posner (1999), which had Lucentio and Tranio galloping across open fields on horseback, courtesy of the enlarged computer screen which Sly was using to access the inner play.

Padua has, however, often been relocated. For example, Canadian versions of Padua include e.g. Guthrie (1954), who placed it in 1900s Canada, Coffey (1979), who set Padua in Halifax, Nova Scotia, where the production was playing, and McCall (1988), who recreated Padua as 'a Saskatoon temperance colony of the 1800s' (Macpherson 29). In Gallant (1968) the inner play was performed 'as visualized by French-Canadians' in a 'stockade-type set' which was 'very English picture-book Quebec' (*Vancouver Province*, 29 January 1968). Ouzounian (1982) made his Padua so specific to Winnipeg that it included a spoof on the then Lieutenant-Governor of Manitoba, Pearl McGonigal, as well as several take-offs of local television personalities: Padua became 'a world of striped awnings and Astro-turf lawns' (*Province*, 7 March 1982) and all the Italian towns were made into Canadian counterparts:

Verona became Toronto; Mantua, Calgary etc. Similarly in Sheard (1998) Padua became (gay) Toronto.

A particularly popular relocation has been to the Wild West, with Annie Oakley-style Katherinas: e.g. Dunn (1979) peopled Padua with 'gunslingers, bandits, dance hall girls and all the stock figures of frontier folklore' and the action included 'shoot-outs, barroom brawls and frontier horseplay' (*San Francisco Examiner*, 31 May 1979). Antoon (1990) also went Wild West and had a 'high-spirited Main Street set, a Hollywood-backlot façade decorated with a mock-Remington mural of stampeding horses' while 'tumbleweeds dance about to a musical score . . . in the Bonanza key' (*NYT* 13 July 1990). Anthony (1965) moved south and placed Padua in Old Mexico with 'mantillas, fans, and flowered guitars' (*New York Herald Tribune*, 24 June 1965) and Fawkes (1985) also chose nineteenth-century Mexico, at fiesta time. The cowboy motif appeared as early as 1927 when Petruchio turned up to his wedding dressed as a cowboy in Massey (1927).

More unexpected relocations include Walford (1987), where Padua became 'modern fantasyland Morocco' (Liverpool *Daily Post*, 6 February 1987). May (1971) set the entire play in a bullring (*Bath and Wilts Chronicle*, 1 April 1971) whereas McKay (1974) chose a wrestling ring setting.

This scene is often set in a tavern, perhaps as a hangover from Sly's scenes, with business with waiters etc. serving drinks, e.g. Bridges-Adams (1920).

Harvey (1913) cut the Tranio/Lucentio dialogue to a bare minimum and disposed of three-quarters of their speeches.

0 s.d. Daly (1887) had Lucentio and Tranio come forward and bow to Sly before beginning their performances (s28), as did Guthrie (1954), Barton (1960). Dews (1981) also had a board paraded around the stage to announce the location of the scene. Ball (1976), which cut the Induction but evoked its metatheatrical effect by keeping a huge commedia troupe onstage throughout the play, opened with a clowning routine involving the entire troupe. Komisarjevsky (1939) had Biondello acting as master of ceremonies and announcing the scene's location. Williams (1973) followed the lead of Sam Taylor's 1929 film and opened 'with two clowns clobbering each other with flower-stuffed truncheons' (*T* 26 September 1973) to entertain Sly.

Lucentio and Tranio have made their first entries by means of many different forms of transportation. Rose (1997) had fog horns and a model of the Statue of Liberty, suggesting Lucentio and Tranio were coming into harbour in New York. Monette (1988): Lucentio arrived in a little red car with a Pisa number plate. Rider (1994): the straw-boatered Lucentio cycled on. Ayliff (1928) stressed the tourist aspect and Lucentio entered wielding a clumsy Kodak, which then had to be folded up. Forward Biancas are sometimes already onstage and on the look out for men; e.g. in Ayliff (1928), and this Bianca clearly immediately registered Lucentio's potential.

2 Kelly (1993) completely de-Italianised the play and 'fair Padua' just became 'this city'. Ball (1976) had cheers every time 'Padua' was mentioned, almost throughout the play.

I am arrived for fruitful Lombardy,
The pleasant garden of great Italy,
And by my father's love and leave am armed   5
With his good will and thy good company –
My trusty servant well approved in all –
Here let us breathe and haply institute
A course of learning and ingenuous studies.
Pisa renownèd for grave citizens   10
Gave me my being and my father first,
A merchant of great traffic through the world,
Vincentio, come of the Bentivolii.
Vincentio's son, brought up in Florence,
It shall become to serve all hopes conceived   15
To deck his fortune with his virtuous deeds.
And therefore, Tranio, for the time I study,
Virtue and that part of philosophy
Will I apply that treats of happiness
By virtue specially to be achieved.   20
Tell me thy mind, for I have Pisa left
And am to Padua come as he that leaves
A shallow plash to plunge him in the deep
And with satiety seeks to quench his thirst.

TRANIO *Mi perdonato*, gentle master mine,   25
I am in all affected as yourself,
Glad that you thus continue your resolve
To suck the sweets of sweet philosophy.

---

  3 Komisarjevsky (1939): addressed to Sly to make things clear to him. Miller (1987): Lucentio
      was consulting his guidebook.
  8 Ball (1976): Lucentio and Tranio did some deep breathing. Allison (1982) followed suit but
      Lucentio started spluttering. Bridges-Adams (1920) took a pause for breath after 'breathe'.
  9 Barton (1960): Sly looked disgusted at this thought.
10 ff. Often trimmed, e.g. Sothern and Marlowe (1905) (S47), Komisarjevsky (1939).
 13 Williams (1973): Sly repeated the exotic 'Bentivolii'.
 18 Allison (1982): Lucentio found himself absent-mindedly embracing a street walker as he
      talked of virtue. By contrast in Kaut-Howson (2001) he had his photograph taken in front of
      two priests.
21a Miller (1987): Tranio attempted to tell Lucentio his mind, but Lucentio carried on talking.
21b Williams (1973) had a running gag whereby people leant whenever Pisa was mentioned.
 25 Antoon (1990): in a Wild West production all Italian became Spanish.

Only, good master, while we do admire
This virtue and this moral discipline,   30
Let's be no stoics nor no stocks, I pray,
Or so devote to Aristotle's checks
As Ovid be an outcast quite abjured.
Balk logic with acquaintance that you have
And practise rhetoric in your common talk;   35
Music and poesy use to quicken you;
The mathematics and the metaphysics –
Fall to them as you find your stomach serves you.
No profit grows where is no pleasure tane:
In brief, sir, study what you most affect.   40
LUCENTIO Gramercies, Tranio, well dost thou advise.
If, Biondello, thou wert come ashore,
We could at once put us in readiness
And take a lodging fit to entertain
Such friends as time in Padua shall beget.   45

31 Komisarjevsky (1939): Sly laughed and pointed to his stockings.

32–5 Vulnerable to cuts and emendations as obscure, e.g. cut in Asche (1899), Carey (1954). 'Chop' replaced 'Balk' in Langham (1962), Monette (pbk 1988). Bridges-Adams (1920) and Payne (1935) replaced 'Aristotle's checks' with 'Aristotle's Ethics'.

40 Ball (1976): Tranio indicated by drawing an hourglass figure that women were what 'you most affect'.

45 s.d. Barton (1960) and Dews (1981) had a mass bow to Sly. Some productions have this entry preceded by noises off: Bridges-Adams (1920) had Katherina screaming; Benson (1890) had her shouting 'I will not.' In Maniutiu (1995) Katherina appeared onstage with a rifle, shot into the sky and a pheasant fell onto the stage. Benthall (1955): Katherina and Bianca both entered in their own sedan chairs but in Benthall (1948) Katherina entered less decorously, wielding a whip, and Bianca began flirting immediately. Morgan (1937), a radio production, had the narrator inform listeners that Bianca entered 'in her light blue silk, her light hair neatly plaited, quiet as a mouse, sweet and a little frightened by the trouble she has caused' (pbk). The 'all the fun of the fair' approach used by Gribble (1935) is suggested by the expanded s.d. here: 'Enter a pantaloon who dances to the music and snapping thumb cymbals. He is followed by Bianca, a lovely white cow of a girl who, at the slightest provocation tucks rosebuds between her breasts. She is surrounded by four Hungarian dwarfs. They have very fierce moustaches and carry each two daggers held at dangerous angles. They form around her a sort of baroque barbed-wire fence' (s65). Meanwhile Katherina did not enter for this scene but delivered her lines from offstage, lurking menacingly just out of sight behind the balcony.

Enter BAPTISTA *with his two daughters* KATHERINA *and* BIANCA;
GREMIO, *a pantaloon, and* HORTENSIO, *suitor to Bianca.*

But stay awhile, what company is this?
TRANIO Master, some show to welcome us to town.
Lucentio and Tranio stand by.
BAPTISTA Gentlemen, importune me no farther
For how I firmly am resolved you know –
That is, not to bestow my youngest daughter   50
Before I have a husband for the elder.
If either of you both love Katherina,

Daly (1887) omitted Katherina from this scene, presumably in order to spare her the humiliation of hearing herself denigrated publicly, and in order to make her first entrance (2.1) a spotlit explosion onto the stage. Sothern and Marlowe (1905) sometimes followed suit but S47 records that Katherina entered 'whip in hand' pursuing Bianca. Anglin (1908) usually delayed Katherina's first entrance until 2.1.176. Asche (1899) delayed Katherina's entry by a few lines to increase the impact: there was 'whistle and whip crack off R Kate enters with two dogs and two stuffed hares' (pbk). She then occupied herself 'with rubbing down the dogs' (*Standard*, 30 November 1904). Gordon Crosse (29) remembers Constance Benson as Katherina here 'carrying a crutch-handled stick with which she laid about her on the slightest provocation'.

In redefining Katherina as a tragic role, Fiona Shaw in Miller (1987) stayed separate from the group which assembled downstage, while she remained upstage, alone, and balancing precariously on the edge of a steeply raked floor, as if emblematising her readiness to topple over into a nervous breakdown. Leach (1978): Meryl Streep entered separately, demonstrated her formidable strength by doing a chin up, stamped on some flowers, pushed over Sly and showed that Katherina was a force to be reckoned with.

Daly (1887): during the next few lines Bartholomew annoyed Sly by fanning himself too violently (S28).

48 The opening line of the play in some versions of Sothern and Marlowe (1905) (S46). Morgan (1937) and Nickell (1950) also opened here, the latter keeping Katherina out of this scene. Gribble (1935): Hortensio and Gremio had lines with which to 'importune' Baptista (S65).

49 Komisarjevsky (1939): the Widow entered and watched.

50 Katherina's shrewishness is often motivated by Baptista treating his 'youngest daughter' very differently from his elder: e.g. Monette (1988) had Bianca the very clear favourite.

51 Ball (1976): Katherina kicked Gremio's stick away from him and he fell over. This gag was repeated several times during the scene, always accompanied by exaggerated sound effects.

52 Ayliff (1928) delayed Katherina's entrance until here. Payne (1935): Katherina slapped Bianca.

                Because I know you well and love you well,
                Leave shall you have to court her at your pleasure.
GREMIO To cart her rather! She's too rough for me.   55
                There, there, Hortensio, will you any wife?
KATHERINA [*To Baptista*] I pray you, sir, is it your will
                To make a stale of me amongst these mates?
HORTENSIO 'Mates', maid? How mean you that? No mates for you
                Unless you were of gentler, milder mould.   60
KATHERINA I'faith, sir, you shall never need to fear.
                Iwis it is not halfway to her heart –
                But if it were, doubt not her care should be
                To comb your noddle with a three-legged stool
                And paint your face and use you like a fool.   65
HORTENSIO From all such devils, good Lord deliver us!
GREMIO And me too, good Lord!
TRANIO [*Aside to Lucentio*]
                Husht, master, here's some good pastime toward;
                That wench is stark mad, or wonderful froward.
LUCENTIO [*Aside to Tranio*] But in the other's silence do I see   70
                Maid's mild behaviour and sobriety.
                Peace, Tranio.
TRANIO [*Aside to Lucentio*]
                Well said, master. Mum! And gaze your fill.
BAPTISTA Gentlemen, that I may soon make good
                What I have said – Bianca, get you in.   75

54 Payne (1935): 'her' was stressed.

55 Komisarjevsky (1939): addressed to Sly.

61–5 Genuinely violent Katherinas, who are comparatively rare, often launch into action here,
        e.g. Asche (1899): Katherina hit Hortensio with the stuffed hares she was carrying, and then
        tended to her dogs, and 'kneeling wipes them with a cloth' (pbk). Benson (1890): Katherina
        stamped on Hortensio's toe at the beginning of the speech. Ball (1976): Katherina was very
        violent but in a pantomime style. Kelly (1993): Katherina threw drink in Hortensio's face.

64 Barton (1960): Katherina was wielding just such a stool against Hortensio and Gremio.

68–73 The distraction of Lucentio's and Tranio's asides are sometimes cut, e.g. Nunn (1967).

71 Sothern and Marlowe (1905) (s47): Katherina saw Lucentio giving a white rose to Bianca
        and snatched the rose away. She then proceeded to pull Bianca's hat awry.

72 Hawthorn (1979) used 'Peace' to cue Katherina screaming very loudly. Bridges-Adams
        (1920): Bianca caught Lucentio's eye, which is why he wanted Tranio to be quiet.

75 Dews (1981): Bianca busied herself collecting together her presents from her suitors, as well

And let it not displease thee, good Bianca,
For I will love thee ne'er the less, my girl.
KATHERINA A pretty peat! It is best put finger in the eye, and she
knew why.
BIANCA Sister, content you in my discontent. 80
Sir, to your pleasure humbly I subscribe.
My books and instruments shall be my company,
On them to look and practise by myself.
LUCENTIO [*Aside*] Hark, Tranio, thou mayst hear Minerva speak!
HORTENSIO Signor Baptista, will you be so strange? 85
Sorry am I that our good will effects
Bianca's grief.
GREMIO   Why will you mew her up,
Signor Baptista, for this fiend of hell,
And make her bear the penance of her tongue?
BAPTISTA Gentlemen, content ye. I am resolved. 90
Go in, Bianca.
                              [*Exit Bianca*]
And, for I know she taketh most delight

as flirting with Lucentio. Harvey (1913): Baptista put his arm round Bianca, signalling her favoured status very clearly (McDonald pbk). Alexander (1992): Bianca was flirting very overtly. Allison (1982) had the crowd go 'Aaaah!' at every mention of Bianca.

76 Ball (1976): a big, disappointed 'Oh' from the entire onstage crowd at being deprived of Bianca.

78 'peat' often becomes 'pet', e.g. in Langham (1962). Bridges-Adams (1920): Katherina pinched Bianca here. Gribble (1935), which kept Katherina in the scene but offstage, had her begin to throw missiles onto the stage here.

80 Sothern and Marlowe (1905): S47 records Bianca 'continues to flirt with Lucentio' and she didn't exit at line 91 but carried on flirting. Asche (1899) had similar business beginning at line 84 with Lucentio throwing a rose to Bianca and making signs to her. Reinhardt (1909): Bianca was in tears, Katherina laughed and Bianca's suitors threw kisses to her.

91 Gribble (1935): Bianca had exited at line 83 but reappeared on the balcony to flirt with Lucentio. Baptista now noticed this.

91 s.d. Biancas often manage to pull faces at and taunt Katherina as they go, e.g. in Alexander (1992). Komisarjevsky (1939) inserted 2.1.26b–37 here, and then later cut the opening sequence of 2.1, thus radically reducing Katherina's early impact in the play. Kyle (1982): Bianca deliberately dropped her handkerchief as she left.

92 Miller (1987): the clinically depressed Katherina started savagely gouging bits out of a bench.

In music, instruments and poetry,
Schoolmasters will I keep within my house
Fit to instruct her youth. If you, Hortensio,   95
Or Signor Gremio you, know any such,
Prefer them hither; for to cunning men
I will be very kind, and liberal
To mine own children in good bringing up.
And so farewell. Katherina, you may stay,   100
For I have more to commune with Bianca.   *Exit*
KATHERINA Why, and I trust I may go too, may I not?
What, shall I be appointed hours as though, belike,
I knew not what to take and what to leave? Ha!   *Exit*
GREMIO You may go to the devil's dam! Your gifts are so good here's   105
none will hold you. There! Love is not so great, Hortensio, but
we may blow our nails together and fast it fairly out. Our cake's
dough on both sides. Farewell. Yet, for the love I bear my sweet
Bianca, if I can by any means light on a fit man to teach her that
wherein she delights, I will wish him to her father.   110
HORTENSIO So will I, Signor Gremio. But a word, I pray. Though
the nature of our quarrel yet never brooked parle, know now,
upon advice, it toucheth us both – that we may yet again have
access to our fair mistress and be happy rivals in Bianca's love –
to labour and effect one thing specially.   115
GREMIO What's that, I pray?
HORTENSIO Marry, sir, to get a husband for her sister.

94 Allison (1982): both Hortensio and Gremio semaphored that they had spotted their
opportunity when Baptista mentioned his need for schoolmasters.

100 Alexander (1990): Katherina took Baptista's arm but he threw her off.

104 'Ha' sometimes becomes a roar, e.g. in Hodgman (1991). Bell (1994) followed it with a
whole series of mocking 'ha's. Sothern and Marlowe (1905) (s47): Katherina knocked off
Hortensio's hat and then knocked Gremio's cane from under him. Bridges-Adams (1920):
Katherina attacked Gremio, slapping his face and mocking him. The self-harming Katherina
in Miller (1987) cut off a lock of her hair and threw it disgustedly; this was one of the few
energetic actions she managed during the entire scene.

105 Guthrie (1954): after 'dam!' Sly interrupted to warn Gremio that Katherina might hear him.
Bogdanov (1978): Sly, who had been watching the scene from a café, now slipped off
(stealing a coat as he did so) in order to make the change to Petruchio.

108–10 'Yet . . .' Barton (1960): played to Sly.

117 Gribble (1935): Katherina was offstage listening to all this, occasionally laughing 'derisively'
and hurling objects onstage, including a golden shoe and a riding boot (s65).

GREMIO A husband? A devil!

HORTENSIO I say a husband.

GREMIO I say a devil. Think'st thou, Hortensio, though her father be   120
very rich, any man is so very a fool to be married to hell?

HORTENSIO Tush, Gremio. Though it pass your patience and mine
to endure her loud alarums – why, man, there be good fellows in
the world, and a man could light on them, would take her with
all faults, and money enough.   125

GREMIO I cannot tell. But I had as lief take her dowry with this
condition: to be whipped at the high cross every morning.

HORTENSIO Faith, as you say, there's small choice in rotten apples.
But come, since this bar in law makes us friends, it shall be so far
forth friendly maintained till by helping Baptista's eldest   130
daughter to a husband we set his youngest free for a husband –
and then have to't afresh. Sweet Bianca! Happy man be his dole!
He that runs fastest gets the ring. How say you, Signor Gremio?

GREMIO I am agreed, and would I had given him the best horse in
Padua to begin his wooing that would thoroughly woo her, wed   135
her, and bed her, and rid the house of her. Come on.

Exeunt Gremio and Hortensio

TRANIO I pray sir, tell me, is it possible
That love should of a sudden take such hold?

118 Sothern and Marlowe (1905): s47 records a heap of extraneous business with flower girls
and the production cut the indecorous references to Katherina in lines 120–8.

120 Komisarjevsky (1939): Sly joined in the discussion and Bartholomew had to drag him back
out of the action.

121 Ayliff (1928): 'very' was stressed.

122 Harvey (1913): Sly repeated 'Tush' (McDonald pbk), as if delighted with a new word.

127 'high cross' became 'market place' in Monette 1988 (pbk).

130 Komisarjevsky (1939): the Widow appeared here for the second time in this scene and
proceeded to chase Hortensio, thus making her intentions towards him clear. Sly became
interested in the Widow and she then speedily exited.

135–6 The 'and bed her' reference to sex was cut, e.g. in Benson (1890).

136 s.d. Dews (1981): Gremio and Hortensio bowed to onstage applause before exiting. Ayliff (1928):
Sly applauded and laughed. Benson (1890) had interplay between Hortensio and the
Widow, who walked past with her duenna, ignoring Hortensio, while her page mocked
him. Daly (1887): Sly fell asleep around here (s28). Gribble (1935): Bianca reappeared to
encourage Lucentio but her guard of four dwarfs prevented him from getting close to her.

137 Ball (1976): absurdly romantic music indicated the onset of love. Allison (1982): Lucentio
attempted to spout Shakespeare's Sonnet 18.

LUCENTIO O Tranio, till I found it to be true
          I never thought it possible or likely.   140
          But see! while idly I stood looking on,
          I found the effect of love-in-idleness,
          And now in plainness do confess to thee
          That art to me as secret and as dear
          As Anna to the Queen of Carthage was –   145
          Tranio, I burn! I pine, I perish, Tranio,
          If I achieve not this young modest girl.
          Counsel me, Tranio, for I know thou canst;
          Assist me, Tranio, for I know thou wilt.
TRANIO Master, it is no time to chide you now;   150
          Affection is not rated from the heart.
          If love have touched you, naught remains but so:
          Redime te captum quam queas minimo.
LUCENTIO Gramercies, lad. Go forward. This contents;
          The rest will comfort, for thy counsel's sound. 155
TRANIO Master, you looked so longly on the maid,
          Perhaps you marked not what's the pith of all.
LUCENTIO O yes, I saw sweet beauty in her face,
          Such as the daughter of Agenor had,
          That made great Jove to humble him to her hand   160
          When with his knees he kissed the Cretan strand.
TRANIO Saw you no more? Marked you not how her sister
          Began to scold and raise up such a storm
          That mortal ears might hardly endure the din?

139 ff. Monette (1988): sentimental music played during this speech and Lucentio sang some of his lines.
144–5 The classical (and suggestive) reference is often cut, e.g. Phelps (1856), Nunn (1967). Alexander (1990): the modern Lord's group giggled at the sentiments.
146–9 Bell (1994) (radio broadcast) played these lines before 137, making matters clearer for listeners.
147 Williams (1973): Lucentio suddenly realised he was strangling Tranio.
151 'rated' became 'driven' in Hodgman (1991).
153 The Latin tag in Guthrie (1954) was delivered directly and impressively to Sly. Alexander (1992): Tranio read the tag from a book.
159–61 The classical reference is sometimes cut, e.g. Phelps (1856). Antoon (1990) substituted a biblical reference to Rebecca and Isaac.

LUCENTIO Tranio, I saw her coral lips to move,   165
    And with her breath she did perfume the air.
    Sacred and sweet was all I saw in her.
TRANIO Nay, then, 'tis time to stir him from his trance.
    I pray, awake, sir. If you love the maid
    Bend thoughts and wits to achieve her. Thus it stands: 170
    Her elder sister is so curst and shrewd
    That, till the father rid his hands of her,
    Master, your love must live a maid at home,
    And therefore has he closely mewed her up,
    Because she will not be annoyed with suitors.   175
LUCENTIO Ah, Tranio, what a cruel father's he!
    But art thou not advised he took some care
    To get her cunning schoolmasters to instruct her?
TRANIO Ay, marry, am I, sir – and now 'tis plotted!
LUCENTIO I have it, Tranio!
TRANIO   Master, for my hand,   180
    Both our inventions meet and jump in one.
LUCENTIO Tell me thine first.
TRANIO   You will be schoolmaster
    And undertake the teaching of the maid –
    That's your device.
LUCENTIO   It is. May it be done?
TRANIO Not possible. For who shall bear your part   185
    And be in Padua here Vincentio's son,
    Keep house, and ply his book, welcome his friends,
    Visit his countrymen and banquet them?
LUCENTIO *Basta*! Content thee, for I have it full.

---

165 Guthrie (1954): Tranio sat on the bed with Sly listening and responding.

165–7 Rose (1997): Bianca appeared as an ethereal vision on the balcony.

168–9 Tranio sometimes slaps Lucentio's face, e.g. Dews (1981), but these lines have sometimes alternatively been addressed to the dozing Sly, e.g. Harvey (1913): Tranio clapped his hands and woke Sly up (McDonald pbk). Ayliff (1928): 169a was shouted in an attempt to wake up Sly in his theatre box.

179–89 Monette (1988): the street-wise Tranio convinced the naïve Lucentio that Tranio was only being obliging in going along with Lucentio's bright ideas. Reinhardt (1909) had Tranio and Lucentio collapsing with merriment, 'ho ho's and 'he he's (pbk). Alexander (1992): as Tranio listed what needed to be done, he realised how desirable a proposition this might be.

We have not yet been seen in any house,   190
Nor can we be distinguished by our faces
For man or master. Then it follows thus:
Thou shalt be master, Tranio, in my stead;
Keep house and port and servants as I should.
I will some other be – some Florentine,   195
Some Neapolitan or meaner man of Pisa.
'Tis hatched and shall be so. Tranio, at once
Uncase thee; take my coloured hat and cloak.
                    [*They exchange clothes.*]
When Biondello comes, he waits on thee,
But I will charm him first to keep his tongue.   200
TRANIO So had you need.
In brief, sir, sith it your pleasure is,
And I am tied to be obedient –
For so your father charged me at our parting:
'Be serviceable to my son', quoth he,   205
Although I think 'twas in another sense –
I am content to be Lucentio,
Because so well I love Lucentio.
LUCENTIO Tranio, be so, because Lucentio loves,

190–4 Barton (1960): largely spoken to Sly. Nunn (1967) had Sly laugh at line 193.

198 Alexander (1992): 'Uncase thee' was an unnecessary command as the eager Tranio was already stripped and ready to exchange clothes. As he was much bigger than Lucentio he then had to try to squeeze into trousers that were far too tight for him.

198 s.d. Often now an opportunity for a 'men dropping trousers' gag, e.g. in Monette (1988) two passing nuns caught both men trouserless. In Bogdanov (1978) Lucentio and Tranio were caught by the café waiter. In Allison (1982), as this sequence was performed in a crowded marketplace, it seemed odd that no one noticed what was going on. In earlier, more modest productions Lucentio and Tranio merely exchanged cloaks and hats, e.g. Benson (1890). In Devine (1954) Sly helped out with the transfer of cloaks, hats and walking cane. Kyle (1982) increased the joke by having Biondello enter early and hear Tranio declare his love for Lucentio in line 208 whilst both men had their trousers down.

206 Ayliff (1928): Tranio was delighted to find a cigar case and cigars in the pockets of his new clothes. In return Lucentio was reduced to cigarettes.

205–6 Komisarjevsky (1939): lines played to Sly.

208 Posner (1999): the pbk comments that the characters embrace 'In a masculine way of course!'

And let me be a slave t'achieve that maid   210
Whose sudden sight hath thralled my wounded eye.

    Enter BIONDELLO.

Here comes the rogue. Sirrah, where have you been?
BIONDELLO Where have I been? Nay, how now, where are you?
 Master, has my fellow Tranio stolen your clothes or you stolen
 his, or both? Pray, what's the news?   215
LUCENTIO Sirrah, come hither. 'Tis no time to jest,
 And therefore frame your manners to the time.
 Your fellow Tranio here, to save my life,
 Puts my apparel and my count'nance on,
 And I for my escape have put on his;   220
 For in a quarrel since I came ashore
 I killed a man, and fear I was descried.
 Wait you on him, I charge you, as becomes,
 While I make way from hence to save my life.
 You understand me?
BIONDELLO   Ay, sir. Ne'er a whit.   225

---

211 Benthall (1955): Tranio slapped Lucentio's face to bring him out of his trance.

211 s.d. Monette (1988): Biondello entered on rollerblades. Sothern and Marlowe (1905): s48 records that Biondello was first heard singing 'Once a farmer and his wife had cause for disputation . . .', entered skipping and was then very confused by the disguises. Asche (1899) had Biondello 'with 3 packages on strapped to his back' (pbk). In Sothern and Marlowe (1905) and Asche (1899), Biondello was subjected to much ear-pulling.

213–15 Harvey (1913): Tranio was admiring himself in his new cloak (McDonald pbk).

218–22 Reinhardt (1909) just cut this fiction and simply turned the speech into an order to Biondello.

221–2 Monette (1988): the joke was that Lucentio's line was so palpably a feeble lie. Ball (1976): as Lucentio stalled from lack of ideas, Tranio mimed a throat-cutting. Daly (1887) cut these lines (s34).

222 Sothern and Marlowe (1905): s47 records that Biondello fell to his knees, crossed himself and put his hands together in prayer. Gribble (1935): Biondello screamed. Williams (1973): Biondello fell flat on the floor. Miller (1987): Biondello made it clear he didn't believe any of it.

223a Alexander (1992): Tranio laughed delightedly at the prospect of being waited upon.

225b The Folio has 'I' instead of 'Ay' and productions often follow the Folio, e.g. Daly (1887) (s34). 'Ne'er a whit' was addressed to Sly in Benthall (1948).

LUCENTIO And not a jot of 'Tranio' in your mouth:
>   Tranio is changed into Lucentio.

BIONDELLO The better for him! Would I were so too.

TRANIO So could I, faith, boy, to have the next wish after –
>   That Lucentio indeed had Baptista's youngest daughter.   230
>   But, sirrah, not for my sake but your master's, I advise
>   You use your manners discreetly in all kind of companies.
>   When I am alone, why then I am Tranio,
>   But in all places else your master Lucentio.

LUCENTIO Tranio, let's go.   235
>   One thing more rests that thyself execute:
>   To make one among these wooers. If thou ask me why,
>   Sufficeth my reasons are both good and weighty.

>   *Exeunt*

>   *The Presenters above speaks.*

LORD My lord, you nod; you do not mind the play.

SLY Yes, by Saint Anne, do I. A good matter surely. Comes there any   240
more of it?

BARTHOLOMEW My lord, 'tis but begun.

SLY 'Tis a very excellent piece of work, madam lady. Would 'twere
done!

>   *They sit and mark.*

238 Reinhardt (1909) had a musical interlude here with a lot of 'tra la la la's (pbk). Once
Lucentio was off in Daly (1887), Biondello mocked Tranio who was very full of his new
status (s28). Sly then snored, yawned, stretched his legs and started falling asleep again.
Alexander (1992): Lucentio gave Tranio his signet ring – a gesture which was reversed in 5.1
when Lucentio resumed his identity, much to Tranio's disappointment.

239 This line is very often given to Bartholomew e.g. Webster (1844), Daly (1887). Harvey (1913):
the line responded to snores by Sly (McDonald pbk).

239–43 Cut by all productions which don't use the Induction, and also cut by productions which
do play the Induction but which double Sly and Petruchio, who is just about to enter. In
productions which set this scene in a tavern, such as Asche (1899), the action sometimes
moves straight into 1.2 with no scene change, although this makes the location of
Hortensio's house (line 4) problematic. Phelps (1856): Sly fell asleep here and servants
carried him off.

ACT I   SCENE 2

Enter PETRUCHIO *and his man* GRUMIO.

PETRUCHIO Verona, for a while I take my leave
To see my friends in Padua, but of all
My best belovèd and approvèd friend,
Hortensio: and I trow this is his house.
Here, sirrah Grumio, knock, I say.   5
GRUMIO Knock, sir? Whom should I knock? Is there any man has
rebused your worship?
PETRUCHIO Villain, I say, knock me here soundly.

---

0 s.d. Petruchio and Grumio often make a sensational first entrance, e.g. Gribble (1935): Petruchio
entered on a horse, manned by two acrobats. Petruchio started his speech and then, as the
horse became unmanageable, had to dismount and start again. Meanwhile the Widow was
coquetting at him. Bogdanov (1987) had a motorcycle entrance, as did Walford (1987).
Monette (1988) reduced Petruchio to a Vespa, and Grumio to a bicycle. Bell (1994) (radio
broadcast) relied on sound effects to suggest Petruchio driving up either on a motorcycle, or
in a clapped-out car.

AS (3.99 s.d.) has *Enter Ferando and his man Sander with a blue coat*: that is, indicating
Sander's servant status. Nunn (1967) used blue coats for servants. Asche (1904) had much
whip-cracking by Petruchio during this scene. Dews (1981) had several false starts for
Petruchio and Grumio, who tried to make a bow to Sly and start performing but kept being
interrupted by Sly. In Hill (1987) 'Sly, who would much rather be devoting all his attention to
his "wife", was drawn into the entertainment when Petruchio did not appear on cue. A copy
of the script was thrust into Sly's hands, he awkwardly began to read the lines, suddenly got
caught up in them, tossed the script away' (Weiss 87). Nunn (1967): Petruchio entered 'as a
blind beggar carrying a hat round the circle of spectators' of the onstage audience (*T* 6 April
1967).

4 Rose (1997): Petruchio recognised the house because the operatic Hortensio was heard
offstage, singing.

6–7 Ball (1976): Grumio warmed up and punched the air ready for a fight.

7 In Allison (1982) Grumio was so palpably showing off with the word 'rebused' that the
malapropism got a laugh from the onstage crowd.

8 Sothern and Marlowe (1905): Petruchio started cracking his whip here, something he then
did enthusiastically for much of the rest of the scene (s47).

GRUMIO Knock you here, sir? Why, sir, what am I, sir, that I should
    knock you here, sir?   10
PETRUCHIO Villain, I say, knock me at this gate,
    And rap me well, or I'll knock your knave's pate!
GRUMIO My master is grown quarrelsome. I should knock you first,
    And then I know after who comes by the worst.
PETRUCHIO Will it not be?   15
    Faith, sirrah, and you'll not knock, I'll ring it.
    I'll try how you can *sol-fa*, and sing it.
        He wrings him by the ears.
GRUMIO Help, mistress, help! My master is mad.
PETRUCHIO Now knock when I bid you, sirrah villain.

          Enter HORTENSIO.

HORTENSIO How now, what's the matter? My old friend Grumio   20
    and my good friend Petruchio! How do you all at Verona?
PETRUCHIO Signor Hortensio, come you to part the fray?
    Con tutto il cuore ben trovato, may I say.
HORTENSIO *Alla nostra casa ben venuto*
    Molto honorato signor mio Petruchio.   25

---

9 Ball (1976): Grumio laughed loudly at the preposterous idea of taking on his Tarzan-like Petruchio.

14 Payne (1935): Sly laughed. This Sly was often in sympathy with Grumio and had to be restrained by Bartholomew from helping Grumio when Petruchio assaulted him, e.g. line 17 s.d.

17 s.d. Guthrie (1954): Sly went to the rescue of Grumio, and attacked Petruchio who responded in kind. Sly continued to interject during the following discussion. Devine (1953): Petruchio held Grumio's ears and knocked the back of his head against the door, using him as a door knocker. Grumio was later held upside down and shaken. Nunn (1967) had a chase here which Sly and the Huntsmen joined in. Alexander (1990): Petruchio dragged Grumio round the stage, something Sly enjoyed watching.

18 'mistress' is often emended to 'master', e.g. Devine (1953), as it is not clear who the 'mistress' is.

19 Allison (1982): Petruchio knocked against the door using Grumio's head.

20 Hortensio didn't recognise Petruchio initially in Miller (1987) because Petruchio and Grumio were indistinguishable, in a heap, fighting on the floor.

23–5 The Italian is often cut, e.g. Asche (1899); line 27 ''tis . . . Latin' is then also cut. Posner (1999) had lots of air-kissing here.

> Rise, Grumio, rise. We will compound this quarrel.

GRUMIO Nay, 'tis no matter, sir, what he ledges in Latin. If this be
not a lawful cause for me to leave his service – look you, sir: he
bid me knock him and rap him soundly, sir. Well, was it fit for a
servant to use his master so, being perhaps, for aught I see, two   30
and thirty, a pip out?

> Whom would to God I had well knocked at first,
> Then had not Grumio come by the worst.

PETRUCHIO A senseless villain! Good Hortensio,

> I bade the rascal knock upon your gate   35
> And could not get him for my heart to do it.

GRUMIO Knock at the gate? O heavens! Spake you not these words
plain: 'Sirrah, knock me here, rap me here, knock me well, and
knock me soundly'? And come you now with 'knocking at the
gate'?   40

PETRUCHIO Sirrah, be gone, or talk not, I advise you.

HORTENSIO Petruchio, patience. I am Grumio's pledge.

> Why this' a heavy chance 'twixt him and you –
> Your ancient, trusty, pleasant servant Grumio.
> And tell me now, sweet friend, what happy gale   45
> Blows you to Padua here from old Verona?

PETRUCHIO Such wind as scatters young men through the world

> To seek their fortunes farther than at home
> Where small experience grows. But, in a few,
> Signor Hortensio, thus it stands with me: 50
> Antonio my father is deceased
> And I have thrust myself into this maze,

26b Payne (1935): addressed to Sly, who was indignant on Grumio's behalf.

30–1 'being . . . out?' is often cut, e.g. Harvey (1913), (McDonald pbk). Even Alexander (1990),
which hardly cut anything, cut this line. Miller (1987): the lines up to line 40 overlapped so
completely that they were unintelligible except as a row.

37 Payne (1935): Grumio played this directly to the sympathetic Sly.

44 Ball (1976): Grumio kissed Hortensio in gratitude.

51 The news of Antonio's death is often played for laughs: for example, Hodgman 1991:
Petruchio exaggeratedly fended off condolences. Bell (1994): Petruchio carried 'his dad's
ashes around in an urn' (*Melbourne Times*, 1 June 1994). Payne (1935): Grumio stood up
and took his hat off in respect. Ball (1976): Petruchio and Grumio performed a big 'hats off,
hand on heart' routine which was repeated at every mention of Antonio or his death from
then on. Gribble (1935): everyone crossed themselves.

Happily to wive and thrive as best I may.
Crowns in my purse I have, and goods at home,
And so am come abroad to see the world.   55
HORTENSIO Petruchio, shall I then come roundly to thee
And wish thee to a shrewd ill-favoured wife?
Thou'dst thank me but a little for my counsel –
And yet I'll promise thee she shall be rich,
And very rich. But th'art too much my friend,   60
And I'll not wish thee to her.
PETRUCHIO Signor Hortensio, 'twixt such friends as we
Few words suffice, and therefore, if thou know
One rich enough to be Petruchio's wife –
As wealth is burden of my wooing dance –   65
Be she as foul as was Florentius' love,
As old as Sibyl, and as curst and shrewd
As Socrates' Xanthippe or a worse,
She moves me not, or not removes at least
Affection's edge in me, were she as rough   70
As are the swelling Adriatic seas.
I come to wive it wealthily in Padua;

53   Ayliff (1928): Hortensio repeated 'to wive' as he spied his opportunity.
54   Ball (1976), Allison (1982): Grumio's derisive 'Ha's during this line made it clear that
      Petruchio was in fact broke.
56–80 By cutting this entire section (and line 178) Harvey (1913) significantly reduced Petruchio's
      mercenariness (McDonald pbk).
57   Ball (1976): both Petruchio and Grumio turned on their heels and prepared to leave. They
      turned round at the word 'rich' (line 59), which was accompanied by a 'ting' from an
      onstage musician.
59   Petruchios often respond enthusiastically to 'rich', e.g. Taylor (1929). In Guthrie (1954)
      Hortensio winked complicitly at Sly. Allison (1982): Petruchio and the crowd gave a big
      knowing 'Aaaah'.
60   Bridges-Adams (1920): Hortensio rubbed his foot remembering that Katherina had stamped
      on it.
66–8 Classical reference often cut, e.g. Ayliff (1928).
67   The *Daily Sketch* (14 September 1927) reported a laugh on 'Sibyl' when Katherina was
      played by Sybil Thorndike in Leigh (1927). Antoon (1990) substituted a reference to
      Methusaleh's wife.
72–3 Rose (1997): 'Padua' was changed to America. Once these lines were made famous by

If wealthily, then happily in Padua.

GRUMIO Nay, look you sir, he tells you flatly what his mind is. Why,
 give him gold enough and marry him to a puppet or an aglet-baby   75
 or an old trot with ne'er a tooth in her head, though she have as
 many diseases as two and fifty horses. Why, nothing comes amiss,
 so money comes withal.

HORTENSIO Petruchio, since we are stepped thus far in,
 I will continue that I broached in jest.   80
 I can, Petruchio, help thee to a wife
 With wealth enough, and young, and beauteous,
 Brought up as best becomes a gentlewoman.
 Her only fault – and that is faults enough –
 Is that she is intolerable curst,   85
 And shrewd and froward so beyond all measure
 That, were my state far worser than it is,
 I would not wed her for a mine of gold!

PETRUCHIO Hortensio, peace. Thou know'st not gold's effect.
 Tell me her father's name and 'tis enough,   90
 For I will board her though she chide as loud
 As thunder when the clouds in autumn crack.

HORTENSIO Her father is Baptista Minola,
 An affable and courteous gentleman.
 Her name is Katherina Minola,   95
 Renowned in Padua for her scolding tongue.

PETRUCHIO I know her father, though I know not her,
 And he knew my deceasèd father well.

Kiss Me, Kate they became almost uncuttable but they are problematic for Petruchios constructed as rejecting the materialist lifestyle of Baptista, e.g. Kelly (1993).

74 ff. Marowitz (1973): Grumio is directed to be *Close, threatening* during this speech (p. 136).

76–7 Patton (1984): Petruchio shook his head 'in disagreement, thus telling us he was not really a gold-digger' (Frey 1985, 488).

88 Rose (1997): Hortensio wept at the thought of Petruchio marrying Katherina (pbk). Leach (1978): Petruchio stopped Hortensio's mouth.

90 Bogdanov (1978), Leach (1978): Grumio began taking notes.

91 Nicer Petruchios play down the threat of rape in this line, e.g. Kelly (1993), or swash their buckles as a distraction, e.g. Dews (1981).

95 Allison (1982): everyone onstage looked terrified at the mention of Katherina's name.

98 Gribble (1935), Payne (1935): 'raising hats in respect' routine. Ball (1976) repeated the business from line 51.

I will not sleep, Hortensio, till I see her,
And therefore let me be thus bold with you   100
To give you over at this first encounter –
Unless you will accompany me thither?

GRUMIO I pray you, sir, let him go while the humour lasts. A' my
word, and she knew him as well as I do, she would think scolding
would do little good upon him. She may perhaps call him half a   105
score knaves or so – why, that's nothing. And he begin once, he'll
rail in his rope-tricks. I'll tell you what, sir, and she stand him
but a little, he will throw a figure in her face and so disfigure her
with it that she shall have no more eyes to see withal than a cat.
You know him not, sir.   110

HORTENSIO Tarry, Petruchio, I must go with thee,
For in Baptista's keep my treasure is.
He hath the jewel of my life in hold,
His youngest daughter, beautiful Bianca,
And her withholds from me and other more –   115
Suitors to her and rivals in my love –
Supposing it a thing impossible,
For those defects I have before rehearsed,
That ever Katherina will be wooed.
Therefore this order hath Baptista tane,   120
That none shall have access unto Bianca
Till Katherine the curst have got a husband.

GRUMIO 'Katherine the curst'!
A title for a maid of all titles the worst.

HORTENSIO Now shall my friend Petruchio do me grace   125
And offer me disguised in sober robes
To old Baptista as a schoolmaster
Well seen in music, to instruct Bianca,
That so I may by this device at least

101–2   Ball (1976): Grumio sprayed Petruchio with scent under the arms and round the groin in
preparation for going into wooing mode. Alexander (1990): Petruchio got a comb, mirror
and perfume bottle from his bag and starting sprucing himself up.

105–9   'She . . . cat' is obscure and often cut or slimmed down, e.g. Benson (1890), Reinhardt (1909).

107   The 'rope-tricks' work well in Wild West productions such as Antoon (1990), where
Petruchio later on lassoed Katherina.

123   Gribble (1935) gave this line to Petruchio.

124   Komisarjevsky (1939) gave this line to Sly.

Have leave and leisure to make love to her   130
And unsuspected court her by herself.

Enter GREMIO, *and* LUCENTIO *disguised* [*as Cambio, a schoolmaster*].

GRUMIO Here's no knavery! See, to beguile the old folks, how the
young folks lay their heads together. Master, master, look about
you! Who goes there, ha?
HORTENSIO Peace, Grumio. It is the rival of my love.   135
Petruchio, stand by a while.
GRUMIO A proper stripling, and an amorous!
[*They stand aside.*]
GREMIO O, very well, I have perused the note.
Hark you, sir, I'll have them very fairly bound –
All books of love, see that at any hand –   140
And see you read no other lectures to her:
You understand me. Over and beside
Signor Baptista's liberality
I'll mend it with a largess. Take your paper too
And let me have them very well perfumed,   145
For she is sweeter than perfume itself
To whom they go to. What will you read to her?
LUCENTIO Whate'er I read to her I'll plead for you
As for my patron, stand you so assured
As firmly as yourself were still in place –   150
Yea and perhaps with more successful words
Than you, unless you were a scholar, sir.
GREMIO O this learning, what a thing it is!
GRUMIO [*Aside*] O this woodcock, what an ass it is!

131 s.d. Lucentio's disguises have included a serious young curate in Ayliff (1928), and a long-robed
priest in Monette (1988). In *Sauny the Scot* the Lucentio character Winlove has a French
accent scripted.
132–3 'here's . . . together', Payne (1935) gave these lines to Sly. Harvey (1913) had them
addressed to Sly (McDonald pbk), as did Devine (1953).
140 Devine (1953): Gremio was 'almost fainting with senile passion when he thinks of Bianca
reading books of love' (*ST* 6 June 1954).
145–6 Ball (1976): the 'fume' part of 'perfume' in each line overwhelmed Lucentio because of
Gremio's bad breath, something which then became a running gag. Benson (1890) had
Gremio shaking a pounce box over a letter, causing Lucentio to sneeze.

PETRUCHIO [*Aside*] Peace, sirrah.   155
HORTENSIO [*Aside*] Grumio, mum.
                                    [*Coming forward.*]
                                    God save you, Signor Gremio.
GREMIO And you are well met, Signor Hortensio.
        Trow you whither I am going? To Baptista Minola.
        I promised to inquire carefully
        About a schoolmaster for the fair Bianca,   160
        And by good fortune I have lighted well
        On this young man, for learning and behaviour
        Fit for her turn, well read in poetry
        And other books – good ones, I warrant ye.
HORTENSIO 'Tis well. And I have met a gentleman   165
        Hath promised me to help me to another,
        A fine musician to instruct our mistress.
        So shall I no whit be behind in duty
        To fair Bianca, so beloved of me.
GREMIO Beloved of me, and that my deeds shall prove.   170
GRUMIO [*Aside*] And that his bags shall prove.
HORTENSIO Gremio, 'tis now no time to vent our love.
        Listen to me, and if you speak me fair,
        I'll tell you news indifferent good for either.
        Here is a gentleman whom by chance I met,   175
                                    [*Presents Petruchio.*]
        Upon agreement from us to his liking,
        Will undertake to woo curst Katherine,
        Yea, and to marry her, if her dowry please.
GREMIO So said, so done, is well.
        Hortensio, have you told him all her faults?   180
PETRUCHIO I know she is an irksome, brawling scold.
        If that be all, masters, I hear no harm.
GREMIO No? Say'st me so, friend? What countryman?
PETRUCHIO Born in Verona, old Antonio's son.

---

171 Sothern and Marlowe (1905) removed any double entendre as Grumio touched a money
    bag here (s47) or they cut 'bags' and substituted 'gold' (s48). Komisarjevsky (1939) gave the
    line to Sly.
177 Dews (1981): the news produced goggle eyes from Gremio. Bridges-Adams (1920): Gremio
    exclaimed 'What!' Leach (1978): Gremio keeled over backwards in surprise.
184–5 Often a reprise of the joke from line 51, e.g. Ball (1976).

My father dead, my fortune lives for me,   185
And I do hope good days and long to see.
GREMIO   O sir, such a life with such a wife were strange.
But if you have a stomach, to't a God's name!
You shall have me assisting you in all.
But will you woo this wildcat?
PETRUCHIO   Will I live?   190
GRUMIO   Will he woo her? Ay, or I'll hang her.
PETRUCHIO   Why came I hither but to that intent?
Think you a little din can daunt mine ears?
Have I not in my time heard lions roar?
Have I not heard the sea, puffed up with winds,   195
Rage like an angry boar chafèd with sweat?
Have I not heard great ordnance in the field,
And heaven's artillery thunder in the skies?
Have I not in a pitchèd battle heard
Loud 'larums, neighing steeds and trumpets' clang?   200
And do you tell me of a woman's tongue,
That gives not half so great a blow to hear
As will a chestnut in a farmer's fire?
Tush, tush, fear boys with bugs!
GRUMIO   For he fears none.
GREMIO   Hortensio, hark.   205
This gentleman is happily arrived,
My mind presumes, for his own good and yours.
HORTENSIO   I promised we would be contributors
And bear his charge of wooing, whatsoe'er.

---

188   'God' became 'Heavens' in Webster (1844), Daly (1887).

191   Williams (1973): Grumio patted Gremio on the back, which caused his toupee to fall
off. Sothern and Marlowe (1905) (s47): Grumio responded to the umpteenth crack of
Petruchio's whip by rolling on his back with his feet in the air.

192–204   Grumio sometimes provides sound effects, e.g. Heap (1985). As Rider (1994) had Petruchio
as a Second World War returned serviceman, his recent military experience added authority
to this speech. Barton (1960): Petruchio leapfrogged downstairs over Gremio. Grumio
sometimes answers Petruchio's rhetorical questions with 'yes' or 'no', e.g. Payne (1935).

204   Komisarjevsky (1939): Sly repeated 'bugs' and started searching for them in his bed. Anglin
(1908) started a new scene here, bringing down the curtain as Grumio fell into an onstage
well.

GREMIO And so we will – provided that he win her.   210
GRUMIO I would I were as sure of a good dinner.

Enter TRANIO *[disguised as Lucentio] and* BIONDELLO.

TRANIO Gentlemen, God save you. If I may be bold,
                 Tell me, I beseech you, which is the readiest way
                 To the house of Signor Baptista Minola?
BIONDELLO He that has the two fair daughters – is't he you mean?   215
TRANIO Even he, Biondello.
GREMIO Hark you, sir, you mean not her to –
TRANIO Perhaps him and her, sir. What have you to do?
PETRUCHIO Not her that chides, sir, at any hand, I pray.
TRANIO I love no chiders, sir. Biondello, let's away.   220
LUCENTIO *[Aside]* Well begun, Tranio.
HORTENSIO   Sir, a word ere you go.
                 Are you a suitor to the maid you talk of, yea or no?
TRANIO And if I be, sir, is it any offence?
GREMIO No, if without more words you will get you hence.
TRANIO Why, sir, I pray, are not the streets as free   225
                 For me as for you?
GREMIO   But so is not she.
TRANIO For what reason, I beseech you?
GREMIO For this reason, if you'll know –
                 That she's the choice love of Signor Gremio.

211 s.d. Alexander (1992): Tranio entered consulting a tourist map but Tranios often make a showy
          entry. Ayliff (1928) had a car honking its horn offstage before Tranio arrived. Monette
          (1988): Biondello carried flowers and a heart-shaped box of chocolates for Tranio to give to
          Bianca. Rose (1997): Tranio arrived in a large fake car, strapped onto the shoulders of Tranio
          and his chauffeur. Sothern and Marlowe (1905) had four musicians accompany Tranio.
          Benson (1890): Biondello recognised an old friend in Grumio and shook his hand.
               Daly (1887) cut all this section to line 267 and gave Tranio's subsequent lines to Petruchio
          (s34). Lloyd (1956) cut most of the rest of the scene, relocating the explanation of Tranio-as-
          Lucentio's intentions (1.2.221b–39) to 2.1.94.
215–16 Often played as pre-rehearsed, with Biondello not very good at his part, e.g. in Barton
          (1960) Biondello had to be nudged to get him going. 215 is sometimes given to Gremio, e.g.
          Webster (1844), Reinhardt (1909).
   217 Some productions insert 'woo' at the end of the line, e.g. Ball (1976), Trevis (1985).
   218 Kyle (1982): Tranio was very camp when disguised, which gave added meaning to this line.
   221a Dews (1981): Lucentio's comment was sarcastic as Tranio was trying too hard.

HORTENSIO That she's the chosen of Signor Hortensio.　230
TRANIO Softly, my masters! If you be gentlemen,
 Do me this right – hear me with patience.
 Baptista is a noble gentleman
 To whom my father is not all unknown,
 And were his daughter fairer than she is,　235
 She may more suitors have, and me for one.
 Fair Leda's daughter had a thousand wooers;
 Then well one more may fair Bianca have.
 And so she shall: Lucentio shall make one,
 Though Paris came in hope to speed alone.　240
GREMIO What, this gentleman will out-talk us all!
LUCENTIO Sir, give him head. I know he'll prove a jade.
PETRUCHIO Hortensio, to what end are all these words?
HORTENSIO Sir, let me be so bold as ask you,
 Did you yet ever see Baptista's daughter?　245
TRANIO No, sir, but hear I do that he hath two,
 The one as famous for a scolding tongue
 As is the other for beauteous modesty.
PETRUCHIO Sir, sir, the first's for me; let her go by.
GREMIO Yea, leave that labour to great Hercules,　250
 And let it be more than Alcides' twelve.
PETRUCHIO Sir, understand you this of me in sooth:
 The youngest daughter, whom you hearken for,
 Her father keeps from all access of suitors
 And will not promise her to any man　255
 Until the elder sister first be wed.
 The younger then is free, and not before.
TRANIO If it be so, sir, that you are the man
 Must stead us all, and me amongst the rest,
 And if you break the ice and do this feat –　260
 Achieve the elder, set the younger free
 For our access – whose hap shall be to have her
 Will not so graceless be to be ingrate.

230　Williams (1973) had a comic fight here.
237–40　The classical allusion is sometimes cut, e.g. Benson (1890).
242　Kelly (1993) cut, which makes sense as Lucentio-as-Cambio claiming knowledge of Tranio-as-Lucentio could give their game away.
251　One of the commonest cuts in the entire history of the play, e.g. Asche (1899), and it is rare to find a twentieth-century production that plays this line, although Sackler (1960) did.

HORTENSIO Sir, you say well, and well you do conceive;
And since you do profess to be a suitor,   265
You must, as we do, gratify this gentleman
To whom we all rest generally beholding.
TRANIO Sir, I shall not be slack; in sign whereof,
Please ye we may contrive this afternoon
And quaff carouses to our mistress' health,   270
And do as adversaries do in law,
Strive mightily, but eat and drink as friends.
GRUMIO   ⎱ O excellent motion! Fellows, let's be gone.
BIONDELLO   ⎰
HORTENSIO The motion's good indeed, and be it so.
Petruchio, I shall be your *ben venuto*.   275

Exeunt

268 Bogdanov (1978): as Tranio took out money Lucentio dropped his books in shock at the
amount.
275 Sothern and Marlowe (1905) s47 had Petruchio and Hortensio sing 'To church away . . .' and
dance off. Using an inn setting, Asche (1899) had much toasting of healths to Bianca, with
Petruchio then insisting on toasting Katherina, business followed by Bridges-Adams (1920).
Reinhardt (1909) finished the scene with another bout of singing 'tralalala' (pbk), something
his Tranio and Biondello were rather prone to do. Komisarjevsky (1939) also finished the
scene with a song and dance. Gribble (1935): there was a song, some 'whooping up',
Petruchio was seen helping Hortensio into his disguise and then a 'daisy chain' of people
went off to Baptista's house (pbk). Devine (1953): Sly went over to the fake property
drinking-fountain and statue to get a drink. Devine (1954): as the set was struck, Sly fell over
as he was leaning on the moving statue.

A version of *AS* Interlude 1 (see Appendix 1, p. 236) is often played here, e.g. Payne (1935),
Benthall (1948). Daly (1887): this moment was the first major scene break, because 1.1 ran
straight into 1.2 and so this was the point at which Sly left (s34). There was a curtain, a
change of scenery and 'the characters of the Induction dropped out of sight' (*NYT* 19
January 1887). However, Haring-Smith (71) records that for the 1893 revival in London, Sly
'remained sitting on the prompter's side of the stage for the entire performance'.

Enter KATHERINA *and* BIANCA [*with her hands tied*].

BIANCA Good sister, wrong me not, nor wrong yourself
　　　　To make a bondmaid and a slave of me.
　　　　That I disdain. But for these other gauds –

0 s.d. Daly (1887): this was Katherina's first entrance and she entered 'in a rage, sweeping round
the stage and Bianca following her' (S34). Odell thought Ada Rehan's entrance 'with her
flaming red hair and her rich dress of superb mahogany-coloured damask, was the most
magnificent stage-entry I have ever seen' (XIII, 216). However, *Punch* (30 June 1888) felt that
the 'pantomime "hurry" music played' was a 'mistake'. Less-dignified Katherinas than
Rehan's assault Biancas in a variety of ways: in Ayliff (1928) Katherina wielded a hairbrush
and spanked Bianca with it. More spectacularly in Antoon (1990), the gun-slinging Katherina
used Bianca as 'the centrepiece of a balloon-popping marksmanship exhibition' (*NYT* 13 July
1990). Kellman (1977): Katherina 'dunked' Bianca 'repeatedly' in a fountain (Gaines 240).
Hawthorn (1979): Katherina swung Bianca 'around by a rope like a calf' (*Kitchener-
Waterloo Record*, 3 July 1979). Maniutiu (1995): Katherina tortured Bianca by tickling her
with a feather (*DT* 3 May 1995). Heap (1985) (where both characters were played by men)
had a 'girly' fight with flying hands but no actual contact. Kelly (1993) set the scene in a
cruise-ship gym and the sisters, equipped with fencing masks, fenced vigorously, even
though Katherina was wearing a surgical boot. Guthrie (1954): Sly gallantly attempted to
rescue Bianca and got into trouble with Katherina himself. Nickell (1950): Katherina in
riding-breeches wielded a riding-crop and beat Bianca with it. Alexander (1990): Bianca was
tied up, hooded, and Katherina was brandishing a noose (pbk). Midgley (1990) had
Katherina lock 'her legs around Bianca's waist in a vice-like stranglehold' (*Eastbourne
Gazette*, 8 August 1990) – as the Katherina, Toyah Wilcox, had recently practised wrestling
skills for the role of Trafford Tanzi, that grip could have been impressive.

　　Anglin (1908) cut this sequence in some revivals and Katherina's first entrance in the play
was then to meet Petruchio at line 176. Gribble (1935) cut the beginning of this scene deeply
and brought Baptista on straight away. Fiona Shaw, Katherina in Miller (1987), saw this
scene as 'humiliating' for Katherina 'with its rather dirty-mac desire to hear who Bianca's
keen on' (Rutter 9). This is the opening scene in Marowitz (1973).

3 'gauds': Leach (1978) had Katherina first snatch Bianca's pearl head-dress and then her
necklace. Benthall (1955) cut 3–5, and Bianca was then locked into a small offstage room by
Katherina. Baptista, who entered as early as line 17, slapped Katherina hard. Ball (1976),
Allison (1982) cut much of 3–20 and replaced the cut lines with physical comedy.

Unbind my hands, I'll pull them off myself,
Yea, all my raiment, to my petticoat,   5
Or what you will command me will I do,
So well I know my duty to my elders.
KATHERINA Of all thy suitors here I charge thee tell
Whom thou lov'st best. See thou dissemble not.
BIANCA Believe me, sister, of all the men alive   10
I never yet beheld that special face
Which I could fancy more than any other.
KATHERINA Minion, thou liest! Is't not Hortensio?
BIANCA If you affect him, sister, here I swear
I'll plead for you myself but you shall have him.   15
KATHERINA O then, belike, you fancy riches more:
You will have Gremio to keep you fair.
BIANCA Is it for him you do envy me so?
Nay then, you jest, and now I well perceive
You have but jested with me all this while.   20
I prithee, sister Kate, untie my hands.
                    [*Katherina*] *strikes her.*
KATHERINA If that be jest, then all the rest was so.

                    Enter BAPTISTA.

---

5 Indecorous reference to a 'petticoat' cut in e.g. Phelps (1856).

13 Monette (1988): Bianca was tied to a chair and Katherina slowly pulled the limbs off
    Bianca's teddy bear. Bridges-Adams (1920): Katherina jabbed Bianca with a pin.

21 s.d. Guthrie (1954): Sly shouted out for help for Bianca. Kelly (1993): Katherina pushed Bianca
    sprawling across a gym horse and then whacked her behind with a racquet. In Bogdanov
    (1978) the fight was very serious and prolonged. Devine (1953): Katherina slashed Bianca's
    hands with a knotted rope and then smacked her behind. Benthall (1948): Katherina
    tweaked Bianca's nose. Kyle (1982): Katherina attacked Bianca with her teddy bear (pbk).
    Constance Benson's (1890) 'manner of threatening Bianca with a pin was such raw realism
    that one felt inclined to cry 'Don't'.' (Beerbohm 341). In Daly (1887) Katherina was poised to
    strike Bianca, but she was interrupted by Baptista's arrival.

22 Phelps (1856): Katherina stressed 'that' very heavily.
    Some productions change setting here: e.g. Rose (1997), Monette (1988) moved from the
    sisters' bedroom where the scene opened. Ayliff (1928) moved on after opening in 'A
    corridor in Baptista's house' (pbk).

22 s.d. Alexander (1992): Bianca emitted a very prolonged scream as soon as she realised Baptista
    was onstage.

BAPTISTA Why, how now, dame! Whence grows this insolence?
      Bianca, stand aside. Poor girl, she weeps.
         [*He unties her hands.*]
      Go, ply thy needle; meddle not with her.   25
      For shame, thou hilding of a devilish spirit!
      Why dost thou wrong her that did ne'er wrong thee?
      When did she cross thee with a bitter word?
KATHERINA Her silence flouts me, and I'll be revenged.
         Flies after Bianca.
BAPTISTA What, in my sight? Bianca, get thee in.   30
         Exit [*Bianca*]
KATHERINA What, will you not suffer me? Nay, now I see
      She is your treasure, she must have a husband.
      I must dance barefoot on her wedding day
      And, for your love to her, lead apes in hell.
      Talk not to me! I will go sit and weep   35
      Till I can find occasion of revenge.   [*Exit*]
BAPTISTA Was ever gentleman thus grieved as I?
      But who comes here?

25 Monette (1988): 'ply thy needle' carried the suggestion of mending the mutilated teddy bear. In Ball (1976) the phrase was addressed to Katherina, who seemed unlikely to oblige.

29 Sothern and Marlowe (1905): Katherina threw an embroidery frame (s45).

30 Many Biancas manage to aggravate Katherina further before they leave, e.g. Bianca stuck her tongue out in Bridges-Adams (1920), Payne (1935).

31 ff. Ayliff (1928): Katherina was shaking and maltreating Baptista during this speech. Rider (1994): Katherina said these lines quietly and sadly.

35 Sothern and Marlowe (1905) (s47): Katherina threw a chair before exiting. There was an overlap between her exit and the line 38 s.d. mass entrance, which enabled the men to indicate 'to Petruchio, in pantomime, that this is the one he is to court, keeping their eyes on him closely to note the effect her temper is having on him' (s48).

36 Hodgman (1991): Katherina roared and stamped. Lynch (1991): Katherina went into a mad, spinning tantrum. Kyle (1982): Katherina banged her head on the floor.

37 Guthrie (1954): Baptista blubbered. Monette (1988): Baptista was harangued by his maid in Italian. Barton (1960), Nunn (1967) played part of *AS* Interlude 1 here.

38 s.d. Hortensio's disguises have included: a Left Bank, beret-wearing, arty double bass player (Monette 1988); a country-and-western 'rhinestone cowboy' (Hawthorne 1984, see *SAG* 681); a zoot-suited, jazz sax player (Dillon 1979). Dews (1981) had false cheeks and spectacles, which Hortensio had difficulty dealing with.

Enter GREMIO, LUCENTIO *in the habit of a mean man* [*disguised as Cambio*], PETRUCHIO *with* [HORTENSIO *disguised as Litio,*] TRANIO [*disguised as Lucentio,*] *with his boy* [BIONDELLO] *bearing a lute and books.*

GREMIO   Good morrow, neighbour Baptista.
BAPTISTA   Good morrow, neighbour Gremio. God save you, gentlemen.   40
PETRUCHIO   And you, good sir. Pray have you not a daughter
    Called Katherina, fair and virtuous?
BAPTISTA   I have a daughter, sir, called Katherina.
GREMIO   You are too blunt; go to it orderly.
PETRUCHIO   You wrong me, Signor Gremio. Give me leave.   45
    [*To Baptista*] I am a gentleman of Verona, sir,
    That hearing of her beauty and her wit,
    Her affability and bashful modesty,
    Her wondrous qualities and mild behaviour,
    Am bold to show myself a forward guest   50
    Within your house, to make mine eye the witness
    Of that report which I so oft have heard.
    And for an entrance to my entertainment,
    I do present you with a man of mine,
        [*Presents Hortensio.*]
    Cunning in music and the mathematics,   55

Komisarjevsky (1939) opened the scene here, having played a small section of it at 1.1.91, thus much reducing Katherina's impact as a shrew. As Daly (1887) cut Tranio from the previous scene, this was his first appearance in his disguise.

40   Daly (1887): 'God' became 'Heaven' (s34).

42   Baptista's reaction to this line is often incredulous, e.g. in Ball (1976) Baptista mugged at the audience. Hodgman (1991): Katherina screamed offstage, something which was repeated at line 48. Alexander (1990): everyone apart from Petruchio tittered. May (1971): the 'frock-suited Baptista' let 'his monocle fall from his eye' in astonishment (*Bristol Evening News*, 1 April 1971).

45   Bridges-Adams (1920): Petruchio placed a bouquet on the table and of Wilfrid Walter, Petruchio in the 1927 revival, a reviewer commented 'His entrance with the bunch of flowers and his subsequent gesticulations with them as he wooes this living volcano is an excellent piece of business' (*SUAH* 12 August 1927).

48   Dews (1981): Baptista checked his ears. Reinhardt (1909): there were onstage titters from those listening to Petruchio.

55   Bell (1994): the claim to skill in maths came as a shock to Hortensio (radio broadcast). Ball

To instruct her fully in those sciences,
Whereof I know she is not ignorant.
Accept of him, or else you do me wrong.
His name is Litio, born in Mantua.

BAPTISTA Y'are welcome, sir, and he for your good sake,   60
But for my daughter Katherine, this I know:
She is not for your turn, the more my grief.

PETRUCHIO I see you do not mean to part with her,
Or else you like not of my company.

BAPTISTA Mistake me not; I speak but as I find.   65
Whence are you, sir? What may I call your name?

PETRUCHIO Petruchio is my name, Antonio's son,
A man well known throughout all Italy.

BAPTISTA I know him well. You are welcome for his sake.

GREMIO Saving your tale, Petruchio, I pray   70
Let us that are poor petitioners speak too.
Backare! You are marvellous forward.

PETRUCHIO O pardon me, Signor Gremio, I would fain be doing.

GREMIO I doubt it not, sir, but you will curse your wooing.
[*To Baptista*] Neighbour, this is a gift very grateful, I am sure of it.   75
To express the like kindness, myself, that have been more kindly
beholding to you than any, freely give unto you this young scholar

(1976): Petruchio listed the qualifications very fast as if they didn't bear scrutiny.
Komisarjevsky (1939): Hortensio prompted Petruchio here.

59 Many productions suggest Petruchio and Hortensio haven't prepared their story sufficiently:
e.g. in Sothern and Marlowe (1905) Hortensio whispered a name to Petruchio (s48). Heap
(1985): a big pause before 'Litio' suggested Petruchio was struggling to think of a name.
Carey (1954) used a sneeze gag, whereby the name 'Litio' was inspired by Hortensio
sneezing, a joke J. C. Trewin thought very funny although 'it sounds nothing whatever in
print' (*ILN* 11 December 1954). Benthall (1955) also used this joke. Allison (1982) had Lice-io,
suggested to Petruchio as Hortensio scratched at his head. In Guthrie (1954) it was Sly who
suggested 'Mantua'.

62 Guthrie (1954): 'the more my grief' was addressed to Sly.

64 Sothern and Marlowe (1905): Petruchio made as if to leave and everyone frantically tried to
stop him (s48). In Gribble (1935) Baptista grabbed Petruchio quickly to prevent him leaving.

67 Ayliff (1928): Petruchio noticed that Hortensio was sitting, which was inappropriate for his
new status as a music master, and kicked him. Gribble (1935), Ball (1976) repeated the
'Antonio's dead' joke routines from 1.2.51.

[*Presents Lucentio.*] that hath been long studying at Rheims, as
cunning in Greek, Latin and other languages as the other in music
and mathematics. His name is Cambio. Pray accept his service.   80
BAPTISTA A thousand thanks, Signor Gremio. Welcome, good Cambio.
[*To Tranio*] But, gentle sir, methinks you walk like a stranger.
May I be so bold to know the cause of your coming?
TRANIO Pardon me, sir, the boldness is mine own
         That, being a stranger in this city here,   85
         Do make myself a suitor to your daughter,
         Unto Bianca, fair and virtuous.
         Nor is your firm resolve unknown to me
         In the preferment of the eldest sister.
         This liberty is all that I request   90
         That, upon knowledge of my parentage,
         I may have welcome 'mongst the rest that woo,
         And free access and favour as the rest,
         And toward the education of your daughters
         I here bestow a simple instrument   95
         And this small packet of Greek and Latin books.
         [*Biondello steps forward with the lute and books.*]
         If you accept them, then their worth is great.

78 Bogdanov (1978): Lucentio said 'Rheims' first, making sure Gremio got it right. Ayliff (1928):
     Tranio giggled at the lie.
79 Kaut-Howson (2001): Lucentio obligingly spouted some Greek, Latin and French.
80 Lucentio sometimes needs to remind Gremio of his name, e.g. Bridges-Adams (1920).
82 Kyle (1982): this line was appropriate as Tranio in disguise was camp and walked affectedly.
86 Leiber (1921, 1930): Baptista responded to this line by asking 'Katherine?', which mistake
     Tranio corrected in the next line. Tranio also took this moment to explain 'My name is
     Lucentio.'
88–93 The recapitulation of these lines was cut in e.g. Sothern and Marlowe (1905) S47, Benson
     (1890), Ball (1976).
95 The 'simple instrument' in Gribble (1935) was a huge lute.
96 In *Sauny the Scot* the books are 'French Romances' (2.2.59). In Anglin (1908) Biondello,
     played by Sydney Greenstreet, fooled around 'with the load of books that would fall from
     between his fat arms and his fat chin' (*Boston Transcript*, 6 March 1914), and he reacted
     strongly to Tranio's description of a 'small packet'.
96 s.d. In modern-dress productions the lute often becomes a guitar, e.g. Ayliff (1928).
97 Baptista has not been told Tranio's assumed name by line 98 and so his knowledge of it is
     puzzling. Bogdanov (1978) solved this problem by Tranio handing out visiting cards here.

BAPTISTA Lucentio is your name. Of whence, I pray?
TRANIO Of Pisa, sir, son to Vincentio.
BAPTISTA A mighty man of Pisa. By report   100
    I know him well. You are very welcome, sir.
    [*To Hortensio*] Take you the lute, [*To Lucentio*] and you the
        set of books;
    You shall go see your pupils presently.
    Holla, within!

Enter a SERVANT.

          Sirrah, lead these gentlemen
    To my daughters, and tell them both   105
    These are their tutors. Bid them use them well.
        [*Exeunt Servant, Hortensio, Lucentio*]
    We will go walk a little in the orchard
    And then to dinner. You are passing welcome,
    And so I pray you all to think yourselves.
PETRUCHIO Signor Baptista, my business asketh haste,   110
    And every day I cannot come to woo.
    You knew my father well, and in him me,
    Left solely heir to all his lands and goods,
    Which I have bettered rather than decreased.
    Then tell me, if I get your daughter's love,   115

Baptista glanced at the books and got the name 'Lucentio' from there in, e.g. Sothern and Marlowe (1905) (S45), Anglin (1908), Ball (1976). Some productions give 98a to Tranio and change 'your name' to 'my name', e.g. Asche (1899), Cottrell (1973). Komisarjevsky (1939): Biondello introduced Tranio to Baptista.

    Sothern and Marlowe (1905): as Lucentio stood forward when his name was mentioned, Tranio had to nudge Biondello to drop the books and create a diversion to cover up this slip (S47). This joke, playing on Lucentio forgetting he was in disguise, recurred many times in this production.

99 Ball (1976): there was a huge sensation on 'Vincentio'. Rose (1997): Tranio was immediately, and respectfully, offered a seat.

102a Kyle (1982): there was a pause as everyone looked at Litio expecting him to play. As he couldn't oblige, he resorted to sighing rapturously and leaving quickly.

110 This is approximately where *C&P* opens.

112 Ball (1976) repeated the joke from 1.2.51.

115–21 Daly (1887) cut, reducing the focus on the economics of the marriage.

What dowry shall I have with her to wife?
BAPTISTA After my death, the one half of my lands,
        And in possession twenty thousand crowns.
PETRUCHIO And for that dowry I'll assure her of
        Her widowhood, be it that she survive me,   120
        In all my lands and leases whatsoever.
        Let specialties be therefore drawn between us,
        That covenants may be kept on either hand.
BAPTISTA Ay, when the special thing is well obtained,
        That is, her love, for that is all in all.   125
PETRUCHIO Why, that is nothing, for I tell you, father,
        I am as peremptory as she proud-minded,
        And where two raging fires meet together
        They do consume the thing that feeds their fury.
        Though little fire grows great with little wind,   130
        Yet extreme gusts will blow out fire and all.
        So I to her, and so she yields to me,
        For I am rough and woo not like a babe.

117 Ball (1976): Baptista looked sad at the thought of his own death but one of the onstage
     musicians made a derisory noise. Leach (1978): Grumio was taking notes. Gribble (1935):
     Petruchio shook his head to indicate the offer was not enough.
118 There is often a reaction to the amount of money mentioned indicating that it is generous,
     e.g. Barton (1960). Gribble (1935): Baptista agonised over whether to offer 20,000 or 30,000
     crowns.
119 Bogdanov (1978): Grumio got a ready-prepared contract out of his case.
124-37 There are often loud noises-off during these lines, a tradition which starts at least as early as
     C&P (1.79-80). The insults from 148, 153-4 are sometimes shouted offstage, e.g. Sothern
     and Marlowe (1905) (s47), and s48 records that the noise of breaking the lute was 'made by
     smashing cigar boxes'. Benthall (1955) had loud crashes, Hodgman (1991) had screams and
     growls. Allison (1982) had a big chase with Katherina pursuing Hortensio onstage,
     brandishing the lute and pushing him into a fountain. In *AS* this scene is played onstage,
     although it appears after Kate's and Ferando's (Petruchio's) first encounter, and Kate only
     offers to strike Valeria (Tranio) *with the lute* and then *throws it down* (*AS* 4.34 s.d.).
126 'father' was very familiarly stressed in Reinhardt (1909), also e.g. in Heap (1985). Ball (1976):
     Petruchio gave Baptista a big hug. Sothern and Marlowe (1905) (s47): Gremio repeated the
     word 'father' with 'great gusto'.
132 Alexander (1992): Petruchio was genuinely working out his strategy here.
133 This line was 'given full weight' in Miller (1987) (*I* 8 September 1988).

BAPTISTA Well mayst thou woo, and happy be thy speed!
   But be thou armed for some unhappy words.   135
PETRUCHIO Ay, to the proof, as mountains are for winds,
   That shakes not though they blow perpetually.

     Enter Hortensio with his head broke.

BAPTISTA How now, my friend! Why dost thou look so pale?
HORTENSIO For fear, I promise you, if I look pale.
BAPTISTA What, will my daughter prove a good musician?   140
HORTENSIO I think she'll sooner prove a soldier!
   Iron may hold with her, but never lutes.
BAPTISTA Why then, thou canst not break her to the lute?
HORTENSIO Why no, for she hath broke the lute to me.
   I did but tell her she mistook her frets   145
   And bowed her hand to teach her fingering,
   When, with a most impatient devilish spirit,
   'Frets, call you these?' quoth she, 'I'll fume with them!'
   And with that word she struck me on the head,
   And through the instrument my pate made way,   150
   And there I stood amazèd for a while,
   As on a pillory, looking through the lute,
   While she did call me rascal fiddler
   And twangling Jack, with twenty such vile terms,
   As had she studied to misuse me so.   155

135 Gribble (1935): Bianca, Lucentio, four dwarfs, dashed on followed by Hortensio and
 Katherina. Katherina smashed the huge lute over Hortensio's head after delivering a speech
 cobbled together from Hortensio's report of the incident and some lines borrowed from
 Petruchio's treatment of the Tailor (4.3).
137 Daly (1887) inserted *C&P* 1.79–85. s.d. It is traditional for Hortensio to enter with a broken
 lute or guitar over his head, e.g. Asche (1899). Webster (1844) had Katherina 'heard
 scolding' and then Hortensio 'runs in with his head through the lute roaring lustily' (pbk).
 Burrell (1947): Hortensio collapsed as soon as he was onstage. Sothern and Marlowe (1905)
 (s47): half a dozen books were hurled onstage after Hortensio. Alexander (1992): Hortensio
 was staggering wildly as if reeling from the force of the blow.
149 Nunn (1967): Hortensio demonstrated what had happened by smashing the lute over the
 hapless Baptista's head.
155 Reinhardt (1909): a door opened and then a second musical instrument was hurled onstage
 followed by a package of music scores.

PETRUCHIO Now, by the world, it is a lusty wench!
　　　　I love her ten times more than e'er I did.
　　　　O how I long to have some chat with her.
BAPTISTA [*To Hortensio*]
　　　　Well, go with me, and be not so discomfited.
　　　　Proceed in practice with my younger daughter;　　　　　　160
　　　　She's apt to learn and thankful for good turns.
　　　　Signor Petruchio, will you go with us,
　　　　Or shall I send my daughter Kate to you?
PETRUCHIO I pray you do. I'll attend her here –
　　　　　　　　　　[*Exeunt all but Petruchio*]
　　　　And woo her with some spirit when she comes!　　　　　　165

156　Guthrie (1954): 'is' was stressed. Dews (1981): Petruchio roared this speech.

157　There are often surprised reactions to this line, e.g. Bridges-Adams (1920), Payne (1935) everyone exclaimed 'What!'

158　Brighton (1981): instead of the popular buccaneering delivery, this line was 'flat with ironic dread' (*GM* 12 February 1981). Bridges-Adams (1920): everyone repeated the word 'chat' in disbelief. Daly (1887) inserted *C&P* 1.107–13. Leach (1978) had a pause before 'chat' as Petruchio searched for the appropriate word.

160a　Bridges-Adams (1920): Hortensio responded with horror until he realised he was not being asked to return to Katherina.

163　Ball (1976): Baptista laughed as he left Petruchio to his fate.

164 s.d.　Sothern and Marlowe (1905) (s47): the men looked at Petruchio 'mournfully as if for the last time'. At the equivalent point in Mrs C. H. Jones's scenario for a silent movie, Petruchio hid on hearing Katherina's voice (s60). Miller (1987): Grumio handed Petruchio a stiff drink to fortify him. Gribble (1935): Alfred Lunt as Petruchio was 'masterful' but 'also indicates – and it is the most amusing feature of his performance – that Petruchio is really scared stiff of this terror whom he is courting' (*San Francisco Chronicle*, 14 November 1939). In *Sauny the Scot* (2.2), Sauny (Grumio) did not exit but stayed on for Petruchio's and Margaret's (Katherina's) first scene together, making crude comments and getting his ears boxed by Margaret. Reinhardt (1909): Petruchio was terrified at this point.

165 ff.　Petruchio's first soliloquy/address to the audience is crucial in establishing sympathy, or otherwise, with his project. Ayliff (1928) had Petruchio move right downstage. In Guthrie (1954) Katherina entered early and overheard part of the very nervous Petruchio's speech, something which allowed her to understand what subsequently happened to her. Farjeon (66) disapproved of the fact that in Guthrie's earlier 1939 Old Vic production Petruchio was 'quaking with fear before he meets Katherine for the first time'. Ball (1976): Petruchio stripped off his top, revealing a very muscular chest and flexing his muscles for the oncoming fray. Devine (1953): most of this speech was addressed to Sly. Allison (1982) had direct address to the camera. Alexander (1992): Petruchio held a chair as if about to tame a

Say that she rail, why then I'll tell her plain
She sings as sweetly as a nightingale.
Say that she frown, I'll say she looks as clear
As morning roses newly washed with dew.
Say she be mute and will not speak a word,   170
Then I'll commend her volubility
And say she uttereth piercing eloquence.
If she do bid me pack, I'll give her thanks
As though she bid me stay by her a week.
If she deny to wed, I'll crave the day   175
When I shall ask the banns, and when be married.

Enter Katherina.

But here she comes, and now, Petruchio, speak.
Good morrow, Kate, for that's your name, I hear.

lion, but then turned and shared his plan with the audience. In Marowitz (1973) the speech is reconfigured as Petruchio being catechised by Grumio and Hortensio (139).

176 s.d. A loud slam of a door often precedes Katherina's arrival, e.g. Ayliff (1928). Williams (1973): Katherina entered and fired a gun in the air. Productions which play the couple instantly falling in love often take a big pause here, e.g. Asche (1899). Ball (1976): Katherina walked round Petruchio, eyed him up and down, grinned at the audience in approbation and then resumed her surly frown, business that was used at least as early as Reinhardt (1909). In *C&P* Catharine enters bemoaning her fate but she states appreciatively of Petruchio 'yet the man's a man' (1.139). Gribble (1935): Katherina appeared on her balcony wielding a huge musical instrument: a 'breakaway serpent' (pbk). Schaefer (1956) had this first encounter played as if in a boxing-ring. Maurice Evans, the Petruchio, remembered that 'Cheered on by the villagers, the two of us played the scene as if sparring for a fight, retiring to our "corners" periodically to be revived by our "seconds" ' (Evans 248).

Katherinas reluctant to meet Petruchio also occur: *K&P* has Katherina protesting as Baptista forces her onstage. Daly (1887) (s34) had similar protests, as did e.g. Payne (1935). Benthall (1955): Katherina was pushed on by Baptista, who then locked the door on her. Meanwhile Petruchio was so busy practising what kind of bow he was going to make that he didn't realise Katherina had arrived. Sybil Thorndike in Leigh (1927) gave Katherina a 'bewildered look of fear' (*T* 13 September 1927) and 'an indication of nervousness' (*ILN* 24 September 1927).

This moment was used as Katherina's very first entrance in Anglin (1908) (*NYT* 20 March 1914).

177 Komisarjevsky (1939) gave this line to Sly. Gribble (1935) gave 177b to Sly.

178 The use of the familiar 'Kate' sometimes pulls Katherina up short, e.g. Sothern and Marlowe

KATHERINA Well have you heard, but something hard of hearing –
            They call me Katherine that do talk of me.   180
PETRUCHIO You lie, in faith, for you are called plain Kate,
            And bonny Kate, and sometimes Kate the curst.
            But Kate, the prettiest Kate in Christendom,
            Kate of Kate-Hall, my super-dainty Kate –
            For dainties are all Kates – and therefore, Kate,   185
            Take this of me, Kate of my consolation:
            Hearing thy mildness praised in every town,
            Thy virtues spoke of and thy beauty sounded –
            Yet not so deeply as to thee belongs –
            Myself am moved to woo thee for my wife.   190

(1905) where Katherina was 'amazed at his impudence' (s48). Robertson/Selbie (1986), Bell (1994) used the pronunciation 'cat'.

179 Reinhardt (1909): Katherina hit Petruchio on his ear.

181 Rider (1994): the slightly built Petruchio backpedalled at Katherina's look in response to 'plain Kate'.

183 Gribble (1935): Katherina hurled her musical instrument, a 'breakaway serpent', at Petruchio 'who quickly ducks under Balcony and groans as though he had been hit. Katharine, becoming quite concerned, comes down steps L. and goes under the Balcony, where Petruchio with a wild whoop grabs her and brings her out on stage' (s65).

184 Dews (1981): Petruchio amused Katherina first by dancing on 'super-dainty', and then by the sheer outrageousness of his speech. She was also visibly affected by his reference to her 'beauty' at line 188.

186 Sothern and Marlowe (1905) (s47): on this line Petruchio tried to kiss Katherina's hand and she 'hits his hand with a book'. Asche (1899): Katherina took Petruchio's pewter tankard and she 'throws contents in Petruchio's face and throws pewter down angrily', actions which made the next line more absurd. Gribble (1935): Petruchio slapped Katherina on the behind, hard. Spanking became central to the narrative of *Kiss Me, Kate*, which was largely inspired by this production.

188 Miller (1987): this was the first line Katherina really attended to, as the shock of hearing herself described as beautiful jolted her out of her traumatised state. Petruchio was 'offhand, formulaic, and with his back to her, until he idly turned on "thy beauty" and was thunderstruck' (Gay 1994, 117). Morgan (1937): the pbk specifies that after speaking the previous line 'ironically' Petruchio speaks 'sincerely' of Katherina's 'beauty'.

190 Carey (1954): Petruchio kneeled. This also made it easier for him to grab Katherina for 'Come sit on me' (line 194).

KATHERINA 'Moved' – in good time! Let him that moved you hither
    Remove you hence. I knew you at the first
    You were a movable.
PETRUCHIO   Why, what's a movable?
KATHERINA A joint stool.
PETRUCHIO   Thou hast hit it. Come sit on me.
KATHERINA Asses are made to bear, and so are you.   195
PETRUCHIO Women are made to bear, and so are you.
KATHERINA No such jade as you, if me you mean.
PETRUCHIO Alas, good Kate, I will not burden thee,
    For, knowing thee to be but young and light –
KATHERINA Too light for such a swain as you to catch,   200
    And yet as heavy as my weight should be.
PETRUCHIO 'Should be'! Should – buzz!
KATHERINA   Well tane, and like a buzzard.
PETRUCHIO O slow-winged turtle, shall a buzzard take thee?
KATHERINA Ay, for a turtle, as he takes a buzzard.
PETRUCHIO Come, come, you wasp! I'faith you are too angry.   205
KATHERINA If I be waspish, best beware my sting.
PETRUCHIO My remedy is then to pluck it out.
KATHERINA Ay, if the fool could find it where it lies.
PETRUCHIO Who knows not where a wasp does wear his sting?
    In his tail.
KATHERINA   In his tongue.

191 Leach (1978): Katherina played over the top as if overcome by the compliment, fanning herself and curtseying in a fluster.

193 Barton (1960): Katherina kicked away the stool Petruchio was sitting on: Peter O'Toole as Petruchio composedly remained sitting on air.

194 'Come sit on me' is often an invitation to sit on Petruchio's lap, e.g. Benson (1890). This can be made very lewd, e.g. Dews (1981).

196 Sothern and Marlowe (1905) (s47): Katherina threw a book at Petruchio.

197–229 Often cut heavily for obscurity and indecency, e.g. Benson (1890) and the intricacies of this sequence of jokes are often lost in productions which emphasise physical comedy, e.g. Zeffirelli (1967).

201 Burrell (1947): Katherina bounced heavily on Petruchio's lap and he let her fall through his legs.

206 Nickell (1950); on 'sting' Katherina bit Petruchio. Komisarjevsky (1939): Katherina tried to scratch his face.

PETRUCHIO Whose tongue? 210
KATHERINA Yours, if you talk of tales, and so farewell.
[*She turns to go.*]
PETRUCHIO What, with my tongue in your tail? Nay, come again.
Good Kate, I am a gentleman –
KATHERINA That I'll try.
She strikes him.
PETRUCHIO I swear I'll cuff you if you strike again.
[*He holds her.*]
KATHERINA So may you lose your arms. 215
If you strike me, you are no gentleman,
And if no gentleman, why then no arms.
PETRUCHIO A herald, Kate? O put me in thy books.
KATHERINA What is your crest – a coxcomb?
PETRUCHIO A combless cock, so Kate will be my hen. 220
KATHERINA No cock of mine; you crow too like a craven.
PETRUCHIO Nay, come, Kate, come; you must not look so sour.

210 Nickell (1950): Petruchio goosed Katherina on 'tail'.

212 Often cut for indecency until the late twentieth century, e.g. Webster (1844). Reinhardt (1909) simply cut all references to tails and made it a discussion about tongues. When uncut, most Katherinas express shock at Petruchio's crudity, e.g. Ball (1976).

213 s.d. Even dignified Katherinas let rip here. Daly (1887) gave 'That I'll try' to Petruchio (s32) as an accompaniment to an attempt to kiss Katherina, and Ada Rehan's outrage was awe-inspiring (Daly 465). In Heap (1985) Katherina (Mark Heap) was so much heftier than 'her' Petruchio that this blow was very threatening. Allison (1982): Katherina swung a big punch at Petruchio and he had to fight to stop himself hitting her back. Nunn (1967): Katherina hit Petruchio so hard he appeared to pass out and she spent several moments trying to revive him. Fiona Shaw in Miller (1987) felt Katherina was 'really appalled' at Petruchio's comment and that 'That slap is the first clue that Kate's behaviour is, ironically, a plea for dignity' (Rutter 11).

214 Rose (1997): Katherina hit Petruchio, broke an egg on his head, and then Petruchio handcuffed her. The handcuffs were on a chain, and Petruchio subsequently dragged Katherina around the stage like a leashed dog. Ball (1976): Katherina immediately hit Petruchio again, knocking him to the floor so line 216 was then used to stop him hitting her.

216 Nickell (1950): Charlton Heston's Petruchio struck Katherina hard across the face several times.

217 Benthall (1948): Katherina let fly with a series of missiles including plates, plants and baskets of fruit. She also broke a chair across Petruchio's back.

222 Burrell (1947): Petruchio walked sideways to cue the crab joke.

KATHERINA It is my fashion when I see a crab.
PETRUCHIO Why, here's no crab, and therefore look not sour.
KATHERINA There is, there is.   225
PETRUCHIO Then show it me.
KATHERINA   Had I a glass I would.
PETRUCHIO What, you mean my face?
KATHERINA   Well aimed of such a young
       one.
PETRUCHIO Now, by Saint George, I am too young for you.
KATHERINA Yet you are withered.
PETRUCHIO   'Tis with cares.
KATHERINA   I care not.
PETRUCHIO Nay, hear you, Kate – in sooth you scape not so.   230
KATHERINA I chafe you if I tarry. Let me go.
PETRUCHIO Nay, not a whit. I find you passing gentle.
       'Twas told me you were rough and coy and sullen,
       And now I find report a very liar,
       For thou art pleasant, gamesome, passing courteous,   235
       But slow in speech, yet sweet as springtime flowers.
       Thou canst not frown, thou canst not look askance,
       Nor bite the lip as angry wenches will,
       Nor hast thou pleasure to be cross in talk,
       But thou with mildness entertain'st thy wooers,   240
       With gentle conference, soft and affable.
              [*He lets her go.*]
       Why does the world report that Kate doth limp?

225 Alexander (1992) turned this into a childish tantrum with the line repeated several times.

226 Katherina sometimes mimes holding a mirror up, e.g. Sothern and Marlowe (1905) (s48).

228 Dews (1981): Katherina appeared insulted by this slur on her age. Alexander (1992): Petruchio walked off, as if giving up. Katherina's next line then became an indication of interest in him.

229 Lynch (1991): on 'withered' Katherina gestured at Petruchio's groin.

230 Benthall (1948): Petruchio lassoed Katherina.

233 Hodgman (1991): Katherina kicked Petruchio hard in the crotch.

238 Leach (1978): Petruchio got hold of Katherina's foot and started tickling her, reducing her to giggling helplessness.

242 Productions sometimes show Katherina receiving the injury that makes her limp: e.g. in Benthall (1948) the limp resulted from Katherina stamping her foot angrily. In Nunn (1967) it

O sland'rous world! Kate like the hazel twig
Is straight and slender, and as brown in hue
As hazel-nuts and sweeter than the kernels.   245
O let me see thee walk. Thou dost not halt.
KATHERINA Go, fool, and whom thou keep'st command.
PETRUCHIO Did ever Dian so become a grove
    As Kate this chamber with her princely gait?
    O be thou Dian, and let her be Kate,   250
    And then let Kate be chaste and Dian sportful!
KATHERINA Where did you study all this goodly speech?
PETRUCHIO It is extempore, from my mother-wit.
KATHERINA A witty mother! Witless else her son.
PETRUCHIO Am I not wise?
KATHERINA   Yes, keep you warm.   255
PETRUCHIO Marry, so I mean, sweet Katherine, in thy bed.
    And therefore, setting all this chat aside,

was a result of her kicking the table. Ball (1976): the limp came after Petruchio stamped on
her foot. This production also used clichés from professional wrestling with both characters
appearing very adept at this sport. In Kelly (1993) this line had a different resonance as
Katherina had a surgical boot, and really did limp. Kyle (1982): Katherina limped because
Petruchio had thrown her shoe into the onstage swimming pool (pbk).

244 'straight and slender': in Leach (1978) Petruchio had Katherina in a *Gone with the Wind*
    embrace and ran his hand along her body.

246a It became traditional for Katherina to pace the room but then to stop short at Petruchio's
    request, e.g. Webster (1844). In Asche (1899) this line 'absolutely convulsed the house' after
    Katherina had 'been pacing up and down the room like a caged lion' (*The Sportsman*, 30
    November 1904).

248 ff. Bogdanov (1978): Petruchio pretended to use a bell on Baptista's desk as a microphone and
    sang these lines into it: Katherina was amused and intrigued by this. Hodgman (1991):
    Petruchio executed a balletic dance. Alexander (1992): Petruchio struck attitudes. Nunn
    (1967): Petruchio took a round of applause from his onstage audience after this virtuoso
    burst of poetry.

256 Cottrell (1973): Katherina hit Petruchio again at 'bed' (radio broadcast). Reinhardt (1909):
    Katherina went for Petruchio with her nails. Daly (1887) replaced 'bed' with 'arms' (534).
    Kyle (1982): Katherina pushed Petruchio into the onstage swimming pool (pbk). Marowitz
    (1973) has *Petruchio grabs Kate's crotch. She is momentarily stunned by the suddenness of
    this brutish move* (143).

Thus in plain terms: your father hath consented
That you shall be my wife, your dowry 'greed on,
And will you, nill you, I will marry you.   260
Now Kate, I am a husband for your turn,
For, by this light whereby I see thy beauty –
Thy beauty that doth make me like thee well –
Thou must be married to no man but me,
For I am he am born to tame you, Kate,   265
And bring you from a wild Kate to a Kate
Conformable as other household Kates.

Enter Baptista, Gremio and Tranio.

Here comes your father. Never make denial –
I must and will have Katherine to my wife.

BAPTISTA

Now, Signor Petruchio, how speed you with my daughter?   270

259 Dews (1981): Katherina looked shell-shocked. Bridges-Adams (1920): Katherina screamed 'No!' Ayliff (1928): Katherina was now in tears and her spirit was broken. She sobbed broken-heartedly for the rest of this speech although she screamed when Baptista arrived onstage. Leach (1978): Katherina had stormed off but on hearing this line she stormed back onstage, absolutely furious.

260 Lynch (1991): this line was roared and Petruchio whirled his arm around ferociously. Monette (1988): Katherina screamed (pbk). Miller (1987): Katherina made a little, distressed, helpless gesture and Fiona Shaw, who played Katherina, comments 'she says nothing. The problem is how to occupy that silence. I think she's stunned' (Rutter 11). Kaut-Howson (2001): the breathless Katherina was on the floor and Petruchio was on top of her in missionary position when he said this line.

261 Often said with great seriousness, e.g. Monette (1988). In Kelly (1993) both Katherina and Petruchio were now in the onstage swimming pool but Petruchio held Katherina's face in his hands here to impress on her that he meant what he said.

263 Daly (1887): s30, which is marked up for Petruchio, notes that this line is 'sincere'.

264 Kelly (1993): Petruchio 'baptized' Katherina, ducking her in the swimming pool. The *Stage* (6 May 1993) thought 'just to see Nichola McAuliffe wringing her skirt dry is worth the price of admission'. Barton (1960): Petruchio was about to kiss the now yielding Katherina but teasingly drew back at the last minute; Katherina's subsequent shrewish behaviour thus appeared to result from pique at being denied a kiss.

269 In *Sauny the Scot*, Margaret (Katherina), having encountered extremely violent threats from her Petruchio, reflects, 'The Devil's in this fellow, he has beat me at my own Weapon. *I* have a good mind to marry him to try if he can *Tame* me' (2.2.252–4).

PETRUCHIO How but well, sir? How but well?
　　　　　It were impossible I should speed amiss.
BAPTISTA Why, how now, daughter Katherine, in your dumps?
KATHERINA Call you me 'daughter'? Now I promise you
　　　　　You have showed a tender fatherly regard   275
　　　　　To wish me wed to one half lunatic,
　　　　　A mad-cap ruffian and a swearing Jack
　　　　　That thinks with oaths to face the matter out.
PETRUCHIO Father, 'tis thus: yourself and all the world
　　　　　That talked of her have talked amiss of her.   280
　　　　　If she be curst, it is for policy,
　　　　　For she's not froward, but modest as the dove;
　　　　　She is not hot, but temperate as the morn;
　　　　　For patience she will prove a second Grissel,
　　　　　And Roman Lucrece for her chastity.   285
　　　　　And, to conclude, we have 'greed so well together
　　　　　That upon Sunday is the wedding day.
KATHERINA I'll see thee hanged on Sunday first!

272 Guthrie (1954): Petruchio tangoed with Katherina through these lines.
273 Ball (1976): Baptista was laughing at this. Reinhardt (1909) took a very big pause here
　　　before Katherina replied. Miller (1987): Katherina was constantly in depression or the
　　　'dumps' until Petruchio came to her rescue.
275 Benson (1890): Katherina beat and threw cushions. Gribble (1935): Katherina started very
　　　sweetly before rising to her feet and screaming line 276, 'half lunatic'. She then grabbed a
　　　sword and attacked Petruchio before he disarmed her.
278 In the equivalent moment in *AS* (3.168 s.d.), Kate *turns aside and speaks*, which, as
　　　Marcus (109) points out, is more direct address to the audience than the Folio gives
　　　Katherina. Kate comments: 'But yet I will consent and marry him, / For I methinks have lived
　　　too long a maid, / And match him too, or else his manhood's good' (3.169–71).
279 'Father' often gets a big laugh by being heavily stressed, e.g. Dews (1981).
281 Daly (1887): Katherina threw herself onto a seat in exasperation (s28).
282 Bell (1994): loud screams from Katherina.
284–5 These literary lines are often cut, e.g. Sothern and Marlowe (1905) (s48). Leach (1978):
　　　Katherina lay on the floor, legs unchastely wide open, laughing mockingly.
288 Sothern and Marlowe (1905): as Katherina shook her fist in Petruchio's face, he caught her
　　　hand and kissed it. She then tried to stamp on his foot and he hopped from one foot to
　　　another whilst continuing to kiss her hands (s47).

GREMIO Hark, Petruchio, she says she'll see thee hanged first.
TRANIO Is this your speeding? Nay then, goodnight our part.   290
PETRUCHIO Be patient, gentlemen. I choose her for myself.
   If she and I be pleased, what's that to you?
   'Tis bargained 'twixt us twain, being alone,
   That she shall still be curst in company.
   I tell you, 'tis incredible to believe   295
   How much she loves me – O the kindest Kate!
   She hung about my neck, and kiss on kiss
   She vied so fast, protesting oath on oath,
   That in a twink she won me to her love.
   O you are novices! 'Tis a world to see   300
   How tame, when men and women are alone,
   A meacock wretch can make the curstest shrew.
   Give me thy hand, Kate. I will unto Venice,

290 Bridges-Adams (1920): in the 1933 revival, Katherina and Baptista argued and threw paper at each other, which *SUAH* though 'poor, unworthy stuff' (26 May).

293 Alexander (1992): Petruchio was confiding in the men in a freemasonry which excluded Katherina.

294 Katherina often reacts strongly to this manoeuvre: in Payne (1935) she exclaimed out loud, in Edwards (1995) she groaned, while in Leach (1978) all the men 'Aaahed' understandingly. *C&P* (1.244–5) had Catharine decide to marry Petruchio for 'revenge' and to 'tame' him, something followed in Daly (1887) (S34).

295 Hodgman (1991): Petruchio took the rest of the chaps aside confidentially. Daly (1887): S30, which is marked up for Petruchio, notes that this line is spoken quietly and sincerely.

299 Ball (1976): the wrestling match between Katherina and Petruchio which carried on throughout this section included moves from professional wrestling and now climaxed as Petruchio triumphantly held Katherina horizontal above his head. Miller (1987): Petruchio stressed the 'she', 'me', and 'her', making Katherina sound assertive and active – quite the opposite of the depressed Katherina he was actually dealing with.

300 Guthrie (1954): Petruchio's hand was over Katherina's mouth. Carey (1954): Petruchio stressed 'O you *are* novices', which was enjoyed by *ILN* (11 December 1954).

302 As Katherina raised her hand to strike Petruchio, he caught it and this cued the next line in e.g. Bridges-Adams (1920).

303 Asche (1899): Petruchio took Katherina's hands and forced her onto her knees. Rider (1994): Katherina refused, and put her hands behind her back, but on line 307 she paused, held the moment, changed her mind and deliberately gave her hand. Alexander (1992): Katherina spat on Petruchio's hand. Leach (1978): Katherina leapt onto Petruchio's back and attacked him.

> To buy apparel 'gainst the wedding day.
> Provide the feast, father, and bid the guests.   305
> I will be sure my Katherine shall be fine.
> BAPTISTA I know not what to say, but give me your hands.
> God send you joy, Petruchio! 'tis a match.
> GREMIO⎫
> TRANIO⎭ Amen say we. We will be witnesses.
> PETRUCHIO Father, and wife, and gentlemen, adieu.   310
> I will to Venice – Sunday comes apace.
> We will have rings, and things, and fine array,
> And kiss me, Kate, 'We will be married a' Sunday.'

---

305 Daly (1887) inserted *C&P* 1.256–61 (s34).

307 Hodgman (1991): Katherina was in serious shock.

308 'Heaven' was substituted for 'God' in e.g. Webster (1844). Bogdanov (1978): Grumio took a photograph.

309 Sothern and Marlowe (1905): Katherina bit first Baptista and then Petruchio (s47). This line is sometimes split between Gremio and Tranio: e.g. Nunn (1967). Once the betrothal has been witnessed, with no verbal protest from the bride, Katherina is committed to Petruchio, which is why Gremio and Tranio are eager to be formal witnesses. Some Katherinas are silent here because they *are* choosing to risk life with Petruchio, e.g. Rider (1994). However, Rose (1997) had Katherina's silence a result of her exhaustion and desperation at Baptista's betrayal of her, and in Dews (1981) Katherina was screaming 'No'. Ball (1976), which had conducted most of the preceding action as a professional wrestling match, now had the couple's hands raised high as if in a declaration of victory. After this line Daly (1887) inserted *C&P* 1.263–8 (s34).

310 Hodgman (1991): Petruchio stressed 'wife' and got a big laugh.

313 Daly (1887), following *C&P*, had the wedding announced for 'tomorrow' and Katherina boxed Petruchio's ear for the second time in the scene before exiting (s32). Dews (1981): Petruchio swung Katherina into the *Gone with the Wind* poster position and kissed her. Devine (1953) had a tango sequence. By contrast in Bogdanov (1978) Katherina slapped Petruchio's face. In Leach (1978) she spat at him, and he then licked up the spittle as if relishing it. Kyle (1982): Katherina kicked Petruchio hard in the crotch, only to be pushed by him into the onstage swimming pool. 313b became a response to this attack, as if Petruchio were suggesting that it was in Katherina's own interests not to damage him. Boleslavsky (1925): Petruchio swung Katherina left and right and finally flung 'her violently into her father's arms' providing a 'sententious curtain' (*NYT* 19 December 1925). Barton (1960): as Petruchio 'Mr. O'Toole made this the best throw-away line I have ever heard in the theatre' (*Evening News*, 22 June 1960). Katharine Hepburn in Benthall (1955) fell into a faint and was

> *Exeunt Petruchio and Katherina [separately]*

GREMIO Was ever match clapped up so suddenly?
BAPTISTA Faith, gentlemen, now I play a merchant's part,   315
And venture madly on a desperate mart.
TRANIO 'Twas a commodity lay fretting by you.
'Twill bring you gain, or perish on the seas.
BAPTISTA The gain I seek is quiet in the match.
GREMIO No doubt but he hath got a quiet catch!   320
But now, Baptista, to your younger daughter:
Now is the day we long have looked for;
I am your neighbour and was suitor first.

carried off. Payne (1935): Katherina exited screaming. Miller (1987): Katherina 'takes her scissors and snips off all the buttons on [Petruchio's] jerkin in a symbolic act of castration' (*Jewish Chronicle*, 16 September 1988). The pbk confirms this but the archival video merely shows Katherina wiping the traces of the kiss from her hand. Posner (1999): Katherina spat at Baptista in disgust. Gribble (1935): Katherina bit Petruchio's cheek, gouged his foot with her heel and Sly, quite reasonably confused, asked 'Must they now be married?', a version of *AS* Interlude 2, while Baptista, Tranio and Gremio danced for joy.

313 s.d. Sothern and Marlowe (1905) cut the rest of the scene with Katherina throwing books and a vase of flowers after Petruchio (S47). The production, which minimised the Bianca narrative, then also cut 3.1. Anglin (1908) also had a curtain here with Katherina throwing a shoe after Petruchio. A new scene then opened set in Baptista's garden and this ran on into 3.1. Asche (1899): Katherina slapped Petruchio's face and exited quickly, slamming the door – meanwhile the picture of Petruchio's departure, laughing, was held, before a new scene started, in Baptista's garden. Webster (1844) had music here to break up this very long scene. Harvey (1913) ended the scene here as Katherina slapped Petruchio, he kissed her, she threw a slipper at him, this hit Sly, and Bartholomew then had to pacify him (McDonald pbk). Lloyd (1956) finished the scene and Petruchio departed after shaking hands with the men and taking possession of a marriage contract.

In *C&P*, after Petruchio exits, Catharine confides in the audience that she will 'tame this haggard' (line 285) Petruchio, and if she fails she will 'tie her tongue up and pare down her nails' (line 286). She thus explicitly *chooses* to marry Petruchio. Taylor (1929) used these lines and the film's Katherina, Mary Pickford, was indeed shown taming her Petruchio.

315 Barton (1960): Baptista, Gremio and Tranio indulged in a celebratory dance. Alexander (1992): Bianca came on and stood and listened attentively through all the bargaining over her. The situation was further complicated as Tranio and Bianca were strongly attracted to each other.

TRANIO And I am one that love Bianca more
   Than words can witness, or your thoughts can guess. 325
GREMIO Youngling, thou canst not love so dear as I.
TRANIO Greybeard, thy love doth freeze.
GREMIO   But thine doth fry.
   Skipper, stand back! 'Tis age that nourisheth.
TRANIO But youth in ladies' eyes that flourisheth.
BAPTISTA Content you, gentlemen; I will compound this strife. 330
   'Tis deeds must win the prize, and he of both
   That can assure my daughter greatest dower
   Shall have my Bianca's love.
   Say, Signor Gremio, what can you assure her?
GREMIO First, as you know, my house within the city 335
   Is richly furnishèd with plate and gold,
   Basins and ewers to lave her dainty hands;
   My hangings all of Tyrian tapestry;
   In ivory coffers I have stuffed my crowns,
   In cypress chests my arras counterpoints, 340
   Costly apparel, tents and canopies,
   Fine linen, Turkey cushions bossed with pearl,

---

325 Allison (1982): 'your thoughts' was pointedly addressed to Gremio.

330 Leach (1978): Baptista was getting a headache from the row and put his hands over his ears.

335 ff. Reinhardt (1909): Baptista repeated all the vital statistics ('a hundred', 'six score' etc.). Bridges-Adams (1920): Baptista took notes and muttered to himself. Bogdanov (1978) used a 'huge old fashioned adding machine' (McLuskie 39) which had exploded by line 369. Rider (1994) used a cash till and Lloyd (1956) had the ringing of a cash register offstage (*NYT* 6 August 1956). Bell (1994): Baptista switched his computer on and Tranio (as Lucentio) had 'a computer disk to list his assets' (*Australian*, 3 May 1994). Kyle (1982) had a conveyer belt gliding past, carrying exhibits indicative of Gremio's wealth, something which evoked a contemporary TV show, *The Generation Game*. While the material excesses of Gremio and Tranio-as-Lucentio's bidding competition can be both funny and important for class consciousness, they are very susceptible to cuts, e.g. Phelps (1856). Miller (1980): Baptista was so delighted to be rid of Katherina, he hardly listened to what anyone was saying. Freedman (1960): Gremio was 'barely able to muster enough breath to list his merits as bridegroom' (*NYT* 20 August 1960). Rose (1997) had Bianca on the balcony listening to this bargaining.

341–50 Ball (1976): Gremio gradually gathered speed, ending up sounding like a commentator on a horse race.

Valance of Venice gold in needlework,
Pewter and brass, and all things that belongs
To house or housekeeping. Then at my farm   345
I have a hundred milch-kine to the pail,
Six score fat oxen standing in my stalls,
And all things answerable to this portion.
Myself am struck in years I must confess,
And if I die tomorrow this is hers,   350
If whilst I live she will be only mine.
TRANIO That 'only' came well in. Sir, list to me:
I am my father's heir and only son.
If I may have your daughter to my wife,
I'll leave her houses three or four as good   355
Within rich Pisa walls as any one
Old Signor Gremio has in Padua,
Besides two thousand ducats by the year
Of fruitful land, all which shall be her jointure.
What, have I pinched you, Signor Gremio?   360
GREMIO Two thousand ducats by the year of land?
[*Aside*] My land amounts not to so much in all! –
That she shall have, besides an argosy
That now is lying in Marsellis' road. –
What, have I choked you with an argosy?   365
TRANIO Gremio, 'tis known my father hath no less
Than three great argosies, besides two galliasses
And twelve tight galleys. These I will assure her,

---

344 Gribble (1935): Tranio repeated 'brass' scornfully.

348 Cottrell (1973): a big yawn here from Tranio.

349 Allison (1982): Gremio coughed feebly before this line.

355 Bridges-Adams (1920): Baptista started a new sheet of paper to make notes on Tranio-as-Lucentio's offerings.

358 Rider (1994): Baptista's cash till could hardly keep up.

363 Antoon (1990) changed the offer here to suit his Wild West setting. Instead of an argosy Gremio offered a team of stallions and Tranio responded with an offer of three teams of stallions plus twelve mustangs and two fringed surreys.

367 Komisarjevsky (1939): Gremio fainted, a servant revived him with snuff, whereupon he had a sneezing fit. Heap (1985): Gremio not only 'choked' (line 365) but had a minor heart attack, thrashing around on the floor.

And twice as much whate'er thou off'rest next.
GREMIO Nay, I have offered all. I have no more,   370
        And she can have no more than all I have.
        If you like me, she shall have me and mine.
TRANIO Why, then the maid is mine from all the world
        By your firm promise. Gremio is out-vied.
BAPTISTA I must confess your offer is the best,   375
        And, let your father make her the assurance,
        She is your own; else, you must pardon me.
        If you should die before him, where's her dower?
TRANIO That's but a cavil. He is old, I young.
GREMIO And may not young men die as well as old?   380
BAPTISTA Well, gentlemen, I am thus resolved.
        On Sunday next you know
        My daughter Katherine is to be married.
        Now, on the Sunday following shall Bianca
        Be bride to you, if you make this assurance.   385
        If not, to Signor Gremio.
        And so I take my leave, and thank you both.
GREMIO Adieu, good neighbour.

                                                    Exit Baptista
                    Now I fear thee not.

374 Williams (1973): Gremio put his toupee on the table in defeat.
375 Gremio prompted Baptista by whispering 'father' to him in e.g. Benson (1890).
379 Daly (1887): Tranio executed a pirouette (s34); when Gremio attempted to follow suit at the end of line 380 he got into difficulties.
381 Williams (1973): 'Baptista awards Bianca to the disguised Tranio with a tap of an auctioneer's hammer, and then uses the same instrument to flail away at what looks like a gruesome hairy spider, but is in fact Gremio's fallen toupee' (*New Statesman*, 5 October 1973).
382 Benson (1890) followed *C&P* and had 'This afternoon' replace 'On Sunday next', speeding up the sequence of events.
383 Barton (1960): Baptista laughed loudly. Dews (1981): Baptista smiled broadly but cut back the smile to resume serious negotiations. Monette (1988): Baptista wrote the date down in his diary. Allison (1982): Baptista crossed himself.
388 s.d. Alexander (1992): Bianca, who had been onstage listening to the bargaining, now left with Baptista.

Sirrah, young gamester, your father were a fool
To give thee all and in his waning age   390
Set foot under thy table. Tut, a toy!
An old Italian fox is not so kind, my boy.   *Exit*

TRANIO A vengeance on your crafty withered hide!
Yet I have faced it with a card of ten.
'Tis in my head to do my master good: 395
I see no reason but supposed Lucentio
Must get a father called supposed Vincentio.
And that's a wonder – fathers commonly
Do get their children, but in this case of wooing
A child shall get a sire, if I fail not of my cunning.   *Exit*   400

394 Often gets cut or modernised as too obscure: e.g. Langham (1962) rendered it 'thus far I
     have brazed it out' (pbk), Dews (1981) 'I have bluffed them with a clever lie' (pbk).
396 ff. Gribble (1935) played to Sly.
398a Komisarjevsky (1939) gave this to Sly.
400 Daly (1887) inserted *C&P* 1.135–9a, followed by 269–72 and a version of 281–6. This gave
     Ada Rehan's Katherina the curtain speech (534). Dews (1981) played a version of *AS*
     Interlude 1 (see Appendix 1, p. 236).
     Benson (1890) went straight from 2.1 into 3.1 without a scene break, with Tranio coughing
     to warn the approaching Lucentio that Hortensio was about to appear.

ACT 3   SCENE 1

Enter LUCENTIO [*as Cambio*], HORTENSIO [*as Litio*] *and* BIANCA.

LUCENTIO Fiddler, forbear! You grow too forward, sir.
　　　　Have you so soon forgot the entertainment
　　　　Her sister Katherine welcomed you withal?
HORTENSIO But, wrangling pedant, this is
　　　　The patroness of heavenly harmony.　　　　　　　　　　5
　　　　Then give me leave to have prerogative,
　　　　And when in music we have spent an hour,
　　　　Your lecture shall have leisure for as much.
LUCENTIO Preposterous ass, that never read so far
　　　　To know the cause why music was ordained!　　　　　　10
　　　　Was it not to refresh the mind of man
　　　　After his studies or his usual pain?
　　　　Then give me leave to read philosophy
　　　　And, while I pause, serve in your harmony.

0 s.d. Rose (1997) had a Hortensio who was an accomplished singer, and who played this scene as a mad music professor, opening with loud and impressive singing. Reinhardt (1909): Hortensio sang scales and in Harvey (1913) Hortensio hit a long top note to show off his prowess (McDonald pbk). In Massey (1927) the modern-dress Bianca was learning the saxophone (*Boston Evening Transcript*, 4 May 1927) and in Leach (1978) Bianca was warming up her singing, and carried on with this through much of the opening of the scene. Kelly (1993): Bianca was riding a large rocking horse. Ball (1976): Bianca was grabbed by Lucentio and then Hortensio repeatedly during the first fifteen lines but through it all she kept smiling sweetly. Kyle (1982): Bianca smiled and played with a yo-yo, enjoying the mayhem she was causing. Sothern and Marlowe (1905) cut this scene entirely as part of their deep cutting of the Bianca plot (s47). Consequently the audience didn't see Lucentio revealing his identity to Bianca.

　　Gribble (1935) opened with an *AS* collage and had Sly very active in this scene – s35 gives him several lines, mostly expressing hostility towards Hortensio. *AS* has a music lesson scene (scene 4) between Kate and Valeria (Tranio), but this intersects more with the offstage Folio scene between Katherina and Hortensio (2.1.106–37) than with this scene.

1 Langham (1962): Lucentio warmed up with a few extra 'hic ibat's before beginning his speech.

9a Gribble (1935) gave this to Sly.

HORTENSIO Sirrah! I will not bear these braves of thine!   15
BIANCA Why, gentlemen, you do me double wrong
　　　To strive for that which resteth in my choice.
　　　I am no breeching scholar in the schools:
　　　I'll not be tied to hours nor 'pointed times
　　　But learn my lessons as I please myself.   20
　　　And, to cut off all strife, here sit we down.
　　　Take you your instrument; play you the whiles;
　　　His lecture will be done ere you have tuned.
HORTENSIO You'll leave his lecture when I am in tune?
LUCENTIO That will be never. Tune your instrument.   25
BIANCA Where left we last?
LUCENTIO Here, madam. [*He reads.*]
　　　Hic ibat Simois, hic est Sigeia tellus,
　　　Hic steterat Priami regia celsa senis.
BIANCA Conster them.   30
LUCENTIO *Hic ibat* – as I told you before; *Simois* – I am Lucentio;
　　　hic est – son unto Vincentio of Pisa; *Sigeia tellus* – disguised thus
　　　to get your love. *Hic steterat* – and that Lucentio that comes a-
　　　wooing; *Priami* – is my man Tranio; *regia* – bearing my port;
　　　celsa senis – that we might beguile the old pantaloon.   35
HORTENSIO Madam, my instrument's in tune.
BIANCA Let's hear. [*He plays.*] O fie! The treble jars.
LUCENTIO Spit in the hole, man, and tune again.

---

15 Dews (1981): Lucentio and Hortensio slapped each other's faces. Ayliff (1928): Hortensio bit Lucentio's hand.

16–21 Shrewish Biancas often give a hint of their true temperament here, e.g. Hodgman (1991).

25 Allison (1982): as Bianca ran her fingers up and down the lute strings suggestively, the prospect of tuning his instrument became very attractive to Hortensio, business Bianca repeated at line 38. 25b Gribble (1935) gave to Sly. Leiber (1921, 1930): Hortensio responded to this line by threatening to brain Lucentio with the lute.

28–9 The Latin is often sent up in modern productions: e.g. Dews (1981) had the 'Hic's delivered loud and high, sounding like a hiccup, and making everyone jump. In Gribble (1935) Sly responded to this with Grumio's line from 1.2.27 ''tis no matter . . . what he ledges in Latin'.

30 'Construe' usually replaces the less familiar 'conster', e.g. Ball (1976).

31–2 Ball (1976): Bianca registered Vincentio's importance and realised what a catch Lucentio was.

33 Burrell (1947); Tranio-as-Lucentio appeared at a window, and at line 35 Gremio appeared.

38 Cut in Asche (1899), possibly as suggestive. Given to Sly in Gribble (1935), Payne (1935).

BIANCA Now let me see if I can conster it. *Hic ibat Simois* – I know
you not; *hic est Sigeia tellus* – I trust you not; *Hic steterat Priami* –   40
take heed he hear us not; *regia* – presume not; *celsa senis* –
despair not.
HORTENSIO Madam, 'tis now in tune.
                    [*He plays again.*]
LUCENTIO   All but the bass.
HORTENSIO The bass is right; 'tis the base knave that jars.
           [*Aside*] How fiery and forward our pedant is!   45
           Now, for my life, the knave doth court my love.
           Pedascule, I'll watch you better yet.
BIANCA In time I may believe, yet I mistrust.
LUCENTIO Mistrust it not, for sure Aeacides
           Was Ajax, called so from his grandfather.   50
BIANCA I must believe my master, else, I promise you,
           I should be arguing still upon that doubt.
           But let it rest. Now, Litio, to you.
           Good master, take it not unkindly, pray,
           That I have been thus pleasant with you both.   55
HORTENSIO [*To Lucentio*]
           You may go walk, and give me leave awhile.
           My lessons make no music in three parts.
LUCENTIO Are you so formal, sir? Well, I must wait –
           [*Aside*] And watch withal, for, but I be deceived,
           Our fine musician groweth amorous.   60
HORTENSIO Madam, before you touch the instrument
           To learn the order of my fingering,
           I must begin with rudiments of art,

41 'presume not' is sometimes a response to an attempted kiss, e.g. Guthrie (1954).
43b Given to Sly in Gribble (1935).
45–7 Benthall (1948): Hortensio delivered these lines as a confidence to Sly.
49–52 The classical reference is sometimes cut, e.g. Kelly (1993).
59–60 Gribble (1935) gave these lines to Sly.
61 Dews (1981): 'instrument' got a laugh as Bianca was sitting on the floor and Hortensio
     moved his lute at just the right moment so that she ended up with her face in his groin. In
     Monette (1988) Hortensio's instrument was a double bass and there was much business as
     he arranged Bianca's legs so that she could play the instrument.
62 Bridges-Adams (1920): Hortensio broke the first of several strings.

To teach you gamut in a briefer sort,
More pleasant, pithy and effectual   65
Than hath been taught by any of my trade;
And there it is in writing, fairly drawn.
BIANCA Why, I am past my gamut long ago.
HORTENSIO Yet read the gamut of Hortensio.
BIANCA [*Reads*]
    '*Gamut* I am, the ground of all accord: 70
    A re, to plead Hortensio's passion;
    B mi, Bianca, take him for thy lord;
    C fa ut, that loves with all affection;
    D sol re, one clef, two notes have I;
    E la mi, show pity or I die.'   75
Call you this 'gamut'? Tut, I like it not!
Old fashions please me best. I am not so nice
To change true rules for odd inventions.

        Enter a SERVANT.

SERVANT Mistress, your father prays you leave your books,
And help to dress your sister's chamber up.   80

69 Hortensios often flash their real identity at Bianca here: e.g. in Heap (1985) Hortensio flung
open his black cape and revealed his habitual bright white costume underneath. Kyle
(1982): Hortensio revealed his distinctive leopard-skin leggings.

70–5 The gamut in Monette (1988) was done as a rap. In Rose (1997) it became a mock opera
showpiece. Kelly (1993) used a version of 'Do re mi' from *The Sound of Music*. Ball (1976)
had Hortensio sing the lines he had written and he got so carried away that Bianca had to
shut him up by stuffing his gamut in his mouth. Komisarjevsky (1939): Hortensio moved his
chair closer with each line, while Bianca moved her chair away. Williams (1973): Bianca sang
the gamut and Sly joined in the last line. Leach (1978): Bianca sang the gamut
enthusiastically, trilling impressively. Miller (1980): once he'd been rejected Hortensio ate
his gamut. Asche (1899) cut the gamut entirely.

78 Instead of a servant Harvey (1913) had Baptista come and hurry Bianca along. Baptista then
stayed on and the scene played straight on without a break into 3.2. (s58, and McDonald
pbk). Schaefer (1956): Hortensio attempted to embrace Bianca whereupon she broke his
lute over his head, thus revealing 'that behind her pink and white façade there's some of the
shrew in her, too' (final pbk).

79–81 Barton (1960): these lines were given to the Prompter, an otherwise silent but very visible
presence in this production, who spoke the lines very fast, panicking at suddenly being
centre stage.

You know tomorrow is the wedding-day.
BIANCA Farewell, sweet masters both, I must be gone.
                              [*Exeunt Bianca and Servant*]
LUCENTIO Faith, mistress, then I have no cause to stay.   [*Exit*]
HORTENSIO But I have cause to pry into this pedant:
          Methinks he looks as though he were in love.   85
          Yet if thy thoughts, Bianca, be so humble
          To cast thy wand'ring eyes on every stale,
          Seize thee that list! If once I find thee ranging
          Hortensio will be quit with thee by changing.   *Exit*

81 Benson (1890), following *C&P*, brought Katherina's wedding-day forward to 'today' (see also 2.1.382).

83–end Ayliff (1928) ran 4.2.37–42, which meant that Hortensio from this point on was no longer interested in Bianca. Gribble (1935) had the Tranio and Lucentio discussion from 3.2.128–38 here.

89 *Sauny the Scot* runs this scene straight on into Katherina's wedding, as did e.g. Daly (1887). Ayliff (1928) used some of *AS* Interlude 1 here, Williams (1973) used *AS* Interlude 2 (see Appendix 1, p. 236). Kelly (1993) used an *AS* collage and closed with Sly trying to kiss Bartholomew, and then chasing him offstage.

Enter BAPTISTA, GREMIO, TRANIO [*disguised as Lucentio*],
KATHERINA, BIANCA, [LUCENTIO *disguised as Cambio,*] *other*
GUESTS *and* ATTENDANTS.

BAPTISTA [*To Tranio*]   Signor Lucentio, this is the 'pointed day
       That Katherine and Petruchio should be married,

---

0 s.d. Many productions bring on Hortensio, which makes sense as his friend Petruchio is getting
married, although sometimes it is difficult for Hortensio to change from his disguise in 3.1 in
time to make the opening entry. Several productions have also assigned Hortensio lines
appropriate to his role as friend to Petruchio (see comments on improved continuity at 1, 7,
21–5, 64, 79–80, 114–16), although the Folio gives them to Tranio, who has only recently met
Petruchio. This practice started as early as *C&P*.

The grander the wedding, the greater the humiliation for Katherina when Petruchio
doesn't show up. Daly (1887) reduced some of Katherina's embarrassment by cutting her
from the opening of 3.2 (which played straight on from 3.1) and instead presenting simply a
dialogue between Baptista and Tranio (s34). Sothern and Marlowe (1905) had the widow in
attendance (s48). Ayliff (1928) also added the widow, dressed very fashionably, plus a
character identified as 'Auntie', among the guests. Langham (1962) had red carpet and lively
choirboys 'leaping upon one another's shoulders and skipping rope in their bright red
cassocks' (*New York Herald Tribune*, 21 June 1962). Monette (1988) had several newspaper
photographers present, and Biondello was keeping watch with binoculars.

Devices used to emphasise how late Petruchio is include: Lynch (1991) had tableaux of
bored guests waiting, with blackouts to indicate time passing; Ayliff (1928), Monette (1998)
had a crowd sensation at the noise of an approaching car and then huge disappointment
when the car didn't stop. Schaefer (1956): Baptista, Katherina, Bianca and Lucentio all
scanned the horizon with telescopes (pbk). Eyre (1971), which was set in an Edwardian pub,
had the pub pianist play 'There was I waiting at the church . . .' (*Listener*, 20 December
1973). Kaut-Howson (2001): as the guests all stood waiting there were comic routines with
the buzzing from, and then killing of, two flies.

Some Katherinas are still resistant: e.g. in Kyle (1982) Katherina's wedding dress was
black. Bogdanov (1978) also struck a gloomy note with a preponderance of black umbrellas
onstage. Marowitz (1973) has an opening ceremony of Kate being dressed like a doll with *a
vague sense of being the victim of some grim, unwanted social ceremony* (Marowitz 51).
The huge-skirted 1950s wedding frock in Hodgman (1991) created added comedy as
Katherina stormed around the stage, creating a minor whirlwind.

And yet we hear not of our son-in-law.
What will be said? What mockery will it be
To want the bridegroom when the priest attends   5
To speak the ceremonial rites of marriage!
What says Lucentio to this shame of ours?
KATHERINA No shame but mine. I must, forsooth, be forced
To give my hand, opposed against my heart,
Unto a mad-brain rudesby, full of spleen,   10
Who wooed in haste and means to wed at leisure.
I told you, I, he was a frantic fool,
Hiding his bitter jests in blunt behaviour.
And to be noted for a merry man,
He'll woo a thousand, 'point the day of marriage,   15
Make feast, invite friends, and proclaim the banns,
Yet never means to wed where he hath wooed.
Now must the world point at poor Katherine
And say, 'Lo, there is mad Petruchio's wife
If it would please him come and marry her!'   20

Gribble (1935), picking up on Grumio's opening speech in 4.1 decided it was winter and opened with wind howling, snow falling and 'people marching to keep warm, rubbing hands, stamping feet' (s65). Baptista and Gremio had colds. Katherina had the production's four male dwarfs as bridesmaids, dressed in 'snowwhite and wearing orange blossoms' (*San Francisco Examiner*, 14 November 1939).

1 'Lucentio' here and in line 7 is sometimes changed to 'Hortensio', e.g. Bogdanov (1978). Benson (1890): the real Lucentio stepped forward and realised his mistake. Kyle (1982) changed 'Lucentio' to 'Licio' (also at line 7) (pbk), which seems to create as many problems as it solves.

7 'Lucentio' is sometimes changed to 'Hortensio', e.g. Cottrell (1973).

10 Allison (1982): Katherina was heart-broken, which seemed odd as she had been very resistant to the marriage at her last appearance. Over the years that Bridges-Adams (1920) flourished the *Stratford-Upon-Avon Herald* (e.g. 12 August 1927, 13 July 1928) repeatedly discussed why on earth Katherina turns up to her wedding when she hasn't agreed to wed Petruchio.

12 Gribble (1935): Katherina started hitting her attendant dwarfs with her bouquet.

17 Ayliff (1928): 'Auntie' voiced her sympathy for Katherina.

18 Trevis (1985): the Widow and Bianca, who were holding the wedding canopy, gave up and put it down.

20 Benson (1890): Bianca went to comfort Katherina, who slapped her hard on the hand. Guthrie (1954): the Cook had a comic crying routine here. Ball (1976): Katherina turned the final 'r' of 'her' into a growl and ran off.

TRANIO Patience, good Katherine, and Baptista too.
Upon my life, Petruchio means but well,
Whatever fortune stays him from his word.
Though he be blunt, I know him passing wise;
Though he be merry, yet withal he's honest.   25
KATHERINA Would Katherine had never seen him though!
Exit weeping [followed by Bianca and others]
BAPTISTA Go, girl. I cannot blame thee now to weep,
For such an injury would vex a very saint,
Much more a shrew of thy impatient humour.

Enter BIONDELLO.

BIONDELLO Master, master, news! And such old news as you never   30
heard of!
BAPTISTA Is it new and old too? How may that be?
BIONDELLO Why, is it not news to hear of Petruchio's coming?
BAPTISTA Is he come?
BIONDELLO Why no, sir.   35
BAPTISTA What then?
BIONDELLO He is coming.
BAPTISTA When will he be here?
BIONDELLO When he stands where I am and sees you there.
TRANIO But say, what to thine old news?   40
BIONDELLO Why, Petruchio is coming in a new hat and an old jerkin;

21-5 Sometimes given to Hortensio, e.g. Cottrell (1973). Others, e.g. Carey (1954), cut 24–5, the
lines which suggest close knowledge of Petruchio.

29 Sothern and Marlowe (1905): Katherina threw her bouquet of white roses at Baptista before
taking a late exit (s47). Gribble (1935) inserted 4.2.1–53a here, advancing the Bianca plot,
and having Hortensio withdraw from the competition.

30 Komisarjevsky (1939) gave all of Biondello's speeches up to line 76 to 'Baptista's Servant'.

41-56 A *tour de force* in the right hands, this speech makes very big demands on Biondello.
Gribble (1935) had huge crowd reactions, and Guthrie (1954) played up the *effects* of the
speech as 'a whole stageful of people staggered under the scatter-shot of Biondello's verbal
assault, sinking at last into exhaustion' (Robertson Davies, 53). Biondellos often enact the
horse's diseases: e.g. Ball (1976), Rose (1997); the latter also had three journalists taking
notes. Cass (1935) had Biondello rattle off the speech 'with the machine gun speed of a
Gilbert and Sullivan patter song' (Williamson 1948, 8). Many productions slim down the
speech: e.g. Ayliff (1928) cut two thirds. Miller (1980): as Katherina stayed on and heard this
speech, presumably Petruchio's appearance was less of a surprise to her. Kyle (1982):
Baptista kept attempting, but failing, to interrupt.

a pair of old breeches thrice turned; a pair of boots that have been
candle-cases, one buckled, another laced; an old rusty sword tane
out of the town armoury, with a broken hilt and chapeless; with
two broken points; his horse hipped – with an old mothy saddle   45
and stirrups of no kindred – besides, possessed with the glanders
and like to mose in the chine; troubled with the lampass, infected
with the fashions, full of windgalls, sped with spavins, rayed with
the yellows, past cure of the fives, stark spoiled with the staggers,
begnawn with the bots, swayed in the back and shoulder-shotten,   50
near-legged before, and with a half-cheeked bit and a headstall of
sheep's leather, which, being restrained to keep him from stum-
bling, hath been often burst and now repaired with knots; one
girth six times pieced, and a woman's crupper of velour, which
hath two letters for her name fairly set down in studs, and here and   55
there pieced with packthread.

BAPTISTA Who comes with him?

BIONDELLO O sir, his lackey, for all the world caparisoned like the
horse, with a linen stock on one leg and a kersey boot-hose on the
other, gartered with a red and blue list; an old hat and the humour   60
of forty fancies pricked in't for a feather; a monster, a very monster
in apparel, and not like a Christian footboy or a gentleman's lackey.

TRANIO 'Tis some odd humour pricks him to this fashion,
    Yet oftentimes he goes but mean-apparelled.

BAPTISTA I am glad he's come, howsoe'er he comes.   65

BIONDELLO Why, sir, he comes not.

BAPTISTA Didst thou not say he comes?

BIONDELLO Who? That Petruchio came?

BAPTISTA Ay, that Petruchio came.

---

45 Bogdanov (1978): there was a big reaction in this modern-dress production to 'horse'.
Petruchio did subsequently enter accompanied by a pantomime horse, and leading a brass
band.

46 ff. Dews (1981) and several subsequent Stratford, Ontario, productions substituted modern
terms for many unfamiliar words in this speech such as 'pustules' for 'glanders'.

58–62 Kyle (1982): this speech was delivered as a racing commentary with Biondello standing
crouched like a jockey on a horse.

59–61 'with . . . feather' cut in many modern-dress productions, e.g. Ayliff (1928).

64 This line suggests someone who has known Petruchio a long time and so it is sometimes
given to Hortensio, e.g. Monette (1988 pbk).

69 Reinhardt (1909): the stressed Baptista screamed this line.

BIONDELLO No, sir, I say his horse comes with him on his back.   70
BAPTISTA Why, that's all one.
BIONDELLO Nay, by Saint Jamy,
　　　　I hold you a penny,
　　　　A horse and a man
　　　　Is more than one,   75
　　　　And yet not many.

70　Lloyd (1956): Baptista threw Biondello into the orchestra.

72–6　Gribble (1935) made this into a big sing-song, but the lines are often cut, e.g. Bridges-Adams (1920). Williams (1973) added a 'Hey nonny no' at the end.

76 s.d.　In Phelps (1856), Sothern and Marlowe (1905) (s47) Petruchio *and* Grumio were wielding whips, and there is some justification for this if the whips are linked to the descriptions of Petruchio's wretched horse, which presumably needs whipping in order to get it to move. Pantomime horses often appear, e.g. in Benthall (1948). Hauser (1960) had Brewster Mason as a 'virile and resonantly braggadocio' Petruchio (*Oxford Times*, 29 April 1960) make a show-stopping entrance here on a horse 'built around the actor, with ridiculously short dummy legs hugging its middle' (*Oxford Mail*, 27 April 1960). Walford (1987): Petruchio appeared as 'the front legs of a camel' with 'a talking parrot on his shoulder' (Liverpool *Daily Post*, 6 February 1987). Monette (1988): Petruchio had fitted a huge plastic horse shape onto his Vespa, while Grumio wore a horse-shaped swimming ring. Guthrie (1954) had a Wild West pantomime horse with Petruchio and Grumio dangerously brandishing pistols, while Rose (1997) had Petruchio and Grumio as cowboys with fake guns and fake horses. Bell (1994): the hippie Petruchio arrived 'at the wedding with his overladen, gypsy bicycle-drawn cart' (*Theatre Australasia*, June 1994). Allison (1982): Petruchio arrived on a cart pulled by Grumio pretending to be a horse.

Petruchio's sartorial excesses have included Gascon (1973): Petruchio wore 'a striped bathing suit of 1900 vintage and a plumed Roman helmet' with 'ribbons, scabbard and sword' (*Sarnia Observer*, 5 June 1973); Antoon (1990): Petruchio looked like 'a hybrid of Davy Crockett, Pancho Villa and Sitting Bull' (*NYT* 13 July 1990); Kelly (1993): Petruchio was a fertility figure on stilts, dressed in green, covered in flowers and with a sheep's-head hat. Kyle (1982): Petruchio was accompanied by Morris dancers and Grumio wore a white wedding dress. Grumio was also dressed as a woman in Martin-Harvey (1934) (*Oxford Mail*, 8 March 1934). Marowitz (1973) had Petruchio in a wedding dress (Marowitz 152), and in Posner (1999) both Petruchio and Grumio wore Elizabethan dresses, with Petruchio's looking very similar to the dress Katherina had been wearing earlier. Guthrie (1939): Petruchio wore Victorian corsets in red, white and blue (Trewin 178). Norman Marshall commented that in Ayliff (1928) the insult to Katherina was particularly clear when 'Petruchio, dressed in a top hat, a red handkerchief round his neck, morning coat, highly coloured pullover, a pair of khaki breeches, a riding boot on one foot and a patent leather

Enter PETRUCHIO *and* GRUMIO.

PETRUCHIO Come, where be these gallants? Who's at home?

BAPTISTA You are welcome, sir.

PETRUCHIO   And yet I come not well.

BAPTISTA And yet you halt not.

TRANIO   Not so well apparelled

    As I wish you were.   80

PETRUCHIO Were it better, I should rush in thus.

    But where is Kate? Where is my lovely bride?

    How does my father? Gentles, methinks you frown,

    And wherefore gaze this goodly company

    As if they saw some wondrous monument,   85

    Some comet or unusual prodigy?

BAPTISTA Why, sir, you know this is your wedding-day.

    First were we sad, fearing you would not come,

    Now sadder that you come so unprovided.

    Fie, doff this habit, shame to your estate,   90

    An eye-sore to our solemn festival.

TRANIO And tell us what occasion of import

    Hath all so long detained you from your wife

shoe on the other, was seen against a crowd dressed with the formal correctitude of the guests at a fashionable wedding at St George's, Hanover Square' (Marshall 172). *AS* has *Enter* FERANDO *basely attired and a red cap on his head* (*AS* 4.107 s.d.).

    As was appropriate in a commedia production, Reinhardt (1909) had Grumio executing lots of gambols during this sequence. Ball (1976): Petruchio swung onstage on a rope, Tarzan style. Miller (1987): everyone crowded upstage to catch the first glimpse of the staggering sight, while Petruchio and Grumio casually entered downstage.

  77 Langham (1962) played *AS* Interlude 2 (see Appendix 1, p. 236) here.

79b–80a Sometimes given to Hortensio, e.g. Cottrell (1973), as Petruchio's friend.

  81 Nunn (1967) inserted 'not' after 'it'.

  83 Hodgman (1991): Petruchio gave Baptista a big kiss after 'father'. Ayliff (1928) had cries of shame from Bianca, the Widow and 'Auntie'. Guthrie (1954): Petruchio pointed his pistol at Baptista causing a great sensation as Petruchio appeared to be not in full control of this weapon, which went off several times during the next few lines.

  89 Benthall (1955): Grumio knelt and polished Petruchio's shoes, and then brushed his clothes in response to this criticism.

92ff. *C&P* (2.83–5) gave this speech to Hortensio.

And sent you hither so unlike yourself.

PETRUCHIO Tedious it were to tell, and harsh to hear.   95
Sufficeth I am come to keep my word
Though in some part enforcèd to digress,
Which at more leisure I will so excuse
As you shall well be satisfied with all.
But where is Kate? I stay too long from her.   100
The morning wears, 'tis time we were at church.

TRANIO See not your bride in these unreverent robes;
Go to my chamber, put on clothes of mine.

PETRUCHIO Not I, believe me; thus I'll visit her.

BAPTISTA But thus, I trust, you will not marry her.   105

PETRUCHIO Good sooth, even thus. Therefore ha' done with words;
To me she's married, not unto my clothes.
Could I repair what she will wear in me
As I can change these poor accoutrements,
'Twere well for Kate and better for myself.   110
But what a fool am I to chat with you
When I should bid good morrow to my bride
And seal the title with a lovely kiss!

Exit [*with Grumio*]

97–9 Often cut, e.g. Burrell (1947).

101 Ball (1976): Petruchio attempted to rush off but was stopped by the crowd. This was repeated at line 104 and he finally fought his way through to exit at line 113.

102–3 *C&P* (2.90–1) gave this speech to Hortensio. Devine (1953) gave the lines to Baptista.

107 Miller (1980) identified this as the most important line in the play (Hallinan 139). Shouted in Alexander (1992); Petruchio then said the rest of the speech with deadly seriousness. Schaefer (1956) imported Petruchio's lines from 4.3.169–72, which reiterate his argument that appearance is not important.

113 *C&P* (2.102) introduced 'What ho! my Kate!' here, while *K&P* first records the joke of Grumio echoing what Petruchio says. It became traditional for Grumio to repeat Petruchio's phrases 'parrot-like' (*St James's Gazette*, 30 November 1904), to copy his gestures, and while Petruchio called out for his 'bonny, bonny Kate', Grumio substituted 'bony' for 'bonny' (Benson (1890) s42). Asche (1899) took a scene break here and moved the action indoors with Lucentio 'discovered' sitting in a window seat with Tranio standing (pbk). This was also a scene break in e.g. Harvey (1913).

113 s.d. Rose (1997): there was an offstage scream from Katherina, as she first caught sight of Petruchio.

TRANIO He hath some meaning in his mad attire.
         We will persuade him, be it possible,   115
         To put on better ere he go to church.
BAPTISTA I'll after him and see the event of this.

                Exit [with Gremio, Biondello and Attendants]

TRANIO [To Lucentio] But, sir, to love concerneth us to add
         Her father's liking, which to bring to pass,
         As I before imparted to your worship,   120
         I am to get a man – whate'er he be
         It skills not much, we'll fit him to our turn –
         And he shall be Vincentio of Pisa
         And make assurance here in Padua
         Of greater sums than I have promisèd.   125

---

114 Dews (1981) had an offstage peal of church bells, followed by Petruchio dragging Katherina
     across the stage at full gallop with the entire wedding party following.

114–16 *C&P* (2.103–5) gave this speech to Hortensio but e.g. Monette (1988) cut the lines. Gribble
     (1935): Petruchio's lines as reported by Gremio, plus Latin from the priest, music and
     general noise could be heard offstage.

117 *AS* Interlude 2 (see Appendix 1, p. 236) is often played around here, e.g. Payne (1935).

118 This transition, as Ann Thompson's commentary suggests, is 'very awkward' and many
     productions – e.g. Ayliff (1928) – simply started a new scene here. Tranio appears to be mid-
     speech and, unless he and Lucentio have been seen to be conferring earlier, this is
     unexpected. Wells and Taylor argue that 3.2 shows signs of rewriting and discuss the
     attempt in Nunn (1967) to improve continuity by adding 'a new bridging speech for
     Lucentio' to make the sense clearer (361). Burrell (1947) had a wild, wordless Sly section
     which involved Sly chasing 'his 'wife', catching 'her' and spanking 'her', the Lord killing a flea
     and everyone applauding. After an interlude as lively as this, the jolting transition would not
     be so noticeable. Antoon (1990) added a speech for Lucentio 'Now to our business'. Sothern
     and Marlowe (1905) (s47) had Tranio begin after a very big processional exit, s49 recording
     that 'Petruchio is pulling Katherine to church against her will'. Productions such as Anglin
     (1908), which start a new scene here, have fewer problems and, as the pbk for Jewett (1915)
     indicates, can use the 'curtain lowered to indicate lapse of time' before Gremio's account of
     the wedding (s59). Miller (1987) had a straightforward exit, a parade of the wedding
     procession across the stage, with Katherina being dragged entirely unwillingly to the
     wedding by Baptista, and a re-entrance by Tranio and Lucentio. Many filmed productions
     stage the whole wedding, e.g. Taylor (1929). Morgan (1937), a radio production, had much
     crowd chatter from outside the church to cover the wedding and then the narrator stepped
     in with a description of what was going on.

>   So shall you quietly enjoy your hope
>   And marry sweet Bianca with consent.
> LUCENTIO Were it not that my fellow schoolmaster
>   Doth watch Bianca's steps so narrowly,
>   'Twere good, methinks, to steal our marriage,   130
>   Which once performed, let all the world say no,
>   I'll keep mine own despite of all the world.
> TRANIO That by degrees we mean to look into
>   And watch our vantage in this business.
>   We'll overreach the greybeard Gremio,   135
>   The narrow-prying father Minola,
>   The quaint musician, amorous Litio,
>   All for my master's sake, Lucentio.

> *Enter Gremio.*

>   Signor Gremio! Came you from the church?
> GREMIO As willingly as e'er I came from school.   140
> TRANIO And is the bride and bridegroom coming home?
> GREMIO A bridegroom, say you? 'Tis a groom indeed –
>   A grumbling groom, and that the girl shall find.
> TRANIO Curster than she? Why, 'tis impossible.
> GREMIO Why, he's a devil, a devil, a very fiend!   145
> TRANIO Why, she's a devil, a devil, the devil's dam!
> GREMIO Tut, she's a lamb, a dove, a fool, to him.
>   I'll tell you, Sir Lucentio: when the priest
>   Should ask if Katherine should be his wife,
>   'Ay, by gogs-wouns!' quoth he, and swore so loud   150
>   That, all-amazed, the priest let fall the book,

127 Hawthorn (1979): reaction off, suggestive of the cuffing of the priest (cf. 153–4).

132 Hawthorn (1979): reaction off, suggestive of wine thrown in the sexton's face (cf. 162–3).

138 Ayliff (1928) started a third scene here, and a wedding photographer entered. Trevis (1985): Lucentio and Tranio embraced, and then hastily parted as Gremio entered. Bogdanov (1978): Biondello warned that Gremio was approaching so Lucentio and Tranio resumed the disguises they had doffed at line 118. Cottrell (1973): on radio the shift from Tranio's 'normal' voice to his assumed posh voice was very pronounced. Komisarjevsky (1939) played most of 4.2.59–end here, considerably advancing the Bianca plot.

142 Dews (1981): Gremio milked a helpless laughter routine.

151 Guthrie (1954): Sly interjected 'He didn't' at the end of the line.

And as he stooped again to take it up,
This mad-brained bridegroom took him such a cuff
That down fell priest and book, and book and priest!
'Now take them up', quoth he, 'if any list.'   155
TRANIO What said the wench when he rose again?
GREMIO Trembled and shook, for why he stamped and swore
As if the vicar meant to cozen him.
But after many ceremonies done
He calls for wine. 'A health', quoth he, as if   160
He had been aboard, carousing to his mates
After a storm; quaffed off the muscadel
And threw the sops all in the sexton's face,
Having no other reason
But that his beard grew thin and hungerly   165
And seemed to ask him sops as he was drinking.
This done, he took the bride about the neck
And kissed her lips with such a clamorous smack
That at the parting all the church did echo.
And I, seeing this, came thence for very shame,   170
And after me, I know, the rout is coming.
Such a mad marriage never was before!
          Music plays.
Hark, hark! I hear the minstrels play.

Enter Petruchio, Katherina, Bianca, Hortensio [as Litio], Baptista,
[Grumio and others].

155 Miller (1987): Tranio had to signal to Lucentio to resume wearing his disguise spectacles.
172 Ayliff (1928) had a collage of lines transposed from the end of the scene and newly invented
    lines for the crowd's re-entry, accompanied by bells, posed flash photographs and kisses
    from Katherina to 'Auntie' and the Widow. Bogdanov (1978) had a band playing the wedding
    march, wedding photographs and confetti. Webster (1844) had a procession and 'All dance
    to music around the stage' (S9). Phelps (1856) had 'Haste to the wedding' (pbk) and a mass
    dance. Sothern and Marlowe (1905) (S47): Petruchio whirled the priest around, bumped
    into the sexton and they both fell over. Harvey (1913) mustered 12 children, 8 minstrels and a
    full bridal procession (McDonald pbk). In Daly (1887) this was Katherina's first entrance in
    3.2, she 'did not appear till the moment of the tumultuous return of the guests' (Winter 1915,
    523–4), which slightly reduced her public humiliation.
173 Devine (1953) played *AS* 12.1, 'Look Sim, the fool is come again now!'

PETRUCHIO Gentlemen and friends, I thank you for your pains.
  I know you think to dine with me today   175
  And have prepared great store of wedding cheer,
  But so it is, my haste doth call me hence,
  And therefore here I mean to take my leave.
BAPTISTA Is't possible you will away tonight?
PETRUCHIO I must away today, before night come.   180
  Make it no wonder; if you knew my business,
  You would entreat me rather go than stay.
  And, honest company, I thank you all
  That have beheld me give away myself
  To this most patient, sweet and virtuous wife.   185
  Dine with my father, drink a health to me,
  For I must hence, and farewell to you all.
TRANIO Let us entreat you stay till after dinner.
PETRUCHIO It may not be.
GREMIO   Let me entreat you.
PETRUCHIO It cannot be.
KATHERINA   Let me entreat you.   190
PETRUCHIO I am content.
KATHERINA   Are you content to stay?

174 Guthrie (1954) staged a massed wedding photograph before Petruchio's speech. Leach (1978): Katherina was trying to pull off her wedding ring.

178 The unpublished Stage Journal of Flora Macdonald Mayor (stage name Mary Strafford) for January 1901 relates that as 'a lady of the household' in Benson (1890): 'We have to make a commotion at Petruchio's refusal to stay for the banquet . . . When Petruchio draws his sword we all get terrified – one faints, another supports her, two jump up on the seats, I crouch and pray and cover my eyes, the men draw their swords, one falls wounded and the Lady ministers to him.' In addition walkers-on were expected to keep up 'an animated flow' of reaction dialogue (quoted in Oldfield 78).

185 Sothern and Marlowe (1905): at each adjective the guests gave suppressed laughs (s48).

188 Alexander (1990) gave this line to Hortensio.

189b Harvey (1913) gave this line to Baptista (McDonald pbk).

190 Daly (1887): said 'tenderly' (s34).

191a Rider (1994): Katherina sat down, relieved; she then realised the catch. Miller (1987) had the signing of the marriage register onstage at this point. Petruchio signed on line 189a, Katherina on line 191a, Petruchio's 'I am content' (pbk). Once Katherina had signed and was committed to the marriage, Petruchio's real meaning was made clear to her.

PETRUCHIO I am content you shall entreat me stay –
　　　　But yet not stay, entreat me how you can.
KATHERINA Now, if you love me, stay.
PETRUCHIO　　　　　　　　Grumio, my horse!
GRUMIO Ay, sir, they be ready – the oats have eaten the horses.　　　195
KATHERINA Nay then,
　　　　Do what thou canst, I will not go today!
　　　　No, nor tomorrow – not till I please myself.
　　　　The door is open, sir, there lies your way;
　　　　You may be jogging whiles your boots are green.　　　200
　　　　For me, I'll not be gone till I please myself.
　　　　'Tis like you'll prove a jolly surly groom
　　　　That take it on you at the first so roundly.
PETRUCHIO O Kate, content thee; prithee be not angry.
KATHERINA I will be angry. What hast thou to do?　　　205
　　　　– Father, be quiet. He shall stay my leisure.

193 Dews (1981): Sly laughed and clapped.
194a Hodgman (1991): on 'stay' Katherina pointed sternly to the floor, as if addressing a dog. Bell (1994): Katherina said her part of the line very uncertainly and tremulously and Petruchio's response was equivalent to a slap in the face. Heap (1985): the crowd registered Petruchio's response as indicating he didn't love Katherina. Patton (1984): Frey (1985, 488) records 'after Kate's line, Petruchio started to kiss her. She turned away. Only then, in reaction, did Petruchio call for his horse, at which point Kate acted out a tantrum.' Daly (1887): this line was said 'imploringly' (S34) and Speaight (80) remembered Rehan's voice, which elsewhere 'could cut like a knife or ring like a bell', suddenly softening on this line. Winter (1915, 524) thought Rehan's tone 'a singular blending of dread and supplication . . . spoken as though intended for [Petruchio's] hearing only'.
194b Leach (1978): Katherina went into a screaming fit, thrashing around on the floor so violently that 'she all but kicks a hole in the stage' (*NYT* 18 August 1978) and all the other characters ran away.
196 ff. Reinhardt (1909): Petruchio whistled and sang through this speech.
197 Patton (1984): Katherina threw a tantrum on 'I will not go today!'; when Petruchio used the same line at 4.3.188 he mocked 'Kate's tantrum at the Church' (Frey 488).
202–3 Sothern and Marlowe (1905): S45 records that Petruchio made kissing noises here.
203 Ayliff (1928): the Widow laughed loudly.
205 Guthrie (1954): Katherina hit both Petruchio and Baptista.
206 'Father, be quiet' is often said before Baptista has even half started to say anything, e.g. Barton (1960).

GREMIO Ay, marry, sir, now it begins to work.

KATHERINA Gentlemen, forward to the bridal dinner.
    I see a woman may be made a fool
    If she had not a spirit to resist.   210

PETRUCHIO They shall go forward, Kate, at thy command.
    Obey the bride, you that attend on her.
    Go to the feast, revel and domineer,
    Carouse full measure to her maidenhead,
    Be mad and merry – or go hang yourselves.   215
    But for my bonny Kate, she must with me.
    Nay, look not big, nor stamp, nor stare, nor fret;
    I will be master of what is mine own.
    She is my goods, my chattels; she is my house,
    My household-stuff, my field, my barn,   220
    My horse, my ox, my ass, my anything,
    And here she stands. Touch her whoever dare,
    I'll bring mine action on the proudest he
    That stops my way in Padua. Grumio,

209–10 Hodgman (1991): Katherina spoke these lines directly to the audience.

210 Sothern and Marlowe (1905): at the end of Katherina's speech there were 'murmurs of approval from Ladies' (s47).

211–28 Rose (1997): as Petruchio delivered this speech through a microphone it was extremely emphatic. The speech functioned as a conventional wedding address and as a party political broadcast. Ball (1976): Petruchio delivered the first four lines as if crushed, defeated and depressed, which made the turn around at line 215 more striking. Marowitz (1973): as Petruchio delivers this speech he strips off his wedding dress *revealing his male attire underneath* (Marowitz 155).

212 Benthall (1955): Petruchio began winding Katherina up in her own wedding train in which he then carried her off.

214 The reference to 'maidenhead' used to be routinely cut, e.g. Webster (1844).

216 Burrell (1947), one of very few productions where Baptista and his friends actually attempt to rescue Katherina, degenerated into a tug of war over her, and ended with most characters on the floor. Antoon (1990): the cowboy Petruchio lassoed Katherina here.

218 Miller (1987) spelt out his vision of early modern Puritan ideals here by having Petruchio take a prayer book from the Priest and flourish it, as if it backed up every word he said.

221 Sothern and Marlowe (1905): 'Exclamation of horror from guests' (s48). Lloyd (1956): on 'ass' Katherina kicked Petruchio.

224 In Rider (1994), where Petruchio was a Second World War returned serviceman, he and Grumio did a fixed-bayonets charge.

Draw forth thy weapon – We are beset with thieves!   225
Rescue thy mistress, if thou be a man.
– Fear not, sweet wench, they shall not touch thee, Kate;
I'll buckler thee against a million!

225 Ayliff (1928): the blackshirted, fascist-looking Grumio drew a revolver. Barton (1960):
Petruchio got out his whip, while Grumio was wielding a blunderbuss.

226 Rose (1997): Grumio's gun let off a bullet which ricocheted around and caused a member of
the wedding party to have a heart attack. The victim's widow later married Hortensio.

228 s.d. It is traditional for Petruchio to throw Katherina over his shoulders, in classic caveman style,
and charge out, although the *Daily Express* (30 November 1904) thought the applause for
Oscar Asche's rendition of this exit was 'remarkable in these days of feminism'. Productions
going for a strong curtain for Petruchio and Katherina finish the scene here (e.g. Benson
1890). Payne (1935) finished here and had Sly exit carrying Bartholomew in imitation of
Petruchio. Burrell (1947) also finished here and had almost everyone else on stage fall on
their backs, waving their legs in the air, while Sly cheered, arms held high. Sothern and
Marlowe (1905): in New York they exited on a horse with Grumio on a donkey (s47). Harvey
(1913) was originally contemplating using a horse (s58) but instead settled for 'the cheers of
a group of 12 children and a fanfare from the musicians' (Macdonald 70). Edith Evans in
Gurney (1937) was carried off on a pantomime horse (*ILN* 10 April 1937). Gribble (1935):
Petruchio and Grumio formed a cat's cradle to lift Katherina and place her facing backwards
onto the pantomime horse, where she was 'nearly bounced out of her clothes as she and
the horse exit', while acrobats tumbled all around (s65). Webster (1844): Buckstone as
Grumio received three rounds of applause for 'the way in which he drew his sword and
followed *Petruchio* off the stage' (*Morning Post*, 18 March 1844) and the *Morning Herald* (18
March 1844) stated that the production's 'most effective scene' was where Petruchio 'bears
[Katherina] off sword in hand, after their return from church'. Williams (1973) had Katherina
'rolled away, after the marriage, in a tub' (*BP* 26 September 1973). Daly (1887): Ada Rehan's
Katherina was carried off hoisted high, facing front and held up by the waist, presumably to
avoid the indignity of her being bundled over Petruchio's shoulder (s28). Sothern and
Marlowe (1905): Katherina sought to escape from Petruchio by climbing onto a seat, thus
making it easier for Petruchio to hoist her onto his shoulders (s47).

Some modern productions have tried to indicate that Katherina takes the decision herself
to go with Petruchio: Liz Taylor in Zeffirelli's 1967 film had ample opportunity to abandon
her marriage, as Petruchio and Grumio galloped off without her, but she took a considered
decision to follow them and leave Paduan life behind. Hodgman (1991) certainly gave all the
initiative here to Katherina. She got on Petruchio's Vespa, he had to scramble to get on the
back, and, after hitching up her huge bridal dress, she drove off. At the very end of the
scene, when the stage had cleared, the Vespa roared across the stage again, with Katherina

Exeunt Petruchio, Katherina [and Grumio]

BAPTISTA Nay, let them go – a couple of quiet ones!

GREMIO Went they not quickly, I should die with laughing.   230

TRANIO Of all mad matches never was the like.

LUCENTIO Mistress, what's your opinion of your sister?

BIANCA That being mad herself, she's madly mated.

GREMIO I warrant him, Petruchio is Kated.

BAPTISTA

    Neighbours and friends, though bride and bridegroom
        wants   235

    For to supply the places at the table,

    You know there wants no junkets at the feast.

    [*To Tranio*] Lucentio, you shall supply the bridegroom's
        place,

still driving and Petruchio as passenger. In Lynch (1991) Katherina was left alone onstage, thought hard about her situation and then took the decision to follow Petruchio. Rider (1994): Petruchio got onto his Vespa, started to ride off on his own but then stopped and looked back. Katherina decided he was worth the gamble, but she had 'to run to jump on the back' of the Vespa (*Theatre Australasia*, May 1994). A disempowered version of Katherina choosing her own destiny appeared in Miller (1987) where Katherina walked off, presumably in the direction of Verona, after 'Petruchio . . . thumbs through a Bishop's Bible to justify his view of a wife's role . . . Kate then seizes the Bible from him to see if that is what it really says before hurling it at the priest's feet in angry resignation' (*G* 8 September 1988). Fiona Shaw, who played Katherina, believed 'it's a tough revelation to discover that your protection, the bible, is also your danger – a book telling you you're nothing. . . . [a]nd that's why I throw the bible down and *choose* to go with Petruchio' (Rutter 14).

    Daly (1887) finished the scene here but used some of 3.2's remaining lines to open the next act, running 4.2 and 4.4 before then running 4.1 (534). 532 includes the direction that Katherina 'takes his whip from [Petruchio's] belt: lashes him', business which had become popular in productions of *C&P*.

    In *Sauny the Scot* the strong exit speech was given to Sauny (Grumio) (3.1.252–4).

229 Bogdanov (1978): some of the wedding party moved as if to rescue Katherina but Baptista's line stopped them.

230 Allison (1982) finished the scene on this line as Gremio nearly collapsed into the fountain. Komisarjevsky (1939) gave the line to Sly, also line 234.

238 Heap (1985): both Lucentio and Tranio stepped forward when Baptista mentioned the name 'Lucentio'.

And let Bianca take her sister's room.
TRANIO Shall sweet Bianca practise how to bride it?   240
BAPTISTA She shall, Lucentio. Come, gentlemen, let's go.

Exeunt

240 Bogdanov (1978): Tranio kissed Bianca's hand and got a poke with an umbrella from
     Lucentio. In Alexander (1992) Tranio accepted the invitation with glee, despite Lucentio's
     frantic signals that he shouldn't, and kissed Bianca with enthusiasm.

241 This is where the interval is usually taken, often after a big clap trap. Monette (1988) had an
     Italian song and dance routine. Rose (1997) closed with the announcement of Petruchio's
     Alitalia flight to Italy departing from gate 37. Ayliff (1928): the gum-chewing photographer
     was chased by 'the entire wedding party' down 'through the auditorium' (Cochrane 134)
     and everything was filmed by a newsreel camera man. Harvey (1913): the scene ended with
     a 'view of the bridal procession across the terrace at the far end of the apartment' in the
     Lord's mansion where the travelling players were performing (*Eastern Morning News*, 5
     March 1913), although Poel had originally suggested an exit on horseback (s58) and that Sly
     should climb up on the stage and demand in pantomime that 'the leading actor and
     actress . . . be brought before him'. Then 'Sly congratulates them and offers them drink'
     which Katherina refuses and Petruchio 'can laughingly accept' before 'They all retire
     together' (s58). Komisarjevsky (1939) went into the interval with a nonsense song
     performed by Sly.

     In *Sauny the Scot*, 3.2 led straight into the equivalent of 4.2.

     Unusually Alexander (1992) did not take the interval here but carried on until after 4.1,
     where the production started forcing the 'Lords' to participate in the play acting. 3.2 closed
     with everyone onstage gazing out across the stalls as if following the progress of Katherina,
     Petruchio and Grumio off into the distance.

ACT 4   SCENE 1

Enter GRUMIO.

GRUMIO   Fie, fie on all tired jades, on all mad masters, and all foul ways!
Was ever man so beaten? Was ever man so rayed? Was ever man so

The journey to Petruchio's house, although not a scene written by Shakespeare, has often
been played on film. Taylor (1929): Katherina, on arriving at Petruchio's house, fell off the
back of his horse and into the mud, in which pigs were wallowing. Zeffirelli (1967):
Katherina tumbled into a pond after urging her donkey to a take a precipitous short cut, in
order to overtake Petruchio. In the theatre, in Gascon (1973) Katherina travelled to
Petruchio's house on a 'horse', played by two actors: the horse 'stumbles and falls upon her,
and is berated by Petruchio' (*Sarnia Observer*, 5 June 1973) but then a rainbow banner
opened, and a chorale started. Edwards (1995) reprised the stormy opening of her
production, thus reminding the audience of the Sly framework.

Petruchio's house has offered many horrors to Katherina including, in Kelly (1993), a
Jackson Pollock-style studio, awash with canvases and paint. Bell (1994) had a hippie
commune, signalled by sitar music in the radio broadcast. Kaut-Howson (2001) had a biker
household, full of hairy, crusty, head-banging servants. Rose (1997) opened with a flight
attendant's announcement, in Italian, that they had arrived in Verona. The action then
moved to a brown, drab, rustic home, lit by torches of fire and inhabited by Bosch-like
grotesques, a far cry from Baptista's elegant New Padua (New York) home, and here
Katherina was to be tamed partly 'by depriving her of the luxuries of her American home'
(*G&M*, 5 June 1997). Mellor (1989): Petruchio's home was 'as macabre and grotesque as the
castle of Gormenghast and with the roughest rugby team of servants you ever saw' (*Courier
Mail*, 19 August 1989). Antoon (1990) played this as 'a lovely, wintry nocturnal scene' and
Grumio's stories were told 'while his audience of cowpokes thaws out by a warm stove'
(*NYT* 13 July 1990). Monette (1988) had a chintzy house, equipped with a Welsh dresser full
of crockery.

Coughing and sneezing gags by Grumio have been popular, e.g. Bridges-Adams 1920, but
generally the scene is vulnerable to deep cutting, e.g. Harvey (1913), because some jokes
have not worn well, and because not all casts can summon up that many servants: e.g.
Lynch (1991) had audience members reading some servants' lines. Petruchio's servants
number eleven if all the speech headings (Nathaniel, Philip, Joseph, Nicholas) are added to
all those named (Walter, Sugarsop, Gregory, Gabriel, Peter, Adam, Rafe) and commercial
productions usually downsize them. Rose (1997) Italianised the servants into Antonio,
Guiseppe, Pietro and Aldo.

weary? I am sent before to make a fire, and they are coming after to
warm them. Now were not I a little pot and soon hot, my very lips
might freeze to my teeth, my tongue to the roof of my mouth, my   5
heart in my belly, ere I should come by a fire to thaw me. But I with
blowing the fire shall warm myself, for, considering the weather, a
taller man than I will take cold. Holla, ho! Curtis!

Enter CURTIS.

CURTIS Who is that calls so coldly?

GRUMIO A piece of ice. If thou doubt it, thou mayst slide from my   10
      shoulder to my heel with no greater a run but my head and my
      neck. A fire, good Curtis.

CURTIS Is my master and his wife coming, Grumio?

GRUMIO O ay, Curtis, ay, and therefore fire, fire! Cast on no water.

CURTIS Is she so hot a shrew as she's reported?   15

GRUMIO She was, good Curtis, before this frost. But thou know'st
      winter tames man, woman and beast; for it hath tamed my old
      master, and my new mistress, and myself, fellow Curtis.

CURTIS Away, you three-inch fool, I am no beast!

GRUMIO Am I but three inches? Why, thy horn is a foot, and so long am   20
      I at the least. But wilt thou make a fire, or shall I complain on thee
      to our mistress, whose hand – she being now at hand – thou shalt
      soon feel, to thy cold comfort, for being slow in thy hot office.

Daly (1887) played 4.2 before 4.1 and then ran all the Petruchio's house scenes (4.1, 4.3.)
together, reducing the number of scene changes needed. This was followed in Sothern and
Marlowe (1905). Sothern and Marlowe (1905) opened 4.1 with (a female) Curtis discovered
trying to decide on a suitable dress for the occasion (s47) and Grumio entered carrying a
saddle (s47).

    Line 3 of *AS* Interlude 2 (see Appendix 1, p. 236) has been, used here, e.g. Barton (1960).

  4 'little': in her commentary Thompson suggests that the original performer of the role of
Grumio was short. See also lines 8 and 19–20.

  8 Gribble (1935) had a curtain, and moved from the exterior of Petruchio's house to the
interior.

8 s.d. For 150 years after *C&P* Curtis was a woman. In Ayliff (1928) Grumio summoned Curtis by
blowing down a speaking tube. In Alexander (1990, 1992) Curtis was the first role to be
forced upon the reluctant Lord's party, who participated grudgingly and incompetently.

20–1 Some productions cut, e.g. Reinhardt (1909), but in Lynch (1991) Grumio and Curtis turned
their backs on the audience and compared their 'three inches'. In Alexander (1992) the line
generated dirty laughs from the onstage audience.

CURTIS I prithee, good Grumio, tell me, how goes the world?

GRUMIO A cold world, Curtis, in every office but thine, and   25
therefore, fire. Do thy duty, and have thy duty, for my master
and mistress are almost frozen to death.

CURTIS There's fire ready, and therefore, good Grumio, the news.

GRUMIO Why, 'Jack boy, ho boy!' and as much news as wilt thou.

CURTIS Come, you are so full of cony-catching.   30

GRUMIO Why, therefore fire, for I have caught extreme cold.
Where's the cook? Is supper ready, the house trimmed, rushes
strewed, cobwebs swept, the servingmen in their new fustian,
their white stockings, and every officer his wedding garment on?
Be the Jacks fair within, the Jills fair without, the carpets laid,   35
and everything in order?

CURTIS All ready, and therefore, I pray thee, news.

GRUMIO First know my horse is tired, my master and mistress fallen
out.

CURTIS How?   40

GRUMIO Out of their saddles into the dirt, and thereby hangs a tale.

CURTIS Let's ha't, good Grumio.

GRUMIO Lend thine ear.

CURTIS Here.

GRUMIO There.   45

[*He boxes Curtis's ear.*]

CURTIS This 'tis to feel a tale, not to hear a tale.

GRUMIO And therefore 'tis called a sensible tale; and this cuff was but
to knock at your ear and beseech listening. Now I begin. *Imprimis*
we came down a foul hill, my master riding behind my mistress.

CURTIS Both of one horse?   50

GRUMIO What's that to thee?

CURTIS Why, a horse.

GRUMIO Tell thou the tale. But hadst thou not crossed me, thou

24 Burrell (1947): the *Morning Advertiser* (10 November 1947) reported great hilarity when the
aged retainer 'pauses to ask: "How goes the world?" when there is an urgent need for him
to prepare a fire'.

28 Ayliff (1928): Curtis 'produced an electric stove' (Marshall 171).

45 s.d. This had added impact in Alexander (1990) where Curtis was being played by one of the
Lord's party.

53 ff. Benthall (1948): this narrative was played to Sly. Alexander (1992): after saying 'Tell thou the
tale', Grumio walked off and abandoned Curtis (played by one of the Lord's party) who was
left completely floundering.

shouldst have heard how her horse fell, and she under her horse;
thou shouldst have heard in how miry a place, how she was   55
bemoiled, how he left her with the horse upon her, how he beat
me because her horse stumbled, how she waded through the dirt
to pluck him off me, how he swore, how she prayed that never
prayed before, how I cried, how the horses ran away, how her
bridle was burst, how I lost my crupper – with many things of   60
worthy memory which now shall die in oblivion, and thou
return un-experienced to thy grave.

CURTIS By this reckoning he is more shrew than she.

GRUMIO Ay, and that thou and the proudest of you all shall find
when he comes home. But what talk I of this? Call forth   65
Nathaniel, Joseph, Nicholas, Philip, Walter, Sugarsop and the
rest. Let their heads be slickly combed, their blue coats brushed,
and their garters of an indifferent knit. Let them curtsy with
their left legs, and not presume to touch a hair of my master's
horse-tail till they kiss their hands. Are they all ready?   70

CURTIS They are.

CRUMIO Call them forth.

CURTIS Do you hear, ho? You must meet my master to countenance
my mistress.

GRUMIO Why, she hath a face of her own.   75

CURTIS Who knows not that?

GRUMIO Thou, it seems, that calls for company to countenance her.

CURTIS I call them forth to credit her.

GRUMIO Why, she comes to borrow nothing of them.

Enter four or five SERVINGMEN.

NATHANIEL Welcome home, Grumio.   80
PHILIP How now, Grumio.

---

59 Rider (1994): Grumio paused before admitting he 'cried'. Nunn (1967): Sly reacted strongly
to this narrative.

60 The bridle and crupper get cut in modern-dress productions, e.g. Ayliff (1928).

64 In Alexander (1990, 1992) 'the proudest of you all' was addressed to the Lord's party.

79 s.d. Lynch (1991) used audience members to read out some of the servants' lines, as did
Midgley (1990) (*I* 19 July 1990). Alexander (1990, 1992) used more of the Lord's party. Ayliff
(1928) converted Petruchio's servants into women and inspired a diatribe from W. J.
Lawrence (*Stage*, 2 June 1928), who argued that the absence of female servants from
Petruchio's house is an important part of Katherina's suffering. Drinkwater (1918) also made
the servants female because of the shortage of men due to the war.

JOSEPH What, Grumio.

NICHOLAS Fellow Grumio.

NATHANIEL How now, old lad.

GRUMIO Welcome you; how now you; what you; fellow you; and   85
    thus much for greeting. Now, my spruce companions, is all
    ready, and all things neat?

NATHANIEL All things is ready. How near is our master?

GRUMIO E'en at hand, alighted by this. And therefore be not –
    Cock's passion, silence! I hear my master.   90

Enter PETRUCHIO *and* KATHERINA.

PETRUCHIO Where be these knaves? What, no man at door
    To hold my stirrup, nor to take my horse?
    Where is Nathaniel, Gregory, Philip?

ALL SERVINGMEN Here! Here sir, here sir!

PETRUCHIO 'Here sir, here sir, here sir, here sir'!   95
    You logger-headed and unpolished grooms!
    What, no attendance? No regard? No duty?
    Where is the foolish knave I sent before?

GRUMIO Here sir, as foolish as I was before.

PETRUCHIO You peasant swain! You whoreson malthorse drudge!   100
    Did I not bid thee meet me in the park
    And bring along these rascal knaves with thee?

GRUMIO Nathaniel's coat, sir, was not fully made,

---

83 Daly (1887): Nicholas's line was given to 'Gregory' tying in with line 93 (S34).

90 Noises-off often cue this line: shouts, the sound of a whip cracking, e.g. Harvey (1913)
    (McDonald pbk).

90 s.d. Much whip-cracking often ensues, e.g. Asche (1899). In Rose (1997) the servants sang a
    welcome song for Katherina. In Posner (1999) Katherina entered with a large red streak on
    her upper arm, which was evidently very painful as she winced when Petruchio touched it.
    This production stressed Petruchio's violence and his beatings of Grumio were vicious.

91 Benson (1890): the female Curtis moved to attend to Katherina, who swept her aside and in
    Daly (1887) Katherina frightened Curtis away (S34).

97 Komisarjevsky (1939) had the traditional nineteenth-century gag here, which was to have
    the servants hanging on to each other's coat tails and falling over like dominoes.

103 ff. Often cut, e.g. Sothern and Marlowe (1905) (S47). Devine (1953) tried to rationalise the
    servants here and changed line 104 'Gabriel' into 'Gregory', line 106 'Walter' into 'Philip' and
    line 107 'Adam' and 'Rafe' into 'Peter' and 'Paul'.

And Gabriel's pumps were all unpinked i'th'heel.
There was no link to colour Peter's hat   105
And Walter's dagger was not come from sheathing.
There were none fine but Adam, Rafe and Gregory;
The rest were ragged, old and beggarly.
Yet, as they are, here are they come to meet you.
PETRUCHIO Go, rascals, go, and fetch my supper in.   110

Exeunt Servingmen

[*Sings*] Where is the life that late I led?
Where are those –
Sit down, Kate, and welcome. Food, food, food, food!

Enter Servants with supper.

Why, when, I say? Nay, good sweet Kate, be merry.
Off with my boots, you rogues, you villains! When?   115
[*Sings*] It was the friar of orders grey
As he forth walkèd on his way –
Out, you rogue! You pluck my foot awry.
Take that!

[*He strikes the Servant.*]
And mend the plucking off the other.
Be merry, Kate. Some water here! What ho!   120

Enter one with water.

111 Avoiding the temptation to sing along to Cole Porter, in Dews (1981) Petruchio sang this
     song in a sad, wavery voice. In Monette (1988) he sang in Italian and the servants all joined
     in. In Hodgman (1991) the song was an Elvis impersonation. Burrell (1947) finished the
     broken-off line 112 with 'happy days'.
113 Dews (1981): 'Food, food . . .' was shouted and woke up the dozing Katherina.
114 Kelly (1993): Petruchio banged a gong immediately behind Katherina.
115 Alexander (1992): Petruchio kicked the servant taking off his boot, played by 'Lady Sarah
     Ormsby'.
116 Guthrie (1954): the servants lined up and swayed in time to the song. Devine (1953, 1954)
     added lots of tra la las. Sothern and Marlowe (1905) had Petruchio signal to Curtis that she
     should get fresh clothes for Katherina, who was then taken behind a screen in order to get
     changed (548).
120a A charged line in Miller (1987) where Katherina was manic depressive.

Where's my spaniel Troilus? Sirrah, get you hence
And bid my cousin Ferdinand come hither –
[*Exit a Servant*]
One, Kate, that you must kiss and be acquainted with.
Where are my slippers? Shall I have some water?
Come, Kate, and wash, and welcome heartily.   125
You whoreson villain! Will you let it fall?
[*He strikes the Servant.*]
KATHERINA Patience, I pray you. 'Twas a fault unwilling.
PETRUCHIO A whoreson, beetle-headed, flap-eared knave!
Come, Kate, sit down, I know you have a stomach.

121 'Troilus' is often followed by enthusiastic whistling and shouting to summon the dog, e.g.
Sothern and Marlowe (1905) (s48). Dunlop (1962) brought on a spaniel (*Nottingham
Evening Post*, 7 February 1962). Rose (1997) had a loud bark as if from a great dane offstage.
Kyle (1982): having roused a monstrous, offstage Troilus, Petruchio had to fight with his
crop to keep this beast safe in the wings. Lynch (1991): Troilus was a glove-puppet dog and
suddenly appeared from behind an overturned table. Nunn (1967) was praised by the
Spectator (11 August 1967) for 'the beetleheaded, flap-eared knaves, deaf and blind, none a
day less than ninety, wambling shakily over the stage with hopeless whispering
endearments in search of their master's unbiddable spaniel, Troilus'.

122 Monette (1988): Ferdinand appeared onstage in his pyjamas, 'a drooling, slack-jawed idiot
who never speaks', a 'trick' which was 'simply distasteful' (*Stratford Beacon Herald*, 2 June
1988). By contrast the *Toronto Sun* (3 June 1988) read Ferdinand's presence as showing
Petruchio's compassionate side. Miron (1992): Ferdinand had punk Mohawk hair and
Katherina, despite her own punk appearance, was dismayed at the prospect of kissing him
(*Toronto Star*, 25 September 1992). Kaut-Howson (2001) had a huge, mop-head, hairy beast
of a Ferdinand erupt onstage and tear around: Petruchio and his biker servants spent some
time calming him down and getting him to return to some offstage lair.

126 Katherina often gets a soaking, e.g. Dews (1981), Hodgman (1991), although in pantomime
style Ball (1976) had bits of paper instead of water fall on Katherina. 'Whoreson' was cut
(also line 128): e.g. Daly (1887) (s34) and Gribble (1935) substituted 'stupid'. Alexander
(1990): the servant who got slapped (hard) was played by 'Mrs Ruth Banks-Ellis' from the
Lord's party.

128 Benson (1890): Petruchio kissed Curtis. Female Curtises were usually motherly and when
Benson used a young Curtis the kiss became 'somewhat problematic' for the *Stratford-
Upon-Avon Herald* (28 April 1916). Miller (1987) had a full fight here, with Katherina trying
to stop it, and the servant getting the better of Petruchio.

129 Daly (1887): Petruchio had to repeat the command 'sit down' three times before he got a
response (s34). Rehan's Katherina also reacted to 129b by turning away, and her 'shudder

Will you give thanks, sweet Kate, or else shall I?   130
What's this? Mutton?
FIRST SERVINGMAN   Ay.
PETRUCHIO   Who brought it?
PETER   I.
PETRUCHIO 'Tis burnt, and so is all the meat.
What dogs are these! Where is the rascal cook?
How durst you villains bring it from the dresser

---

indicated plainly that even in the outspoken age of Shakespeare, women do not like to be told such trite truths' (*NYT* 19 January 1904).

130   Barton (1960): grace was said in Latin very fast. Monette (1988): grace went on for a very long time, with repeated false finishes. Carey (1954) had everyone in two lines, palms together and after Petruchio said grace Katherina added 'Ah! Men!' (*ILN* 11 December 1954). Sothern and Marlowe (1905): Petruchio beckoned Katherina to bow her head; she would not 'whereupon Petruchio with his hand forces down her head. Katherine raises her head indignantly' (s48).

In the 1756 production of Garrick *C&P*, Woodward, when Petruchio 'and his bride are at supper' actually 'stuck a fork, it is said, in Mrs Clive's finger; and in pushing her off the stage he was so much in earnest that he threw her down: as it is well known that they did not greatly respect one another, it was believed that something more than chance contributed to these excesses' (Thomas Davies I, 312).

132   Webster (1844): after calling for the Cook 'Petruchio rushes at him and seizes him by the ear, and rubs the shoulder or leg of mutton in his face, blackening his nose &c.' (*Morning Chronicle*, 18 March 1844). The burnt mutton joke was still being used as late as Williams (1931), which still had 'the traditional leg of mutton that tantalises poor Kate . . . hard and soot-encrusted as of old' (*O* 18 October 1931). As the *Athenaeum* repeatedly pointed out (e.g. 15 October 1870, 26 June 1875) this makes Petruchio's reaction reasonable, when he is meant to be acting *unreasonably*. The *Pall Mall Gazette* (30 November 1904) applauded Asche (1899) for being 'almost revolutionary' in not having mutton 'burnt to a cinder' but then could not understand why Asche used chicken instead of mutton. Unwin (1998) had a banquet of takeaway burgers and pizzas. Bogdanov (1978): Petruchio tore the meat apart. Robertson (1983) had the meat as too hot to handle and it was thrown round the room, 'until an excited Sly ran up, caught the meat, and took it back to his chair to nibble on it as the play continued' (Hageman 223). Williams (1973) started an orgy of food throwing here: which included 'a carrot floating down on a parachute', planted audience members 'pelting the stage with prop vegetables' (*G* 26 September 1973) and Katherina getting a trifle in her face.

133   The 'dogs' were sausages in e.g. Nickell (1950). Daly (1887) had 'hurry' music here (s532).

And serve it thus to me that love it not?   135
There, take it to you, trenchers, cups and all!
[*He throws the food and dishes at them.*]
You heedless joltheads and unmannered slaves!
What, do you grumble? I'll be with you straight.
                                    [*Exeunt Servants*]
KATHERINA I pray you, husband, be not so disquiet.
The meat was well, if you were so contented.   140
PETRUCHIO I tell thee, Kate, 'twas burnt and dried away,
And I expressly am forbid to touch it,
For it engenders choler, planteth anger;
And better 'twere that both of us did fast,
Since, of ourselves, ourselves are choleric,   145
Than feed it with such over-roasted flesh.
Be patient. Tomorrow't shall be mended,
And for this night we'll fast for company.
Come, I will bring thee to thy bridal chamber.
                                            Exeunt

136 s.d. A Charles Kemble copy of *K&P* (s6) has Katharine hiding under the table. Sothern and
Marlowe (1905): Sothern's Petruchio 'apparently in sheer enjoyment of his masterful and
masculine strength, threw the joint clear across the stage into the proscenium box' where it
landed on a young woman's lap (*NYT* 17 October 1905). Benthall (1948): Sly and
Bartholomew joined in the custard-pie throwing. Gribble (1935): the cook had his face
pushed in a plate of mashed potato.

137 Guthrie (1954): Petruchio chased Grumio around Sly's bed.

139 Harvey (1913): Petruchio discovered Katherina hiding under the table, and the picture was
held before she delivered her line (McDonald pbk). Rose (1997): Katherina was careful over
the unfamiliar word 'husband' (pbk). Leach (1978): Katherina started hiding food up her
sleeve.

140 Ayliff (1928): Petruchio and Katherina struggled over possession of the meat.

146 Sothern and Marlowe (1905): as Petruchio crossed behind Katherina he performed a tender
pantomime of kissing his fingers, touching her hair and 'then he pats her head with fingers
of both hands' (s48). Leach (1978): Katherina had the meat in her mouth and as Petruchio
pulled it away from her she was growling like a dog.

149 After Petruchio and Katherina exited, Harvey (1913) had the servants' heads gradually
reappearing 'from various nooks and crannies' (*ES* 12 May 1913). Some Katherinas are very
nervous at this exit: e.g. in Miller (1987) Fiona Shaw as Katherina stressed that 'it's this man
who beats servants now taking her to bed' (Rutter 15). By contrast in Lynch (1991) both

Enter Servants severally.

NATHANIEL Peter, didst ever see the like?   150
PETER He kills her in her own humour.

Enter Curtis.

GRUMIO Where is he?
CURTIS In her chamber,
          Making a sermon of continency to her,
          And rails and swears and rates, that she, poor soul,   155
          Knows not which way to stand, to look, to speak,
          And sits as one new-risen from a dream.
          Away, away, for he is coming hither.
                                                          [*Exeunt*]

Enter Petruchio.

PETRUCHIO Thus have I politicly begun my reign,
          And 'tis my hope to end successfully.   160

Katherina and Petruchio were grinning excitedly. Similarly in Nunn (1967) Petruchio was
enthusiastic: 'he strips to the waist, scratches his chest, and utters a Tarzan mating cry' (*ES* 6
April 1967). *K&P* has Katharine protest, 'Fast? Go to bed without my supper thus?', and
Phelps (1856) elaborated on this: 'Katharine: Oh I want my supper. Petruchio: You want your
supper – you want a fiddlestick', lines Phelps had already used in performances of *K&P* in
1850. Katherina also protested about her loss of supper in e.g. Daly (1887) (534). Devine
(1953, 1954): Katherina successfully stole some bread but in Leach (1978) the food she had
hidden in her clothing now all fell out.

150   Rose (1997): as noises were heard from bridal chamber, the servants sang 'Nessun Dorma'.
       Trevis (1985): the actors gazed up at the ceiling 'to imagine what was happening to Kate in
       the bedroom' (Howard 186). At the equivalent point in *AS* there is the s.d., *Manent
       servingmen and eat up all the meat* (*AS* 6.32 s.d.) and Marcus (112) suggests the players
       were supposed to be hungry enough not to let the food requested in *AS* 1.83–4, and
       provided by the Lord, go to waste.

151   Harvey (1913): Sly warned the servants that Petruchio was returning (McDonald pbk).

152   Burrell (1947) swapped speeches here and rejigged Grumio, who not only had Curtis's
       explanatory words here but remained onstage for Petruchio's 'soliloquy', giving Petruchio a
       tankard at the beginning and sitting, listening, throughout.

156   Gribble (1935): two pillows, sheets and a coverlet came flying out from the balcony. When
       Petruchio entered he was dragging a feather bed with him and Grumio brought him a
       platter of food.

159 ff. This is a crucial speech which will affect how the audience feel about the treatment of
       Katherina. Sometimes the speech is addressed to Sly: e.g. Dews (1981), where Petruchio

joined Sly on his balcony, and Trevis (1985), where Petruchio poured Sly a glass of wine before starting to speak. Gribble (1935): the speech was addressed to Grumio. Bernard Beckerman (333) was disgusted that in Anthony (1965) Petruchio addressed 'his servants, that is, makes a report to the help on how he is doing with his wife'. Benthall (1955) brought on Hortensio, and had the soliloquy addressed to him, while Petruchio ate a sausage. Other Petruchios have fortified themselves with a cigarette and champagne (Bogdanov 1978), or a sandwich (Nickell 1950). Reinhardt (1909): Petruchio appeared nervous but after eating some food ended up singing.

Broad comedy Petruchios include Webster (1844) who had Petruchio speak and crack his horsewhip while his servants were trying to pick up the spilled food (*Morning Chronicle*, 18 March 1844). In Heap (1985) Petruchio delivered part of the speech as a Richard III parody. Komisarjevsky (1939): Petruchio entered carrying all the bedclothes with him. In a top speed comic production the calmness with which this speech was spoken in Ball (1976) contrasted with the frenzied pace of the rest of the play and made it particularly memorable.

The hawking image was made literal in Kyle (1982) where Petruchio carried an actual falcon on his arm; this production's Katherina, Sinead Cusack, thought (Rutter 4) the way Petruchio 'gentled the falcon' was 'liberating her to a role that she was going to enjoy playing', just like Katherina, and the *Guardian* (13 October 1982) commented as 'the speech progresses [Petruchio] lifts the protective mask from the falcon's beak and raises the bird aloft in a gesture of symbolic freedom. The point is clear: by "taming" Kate he has released her true unfettered spirit.' However, Penny Gay (1994, 113) argues that this memorable stage image 'legitimise[s] Petruchio's view of Kate', objectifying her as a bird about to be domesticated.

Attempts to soften the speech have been made: Sothern and Marlowe (1905) had extended, almost fetishistic business whereby Petruchio played lovingly with Katherina's 'soiled stockings', which Curtis had hung up to dry, and kissed the toes of her white slippers several times. At the end of the scene Katherina crept on in the sabots she now had to wear and looked unsuccessfully for food, while Petruchio pretended to snore. As she exited Petruchio kissed her slippers again (S47). Asche (1899), which kept Grumio onstage, had Petruchio going to put Katherina's cloak in front of the fire to dry, in order to indicate his care of her. Monette (1988 pbk) went for inclusive language and changed the repeated 'she' of lines 168–9 to 'we'. Kelly (1993) had Katherina overhear Petruchio, which allowed Katherina to understand what Petruchio thought he was doing. Because Petruchio looked up and saw that Katherina was listening, there was a sense that Katherina was almost agreeing to go along with Petruchio's plans. More gutsily in Taylor (1929) Mary Pickford's Katherina, who also overheard Petruchio, then exited to the bedroom, determined to outdo Petruchio in all his excesses.

Some productions stress Katherina's suffering here, e.g. Edwards (1995), where Katherina appeared upstage, unable to hear Petruchio's words, but clearly a woman in trauma. Allison (1982) was much less serious about Katherina's sufferings but still had

My falcon now is sharp and passing empty,
And till she stoop she must not be full-gorged,
For then she never looks upon her lure.
Another way I have to man my haggard,
To make her come and know her keeper's call,   165
That is, to watch her, as we watch these kites
That bate and beat and will not be obedient.
She ate no meat today, nor none shall eat;
Last night she slept not, nor tonight she shall not.
As with the meat, some undeservèd fault   170
I'll find about the making of the bed,
And here I'll fling the pillow, there the bolster,
This way the coverlet, another way the sheets.
Ay, and amid this hurly I intend
That all is done in reverend care of her.   175
And, in conclusion, she shall watch all night,

Katherina standing behind Petruchio in such a state of exhaustion that she didn't register what he said. Rose (1997): *Petruchio* was seen to be suffering, exhausted, and only faintly hopeful that the plan would work. In Vaughan (1956) Petruchio gasped the opening of the speech 'in such a state of exhaustion that the audience laughs' (*Literary Review*, 25 August 1956).

    The speech almost disappeared from Benson (1890), who cut it apart from the last two lines and went straight into 4.3, and from Zeffirelli (1967) where Richard Burton's drunken Petruchio seemed to have very little idea as to what he was doing with Katherina.

160 Kelly (1993): Petruchio stressed 'hope' making the speech sound quite tentative (*Yorkshire Post*, 20 April 1993).

161–7 The whole hawking metaphor is sometimes cut, e.g. Harvey (1913).

169 Heap (1985) got a dirty laugh.

170 ff. In *Sauny the Scot*, the wrecking of the bed is played onstage 'in a Bed-Chamber' (3.3.0 s.d.) after Margaret (Katherina) has been threatened with being undressed by manservants. Margaret is then forced to drink beer and smoke tobacco. The wrecking of the nuptial bed also featured in the film of Taylor (1929). By contrast Maniutiu (1995) cut 'all the lines about throwing the bed around' while the audience saw a 'duvet heave and roll, in strobe lighting that climaxes with a firework' indicating that athletic sex was what was depriving Katherina of sleep (*T* 28 April 1995).

175 Monette (1988): Petruchio stressed 'in reverend care of her' as if he meant it.

176 A few Katherinas have a sexually exciting wedding night. In Walford (1987) there was 'plenty of fun with the honeymooners under canvas' (*Stage*, 26 February 1987). More usually,

And if she chance to nod I'll rail and brawl
And with the clamour keep her still awake.
This is a way to kill a wife with kindness,
And thus I'll curb her mad and headstrong humour.   180
He that knows better how to tame a shrew,
Now let him speak – 'tis charity to show.   *Exit*

productions stress the couple's sexual abstinence until the marital power struggle is
resolved.

180 Guthrie (1954): Petruchio exited but then returned for the last two lines as an afterthought.

181 Kelly (1993): Petruchio here looked up at Katherina on the balcony, acknowledging that she
     had heard the speech.

182 Petruchios often pause after 'speak' as if in hope of a reply, e.g. Ball (1976). Bogdanov
     (1978): Petruchio's appeal was 'followed by a pause of almost half a minute' (*FT* 30 April
     1979). The video of Leach (1978) records a woman shouting out and suggesting Petruchio try
     a little tenderness. Raúl Juliá, the Petruchio, suggested that would be less dramatic but
     added 'I thank thee for thy advice.' Generally video records of performance document this
     speech being enthusiastically applauded, e.g. Monette (1988). Taylor (1929): Troilus, who
     had been the audience for the speech, barked. Miron (1992) played a blast of the Animals'
     'Don't Let Me Be Misunderstood' (*G&M* 30 September 1992). Asche (1899): Petruchio and
     Grumio toasted Katherina together. Harvey (1913): Sly commented, 'He knows how to tame
     a shrew' (McDonald pbk). Creswell (1935, 1941): on radio Sly noisily applauded Petruchio's
     speech. Ayliff (1928) used a collage of fragments from *AS*, with Sly claiming he now
     knew how to tame a shrew and the Lord reminding him it was only a play. When Balliol
     Holloway's Petruchio, in Leigh (1925), 'took the gallery into his confidence and, with that
     irresistible, all-embracing swagger, detailed the hideous paces he intended to put Kate
     through, it was all one could do not to shout a responsive "Right-o!" ' (*O* 1 November 1925).
     Gurney (1937) had Katherina visible on her bridal couch (formerly Sly's bed) trying to sleep
     'while a group of dancers enact her husband's speech' (*Stage*, 25 March 1937) and 'modish
     fantasts . . . twitch the sheets from Kate's bridal bed and leave her speechless' (*O* 28 March
     1937). Anthony (1965): as Katherina locked the bedroom door, Petruchio had to break it
     down with 'a battering ram as big as a telephone pole' (*New York Herald Tribune*, 24 June
     1965).
     Daly (1887) carried straight on to 4.3 (534), and this transposition was still happening as
     late as Gribble (1935) and Komisarjevsky (1939). Unusually, Alexander (1992) took the
     interval here, after a scene in which the Lord's party had been roughly manhandled. Posner
     (1999) also took the interval here.

ACT 4   SCENE 2

Enter TRANIO [*disguised as Lucentio*] *and* HORTENSIO
[*disguised as Litio*].

TRANIO Is't possible, friend Litio, that mistress Bianca
Doth fancy any other but Lucentio?
I tell you, sir, she bears me fair in hand.
HORTENSIO Sir, to satisfy you in what I have said,
Stand by, and mark the manner of his teaching.   5
[*They stand aside.*]

Enter BIANCA [*and* LUCENTIO *disguised as Cambio*].

LUCENTIO Now, mistress, profit you in what you read?
BIANCA What, master, read you? First resolve me that.
LUCENTIO I read that I profess, *The Art to Love.*
BIANCA And may you prove, sir, master of your art.
LUCENTIO While you, sweet dear, prove mistress of my heart.   10
[*They court.*]

Edwards (1995): during this scene Katherina remained visible upstage, traumatised by her suffering. Ayliff (1928) cut 4.2 very heavily (Hortensio had already renounced his interest in Bianca at the end of 3.1), and transposed what was left of the scene to the beginning of 4.4. Daly (1887) reduced scene changes by reordering the scenes to 4.2, 4.4, 4.1, 4.3 (S34). Sothern and Marlowe (1905) followed suit and had extended business with flower girls in this scene (S47). Benson (1890) ran 4.1, 4.3, 4.2, 4.4. Harvey (1913): Sly was very active in 4.2, commenting on and responding to the action (McDonald pbk). Creswell (1935, 1941) cut Tranio completely and so played this scene between Hortensio and Gremio. In the 1935 script Gremio then had Tranio's lines telling Bianca he had renounced her, a confusing device which Creswell cut when he returned to the play in 1941. This scene also bored the very active Sly who wanted to return to 'the mad knave and his froward wench' (pbk).
5 Guthrie (1954): Hortensio and Tranio ducked behind Sly's bed to observe the goings on, much to the delight of Sly. Lloyd (1956) had birds twittering during Bianca and Lucentio's courting.
10 s.d. The courting was extremely enthusiastic in Dews (1981) where Bianca and Lucentio rolled energetically on the floor, before Bianca ended up on top. Daly (1887) had the lovers exit and be observed offstage (S34).
   In *Sauny the Scot*, Tranio and Geraldo (Hortensio) directly confront Winlove (Lucentio) and Biancha at this point.

HORTENSIO Quick proceeders, marry! Now tell me, I pray,
    You that durst swear that your mistress Bianca
    Loved none in the world so well as Lucentio.
TRANIO O despiteful love, unconstant womankind!
    I tell thee, Litio, this is wonderful.   15
HORTENSIO Mistake no more – I am not Litio,
    Nor a musician as I seem to be,
    But one that scorn to live in this disguise
    For such a one as leaves a gentleman
    And makes a god of such a cullion.   20
    Know, sir, that I am called Hortensio.
TRANIO Signor Hortensio, I have often heard
    Of your entire affection to Bianca,
    And since mine eyes are witness of her lightness,
    I will with you, if you be so contented,   25
    Forswear Bianca and her love for ever.
HORTENSIO See how they kiss and court! Signor Lucentio,
    Here is my hand, and here I firmly vow
    Never to woo her more, but do forswear her
    As one unworthy all the former favours   30
    That I have fondly flattered her withal.
TRANIO And here I take the like unfeignèd oath
    Never to marry with her though she would entreat.
    Fie on her! See how beastly she doth court him.
HORTENSIO Would all the world but he had quite forsworn!   35
    For me, that I may surely keep mine oath,
    I will be married to a wealthy widow

21 Harvey (1913): when Hortensio pulled off his false moustache here Sly protested until it was explained to him that it was part of the play (Mcdonald pbk, s58).

34 Indecorous line cut by e.g. Webster (1844), Daly (1887) (534). Asche (1899) changed 'beastly' to 'basely'. Hodgman (1991): this 1950s style production staged heavy petting here and while Bianca remain fully clothed Lucentio managed to extract her bra.

35 ff. Monette (1988): Hortensio discarded a photograph of Bianca but had a new photo, of the Widow, ready to hand.

37 Some productions prepare for this line by featuring the Widow earlier. Ayliff (1928): the Widow appeared at Katherina's wedding. Rose (1997): the funeral procession for a heart-attack victim who dropped dead at Katherina's wedding now wended its way across the stage. The Widow of the victim dropped her handkerchief for Hortensio, and her cries of grief started to sound more gutturally sexual. Gribble (1935) had the Widow actually present

Ere three days pass, which hath as long loved me
As I have loved this proud disdainful haggard.
And so farewell, Signor Lucentio.   40
Kindness in women, not their beauteous looks,
Shall win my love; and so I take my leave,
In resolution as I swore before.   [*Exit*]
      [*Tranio joins Lucentio and Bianca.*]
TRANIO Mistress Bianca, bless you with such grace
    As 'longeth to a lover's blessèd case!   45
    Nay, I have tane you napping, gentle love,
    And have forsworn you with Hortensio.
BIANCA Tranio, you jest – but have you both forsworn me?
TRANIO Mistress, we have.
LUCENTIO   Then we are rid of Litio.
TRANIO I'faith, he'll have a lusty widow now   50
    That shall be wooed and wedded in a day.
BIANCA God give him joy!
TRANIO Ay, and he'll tame her.
BIANCA   He says so, Tranio?
TRANIO Faith, he is gone unto the taming-school.
BIANCA The taming-school? What, is there such a place?   55
TRANIO Ay, mistress, and Petruchio is the master,
    That teacheth tricks eleven and twenty long
    To tame a shrew and charm her chattering tongue.

during these lines, which was possible as this section was transposed into 3.2, Katherina's wedding.

40 Leach (1978) and Bogdanov (1978) used a version of 54–6 here to enable Hortensio to declare his intention of visiting the taming school. Without such a manoeuvre it is a mystery how Tranio comes by his information.

42 Allison (1982): Hortensio attempted to leave with dignity but then burst into tears.

43 Asche (1899): Bianca and Hortensio made their first entry in this scene at this point, having only been observed offstage up until then.

44 Alexander (1992): Tranio was very bitter, and genuinely jealous. He grabbed crudely at Bianca's crotch at line 46 and the rest of this section was played as a lovers' quarrel between them.

50 Benson (1890) changed 'lusty' to 'wealthy'.

53–8 Cut in e.g. Benthall (1948). The cut makes particular sense for productions omitting Hortensio from 4.3 (e.g. Devine 1954), something which in turn can explain Hortensio's surprise at Katherina's tamed state in 5.2.

Enter BIONDELLO.

BIONDELLO O master, master, I have watched so long
        That I am dog-weary, but at last I spied   60
        An ancient angel coming down the hill
        Will serve the turn.
TRANIO   What is he, Biondello?
BIONDELLO Master, a marcantant, or a pedant,
        I know not what, but formal in apparel,
        In gait and countenance surely like a father.   65
LUCENTIO And what of him, Tranio?
TRANIO If he be credulous and trust my tale,
        I'll make him glad to seem Vincentio
        And give assurance to Baptista Minola
        As if he were the right Vincentio.   70
        Take in your love, and then let me alone.
        [*Exeunt Lucentio and Bianca*]

Enter a MERCHANT.

MERCHANT God save you, sir.
TRANIO   And you, sir. You are welcome.
        Travel you farre on or are you at the farthest?
MERCHANT Sir, at the farthest for a week or two,
        But then up farther, and as far as Rome,   75

---

63 'merchant' is sometimes substituted for 'marcantant', e.g. Bell (1994).

68 Daly (1887) S31: Tranio indicated a bribe had been involved. Tranio also used the past tense
    here as the arrangement with the Pedant (Merchant) was already established (S34). This
    enabled Daly to cut line 74 to the end of the scene, and move straight on into the beginning
    of 4.4.

71 s.d. The Folio reads 'Pedant', Biondello identifies him as a 'marcantant' or a 'pedant' (line 63)
    but while 89–90 suggests this character may be a merchant, stage practice, almost without
    exception, makes the character a pedant or schoolmaster. Traditionally the Pedant
    (Merchant) is often a drunk, e.g. Antoon (1990), and sometimes has a speech impediment,
    e.g. Monette (1988). Sly is sometimes co-opted to play the Pedant (Merchant), e.g. Coffey
    (1979). Bogdanov (1978): the Pedant (Merchant) entered riding a bike and Tranio stopped
    him by making a hissing noise, making him think he had a puncture.

72 Kelly (1993) gave Lucentio extra lines here to explain the plot. Webster (1844) substituted
    'Heaven' for 'God'. Sothern and Marlowe (1905) had business with Tranio bumping into the
    Pedant (Merchant) three times as if by accident before proceeding with the dialogue (S47).

> And so to Tripoli, if God lend me life.
>
> TRANIO What countryman, I pray?
>
> MERCHANT   Of Mantua.
>
> TRANIO Of Mantua, sir? Marry, God forbid!
>
> And come to Padua careless of your life?
>
> MERCHANT My life, sir? How, I pray? For that goes hard.   80
>
> TRANIO 'Tis death for anyone in Mantua
>
> To come to Padua. Know you not the cause?
>
> Your ships are stayed at Venice, and the Duke,
>
> For private quarrel 'twixt your Duke and him,
>
> Hath published and proclaimed it openly.   85
>
> 'Tis marvel – but that you are but newly come,
>
> You might have heard it else proclaimed about.
>
> MERCHANT Alas, sir, it is worse for me than so.
>
> For I have bills for money by exchange
>
> From Florence, and must here deliver them.   90
>
> TRANIO Well, sir, to do you courtesy,
>
> This will I do, and this I will advise you –
>
> First tell me, have you ever been at Pisa?
>
> MERCHANT Ay, sir, in Pisa have I often been,
>
> Pisa renownèd for grave citizens.   95
>
> TRANIO Among them know you one Vincentio?
>
> MERCHANT I know him not, but I have heard of him,
>
> A merchant of incomparable wealth.
>
> TRANIO He is my father, sir, and sooth to say,
>
> In count'nance somewhat doth resemble you.   100
>
> BIONDELLO [*Aside*] As much as an apple doth an oyster, and all one!

---

82 Sothern and Marlowe (1905) upped the stakes for the Pedant (Merchant) as 'Guard with halberd passes . . . Tranio and Biondello stand so as to hide Pedant from guard, Biondello holds out his trousers to mask Pedant' (547). Bridges-Adams (1920): as Biondello indicated the penalty was hanging, the Pedant (Merchant) fainted. Williams (1973): Biondello imitated a death rattle.

83–5 Rose (1997) made this very Mafia: 'ships' became 'shipments'; 'Duke' became 'padre' and then 'Don' etc. and the Pedant (Merchant) was terrorised into agreeing to the deception.

98 Payne (1935): the Pedant (Merchant) bowed in acknowledgement of Vincentio's wealth.

101 'and all one' is often cut, e.g. Devine (1953). Trevis (1985): Biondello addressed this line to Sly.

TRANIO To save your life in this extremity,
        This favour will I do you for his sake –
        And think it not the worst of all your fortunes
        That you are like to Sir Vincentio –   105
        His name and credit shall you undertake,
        And in my house you shall be friendly lodged.
        Look that you take upon you as you should –
        You understand me, sir? So shall you stay
        Till you have done your business in the city.   110
        If this be court'sy, sir, accept of it.
MERCHANT O sir, I do, and will repute you ever
        The patron of my life and liberty.
TRANIO Then go with me to make the matter good.
        This, by the way, I let you understand: 115
        My father is here looked for every day
        To pass assurance of a dower in marriage
        'Twixt me and one Baptista's daughter here.
        In all these circumstances I'll instruct you.
        Go with me to clothe you as becomes you.   120

                                                 Exeunt

102–20 Sothern and Marlowe (1905) had lots of shushing jokes, increasing the idea that the Pedant
        (Merchant) was in real danger. Asche (1899) closed with business where Biondello stole a
        bread roll from the Pedant (Merchant). Nunn (1967) finished with a dance by Tranio and
        Biondello, once the Pedant (Merchant) had safely exited.

ACT 4   SCENE 3

Enter KATHERINA *and* GRUMIO.

GRUMIO No, no, forsooth, I dare not for my life!
KATHERINA The more my wrong, the more his spite appears.
　　　　　What, did he marry me to famish me?
　　　　　Beggars that come unto my father's door
　　　　　Upon entreaty have a present alms;　　　　　　　　　　5
　　　　　If not, elsewhere they meet with charity.
　　　　　But I, who never knew how to entreat,
　　　　　Nor never needed that I should entreat,
　　　　　Am starved for meat, giddy for lack of sleep,
　　　　　With oaths kept waking, and with brawling fed.　　　10

After Daly (1887) (s34) 4.3 sometimes played immediately after 4.1 to reduce scene changes, e.g Benson (1890). Ayliff (1928): Grumio entered cleaning with a carpet sweeper, and eating a banana. Bell (1994) (radio broadcast) piled on the agony for Katherina by opening with the sound of a sizzling barbecue. Kelly (1993): Katherina attacked the padlocked fridge with a crowbar. Lynch (1991): in her frustration Katherina forced the burly Grumio to the floor, pummelled his back and later judo threw him several times. Nickell (1950): Katherina tried to bribe Grumio. Gascon (1973): Katherina spent most of 4.3 dressed only in a bodice and underclothes. Komisarjevsky (1939) cut Hortensio and gave some of his lines to Grumio, thus making better sense of his surprise at Katherina's tamed state in 5.2.

1 Daly (1887) (s34) cut this line, thus creating a soliloquy for Katherina. Giving Katherina a soliloquy – which the play denies her – enables her to appeal directly to the audience in a way she is not permitted to do in the Folio text, and this cut was followed by e.g. Asche (1899), Sothern and Marlowe (1905) (s47), Guthrie (1954), although in the latter her comic yawns may have diverted attention from what Katherina was saying. Benthall (1955) also made the speech a soliloquy but upstaged it with action: Katharine Hepburn as Katherina crept on listening carefully to Petruchio's offstage snoring, climbed on a chair teetering on top of a table, and tried to reach for food that hung on a cross beam high in the air, just out of her reach. Carey (1954) created a soliloquy by having Grumio run on, chased by Katherina, say his line, and then run straight off again. Hodgman (1991): Katherina simply addressed the speech to the audience directly, ignoring Grumio. Dews (1981): Katherina was clearly distraught during her soliloquy and in Edwards (1995) she was in deep trauma. Nickell (1950) had 2–14 as a soliloquy but performed in voiceover, while Lisa Kirk tried to act out the speech's meanings with her face.

4 Kelly (1993): Katherina rummaged through the rubbish bin trying to find food.

And that which spites me more than all these wants,
He does it under name of perfect love,
As who should say, if I should sleep or eat
'Twere deadly sickness or else present death.
I prithee go and get me some repast –   15
I care not what, so it be wholesome food.

GRUMIO What say you to a neat's foot?

KATHERINA 'Tis passing good. I prithee let me have it.

GRUMIO I fear it is too choleric a meat.
How say you to a fat tripe finely broiled?   20

KATHERINA I like it well. Good Grumio, fetch it me.

GRUMIO I cannot tell, I fear 'tis choleric.
What say you to a piece of beef and mustard?

KATHERINA A dish that I do love to feed upon.

GRUMIO Ay, but the mustard is too hot a little.   25

KATHERINA Why then, the beef, and let the mustard rest.

GRUMIO Nay then, I will not. You shall have the mustard,
Or else you get no beef of Grumio.

KATHERINA Then both, or one, or anything thou wilt.

GRUMIO Why then, the mustard without the beef.   30

KATHERINA Go, get thee gone, thou false deluding slave
                        Beats him.
That feed'st me with the very name of meat.
Sorrow on thee and all the pack of you
That triumph thus upon my misery!
Go, get thee gone, I say.   35

14 The entry line for Grumio when Katherina's speech has been rendered a soliloquy, as in e.g.
    Daly (1887) (s34).
16 Bogdanov (1978): Grumio started flicking through a recipe book.
17 Some Katherinas are revolted by the offer of a 'neat's foot' but are so desperate for food
    they agree to it, e.g. Dews (1981). Leach (1978): Katherina was offered a 'pig's foot' to which
    her initial response was 'Yuk!'
31 s.d. Sothern and Marlowe (1905): Katherina seized a whip from the table to attack Grumio (s47).
    Bridges-Adams (1920): Katherina picked up a poker to hurl at Grumio. The narrator in
    Morgan (1937) explained that Grumio 'has received his instructions from Petruchio and
    takes as much pleasure as his master in teasing and torturing his mistress' (pbk).
35 s.d. *AS* has at the equivalent moment (8.23 s.d.): *Enter* FERANDO *with a piece of meat upon his
    dagger's point.* This may reflect original stage business, although Morris (259) dismisses
    this as well as a possible parallel with *1 Tamburlaine*, 4.4.40. Gribble (1935), which played

Enter PETRUCHIO *and* HORTENSIO *with meat.*

PETRUCHIO How fares my Kate? What, sweeting, all amort?
HORTENSIO Mistress, what cheer?
KATHERINA   Faith, as cold as can be.
PETRUCHIO Pluck up thy spirits; look cheerfully upon me.
    Here, love, thou seest how diligent I am
    To dress thy meat myself, and bring it thee.   40
    I am sure, sweet Kate, this kindness merits thanks.
    What, not a word? Nay then, thou lov'st it not,
    And all my pains is sorted to no proof.
    Here, take away this dish.
KATHERINA   I pray you, let it stand.
PETRUCHIO The poorest service is repaid with thanks,   45
    And so shall mine before you touch the meat.
KATHERINA I thank you, sir.
HORTENSIO Signor Petruchio, fie, you are to blame.
    Come, Mistress Kate, I'll bear you company.
PETRUCHIO [*Aside*] Eat it up all, Hortensio, if thou lov'st me –   50
    [*To Katherina*] Much good do it unto thy gentle heart.
    Kate, eat apace. And now, my honey love,
    Will we return unto thy father's house
    And revel it as bravely as the best,

this scene straight on from the end of 4.1, had Petruchio asleep and snoring, while Katherina tried to scavenge some food from the floor. On this line Petruchio awoke in time to prevent Katherina from eating anything and then got up and did his morning exercises.

46 There is often a long pause after line 46, e.g. Cottrell (1973).
47 Sothern and Marlowe (1905): spoken 'as if without hope' (s48). Rose (1997): said in a girly and mocking fashion. Miller (1987) made Katherina repeat the line, as she didn't say it loud enough first time.
50 Petruchio's instruction is sometimes difficult for Hortensio to follow; in Lynch (1991) the problem was solved by the reappearance of the glove-puppet dog Troilus from 4.1. Troilus enthusiastically took all the food, stowing it under the table as fast as Hortensio gave it to him. Williams (1973): Petruchio gave Katherina a single rib to eat. Leach (1978): Katherina held her knife so fiercely in front of Hortensio that he didn't dare take the meat and she managed to eat it.
51 Hodgman (1991): 'gentle heart' got Katherina's attention and distracted her from the food.
52 Rider (1994): Petruchio and Katherina sat at the table, both resisting the food, each of them trying to prove they had the stronger willpower.

With silken coats and caps, and golden rings,   55
With ruffs and cuffs and farthingales and things,
With scarves and fans and double change of brav'ry,
With amber bracelets, beads and all this knav'ry.
What, hast thou dined? The tailor stays thy leisure,
To deck thy body with his ruffling treasure.   60

Enter TAILOR.

Come, tailor, let us see these ornaments.
Lay forth the gown.

Enter HABERDASHER.

What news with you, sir?
HABERDASHER Here is the cap your worship did bespeak.
PETRUCHIO Why, this was moulded on a porringer –
A velvet dish! Fie, fie, 'tis lewd and filthy.   65
Why, 'tis a cockle or a walnut-shell,
A knack, a toy, a trick, a baby's cap.
Away with it! Come, let me have a bigger.
KATHERINA I'll have no bigger. This doth fit the time,
And gentlewomen wear such caps as these.   70
PETRUCHIO When you are gentle you shall have one too,
And not till then.
HORTENSIO [*Aside*]   That will not be in haste.

---

58 Ayliff (1928): Petruchio put one piece of macaroni on a fork and, after dangling it over the
    starving Katherina's mouth, he slowly lowered it 'down her gullet' (*O* 6 May 1928).
59 Rider (1994): Katherina outfaced Petruchio and demanded the food be removed by clicking
    her fingers.
60 s.d. The Tailor and Haberdasher are often reduced to one character, e.g. Phelps (1856), often
    played gay, e.g. Guthrie (1939), Hodgman (1991). The Tailor traditionally had a stutter, e.g.
    Daly (1887) (534). Antoon (1990) played with race stereotypes and had a servile Chinese
    tailor (*Wall Street Journal*, 16 July 1990) whereas Ayliff (1928) had a stereotypical Jewish
    character (Speaight 162). Rose (1997) had a *haute couture* modelling session which
    included a *Seven Year Itch* Marilyn Monroe model, and Petruchio managed to manhandle
    all the glamorous models.
64 Reviewers of Ayliff (1928) were amused that this description so well fitted the cloche hat the
    modern-dress Katherina was so taken with, e.g. *Saturday Review*, 5 May 1928. Daly (1887):
    Petruchio picked the cap up on his whip (534).

KATHERINA Why, sir, I trust I may have leave to speak,
        And speak I will. I am no child, no babe.
        Your betters have endured me say my mind,   75
        And if you cannot, best you stop your ears.
        My tongue will tell the anger of my heart,
        Or else my heart concealing it will break,
        And, rather than it shall, I will be free
        Even to the uttermost, as I please, in words.   80
PETRUCHIO Why, thou say'st true – it is a paltry cap.
        A custard-coffin, a bauble, a silken pie!
        I love thee well in that thou lik'st it not.
KATHERINA Love me or love me not, I like the cap,
        And it I will have, or I will have none.   85
PETRUCHIO Thy gown? Why, ay. Come, tailor, let us see't.
                                    [*Exit Haberdasher*]
        O mercy God! What masking stuff is here?
        What's this – a sleeve? 'Tis like a demi-cannon.
        What, up and down carved like an apple-tart?
        Here's snip and nip and cut and slish and slash,   90

73–80 This speech is often Katherina's last stand. Dews (1981): Katherina climbed on a table to
        declaim the speech very firmly. Kelly (1993): Katherina pulled the cloth and plates off the
        table and then overturned the table for emphasis. Ball (1976): Katherina stood tall and
        declaimed this very proudly. Productions which cut into this speech make Katherina's fight
        back much less impressive, e.g. Phelps (1856). Gribble (1935): as she finished speaking,
        Katherina slapped first the Haberdasher and then Grumio.
  78   Williams (1973): Katherina knocked out the Haberdasher.
  85   Lynch (1991): Katherina went into a tantrum and jumped on the cap. This tantrum was very
        precisely replicated moments later as Petruchio subjected the sleeve of the dress to the
        same treatment. Benthall (1955) also had Katherina jump on her cap, and in Leach (1978)
        Katherina stamped on the cap so hard she 'killed' it and then wept over its mauled state.
        Such business looks forward to Petruchio's command for Katherina to trample on her cap in
        5.2. Ball (1976): Petruchio tore the cap to pieces. Sothern and Marlowe (1905): the cap was
        thrown around the room by the men to tease Katherina (s44). Anglin (1908): Petruchio and
        Hortensio played catch with the cap and then threw it out of the window. Katherina
        retaliated by throwing Hortensio's cap out of the window.
  86   Allison (1982): Grumio modelled the gown.
  87   Guthrie (1954): the effeminate tailor was devastated by the rough treatment his work
        received (*G&M* 1 July 1954).

Like to a censer in a barber's shop.
Why, what a devil's name, tailor, call'st thou this?
HORTENSIO [*Aside*] I see she's like to have neither cap nor gown.
TAILOR You bid me make it orderly and well,
According to the fashion and the time.   95
PETRUCHIO Marry, and did. But if you be remembered,
I did not bid you mar it to the time.
Go, hop me over every kennel home,
For you shall hop without my custom, sir.
I'll none of it. Hence, make your best of it.   100
KATHERINA I never saw a better-fashioned gown,
More quaint, more pleasing, nor more commendable.
Belike you mean to make a puppet of me.
PETRUCHIO Why, true, he means to make a puppet of thee.
TAILOR She says your worship means to make a puppet of her.   105
PETRUCHIO O monstrous arrogance! Thou liest, thou thread, thou
          thimble,
Thou yard, three-quarters, half-yard, quarter, nail!
Thou flea, thou nit, thou winter-cricket thou!
Braved in mine own house with a skein of thread?
Away, thou rag, thou quantity, thou remnant!   110
Or I shall so bemete thee with thy yard
As thou shalt think on prating whilst thou liv'st.

91 Often cut, e.g. Williams (1973).

98 Daly (1887) (S32) notes that it was 'Old bus.' for Petruchio to make the Tailor hop over either
    his sword or whip. Sothern and Marlowe (1905) (S47) had Petruchio using the gown to beat
    the Tailor's legs and make him jump.

101 The traditional business whereby the gown was 'a worn, faded, and ridiculous garment no
    woman of taste or reason would consent to wear' (*Athenaeum*, 15 October 1870) made
    Petruchio's reaction to it reasonable and Katherina's nonsensical.

106 Trevis (1985): Petruchio pulled the tailor around tied up with his own tape measure. Allison
    (1982): Petruchio pulled the dress off Grumio who was modelling it and using apples for
    breasts. Both Grumio and Katherina immediately starting eating the apples.

109 Hodgman (1991): Petruchio let out a roar which was an extremely good imitation of an
    earlier roar emitted by Katherina, and she clearly recognised this. Daly (1887): the pbk
    marked up for Petruchio (S30) notes that this line was addressed to the audience.

110 Guthrie (1939): the Tailor 'listened to Petruchio's railing with indifference, until the insult
    "Thou remnant!" pierced his professional heart and he departed in high dudgeon and in
    tears' (Williamson 1948, 120).

I tell thee, I, that thou hast marred her gown.
TAILOR Your worship is deceived. The gown is made
    Just as my master had direction.   115
    Grumio gave order how it should be done.
GRUMIO I gave him no order; I gave him the stuff.
TAILOR But how did you desire it should be made?
GRUMIO Marry, sir, with needle and thread.
TAILOR But did you not request to have it cut?   120
GRUMIO Thou hast faced many things.
TAILOR I have.
GRUMIO Face not me. Thou hast braved many men; brave not me. I
    will neither be faced nor braved. I say unto thee, I bid thy master
    cut out the gown, but I did not bid him cut it to pieces. *Ergo*,   125
    thou liest.
TAILOR Why, here is the note of the fashion to testify.
PETRUCHIO Read it.
GRUMIO The note lies in's throat if he say I said so.
TAILOR [*Reads*] '*Imprimis*, a loose-bodied gown –'   130
GRUMIO Master, if ever I said 'loose-bodied gown', sew me in the
    skirts of it and beat me to death with a bottom of brown thread.
    I said 'a gown'.
PETRUCHIO Proceed.
TAILOR 'With a small compassed cape.'   135
GRUMIO I confess the cape.

113 Sothern and Marlowe (1905) cut heavily in this section but they did include a tug of war
    which ripped the gown apart (s47). Gribble (1935): Katherina 'surreptitiously stuffs food off
    the table into her bosom and her sleeves' (s65).

116–47 Poel (s58) suggested for Harvey (1913) that Grumio and the Tailor should be 'nose to nose'
    for much of this section. He also suggested that Grumio and the Tailor fight 'as with
    cutlasses'. In Leach (1978) Katherina and Petruchio were taking very little notice of the
    Grumio/Tailor fracas and were looking at each other, thinking things through.

127 Barton (1960) had a huge diagram of the gown displayed.

134–40 Ayliff (1928) produced a modern gown which fitted the description well (*T* 1 May 1928). The
    gown is often ripped to pieces by Petruchio but in this production this happened while
    Katherina was actually wearing the dress. After Petruchio ripped off the sleeves at line 140,
    Katherina stepped out of the gown, threw it on the floor and stood there dressed only in her
    petticoat. Miller (1987): Katherina was dressed in a shift and placed on a pedestal to model
    the gown which was then ripped off her bit by bit.

136 Gribble (1935): Grumio cried on the Tailor's shoulder.

TAILOR 'With a trunk sleeve.'

GRUMIO I confess two sleeves.

TAILOR 'The sleeves curiously cut.'

PETRUCHIO Ay, there's the villainy.   140

GRUMIO Error i'th'bill, sir, error i'th'bill! I commanded the sleeves
should be cut out and sewed up again – and that I'll prove upon
thee, though thy little finger be armed in a thimble.

TAILOR This is true that I say, and I had thee in place where thou
should'st know it.   145

GRUMIO I am for thee straight. Take thou the bill, give me thy mete-
yard and spare not me.

HORTENSIO God-a-mercy, Grumio, then he shall have no odds.

PETRUCHIO Well, sir, in brief, the gown is not for me.

GRUMIO You are i'th'right sir, 'tis for my mistress.   150

PETRUCHIO Go, take it up unto thy master's use.

GRUMIO Villain, not for thy life! Take up my mistress' gown for thy
master's use?

PETRUCHIO Why, sir, what's your conceit in that?

GRUMIO O sir, the conceit is deeper than you think for.   155
Take up my mistress' gown to his master's use?
O fie, fie, fie!

PETRUCHIO [*Aside*] Hortensio, say thou wilt see the tailor paid.
[*To Tailor*] Go, take it hence; be gone and say no more.

---

138 Benthall (1948): the two sleeves were torn out. Gribble (1935): Grumio kissed the Tailor
'French fashion' (s65).

145 Daly (1887) (s34) inserted a version of Garrick *C&P* 3.130–2. Pbk s32 notes 'Old bus.'
whereby the Tailor jumped into his box here, flourished his shears and asked, ' "Would you
hit a man in his own shop?" ' Benthall (1948) had the Tailor trying to sew bits of the dress
back together again.

147 Benson (1890) had the Tailor chased until he fell into his own large basket whereupon
Petruchio's servants carried him off. The fight in *C&P* (3.133–4) is so violent that Catharine
cries out, 'How you fright me.'

148 Leach (1978): Meryl Streep's Katherina handed back the dress of her own accord. Streep
argued that in doing this Katherina was rejecting puppetry or the conventional behaviour
foisted on most women (*Kiss Me, Petruchio*).

151–7 The sexual reference was often cut, e.g Webster (1844). This production had a fight here:
'Grumio flourishes the yard – the tailor the scizzors – they then wrestle – and are separated
by a crack of Petruchio's whip' (pbk).

HORTENSIO [*Aside*] Tailor, I'll pay thee for thy gown tomorrow,   160
Take no unkindness of his hasty words.
Away I say, commend me to thy master.

                                        Exit Tailor

PETRUCHIO Well, come, my Kate, we will unto your father's
Even in these honest mean habiliments.
Our purses shall be proud, our garments poor,   165
For 'tis the mind that makes the body rich,
And as the sun breaks through the darkest clouds,
So honour peereth in the meanest habit.
What, is the jay more precious than the lark
Because his feathers are more beautiful?   170
Or is the adder better than the eel
Because his painted skin contents the eye?
O no, good Kate; neither art thou the worse
For this poor furniture and mean array.
If thou account'st it shame, lay it on me,   175
And therefore frolic! We will hence forthwith
To feast and sport us at thy father's house.
[*To Grumio*] Go call my men, and let us straight to him,

160 Gribble (1935) gave this line to Katherina.

163 Dews (1981): Katherina had fallen asleep with exhaustion and Petruchio shouted in her ear.

166–8 Hodgman (1991): Petruchio stressed this as the lesson of the play.

169–70 Monette (1988): Petruchio said this very seriously to Katherina who was learning to value
what she had not valued before; this was embodied in her response to the onstage presence
of the unfortunate and unappealing cousin Ferdinand. Having hit him repeatedly earlier,
Katherina was now able to hug him. In Edwards (1995) Michael Siberry (Petruchio) saw this
speech as articulating 'a theory [Petruchio] has about values' which is trying to tell Katherina
'that he doesn't care how she looks, or what people have said about her in the past; what
she is, and what she is to him, is wonderful' (Siberry 53). In May (1994) this speech was
spoken 'with unusual kindness and quiet urgency as if it contained the essence of the play's
theme' (*T* 2 July 1994). Ball (1976): this seriously spoken speech contrasted starkly with the
mayhem of the previous section. However, Asche (1899) cut 169–75, which does repeat the
point Petruchio has already made.

175 Hodgman (1991): 'lay . . . me' was spoken tenderly. Ball (1976): Katherina and Petruchio
looked at each other and came near to kissing; she was relieved and happy. Daly (1887) in
the pbk marked up for Petruchio (530) instructs 'give poetic value' in this speech until the
end of this line when the tone turns back to 'colloquial'.

And bring our horses unto Long-lane end,
There will we mount, and thither walk on foot.   180
Let's see, I think 'tis now some seven o'clock,
And well we may come there by dinner-time.
KATHERINA I dare assure you, sir, 'tis almost two,
And 'twill be supper-time ere you come there.
PETRUCHIO It shall be seven ere I go to horse.   185
Look what I speak, or do, or think to do,
You are still crossing it. Sirs, let't alone.
I will not go today, and, ere I do,
It shall be what o'clock I say it is.
HORTENSIO [*Aside*] Why so this gallant will command the sun.   190
                                                [*Exeunt*]

179–80 Sometimes cut in modern-dress productions, e.g. Ayliff (1928), ditto the horse in 185. Kyle (1982) cut and replaced horses with a four-wheel bicycle.

183 Edwards (1995): Michael Siberry's Petruchio was disappointed by Katherina: 'I brushed a bit of hair off her face and tried to be as tender as I could in order to make some impression with what I was saying, in the hope that she might come on board; but she wouldn't, and I stormed off' (Siberry 53). Siberry felt that for Petruchio 'the game is no longer in his control' (53); he wants to stop but he cannot now. In Zeffirelli (1967) Petruchio woke Katherina in the middle of the night for this sequence.

185 Dews (1981): Petruchio said this in a very sinister tone.

187 Rider (1994): Katherina marched out after 'it'.

188 Patton (1984): Petruchio precisely imitated and mocked the tantrum Katherina had thrown on the same line spoken at 3.2.197 (Frey 1985, 488). Sothern and Marlowe (1905): Katherina's unbroken spirit was indicated by the fact that at this line she was in a 'frenzy of anger' (s47), throwing a shawl and hat, which Curtis had given her, in all directions.

189 Guthrie (1954): Hortensio joined the hands of Petruchio and the acquiescent Katherina. By contrast in Heap (1985) Katherina kicked a stool and stormed out. Harvey (1913): Katherina broke a plate (McDonald pbk). Gribble (1935): Petruchio took away the food Katherina had hidden in her sleeves and bosom.

190 Dews (1981): the television version had a close up on Katherina's face as she thought this through and started to laugh. Patton (1984): 'Kate was then left alone to meditate. She figured it all out, saw Petruchio's game' and decided to go along with it (Frey 1985, 488). Monette (1988) also left Katherina onstage for a good while, thinking through the issues. Anglin's 1908 pbk (s57) has a sequence of Katherina and Petruchio sitting on either side of the stage stamping defiance at each other, but William Winter (1915, 537), Augustin Daly's apologist, poured scorn on Anglin for having Katherina 'climbing on a chair and turning

back the hands of a clock, before she would assent to Petruchio's assertion that at two o'clock 'tis seven'. Ayliff (1928) took this business up and had Katherina turning the hands of the clock, which struck 2, then 3, then 4. Sothern and Marlowe (1905) had an extended pantomime here whereby Katherina repeatedly held up seven fingers when Petruchio was looking and two when he was not. As he left the scene thinking he'd won she held her 'right hand high in air with two fingers waving' (s47), which sounds encouragingly defiant. Pbk s46 glosses the moment: 'she pretends to yield now but knows she will have her own way and manage him in the end'. Benthall (1955): Katherina was left alone thinking, but Petruchio was watching her through a crack in the door. Nickell (1950): Katherina thumped the table and stormed off. The Bensons (1890) cut Hortensio's line and then: 'Here it was arranged that in her last burst of temper, "Katherine" should suddenly snatch up a knife and raise it to strike "Petruchio," when the sight of his mocking face, quite unruffled by her fury, breaks down her proud spirit, and plunging the knife into the table, she sinks sobbing at his feet' (Benson 86). Bridges-Adams (1920): as Katherina collapsed sobbing, Petruchio began to feed her but when Dorothy Green played Katherina in this production she 'made the breaking point an almost tragical incident, when, after being baited by Petruchio, she took up a knife to kill him, and collapsed in a flood of hysterical laughter' (*BP* 18 April 1922). Devine (1953) had Katherina and Petruchio stamping defiance at each other before Katherina ran and jumped into Petruchio's arms. Line 190 was given to the Lord as this production cut Hortensio from the scene. In Schaefer (1956) the line was spoken by Katherina. Alexander (1990): Katherina sniffed at a remaining plate for traces of food. As she left, Sly got up to offer her a plate of food from the Lord's area. Nunn (1967) played 4.5.77–9 here and had Hortensio heading off to his widow. Daly (1888) ran straight on into 4.5, with the sun and moon test following on after the telling the time test, thus delaying the departure for Baptista's house until Katherina had fully capitulated (s34).

In *Sauny the Scot* Margaret's (Katherina's) capitulation here was explicitly in order to get home to her father's house where she could rebel once more (4.1.174–5).

ACT 4   SCENE 4

Enter TRANIO *[disguised as Lucentio] and the* MERCHANT, *booted
and bare headed, dressed like Vincentio.*

TRANIO Sir, this is the house. Please it you that I call?
MERCHANT Ay, what else? And, but I be deceived,
       Signor Baptista may remember me
       Near twenty years ago in Genoa
       Where we were lodgers at the Pegasus.   5
TRANIO 'Tis well. And hold your own, in any case,
       With such austerity as 'longeth to a father.
MERCHANT I warrant you.

                    Enter BIONDELLO.

              But, sir, here comes your boy;
          'Twere good he were schooled.
TRANIO Fear you not him. Sirrah Biondello,   10
       Now do your duty throughly, I advise you:
       Imagine 'twere the right Vincentio.

This scene's action is confusing, something explored by Wells and Taylor (353–60). The Folio
has a puzzling entry for 'Peter', a character whose function is unclear and who usually gets
cut by editors. The Folio also has an exit for Biondello followed by a rapid re-entry (see lines
68 and 72), which is very awkward: Ann Thompson (135) suggests that Biondello, and
indeed Lucentio as well, 'just move downstage at this point' rather than rush off and back
onstage so rapidly. Such anomalies are useful reminders that the Folio text is not infallible.
4.4 is often altered or cut as directors try to clarify the action or distract their audiences from
its problems: e.g Rose (1997) had an outbreak of business with actors wearing strap-on
plastic cars involved in traffic jams and a crash. Asche (1899) played up the Pedant
(Merchant)'s drunkenness. Harvey (1913) just cut the scene entirely. To save on scene
changes Daly (1887) ran 4.4 straight after a much cut 4.2; Benson (1890) played 4.4 after 4.5
and then ran straight on into 5.1.

3–5 The Pedant (Merchant) often needs prompting: e.g. in Anthony (1965) he had here to 'sneak
    a look at his notes' (*New York Herald Tribune*, 24 June 1965). Pedants (Merchants)
    sometimes speak very fast, as if they have learnt their lines by rote, e.g. Hodgman (1991).
4–5 Monette (1988 pbk): the Pedant (Merchant) paused before 'Genoa' and 'Pegasus',
    struggling to get the story right. Hawthorn (1979) gave 'at the Pegasus' to Tranio, who was
    still coaching the Pedant (Merchant).

BIONDELLO Tut, fear not me.

TRANIO But hast thou done thy errand to Baptista?

BIONDELLO I told him that your father was at Venice,   15
    And that you looked for him this day in Padua.

TRANIO Th'art a tall fellow; hold thee that to drink.
      [*He gives him money.*]

   Enter BAPTISTA *and* LUCENTIO [*disguised as Cambio*].

   Here comes Baptista. Set your countenance, sir.
   Signor Baptista, you are happily met.
   Sir, this is the gentleman I told you of.   20
   I pray you stand good father to me now:
   Give me Bianca for my patrimony.

MERCHANT Soft, son.
   Sir, by your leave, having come to Padua
   To gather in some debts, my son Lucentio   25
   Made me acquainted with a weighty cause
   Of love between your daughter and himself.
   And – for the good report I hear of you,
   And for the love he beareth to your daughter,
   And she to him – to stay him not too long,   30
   I am content, in a good father's care,
   To have him matched. And if you please to like
   No worse than I, upon some agreement
   Me shall you find ready and willing
   With one consent to have her so bestowed,   35
   For curious I cannot be with you,
   Signor Baptista, of whom I hear so well.

BAPTISTA Sir, pardon me in what I have to say.

18 Nunn (1967): Biondello brushed the Pedant (Merchant) down, ready for action.

23 Ball (1976): the Pedant (Merchant) dried completely here. Allison (1982): the Pedant
(Merchant) performed very enthusiastically and, despite repeated attempts, no one else
could get a word in edgeways which made Baptista's reference to 'shortness' at line 39 a
joke.

25 Gribble (1935): the Pedant (Merchant) forgot his 'son's' name and Tranio had to prompt
him. Leach (1978): Tranio corrected the Pedant (Merchant)'s pronunciation of 'Lucentio'.
Ayliff (1928): Tranio held up an envelope with Lucentio's name on it to make sure the Pedant
(Merchant) got it right.

38 ff. Payne (1935): Sly got hold of the Pedant (Merchant)'s bottle of drink, which Biondello
eventually managed to wrestle back from him. Komisarjevsky (1939) played the Pedant

Your plainness and your shortness please me well.
Right true it is your son Lucentio here   40
Doth love my daughter, and she loveth him –
Or both dissemble deeply their affections –
And therefore, if you say no more than this,
That like a father you will deal with him,
And pass my daughter a sufficient dower,   45
The match is made and all is done:
Your son shall have my daughter with consent.
TRANIO I thank you, sir. Where, then, do you know best
We be affied and such assurance tane
As shall with either part's agreement stand?   50
BAPTISTA Not in my house, Lucentio, for you know
Pitchers have ears, and I have many servants.
Besides, old Gremio is heark'ning still,
And happily we might be interrupted.
TRANIO Then at my lodging, and it like you.   55
There doth my father lie, and there this night
We'll pass the business privately and well.
Send for your daughter by your servant here.
    [*He indicates Lucentio and winks at him.*]
My boy shall fetch the scrivener presently.
The worst is this, that at so slender warning   60
You are like to have a thin and slender pittance.
BAPTISTA It likes me well. Cambio, hie you home,
And bid Bianca make her ready straight,
And, if you will, tell what hath happenèd:
Lucentio's father is arrived in Padua,   65
And how she's like to be Lucentio's wife.

(Merchant) as deaf as well as drunk and Biondello kept making signs to Baptista here to
make him speak up.

42 Allison (1982): Baptista seriously considered this possibility (which is correct, as he is talking
about Tranio-as-Lucentio and Bianca) but then rejected it.

46 Benthall (1955): Tranio put his hand behind his back and Lucentio shook it, signalling to the
audience these two knew what was going on.

62 Alexander (1992): Tranio had to remind Baptista of Cambio's name.

66 Bogdanov (1978): Tranio and Biondello tried to signal to Lucentio that he must go to the
church and Baptista caught Biondello miming his message.

[Exit Lucentio]

BIONDELLO I pray the gods she may, with all my heart!
TRANIO Dally not with the gods, but get thee gone.

Exit Biondello

       – Signor Baptista, shall I lead the way?
       Welcome. One mess is like to be your cheer.   70
       Come sir, we will better it in Pisa.
BAPTISTA I follow you.

Exeunt

Enter Lucentio [disguised as Cambio] and Biondello.

BIONDELLO Cambio!
LUCENTIO What say'st thou, Biondello?
BIONDELLO You saw my master wink and laugh upon you?   75
LUCENTIO Biondello, what of that?
BIONDELLO Faith, nothing – but 'has left me here behind to
    expound the meaning or moral of his signs and tokens.
LUCENTIO I pray thee, moralise them.
BIONDELLO Then thus: Baptista is safe, talking with the deceiving   80
    father of a deceitful son.
LUCENTIO And what of him?
BIONDELLO His daughter is to be brought by you to the supper.
LUCENTIO And then?

---

67 This line is often given to Lucentio, e.g. Daly (1887) (s34). Asche (1899): after Lucentio
    delivered this line, 'Biondello signals to Cambio to remain' onstage (pbk).

68 Gribble (1935) gave this line to Baptista. Wells and Taylor (360) discuss the 1962 revival of
    Barton (1960) where Tranio's attempts to communicate with Lucentio were spotted by a
    confused Baptista.

68 s.d. Leach (1978): after exiting, Biondello rushed back on shouting for 'Cambio'. Watts (1954), a
    radio production, had Biondello remaining on and calling 'Cambio' back.

69 Carey (1954): Tranio did a mime of a church for Lucentio.

72 Sothern and Marlowe (1905) s49: after Tranio left, Biondello beckoned on the Priest, then
    Lucentio and Bianca, and they all exited together. The production then cut to the end of the
    scene but imported some of the beginning of 5.1 (s47).

73 Monette (1988): Biondello's and Lucentio's conversation here was by phone. Rose (1997):
    Biondello hid in a rubbish bin and his message for Lucentio was delivered from there. Daly
    (1887): Biondello took his hat off to Lucentio as he re-entered, reminding the audience of
    their real master/servant relationship (s34).

BIONDELLO The old priest at Saint Luke's church is at your   85
command at all hours.

LUCENTIO And what of all this?

BIONDELLO I cannot tell, except they are busied about a counterfeit
assurance. Take you assurance of her *cum privilegio ad
imprimendum solum.* To the church! Take the priest, clerk and   90
some sufficient honest witnesses.

   If this be not that you look for, I have no more to say,
   But bid Bianca farewell for ever and a day.

LUCENTIO Hear'st thou, Biondello?

BIONDELLO I cannot tarry. I knew a wench married in an afternoon   95
as she went to the garden for parsley to stuff a rabbit. And so
may you, sir; and so adieu, sir. My master hath appointed me to
go to Saint Luke's to bid the priest be ready to come against you
come with your appendix.   *Exit*

LUCENTIO I may and will, if she be so contented.   100
   She will be pleased – then wherefore should I doubt?
   Hap what hap may, I'll roundly go about her.
   It shall go hard if Cambio go without her.   *Exit*

89–90 The Latin is sometimes cut, e.g. Asche (1899). Dews (1981) turned 'imprimendum' into
'impregnatum' (pbk).

100–3 Cut in Daly (1887) although the lines prepare for Bianca's behaviour in the final scene (534).

103 *AS* Interlude 2 (see Appendix 1, p. 236) was used here by e.g. Dews (1981). 5.1.1–5 is
sometimes imported to help the narrative, e.g. Gribble (1935), Benthall (1955).

ACT 4   SCENE 5

Enter PETRUCHIO, KATHERINA, HORTENSIO [*and* SERVANTS].

PETRUCHIO Come on, a God's name! Once more toward our father's.
Good Lord, how bright and goodly shines the moon!

For the journey back to Padua, Constance Benson (1890) had a different, untrained, often unpredictable donkey at every new venue the touring Benson company visited: 'Sometimes [the donkey] would kick violently, and on more than one occasion, it actually sat down. [In] either case, needless to say, the audience roared with laughter, as much at my discomfiture as at the antics of the donkey' (Benson 87). Production photographs show Petruchio pushing the donkey, which is stubbornly standing still, with Katherina sitting sidesaddle. Several servants lie sprawled on the floor as a result of falling over, trying to pull the donkey along. The donkey sometimes took a curtain call on its own (*SUAH* 22 April 1898). In Ayliff (1927, 1928), 4.5 was a highlight and used a cut-out motor car in front of a moving panorama to suggest that the car was travelling along; the panorama reversed when Katherina contradicted Petruchio in order to indicate that the car was now travelling backwards. Massey (1927) also had Katherina and Petruchio travelling by car here, in a flivver (*Boston Evening Transcript*, 4 May 1927). Benthall (1948) had a pantomime horse that had brought Petruchio to his wedding. Devine (1953) had two actors pretending to be horses and allowing the delighted Sly to join in as a third horse. Rose (1997) set this scene on a plane waiting to take off, with two banks of airline seats in the background. Kyle (1982) had everyone travelling on a four-wheel bicycle. Reinhardt (1909) played this entire scene by moonlight and so all references to sun and moon had to be reversed so that the topsy-turvy logic could still be maintained.

As in 4.3, Hortensio is sometimes cut and his lines mostly given to Grumio, e.g. Gribble (1935).

Anglin (1908) opened with business whereby Katherina was discovered sleeping, lying against a log. Petruchio went to wake her by cracking his whip but Hortensio protested. Petruchio then leant over Katherina, kissed her, winked at Hortensio and then cracked his whip to wake her. The *Sydney Morning Herald* (23 November 1908) recorded 'when Petruchio offered to crack his whip over the head of the recumbent beauty an ominous growl from the gallery only fell short of a roar because the actor, lively in his apprehension of danger contented himself with playfully slapping his riding-boot instead'.

1a Ayliff (1927, 1928): this was addressed in exasperation to the starting handle of Petruchio's car. Every time Petruchio started the car and got into the driver's seat the engine stopped again. Miller (1987): the exhausted Katherina lay down to sleep the moment Petruchio stopped.

KATHERINA The moon? The sun! It is not moonlight now.
PETRUCHIO I say it is the moon that shines so bright.
KATHERINA I know it is the sun that shines so bright.   5
PETRUCHIO Now, by my mother's son – and that's myself –
    It shall be moon or star or what I list
    Or e'er I journey to your father's house.
    [*To Servants*] Go on and fetch our horses back again.
    Evermore crossed and crossed, nothing but crossed!   10
HORTENSIO Say as he says, or we shall never go.
KATHERINA Forward, I pray, since we have come so far.
    And be it moon or sun or what you please;
    And if you please to call it a rush-candle,

3 Dews (1981): Katherina slapped her cheek in mock horror as soon as she had said 'sun'; she'd forgotten to apply the lesson she'd learnt at the end of 4.3. Stylised suns and moons make debate slightly less like brainwashing: in Kelly (1993), which had Petruchio as a Jackson Pollock-style artist who summoned the sun or the moon 'at the throw of a yellow paintpot' (*Yorkshire Evening Post*, 24 April 1993), the splash of paint *was* more obviously open to varying interpretations than the actual sun and moon. Williams (1973) had the sun/moon represented by 'a large sunflower on the end of a long stick' (*Evening Standard*, 26 September 1973).

5 Ball (1976): Katherina spoke this line very crossly. Sothern and Marlowe (1905) had Petruchio staging 'affected rage' here (s47).

9 The horses are cut or altered in most modern-dress productions, e.g. Ayliff (1928).

10 Leach (1978): Petruchio threw a big childish tantrum, thrashing around on the floor precisely as Katherina had done earlier.

12 The Petruchio in Edwards (1995), Michael Siberry, identified line 12 as 'in our production, one of the most important things (Katherina) says' (Siberry 55), and he suggests the paraphrase: 'We have come a long way together since our first meeting. . . . and we have now come to an understanding in which we are just beginning to find out about each other; so let us go forward from here.' Siberry then paraphrases Katherina's response as 'Since what you say changes as rapidly as your mind, I'll say whatever you want me to say. But what does it mean if I do? What *does* it mean?' Hodgman (1991): Katherina was in tears and said her lines with great difficulty but some Katherinas take the submission less seriously: e.g. in Rider (1994) Katherina was over the top and having fun. Ball (1976): Katherina shouted this speech so crossly that it was one of the most shrewish-sounding speeches in the entire production. Miller (1987) had an 'Extremely long pause in which Kate works out the rest of her life', a pause which sometimes lasted up to 34.9 seconds (pbk). Holland (6) recalls Katherina 'observed the sun, looking at it through her wedding-ring' and 'silently meditated on her marriage and analysed the relationship before resolving to accept it and value it'.

Henceforth I vow it shall be so for me.   15
PETRUCHIO I say it is the moon.
KATHERINA   I know it is the moon.
PETRUCHIO Nay then you lie, it is the blessèd sun.
KATHERINA Then God be blessed, it is the blessèd sun.
But sun it is not, when you say it is not,
And the moon changes even as your mind.   20
What you will have it named, even that it is,
And so it shall be so for Katherine.
HORTENSIO [*Aside*] Petruchio, go thy ways. The field is won.
PETRUCHIO Well, forward, forward! Thus the bowl should run
And not unluckily against the bias.   25

16b Ball (1976): Katherina said this line with enthusiastic overemphasis.

17 Nunn (1967): at Petruchio's line Katherina 'laughs hysterically for two minutes, lies down full length on the ground' (*FT* 6 April 1967), and was 'kicking her heels with laughter' (*BM* 6 April 1967).

18 Sothern and Marlowe (1905): Katherina who was 'furious' gave 'a little cry of impotent rage' before blurting out the line (s47). Daly (1887) changed 'God' into 'Heaven' (s34). Alexander (1992): the penny dropped for Katherina during this speech and by the end of it she was excited at what she was saying.

22 Devine (1953): an embrace here varied between 15 and 20 seconds (pbk).

24 Ball (1976): Petruchio was a bit uncertain whether he had won or not as Katherina complied with his demands in so exaggerated a manner.

25 Bridges-Adams (1920): Petruchio was about to kiss Katherina but saw Vincentio and decided to take the testing further.

25 s.d. Ayliff (1928): Vincentio was reading a newspaper and walking backwards as if Petruchio's car were coming towards him. He was then run over and emerged from between the front and back wheels to be greeted by Petruchio uttering line 26. Guthrie (1954) also had a car, a cut-out which was walked along sedately by the cigar-smoking Vincentio and his chauffeur.

   One of the problems of running 4.5 straight on from 4.3, as Daly (1887) did, is that the location remains Petruchio's house and that Vincentio's appearance is unexpected. s28 records that Vincentio enters 'as if to enquire his way' and transposes lines 53–63 to run at line 27, which means that Vincentio introduces himself as he enters Petruchio's house, before having the joke played upon him. This echoes *C&P*, where this joke is practised on Baptista, who visits Catharine and Petruchio at home. Radio productions have to signal straightaway that Vincentio is a man in order for the joke to work: e.g. Cottrell (1973) had Vincentio greet everyone, Watts (1954) had Vincentio clear his throat and Morgan (1937), specified that Vincentio should try to interrupt Petruchio 'in a deep bass voice' (pbk).

Enter VINCENTIO.

> But soft, company is coming here.
> [*To Vincentio*] Good morrow, gentle mistress, where away?
> Tell me, sweet Kate, and tell me truly too,
> Hast thou beheld a fresher gentlewoman?
> Such war of white and red within her cheeks!   30
> What stars do spangle heaven with such beauty
> As those two eyes become that heavenly face?
> Fair lovely maid, once more good day to thee.
> Sweet Kate, embrace her for her beauty's sake.

HORTENSIO [*Aside*] A will make the man mad, to make the woman   35
>   of him.

KATHERINA Young budding virgin, fair and fresh and sweet,
> Whither away, or where is thy abode?
> Happy the parents of so fair a child!
> Happier the man whom favourable stars   40
> Allots thee for his lovely bedfellow.

PETRUCHIO Why, how now, Kate! I hope thou art not mad.
> This is a man – old, wrinkled, faded, withered –
> And not a maiden, as thou say'st he is.

KATHERINA Pardon, old father, my mistaking eyes   45
> That have been so bedazzled with the sun

27 Some Katherinas enjoy this joke: e.g. Heap (1985). Gribble (1935): Vincentio tried to assert
his identity by using lines 55–63.

33 Asche (1899): Petruchio kissed Vincentio's bald head.

36 Katherina sometimes kisses Vincentio, e.g. Burrell (1947).

37 Ball (1976): Katherina stressed 'virgin' and got a big laugh. Williams (1973): Katherina's
comic improvisation was completely upstaged as she, Petruchio and Vincentio 'are all
inexplicably teetering on a suspended plank, and the joke has become whether or not one
of them will fall off' (*New Statesman*, 5 October 1973).

40–1 Indecorous reference to a 'bedfellow' cut in e.g. Phelps (1856). Daly (1887) substituted
'wedded wife' for 'bedfellow' (534).

43 Vincentio is often as offended by this description as by 'budding virgin', e.g. Bogdanov
(1978).

46 It is traditional for Katherina either to pause before 'sun' to query it, or to check by looking
questioningly at Petruchio immediately after she has said the word. This business goes back
at least as far as Webster (1844): 'In giving these lines, Mrs Nisbett hesitated as she came to
the last word, and looked at *Petruchio* to see, as it were, if she was right this time' (*Morning*

That everything I look on seemeth green.
Now I perceive thou art a reverend father.
Pardon, I pray thee, for my mad mistaking.
PETRUCHIO Do, good old grandsire, and withal make known   50
Which way thou travellest – if along with us
We shall be joyful of thy company.
VINCENTIO Fair sir, and you, my merry mistress,
That with your strange encounter much amazed me,
My name is called Vincentio, my dwelling Pisa,   55
And bound I am to Padua, there to visit
A son of mine which long I have not seen.
PETRUCHIO What is his name?
VINCENTIO   Lucentio, gentle sir.
PETRUCHIO Happily met – the happier for thy son.
And now by law as well as reverend age   60
I may entitle thee my loving father.
The sister to my wife, this gentlewoman,
Thy son by this hath married. Wonder not,
Nor be not grieved. She is of good esteem,

Chronicle, 18 March 1844). This joke is also gestured at as early as *Sauny the Scot* where
Margaret (Katherina) says her eyes 'have been so dazled with the Moon (*Sun*, I mean)'
(4.3.49–50). In Kyle (1982) the joke reduced Katherina to helpless laughter (pbk).

47 Daly (1887) S32 records an added argument over 'green' and whether this was in fact 'blue'.

49 Leach (1978): Katherina addressed this line to Petruchio as if apologising for her previous
behaviour.

53 Miller (1980): Vincentio queried 'sir', to indicate the possibility a game was still in hand. In
Miller (1987) he queried 'mistress'.

60 ff. Because this section is awkward in terms of continuity – it is unclear how Petruchio has
obtained his information and as Hortensio was last seen forswearing Bianca in the company
of the man he believed was Lucentio (actually Tranio), his equanimity here is surprising –
some productions cut back this speech, e.g. Kelly (1993). Bogdanov (1978) replaced
Petruchio's speech with 'Lucentio, Hey we know him well' (pbk) and only played 68–70 of
the rest of the scene. Schaefer (1956) dealt with this by importing a sequence whereby a
dove, which had witnessed Bianca's and Lucentio's wedding, flew to Petruchio's house, told
a pet parrot the news and had the parrot then proclaim 'Lucentio and Bianca are married!'
(final pbk). Morgan (1937): the omniscient narrator announced the news.

62 Leach (1978): Petruchio stressed 'gentlewoman', as Katherina had now become gentle,
unlike her state at 4.3.71. The 'gentle' of 'gentlewoman' was stressed in Alexander (1992).

Her dowry wealthy, and of worthy birth;   65
Beside, so qualified as may beseem
The spouse of any noble gentleman.
Let me embrace with old Vincentio,
And wander we to see thy honest son,
Who will of thy arrival be full joyous.   70
VINCENTIO But is this true, or is it else your pleasure,
Like pleasant travellers, to break a jest
Upon the company you overtake?
HORTENSIO I do assure thee, father, so it is.
PETRUCHIO Come, go along and see the truth hereof,   75
For our first merriment hath made thee jealous.
                                        Exeunt [all but Hortensio]
HORTENSIO Well, Petruchio, this has put me in heart!
Have to my widow, and if she be froward,
Then hast thou taught Hortensio to be untoward.   *Exit*

68 Some Vincentios take more convincing: e.g. in Hodgman (1991) the still intensely suspicious
     Vincentio prepared to defend himself from the offered 'embrace' with an umbrella and in
     Leach (1978) Vincentio backed off from the proffered enthusiastic embrace.
74 Lloyd (1956), which cut Hortensio from this scene, gave this line to Petruchio. Antoon (1990)
     gave the line to Katherina.
76 Edwards (1995): Petruchio stressed 'our', indicating the moment of fun as a watershed in the
     relationship (Siberry 55).
76 s.d. Ayliff (1928): Hortensio got left behind by Vincentio's car and had to chase after it.
77–9 Guthrie (1954) cut the *Exeunt* so Hortensio addressed this to Petruchio. Webster (1844) s9:
     'The Lord rises – beckons on the Servants, and directs them to remove the Tinker. They bear
     him off' (pbk). Benson (1890) ran 4.5, 4.4, and then 5.1. Constance Benson (86) records that
     after 'the subdued wife meekly echoes her husband's words', Petruchio made 'a triumphant
     exit, with "Katherine" perched on the donkey's back'. Anglin (1908) had Petruchio carry
     Katherina off 'tenderly' (pbk). Winter (538) described how Petruchio 'raised her in his arms,
     wrapped his cloak around her, and supported her from the scene, she, meanwhile, clinging
     to him, with an air of affectionate dependence'.
        The 'Kiss me, Kate' sequence from the end of 5.1 was sometimes played here, e.g. Benson
     (1890), Gribble (1935). Daly (1887) played just 5.1.124–5, thus Ada Rehan avoided having to
     kiss a man in a public street, and then cut Katherina and Petruchio from 5.1, which facilitated
     a big costume change for 5.2. Sothern and Marlowe (1905) (s47) had 4.5 set in Padua, rather
     than on the way there, and they ran straight on into 5.1.

ACT 5   SCENE 1

Enter BIONDELLO, LUCENTIO [*as himself*] *and* BIANCA.
GREMIO *is out before.*

BIONDELLO Softly and swiftly, sir, for the priest is ready.
LUCENTIO I fly, Biondello. But they may chance to need thee at
home; therefore leave us.

Exit Lucentio [*with Bianca*]

BIONDELLO Nay, faith, I'll see the church a'your back, and then
come back to my master's as soon as I can.   *Exit*   5
GREMIO I marvel Cambio comes not all this while.

Enter PETRUCHIO, KATHERINA, VINCENTIO, GRUMIO,
with ATTENDANTS.

PETRUCHIO Sir, here's the door, this is Lucentio's house.
My father's bears more toward the market-place;
Thither must I, and here I leave you, sir.
VINCENTIO You shall not choose but drink before you go.   10
I think I shall command your welcome here,
And by all likelihood some cheer is toward.

He knocks.

0 s.d. The opening of this scene is not clear and directors often adjust it: e.g. Guthrie (1954)
introduced an extended mime, followed by a chase sequence in which Sly became
embroiled. Monette (1988): Lucentio, Bianca and Biondello hid under a huge black
umbrella, confusing Gremio who couldn't detect any rain. Rose (1997) played this in cloak-
and-dagger style and Bianca and Lucentio entered surreptitiously via a grille in the floor.
Lynch (1991): Bianca, Lucentio and Biondello performed an exaggerated 'running on the
spot' routine, while a confused Gremio appeared to be left behind by the runaways (the
actor was actually walking backwards). Ayliff (1928) delayed Gremio's entrance to line 66,
and cut his earlier lines. Bogdanov (1978) placed Gremio on a balcony. Sothern and
Marlowe (1905) played the opening lines of 5.1 at the end of 4.4 (s47) as did e.g. Gribble
(1935).
    Sauny the Scot makes Woodall's (Gremio's) contribution to this scene nastier by having
him and '3 or 4 Fellows' ready to abduct Biancha (4.4.6 s.d.).
6 s.d. Daly (1887) kept Petruchio and Katherina out of this scene, allowing more time for a grand
costume change for the final scene. Hortensio was brought on instead and given Petruchio's
lines (s34).

GREMIO They're busy within. You were best knock louder.

MERCHANT *looks out of the window.*

MERCHANT What's he that knocks as he would beat down the gate?

VINCENTIO Is Signor Lucentio within, sir?   15

MERCHANT He's within, sir, but not to be spoken withal.

VINCENTIO What if a man bring him a hundred pound or two to make merry withal?

MERCHANT Keep your hundred pounds to yourself. He shall need none so long as I live.   20

PETRUCHIO Nay, I told you your son was well beloved in Padua. Do you hear, sir? To leave frivolous circumstances, I pray you tell Signor Lucentio that his father is come from Pisa and is here at the door to speak with him.

MERCHANT Thou liest. His father is come from Mantua and here   25
looking out at the window.

VINCENTIO Art thou his father?

MERCHANT Ay, sir, so his mother says, if I may believe her.

PETRUCHIO [*To Vincentio*] Why, how now, gentleman! Why, this is flat knavery, to take upon you another man's name.   30

MERCHANT Lay hands on the villain. I believe a means to cozen somebody in this city under my countenance.

Enter Biondello.

13 s.d. Dews (1981): at Stratford, Ontario, the Pedant (Merchant) appeared in a skylight window above the balcony, which was occupied by Sly. Traditionally Pedants (Merchants) are often even drunker in this scene than previously, e.g. Benthall (1955), Ball (1976). In Rose (1997) the formerly reluctant Pedant (Merchant) was now happy to be taking part in the Mafia-style scam and had a woman on each arm. The 1928 revival of Bridges-Adams (1920) inspired a rapturous review of the 'excellent fooling' when Arthur Chisholm as the Pedant (Merchant) threw 'himself, like Punch, from side to side when leaning out of the window' (*SUAH* 13 July 1928).

17 Bogdanov (1978) increased the amount to a thousand pounds (also line 19).

25 'Mantua' is wrong for Vincentio and, as the Pedant (Merchant) is currently supposed to believe, life-threatening for the Pedant (Merchant). Bogdanov (1978) played this up, having the Pedant (Merchant) realise he's made a mistake and then attempt to cover up. Various attempts at correction have been made: Daly (1887) corrected to 'from Pisa' (s34), Gribble (1935) had 'to Padua', Asche (1899) 'from Pisa'.

28 Harvey (1913): Sly laughed (McDonald pbk). Cut in some revivals of Daly (1887), e.g. s34.

29–30 Cottrell (1973) gave these lines to Vincentio.

BIONDELLO [*Aside*] I have seen them in the church together – God
  send 'em good shipping! But who is here? Mine old master,
  Vincentio! Now we are undone and brought to nothing!   35
VINCENTIO Come hither, crack-hemp.
BIONDELLO I hope I may choose, sir.
VINCENTIO Come hither, you rogue! What, have you forgot me?
BIONDELLO Forgot you? No, sir. I could not forget you, for I never
  saw you before in all my life.   40
VINCENTIO What, you notorious villain! Didst thou never see thy
  master's father, Vincentio?
BIONDELLO What, my old worshipful old master? Yes, marry, sir,
  see where he looks out of the window.
VINCENTIO Is't so indeed?   45
                  He beats Biondello.
BIONDELLO Help! Help! Help! Here's a madman will murder me!
                                                                [Exit]
MERCHANT Help, son! Help, Signor Baptista!   [*Exit from the window*]
PETRUCHIO Prithee, Kate, let's stand aside and see the end of this
  controversy.
                  [*They stand aside.*]

Enter Merchant [below] with SERVANTS, BAPTISTA *and* TRANIO
                  [*disguised as Lucentio*].

TRANIO Sir, what are you that offer to beat my servant?   50
VINCENTIO What am I, sir? Nay, what are you, sir? O immortal gods! O
  fine villain! A silken doublet, a velvet hose, a scarlet cloak, and a
  copatain hat! O I am undone, I am undone! While I play the good
  husband at home my son and my servant spend all at the university.
TRANIO How now, what's the matter?   55

---

33 'God' became 'Heaven' in Webster (1844).
40 Sothern and Marlowe (1905): Petruchio cracked his whip at Biondello who was trying to
   escape (s47).
45 Ball (1976): Vincentio used a slapstick to beat Biondello.
51 Allison (1982): through habit Tranio immediately took off his hat on seeing his master.
52–3 Modern-dress productions often cut the dress details, e.g. Ayliff (1928). Vincentios react
   differently to the crisis: in Burrell (1947) Vincentio jumped up and down in rage but in
   Allison (1982) he began to sob.

BAPTISTA What, is the man lunatic?

TRANIO Sir, you seem a sober ancient gentleman by your habit, but your
  words show you a madman. Why, sir, what 'cerns it you if I wear
  pearl and gold? I thank my good father, I am able to maintain it.

VINCENTIO Thy father? O villain! He is a sail-maker in Bergamo. 60

BAPTISTA You mistake, sir; you mistake, sir. Pray, what do you think
  is his name?

VINCENTIO His name? As if I knew not his name! I have brought
  him up ever since he was three years old, and his name is Tranio.

MERCHANT Away, away, mad ass! His name is Lucentio and he is 65
  mine only son, and heir to the lands of me, Signor Vincentio.

VINCENTIO Lucentio? O, he hath murdered his master! Lay hold on
  him, I charge you in the Duke's name. O my son, my son! Tell
  me, thou villain, where is my son Lucentio?

TRANIO Call forth an officer. 70

    [*Enter an* OFFICER.]

  Carry this mad knave to the jail. Father Baptista, I charge
    you see that he be forthcoming.

VINCENTIO Carry me to the jail?

GREMIO Stay, officer. He shall not go to prison.

BAPTISTA Talk not, Signor Gremio. I say he shall go to prison. 75

65–6 Benson (1890): the drunken Pedant (Merchant) was so overcome at this thought that he fell
  into Tranio's arms. Leach (1978): Tranio had to correct the Pedant (Merchant)'s
  pronunciation of 'Lucentio'.

70 Rose (1997): a policeman arrived in a strap-on police car. In Antoon (1990) the officer was
  the town sheriff, Hortensio.

71–84 Material from *AS* Interlude 3 (see Appendix 1, pp. 236–7) is often used here, e.g. Harvey
  (1913) (McDonald pbk), Payne (1935). In suggesting the use of the Interlude to Harvey, Poel
  remarked that this is a 'delicious interruption for Sly' (s58). The Interlude is sometimes
  played as stopping the show, with the inner play actors fazed by Sly's vehemence and
  needing a prompt to get going again, e.g. Nunn (1967). In Barton (1960) Sly's intervention
  was particularly vigorous: he chased several characters with a pike, the players' Prompter
  was called upon to help restore order, Sly fell asleep shortly after his bout of strenuous
  exercise and was carried out. Sly's reaction in Trevis (1985) suggested that he had 'himself
  been "inside" ' (Holderness 1989, 47). Gremio's lines sometimes get cut back as redundant
  when *AS* is used but e.g. Payne (1942 revival) kept line 74, with Sly actually picking up on
  Gremio's line, which then prompted his intervention.

GREMIO Take heed, Signor Baptista, lest you be cony-catched in
    this business. I dare swear this is the right Vincentio.

MERCHANT Swear, if thou dar'st.

GREMIO Nay, I dare not swear it.

TRANIO Then thou wert best say that I am not Lucentio.   80

GREMIO Yes, I know thee to be Signor Lucentio.

BAPTISTA Away with the dotard, to the jail with him!

VINCENTIO Thus strangers may be haled and abused. O monstrous
    villain!

        Enter Biondello, Lucentio and Bianca.

BIONDELLO O, we are spoiled, and yonder he is! Deny him,   85
    forswear him, or else we are all undone.

        Exeunt Biondello, Tranio and Merchant, as fast as may be

LUCENTIO Pardon, sweet father.

        Lucentio and Bianca kneel.

VINCENTIO   Lives my sweet son?

BIANCA Pardon, dear father.

BAPTISTA   How hast thou offended?
    Where is Lucentio?

LUCENTIO   Here's Lucentio,
    Right son to the right Vincentio,   90
    That have by marriage made thy daughter mine
    While counterfeit supposes bleared thine eyne.

GREMIO Here's packing, with a witness, to deceive us all!

VINCENTIO Where is that damnèd villain, Tranio,
    That faced and braved me in this matter so?   95

BAPTISTA Why, tell me, is not this my Cambio?

---

76 Bogdanov (1978): Vincentio was severely manhandled and armlocked with a truncheon held
    across his chest by the Officer who was in the pocket of Baptista, a Mafia baron.

84 Reinhardt (1909) had a big fight here with everyone hitting everyone else, and a 'cast of
    thousands' onstage including naughty boys, fools, etc.

87 Ball (1976): Lucentio and Vincentio's reunion was comically rapturous. Alexander (1992):
    Tranio gave Lucentio's signet ring back to him with great reluctance, Lucentio's line was the
    cue for *AS* Interlude 3 (see Appendix 1, pp. 236–7) and at this Sly broke a bottle and was
    prepared to use it as a weapon to enforce his wishes. After the interruption Lucentio
    repeated his line and the action carried on.

BIANCA Cambio is changed into Lucentio.

LUCENTIO Love wrought these miracles. Bianca's love
  Made me exchange my state with Tranio
  While he did bear my countenance in the town, 100
  And happily I have arrived at the last
  Unto the wishèd haven of my bliss.
  What Tranio did, myself enforced him to;
  Then pardon him, sweet father, for my sake.

VINCENTIO I'll slit the villain's nose that would have sent me to the 105
jail!

BAPTISTA But do you hear, sir? Have you married my daughter
without asking my good will?

VINCENTIO Fear not, Baptista, we will content you. Go to. But I will
  in to be revenged for this villainy.   *Exit* 110

BAPTISTA And I, to sound the depth of this knavery. *Exit*

LUCENTIO Look not pale, Bianca, thy father will not frown.
          Exeunt [Lucentio and Bianca]

GREMIO My cake is dough, but I'll in among the rest,
  Out of hope of all but my share of the feast. *[Exit]*

KATHERINA Husband, let's follow, to see the end of this ado. 115

PETRUCHIO First kiss me, Kate, and we will.

KATHERINA What, in the midst of the street?

PETRUCHIO What, art thou ashamed of me?

---

98 ff. Kaut-Howson (2001): while the extremely soppy Lucentio uttered these words, everyone
   else onstage looked very unconvinced.

105–6 Benson (1890) transposed this threat to line 93, which allowed Vincentio to appear mollified
   by the end of the scene. Anglin (1908) cut it.

113–14 Gordon Crosse (25) remembers Lyall Swete in Benson (1890) saying Gremio's lines 'in a
   tone of despairing resignation'.

115–end The degree to which Petruchio's demand for a kiss is difficult for Katherina can depend on
   period setting, cultural location, and the number of people onstage witnessing it: e.g.
   Walford (1987), by setting the play in a conservative Muslim culture, certainly upped the
   stakes on what kissing in public meant. While e.g. Anglin (1908) cut this famous moment,
   Monette (1988) had the onstage policeman turn his back politely while Katherina and
   Petruchio kissed. Lovejoy (1972): the sky turned 'blushing pink' here (*SAG* 674). Edwards
   (1995): this was 'romanticized' and there was 'a big, long "screen" kiss' (Siberry 56). Nickell
   (1950) played this sequence at the beginning of 5.2, making Katherina's bashfulness a lot
   more understandable as the entire wedding party was looking at her.

KATHERINA No sir, God forbid – but ashamed to kiss.
PETRUCHIO Why then, let's home again.   120
        [*To Grumio*] Come, sirrah, let's away.
KATHERINA Nay, I will give thee a kiss.
                [*She kisses him.*]
        Now pray thee, love, stay.
PETRUCHIO Is not this well? Come, my sweet Kate,
        Better once than never, for never too late.   125
                                            Exeunt

---

119 'God' became 'Heaven' in Webster (1844).

122–3 Unlike 3.2.194, this time Katherina *does* persuade Petruchio to stay; productions often stress
        that this is the first time she calls him 'love' by making this moment very tender. In Zeffirelli
        (1967) Katherina 'holds her own, for she gives [Petruchio] a most unsatisfying peck on the
        nose' (Jorgens 70). In Alexander (1992), inspired by Katherina and Petruchio's kiss, Sly
        gently took his 'wife's' hand.

124 Burrell (1947): 'Is not this well?' was played to Grumio who raised his hat in agreement.

125 Harvey (1913) played a version of *AS* Interlude 4 (see Appendix 1, p. 237) here (s58 and
        McDonald pbk) and this is now often performed, e.g. Payne (1935). This scene was in effect
        used in Webster (1844) which played a wordless version of its action (see *Spectator*, 23
        March 1844).

ACT 5   SCENE 2

Enter BAPTISTA, VINCENTIO, GREMIO, *the* MERCHANT, LUCENTIO
and BIANCA, [HORTENSIO] *and the* WIDOW, [PETRUCHIO *and*
KATHERINA], TRANIO, BIONDELLO *and* GRUMIO *with*
SERVINGMEN *bringing in a banquet.*

LUCENTIO   At last, though long, our jarring notes agree,
    And time it is when raging war is done

0 s.d. Katherina and Petruchio have to exit and then immediately re-enter here, a situation
Shakespeare usually avoids, and which also creates a challenge for designers wanting
Katherina to turn up in a magnificent frock for her final scene. This problem is reduced
when the *AS* Interlude 4 (see Appendix 1, p. 237) is played here, as in e.g. Harvey (1913). Sly
then does not witness Katherina's submission speech but as he has already witnessed her
complete capitulation in 4.5, his confidence in the Epilogue that he has learnt how to tame a
shrew can still make sense. Stephen Miller (1998, 113–15) links the fact that Petruchio and
Katherina break the law of re-entry to the staging at Blackfriars, suggesting that even
without Sly there would not be a problem at this indoor theatre where there would be the
need for breaks between acts to trim candles, and this would mask the re-entry.

This scene is very crowded and small casts get very stretched. Trevis (1985) created a
rustic picnic setting, with the cast camped out on the floor, which reduced the problems of
blocking this scene on a traverse stage. Asche (1899) set the scene 'in a room of an Italian
inn, being Lucentio's lodging, and not, as is often the case, in marble halls or gilded palaces.
In this room were two old wooden tables laid out for about twenty guests; the servants
clearing away the last course and everyone partaking of fruit and wine' (Asche 119). Harvey
(1913) had the banquet set up as 'in Leonardo's "Last Supper"' (Carter 263). Daly (1887)
based the scene on 'Paul Veronese's famous picture of the Marriage at Cana' (*NYT* 8 March
1889). The banquet was brilliantly dealt with in Lynch (1991) when an empty table was
instantly transformed by the device of a hinged, double table top being flipped over, and a
table top laden with food appearing. Moments later, with another flip-over, a new underside
– a finished meal – then appeared. In Edwards (1995) people had drunk enough to discuss
'things they would normally never dream of talking about' (Siberry 56). Baptista is
sometimes quite drunk, e.g. Kyle (1982). Bianca was very drunk in Hammond (1984).
Morgan (1937): the narrator described the banquet in terms that suggested *Rape of Lucrece*
and *Cymbeline* as well – they had reached 'that cheerful moment when men, having eaten
and drunk together, are prone to make bets about the superior virtues of the wives whom
they have honored with marriage' (pbk).

The Widow has sometimes been played by a man, e.g. Guthrie (1954). While Phelps
(1856) cut the opening of this scene, starting essentially at line 63, and thus making the

To smile at scapes and perils overblown.
My fair Bianca, bid my father welcome,
While I with selfsame kindness welcome thine.   5
Brother Petruchio, sister Katherina,
And thou Hortensio, with thy loving widow,
Feast with the best, and welcome to my house.
My banquet is to close our stomachs up

Widow very much a token character, by contrast Burrell (1947) opened with a mime of Hortensio on his knee, presumably proposing to the Widow. As the Widow kissed him, the group onstage clapped. Schaefer (1956) cut the Widow, gave her argument with Katherina to a vile-tempered Bianca, and had Lucentio make two unsuccessful attempts to summon his wife before Petruchio summoned Katherina.

Anglin (1908), Jewett (1915), Komisarjevsky (1939): the women were left out of the quarrelsome beginning of the scene and the women are also omitted from the equivalent section of *AS* (scene 14). Bogdanov (1978) had Sly watching the scene, but had to use a double as the original Sly was playing Petruchio.

It became traditional after Daly (1887) (528) to open 5.2 with Bishop's song 'Should he upbraid', e.g. Sothern and Marlowe (1905) (548), Benson (1890). The latter production also featured a minuet which often received so much applause that it encored (*Herald*, 28 April 1893, *Stage*, 30 April 1896). More modern mood-setting music appeared in Monette (1988), which began with Tranio as lounge lizard, singing in Italian and playing piano accordion. Hodgman (1991) had rock and roll with Petruchio and Katherina dressed as a pair of elegant, androgynous rockers. *Sauny the Scot* recasts this scene extensively by having Margaret (Katherina) stage her final rebellion, mock Petruchio and abuse him in company. She is not quelled until Petruchio threatens to have her teeth pulled out, then to bury her alive (an episode derived from Fletcher's *Tamer Tamed*).

1   Heap (1985) took this line very literally and the scene opened with singing in three-part harmony but ending on a false note several times before the singers got their 'jarring notes' in tune. Gribble (1935) had Biondello singing and helping servants set chairs etc. Lucentio's speech was delivered offstage, then the whole company entered at the end of the speech, while dwarfs handed round finger bowls.

1 ff. Ayliff (1928): surrounded by festive streamers and decorations, Lucentio rapped on a table ready to make a formal wedding speech. Kyle (1982): Lucentio read his speech out but had forgotten the name of the Widow. Benthall (1955) gave this speech to Baptista with appropriate adjustments to the personal pronouns. Allison (1982): Lucentio declared 'a toast, a toast' and then began. Reinhardt (1909) had an outbreak of hugging by everyone.

2   Dillon (1979) located the action in post-Second World War Italy with Petruchio as a GI. This line was 'treated as the reconciliation of former enemies' (*Daily Iowan*, 30 October 1979).

After our great good cheer. Pray you, sit down,　10
For now we sit to chat as well as eat.
PETRUCHIO Nothing but sit and sit, and eat and eat!
BAPTISTA Padua affords this kindness, son Petruchio.
PETRUCHIO Padua affords nothing but what is kind.
HORTENSIO For both our sakes I would that word were true.　15
PETRUCHIO Now, for my life, Hortensio fears his widow!
WIDOW Then never trust me if I be afeard.
PETRUCHIO You are very sensible, and yet you miss my sense:
　　I mean Hortensio is afeard of you.
WIDOW He that is giddy thinks the world turns round.　20
PETRUCHIO Roundly replied.
KATHERINA　　　　　　　　Mistress, how mean you that?
WIDOW Thus I conceive by him.
PETRUCHIO Conceives by me! How likes Hortensio that?
HORTENSIO My widow says, thus she conceives her tale.
PETRUCHIO Very well mended. Kiss him for that, good widow.　25
KATHERINA 'He that is giddy thinks the world turns round.'
　　I pray you tell me what you meant by that.
WIDOW Your husband, being troubled with a shrew,
　　Measures my husband's sorrow by his woe –
　　And now you know my meaning.　30
KATHERINA A very mean meaning.
WIDOW　　　　　　　　　Right, I mean you.
KATHERINA And I am mean indeed, respecting you.
PETRUCHIO To her, Kate!

---

14 Daly (1887) (s34) cut much from here until line 47 so the women came on, listened to the song and departed without any indecorous disputes between them. The Widow, however, left wagging her finger reprovingly at Hortensio and this started the competition between the men on the state of their marriages (s34).

15 Allison (1982): Hortensio was already under the thumb of the Widow as she rapped his knuckles with her fan to make him sit down.

17 Alexander (1992): the Widow was played by 'Mrs Ruth Banks-Ellis' from the Lord's party. On being offered a script she pushed it away, confidently assuming the role of the Widow, in contrast with her earlier tentative participation in 4.1 as a servant manhandled by Petruchio.

22–5 Sexual pun cut in e.g. Webster (1844).

25 Miller (1987): Hortensio obeyed and the Widow hit him.

33 Devine (1953): Katherina chased the Widow offstage. Barton (1960) did likewise after Katherina had snatched the Widow's cap. Ball (1976) had a big fight ending in an exit.

HORTENSIO To her, widow!
PETRUCHIO A hundred marks my Kate does put her down.   35
HORTENSIO That's my office.
PETRUCHIO Spoke like an officer. Ha' to thee, lad.
                    He drinks to Hortensio.
BAPTISTA How likes Gremio these quick-witted folks?
GREMIO Believe me, sir, they butt together well.
BIANCA Head and butt! An hasty-witted body   40
          Would say your head and butt were head and horn.
VINCENTIO Ay, mistress bride, hath that awakened you?
BIANCA Ay, but not frighted me; therefore I'll sleep again.
PETRUCHIO Nay, that you shall not. Since you have begun,
          Have at you for a bitter jest or two.   45
BIANCA Am I your bird? I mean to shift my bush,
          And then pursue me as you draw your bow.
          You are welcome all.
                    Exeunt Bianca, [Katherina and Widow]
PETRUCHIO She hath prevented me. Here, Signor Tranio,
          This bird you aimed at, though you hit her not –   50
          Therefore a health to all that shot and missed.
TRANIO O sir, Lucentio slipped me like his greyhound,
          Which runs himself and catches for his master.
PETRUCHIO A good swift simile, but something currish.
TRANIO 'Tis well, sir, that you hunted for yourself –   55

Allison (1982): Katherina stuffed grapes down the front of the Widow's dress and chased her away.

43 Hammond (1984) had a Bianca so drunk that 'she was ready to pass out' rather than 'sleep' (Babula 1985, 360).

46 Hammond (1984): the drunken Bianca here pulled 'up her dress to expose herself and to tease Petruchio' (Babula 1985, 360). Devine (1953): Petruchio grabbed at Bianca but she evaded him. Leach (1978): Bianca threw a drink in Lucentio's face.

48 s.d. Bridges-Adams (1920) had the men sigh with relief once the women had departed but some directors have played with the ambiguous Folio exit, which does not specifiy that Katherina leaves: e.g. Rose (1997), although the pbk indicates that Katherina exited as normal, actually, as the production video reveals, delayed Katherina's exit until line 64 so that she heard the lead up to the bet. Trevis (1985) kept Katherina onstage until line 65 and she heard Petruchio reject the title 'shrew' on her behalf.

55–6 Daly (1887) (s34): Gremio was given this jibe. Monette (1988): Tranio's pelvic thrusting here made it clear he was mocking Petruchio for failing to consummate his marriage.

'Tis thought your deer does hold you at a bay.
BAPTISTA O, O, Petruchio! Tranio hits you now.
LUCENTIO I thank thee for that gird, good Tranio.
HORTENSIO Confess! Confess! Hath he not hit you here?
PETRUCHIO A has a little galled me, I confess,   60
    And as the jest did glance away from me,
    'Tis ten to one it maimed you two outright.
BAPTISTA Now in good sadness, son Petruchio,
    I think thou hast the veriest shrew of all.
PETRUCHIO Well, I say no, and therefore, Sir Assurance,   65
    Let's each one send unto his wife,
    And he whose wife is most obedient
    To come at first when he doth send for her
    Shall win the wager which we will propose.
HORTENSIO Content. What's the wager?
LUCENTIO   Twenty crowns.   70
PETRUCHIO Twenty crowns?
    I'll venture so much of my hawk or hound,
    But twenty times so much upon my wife.
LUCENTIO A hundred then.
HORTENSIO   Content.
PETRUCHIO   A match! 'Tis done.
HORTENSIO Who shall begin?
LUCENTIO   That will I.   75
    Go Biondello, bid your mistress come to me.
BIONDELLO I go.   *Exit*
BAPTISTA Son, I'll be your half Bianca comes.
LUCENTIO I'll have no halves; I'll bear it all myself.

        Enter Biondello.

63 Phelps (1856) started the scene here.

65 'Sir Assurance' often becomes 'for assurance' as in the second Folio, e.g. Benson (1890). Fiona Shaw, Katherina in Miller (1987), felt that 'When Petruchio lays a bet on Kate, maybe that's where he renders himself up: he takes a chance on her. She took a chance on him, she rendered herself up in the sun/moon scene. Now *he* takes a chance on her' (Rutter 23).

74 Bogdanov (1978): money was thrown on a green baize gambling table. This production stressed the gambling motif and had a version of line 72–3 played very early in the Induction.

79 Kaut-Howson (2001): Bianca was heard very clearly offstage shouting at Biondello.

How now, what news?

BIONDELLO   Sir, my mistress sends you word   80
That she is busy, and she cannot come.

PETRUCHIO How? 'She's busy and she cannot come'!
Is that an answer?

GREMIO   Ay, and a kind one too.
Pray God, sir, your wife send you not a worse.

PETRUCHIO I hope better.   85

HORTENSIO Sirrah Biondello, go and entreat my wife
To come to me forthwith.

Exit Biondello

PETRUCHIO   O ho, 'entreat' her!
Nay then, she must needs come.

HORTENSIO   I am afraid, sir,
Do what you can, yours will not be entreated.

Enter Biondello.

Now, where's my wife?   90

BIONDELLO She says you have some goodly jest in hand.
She will not come. She bids you come to her.

PETRUCHIO Worse and worse! 'She will not come'! O vile,
Intolerable, not to be endured!
Sirrah Grumio, go to your mistress.   95
Say I command her come to me.

Exit [Grumio]

HORTENSIO I know her answer.

PETRUCHIO   What?

HORTENSIO   She will not.

PETRUCHIO The fouler fortune mine, and there an end.

86 Allison (1982): Hortensio whispered 'entreat' to Biondello who repeated it loudly. Asche (1899): everyone repeated 'entreat'.

89 Kaut-Howson (2001): the Widow was heard offstage berating Biondello and when he reappeared onstage he had been hit.

96 Monette (1988): Grumio crossed himself before exiting.

97 Hortensio seems to have forgotten what he witnessed in 4.5. Unwin (1998): Grumio was seen briefing Katherina as to what was going on, explaining what she needed to do to get the cash. However, line 91 indicates that the women offstage may be deducing what is going on. Mrs C. H. Jones's scenario for a silent movie (s60) has a scene that *The Shrew* keeps offstage, with the women's first reactions to their summonses.

Enter Katherina.

BAPTISTA Now, by my holidame, here comes Katherina!
KATHERINA What is your will, sir, that you send for me?   100
PETRUCHIO Where is your sister, and Hortensio's wife?
KATHERINA They sit conferring by the parlour fire.
PETRUCHIO Go fetch them hither. If they deny to come,
    Swinge me them soundly forth unto their husbands.
    Away, I say, and bring them hither straight.   105
                 [*Exit Katherina*]
LUCENTIO Here is a wonder, if you talk of a wonder.
HORTENSIO And so it is. I wonder what it bodes.
PETRUCHIO Marry, peace it bodes, and love, and quiet life.
    An awful rule and right supremacy
    And, to be short, what not that's sweet and happy.   110

98 Some Petruchios are very anxious at this stage, e.g. Guthrie (1939) (Farjeon 67). In Barton (1960) there was a very long wait before Katherina appeared, also Bogdanov (1978). Kaut-Howson (2001) made the wait very much reflect the wait at the beginning of 3.2, where the wedding guests were waiting for Petruchio. When Katherina finally did appear Petruchio was so relieved he broke out into a triumphal dance. Sothern and Marlowe (1905): everyone whistled with surprise (s47). Some Grumios prolong the agony for Petruchio: in Devine (1953) Grumio entered, opened his mouth as if to explain Katherina was not coming, and then retreated as she entered. Alexander (1992): Katherina's entrance was made more sensational as she had changed into her smart clothes – at the beginning of the scene she was still bedraggled and in rags.

100 Monette (1988): Katherina laughed slightly as she asked this question, clearly assuming that some game was in hand. In *Sauny the Scot* (5.1.405–6) Margaret (Katherina) is instructed by Petruchio to take possession of the wager money she has won for him.

104 Leach (1978): Katherina smiled at the prospect of swingeing Bianca and the Widow. Alexander (1992): Katherina rubbed her hands in glee.

105 Sothern and Marlowe (1905): Petruchio's 'commanding tone' at the beginning of the line softened after Katherina looked at him and 'they exchange an understanding glance' (s48).

108 Burrell (1947): Petruchio said this line 'in a sudden tired relief, and the exhausted voice of a man who has reached the end of his physical resources' (Williamson 1957, 3).

109 Gribble (1935), Ball (1976) cut this line, making Petruchio's statement far easier for modern audiences to accept. Kyle (1982): Petruchio sent it up 'in hoity-toity tones' (*G* 13 October 1982).

BAPTISTA Now fair befall thee, good Petruchio!
   The wager thou hast won, and I will add
   Unto their losses twenty thousand crowns,
   Another dowry to another daughter,
   For she is changed, as she had never been.   115
PETRUCHIO Nay, I will win my wager better yet,
   And show more sign of her obedience –
   Her new-built virtue and obedience.

   Enter Katherina, Bianca and Widow.

   See where she comes, and brings your froward wives
   As prisoners to her womanly persuasion.   120
   Katherine, that cap of yours becomes you not:
   Off with that bauble – throw it underfoot!

111–18 Gribble (1935) cut this, reducing the financial focus as well as Petruchio's showing off.

114 Allison (1982) emphasised the fact that Petruchio is gaining precisely 'Another dowry' as everyone onstage repeated this phrase together. Miller (1987) also had everyone register the huge amount of money involved.

115 Guthrie (1954): Katherina entered in time to hear Petruchio's next speech. Bogdanov (1978): Baptista immediately wrote out a cheque.

116–18 Benson (1890) cut, making Petruchio less of a show-off. 117–18 is sometimes cut (e.g. Devine 1953) thus eliminating the repetition of 'obedience' at the end of the line.

119 Sothern and Marlowe (1905): Petruchio spoke this line 'with great tenderness' (S47).

121–9 The cap-trampling episode was cut e.g. in Phelps (1856).

122 s.d. The cap is sometimes the one from 4.3. Some Katherinas ensure that the cap will not be damaged: e.g. in Edwards (1995) Katherina hesitated 'before standing on it so lightly that it can come to no harm' (*O* 14 April 1996). Monette (1988): Katherina threw the cap flamboyantly over her head backwards, that is, to safety. By contrast, in Rider (1994) Katherina stamped on the cap ferociously in an exaggerated fashion, as if killing it. Kaut-Howson (2001): Katherina, dressed in bright red, had an almost indestructible, aggressive, extremely spiky cap which reached about two feet above her head and, despite her vigorous trampling of it, suffered no damage at all. Posner (1999): Katherina had the cap off and on the floor before Petruchio had finished the line, her excessive enthusiasm challenging Petruchio to name anything she wouldn't now dare to do. Bridges-Adams (1920): Petruchio caught the cap as Katherina dropped it and put a chain around her neck as a reward for her performance. Mellor (1989): Petruchio's order was tragic: 'The pause before [Katherina] obeyed was indicative of disbelief and sad disappointment' (Gay 1998, 174). *AS* is unequivocal – Kate *takes off her cap and treads on it* (14.86 s.d.).

[*She obeys.*]

WIDOW Lord, let me never have a cause to sigh
            Till I be brought to such a silly pass!
BIANCA Fie, what a foolish duty call you this?   125
LUCENTIO I would your duty were as foolish too.
            The wisdom of your duty, fair Bianca,
            Hath cost me a hundred crowns since supper-time.
BIANCA The more fool you for laying on my duty.
PETRUCHIO Katherine, I charge thee, tell these headstrong women   130
            What duty they do owe their lords and husbands.
WIDOW Come, come, you're mocking. We will have no telling.
PETRUCHIO Come on, I say, and first begin with her.
WIDOW She shall not.
PETRUCHIO I say she shall. And first begin with her.   135
KATHERINA Fie, fie, unknit that threatening unkind brow,

126 Kelly (1993): Bianca slapped Lucentio.

126–9 Dews (1981): Katherina clearly realised now that a bet and money were at stake (Berry 200). Sothern and Marlowe (1905) had Katherina look at Petruchio at line 128 and he 'pats his money pouch' which indicates what's going on (s48).

129 Hammond (1984): the drunken Bianca 'poured a glass of wine on [Lucentio's] head to make her point' (Babula 1985, 360). Ball (1976): Bianca said this line extremely sweetly. Alexander (1992): Bianca went and sat on the couch next to Tranio indicating her preference for the man over the master. Sothern and Marlowe (1905): Petruchio picked up the cap and returned it to Katherina (s47).

131 Sothern and Marlowe (1905): Katherina 'protestingly falls on stool' (s48). Miller (1987): Katherina sat on a stool next to Petruchio and he fed her as he spoke. Morgan (1937): there were 'shouts of approval from men' (pbk).

136 ff. For discussion of this speech see introduction (pp. 34–6). Some productions duck the challenge the speech presents: Robertson Davies (41) complained of Guthrie (1954) that Katherina's speech was 'interrupted and clouded by all kinds of directorial distractions, until the effect of it was almost ruined'. Onstage resistance to Katherina's declarations sometimes occurs: for example, in Bell (1994). The bewilderment of Katherina's onstage audience was strongly registered (*Theatre Australasia*, June 1994) but the production had previously written these characters off as bourgeois materialists so it was hard to respect their viewpoint. In Rose (1997) although Katherina was proud not humbled, the onstage audience's reaction to her speech was to 'laugh, hoot or fall into embarrassed silence' (*G&M* 5 June 1997). Alexander (1992): Katherina used the onstage audience of Hooray Henrys and spoke 'not to the theatre but to a self-possessed 20th-century woman in the closet audience.

And dart not scornful glances from those eyes
To wound thy lord, thy king, thy governor.
It blots thy beauty as frosts do bite the meads,
Confounds thy fame as whirlwinds shake fair buds,   140
And in no sense is meet or amiable.
A woman moved is like a fountain troubled,
Muddy, ill-seeming, thick, bereft of beauty,
And while it is so, none so dry or thirsty
Will deign to sip, or touch one drop of it.   145
Thy husband is thy lord, thy life, thy keeper,
Thy head, thy sovereign; one that cares for thee
And for thy maintenance; commits his body
To painful labour both by sea and land,
To watch the night in storms, the day in cold,   150
Whilst thou li'st warm at home, secure and safe,
And craves no other tribute at thy hands
But love, fair looks and true obedience –

A feminist reaction is one among many in a complex and crowded scene' (*FT* 3 April 1992)
and 'Lady Sarah Ormsby' was seen to start distancing herself from her Petruchio-like
partner, 'Lord Simon Llewellyn'.

However unpalatable this speech may sound to modern audiences, cutting back the
speech deprives the actress of her star turn and very radical cutting, such as that in Phelps
(1856), makes it clear that actually it *is* important that Katherina has a big moment at the
end of the play.

In *Sauny the Scot*, Margaret (Katherina) had no orders to deliver a speech and she
contented herself with three lines on a wife's duty to her husband (5.1.426–8).

138 Daly (1887) (S34): the Widow bowed her head in shame but the Widow is often resistant to
this, e.g. Gribble (1935): the Widow's laughter here earned her a slap from Katherina. Dews
(1981): the Widow glared at Hortensio who was enjoying himself. Bell (1994): the Widow
and Bianca laughed very loudly. Rose (1997): the Widow laughed particularly on the word
'governor' and signalled her disagreement with the entire speech.

146–7 Rider (1994): Katherina shouted 'lord', 'head', 'sovereign'. Morgan (1937): Petruchio
shouted 'Bravo!' (pbk).

147 Ayliff (1928): the Widow laughed at this as a description of Hortensio.

149–50 Leach (1978): Petruchio demurred politely. Gribble (1935): Bianca and the others looked
puzzled and ad libbed around 'labour?'

153 Monette (1988): Katherina stressed '*true* obedience', suggesting only certain kinds of
obedience were called for.

Too little payment for so great a debt.
Such duty as the subject owes the prince,   155
Even such a woman oweth to her husband.
And when she is froward, peevish, sullen, sour,
And not obedient to his honest will,
What is she but a foul contending rebel
And graceless traitor to her loving lord?   160
I am ashamed that women are so simple
To offer war where they should kneel for peace,
Or seek for rule, supremacy and sway,
When they are bound to serve, love and obey.
Why are our bodies soft, and weak, and smooth,   165
Unapt to toil and trouble in the world,
But that our soft conditions and our hearts
Should well agree with our external parts?
Come, come, you froward and unable worms,
My mind hath been as big as one of yours,   170
My heart as great, my reason haply more,
To bandy word for word and frown for frown.

154 Bogdanov (1978): 'hear, hear' from Hortensio and Vincentio.

157–60 Hamilton (1999): Katherina started enthusiastically illustrating these lines, which included swinging punches and kicking out, and Petruchio got caught in the crossfire.

158 In Monette (1988), Katherina stressed 'honest'. In 1991 Judy Gibson as Lynch's Katherina argued Katherina 'doesn't say, just submit to your husband's will, she says "honest will" ', which Gibson translated as 'if . . . he is being honest and direct with you and it feels right, fine, but don't take the rubbish' (*Dominion*, 17 June 1991).

160 Daly (1887): Katherina's speech ended here although after Petruchio's reaction, which included him kneeling and her raising him, she then delivered *C&P* 3.274–5, followed by a version of Shakespeare 5.2.161–4. This gave Rehan the final curtain speech of the production (534). Devine (1953): Katherina addressed this general recantation to Baptista.

161 Morgan (1937): Bianca and the Widow protested by crying 'Nay, nay!' while men's voices called out 'Bravo!' (pbk).

164 Ayliff (1928): the Widow laughed at this line. Reviewers referred to the contemporary debate over whether to retain the promise 'to obey' in the wedding service (e.g. *Daily Herald*, 1 May 1928, *O* 6 May 1928).

165 Rider (1994): Katherina said this very seductively.

169 Dews (1981): Katherina was laughing. Kaut-Howson (2001): Petruchio went to stop her, signalling she'd said plenty, but she held up her hand to prevent his interruption and carried on regardless.

But now I see our lances are but straws,
Our strength as weak, our weakness past compare,
That seeming to be most which we indeed least are.   175
Then vail your stomachs, for it is no boot,
And place your hands below your husband's foot.
In token of which duty, if he please,
My hand is ready, may it do him ease.

173–5 Hodgman (1991): this was stated sadly, as incontrovertible.

175 This line, which might suggest Katherina's speech is not entirely genuine, was cut in e.g.
Benthall (1948), Barton (1960).

179 Modern romantic Katherinas do not kneel: e.g. in Monette (1988) Goldie Semple's
Katherina stood tall, holding her hand up in the air in a grand theatrical gesture, clearly with
no intention of going anywhere near Petruchio's foot. Petruchios often stop Katherinas from
grovelling but unusually in Hammond (1984), when Petruchio did this, the *onstage*
characters applauded Petruchio's gesture (Babula 1985, 360). Julie Taymor (who had played
Katherina herself when at University) felt that in her 1988 production Katherina's 'gesture
was grand and it moved [Petruchio]. It was a private moment as the two slowly waltzed
about the periphery of the stage oblivious to those, players and audience alike, who don't
really get it' (Blumenthal 128). Sometimes Petruchios kneel themselves, sometimes they
embrace Katherina before she has begun to move to the floor and some kind of reciprocity
was suggested in Sothern and Marlowe (1905) when, as Katherina placed her hand on the
floor, Petruchio 'seizes her hand, and places his own on floor. She places her foot on his
hand' (s47).

Katherina's hand gestures sometimes, however, catch Petruchio unawares. Gribble
(1935): 'as she swings her hand to punctuate her meaning, it strikes Petruchio on the cheek'
(s65). A popular variation on this is to have Katherina put her hand down and, as Petruchio
approaches, tip him over, e.g. Lovejoy (1972) (*SAG* 674). A different joke at Petruchio's
expense was suggested by Maniutiu (1995) which had the rifle-wielding Katherina, Josette
Simon, 'decide not to shoot her man', fire her rifle above Petruchio's head, and the giant
cuckold's horns which then descended to hover over the head of the complacent
pipe-smoking Petruchio, plus Katherina's 'broad grin', indicated 'plainly that in the months
ahead she will frolic with any Paduan male who takes her fancy' (*T* 28 April 1995).

Hodgman (1991) had a disturbing moment here as Petruchio lifted his foot, daring
Katherina to do as she said. She obliged but in such a masochistically and overtly sensual
way that she seduced Petruchio into joining her on the floor, and the 'ease' her 'hand' was
going to 'do' him seemed pretty clear. More grimly in Bogdanov (1978) when Katherina
licked 'his foot like a dog', Petruchio moved his foot away (*ES* 5 May 1978). In Mellor (1989),
which cut after 'may it do him ease', Katherina put her *forehead* to Petruchio's foot, 'the
moment was held and disturbed music underlined it before Petruchio pulled away and

PETRUCHIO Why, there's a wench! Come on and kiss me, Kate.   180
LUCENTIO Well, go thy ways, old lad, for thou shall ha't.
VINCENTIO 'Tis a good hearing when children are toward.
LUCENTIO But a harsh hearing when women are froward.
PETRUCHIO Come, Kate, we'll to bed.
    We three are married, but you two are sped.   185
    [*To Lucentio*] 'Twas I won the wager, though you hit
      the white,
    And being a winner, God give you good night.

retreated', Katherina and Petruchio then exited separately (Gay 1998, 174, quoting Mellor). Kaut-Howson (2001): Katherina was very distressed by the time she said this line.

    Edwards (1995) finished on this line, ensuring that Katherina spoke the final words of the production. This big speech still often elicits bursts of applause, e.g. Miller (1987) (*DT* 10 September 1987). Yurcel Erten's 1986 production in Turkey had Katherina collapse at the end of the speech, having cut her wrist and bled to death during it (Elsom 75).

    In *AS*, Kate *lays her hand under her husband's feet* (14.142 s.d.) but Marcus (112) argues this is read as a 'masochistic gesture' which is 'acknowledged as excessive – performed to help her husband win the bet' when Ferando/ Petruchio responds: 'Enough sweet, the wager thou hast won, / And they I am sure cannot deny the same' (14.143–4).

180 Ball (1976): as Katherina lay prone on the floor before him, Petruchio lifted her up and kissed her. Immediately after the kiss Katherina turned and winked broadly at the audience. The wink works better on film, in close-up, than in the theatre and also appeared in Nickell (1950). Mary Pickford in Taylor (1929) first popularised this by winking complicitly at Bianca.

    This line closed the play for e.g. Benson (1890) and in Asche, as Katherina and Petruchio embraced, 'Lucentio offers his face to Bianca to kiss. She smacks it. Hortensio and Widow same business' (pbk). A production photograph of Benson (1890) shows the Widow twisting Hortensio's nose, with her arm raised to strike him. In Devine (1953) Petruchio's line was 'as much a sigh of relief as an expression of conquest' (*BP* 11 June 1953).

181 Kyle (1982): Baptista blew his nose, overcome with emotion.

183 Ayliff (1928): Lucentio kissed Bianca, but many modern productions have Lucentio and Bianca heading towards their first argument, e.g. Alexander (1992).

187 Hawthorn (1979): after Katherina's and Petruchio's exit, Bianca and the Widow stared icily at their husbands (*Beacon Herald*, 3 July 1979). Trevis (1985): both Bianca and the Widow walked off alone, leaving their husbands behind. Kyle (1982): Petruchio passed the money he had won to Katherina and she threw it up in the air before another kiss. Kaut-Howson (2001): Petruchio gathered all the money together and gave it to Lucentio, as if in compensation for his choice of bride, and suggesting that Petruchio wasn't interested in money any longer, but only interested in Katherina.

> *Exeunt Petruchio [and Katherina]*
> HORTENSIO Now, go thy ways; thou hast tamed a curst shrew.
> LUCENTIO 'Tis a wonder, by your leave, she will be tamed so.
>   [*Exeunt*]

Many productions have ended at line 187, e.g. Harvey (1913), which makes bidding farewell to the paying audience easy, and eliminates the suggestion that Katherina's taming is too much of 'a wonder' to be true (although line 189 *can* be played as genuine admiration as well as disbelief). Sothern and Marlowe (1905): Katherina 'holds up her dress and he takes gold he has won and pours all of it into her lap' (s48). Rose (1997) finished with a vision of Petruchio and Katherina in bed on the upper stage, excitedly sharing the money, and then starting to strip off ready for sex. Hodgman (1991) also had a final glimpse of Katherina and Petruchio enthusiastically disrobing. Patton (1984): Petruchio 'threw a bag of money to Kate at "being a winner" ' (Frey 1985, 488).

The Folio actually states 'Exit Petruchio', which, unless Katherina is now totally subsumed into her husband's identity, can be suggestive. Some productions have had the husband and wife exit separately, e.g. Mellor (1989). Leach (1978) had Katherina drag Petruchio off, as if to bed and then after the final curtain call, Meryl Streep was 'defiantly exiting right despite [Raúl] Juliá's vehement gesturing to the left. Finally, with a *Cosi fan tutte* air, he shrugged and followed her' (Ranald 221). Kyle (1982) had a communal dance but Katherina then 'stands apart' for a moment 'with an air of distress that is very touching' (*FT* 3 May 1983).

Kaut-Howson (2001) followed the exit with noises-off of Petruchio whooping with joy, followed by a motorcycle revving up, as the biker Petruchio and Katherina raced off.

Webster (1844) had 'Curtain when the Lord gives the purse to the players'. Burrell (1947): all the players bowed to Sly and then departed. Alexander (1992): Sly's 'wife', 'Rupert Llewellyn', younger brother to the Lord, carried him off and left him to be found by the publican.

EPILOGUE: SCENE 15 FROM *A SHREW*

Then enter two bearing of SLY *in his own apparel again and*
leaves him where they found him and then goes out. Then enter
the TAPSTER

TAPSTER Now that the darksome night is overpast,
And dawning day appears in crystal sky,

Although William Poel and Martin Harvey considered playing a slightly cut version of this
scene in 1913, the Poel marked promptbook notes, 'NB The waking of Sly was not played'
(558). The Epilogue was first restored by Robert Atkins in 1922 at the Old Vic and played
frequently at that theatre from then on. French's acting edition (1925), edited by Robert
Atkins, suggests that at the opening of this scene: 'The Company turn and bow to the Lord.
He advances to them to congratulate them. As he is doing so, two attendants carry Sly on
from door R. in his old attire. The company laugh. When C. the attendants swing Sly to and
fro three times and pitch him clear of Traverse No. 1, which is at once drawn over leaving
him huddled on the floor.' Concern for the safety of the actor playing Sly was more in
evidence in Ayliff (1927) which had Sly remain asleep snoring on 'in the front row of the
orchestra until the last guest of the Garrick Theater had disappeared from the auditorium'
(*New York Sun*, 26 October 1927).

The Tapster is sometimes replaced by the Hostess from the Folio Induction 1, e.g. French's
acting edition (1925). In Creswell (1935, 1941) the Tapster's lines were given to the Lord.
Heap (1985) had the Hostess discover Sly under a table as the travelling players struck their
set. The Players often feature: e.g. in Barton (1960), 'A purse is flung to Epilogue [Baptista]
and he and all the mummers are on their way to Chipping Camden or to Ilmington, leaving
a sprawling, snoring Irish man semi-conscious at a pot-house table to come back to a world
without a dream' (*John O'London*, 30 June 1960). Langham (1962): the actor playing
Petruchio, now out of part, walked 'past Kate without so much as a nod to her. Starting
down the road that will end somewhere in another performance, he throws his arm about
Bianca, who is obviously his real love' (*New York Herald Tribune*, 21 June 1962). Nunn
(1967): Sly was 'laid gently in the snow. He turns a little, awakes – one might almost say, as if
to dream again. And the players, their tackle packed up, troop away, past the beam of a
lantern, away from the tavern warmth, into the frosty night, their good work very well done.
It is a moving close' (*Stage*, 13 April 1967). Trevis (1985): Sly rushed to congratulate the
players. Although the Lord contemptuously dropped coins at Sly's feet, Sly was generous
enough, and sufficiently sensitive to class solidarity, to offer some of the money to the
actress playing Katherina (Holderness 1989, 48). Guthrie (1954) had a mimed farewell to

Now must I haste abroad. But soft, who's this?
What, Sly? O wondrous, hath he lain here all night?
I'll wake him. I think he's starved by this,   5
But that his belly was so stuffed with ale.
What ho, Sly? Awake for shame.

SLY   Sim, gi's some more wine. What's all the players gone?
Am not I a lord?

TAPSTER   A lord with a murrain! Come, art thou drunken still?   10

SLY   Who's this? Tapster? O Lord, sirrah,
I have had the bravest dream tonight
That ever thou heardest in all thy life.

TAPSTER   Ay marry, but you had best get you home,

the players: 'at the end of the play, the Lord covered his strange guest (Sly) and, after paying off the players, bade him a silent goodnight' (Robertson Davies, 58). Alexander (1992) had Sly brought on by 'Rupert Llewellyn', the younger brother of the Lord, who had been forced to play Sly's 'wife', and Sly woke in time to see the players arriving for a post-performance drink. The evidence is confusing in relation to Webster (1844), the earliest production to reinstate Sly, and this may reflect changes in performance. The *Spectator* (23 March 1844) describes how at the end, 'being clothed in his own dirty rags, [Sly] is brought on in the last scene as though being carried out to wallow in the mire' until finally 'The Lord bestows a purse upon the actors after all is done'. Planché (297) also claims that Sly was carried out at the end of Act 5; however pbk s9 indicates that Sly was carried offstage at the end of Act 4. Gribble (1935): 'Everyone on stage applauds as the Lord with the huntsmen enters from down L. They have their brass pot with coins' (s65). The actors then 'set out for the road again, looking for a new audience, swinging along in the spirit of gay adventure' (*Oakland Tribune*, 29 October 1939). There was then an extravagant transformation scene, which had little to do with the play, whereby 'Alfred Lunt and Lynn Fontanne, disciples of connubial bliss' were 'translated to heaven in a golden chariot in all the splendor of a magnificent sunburst' accompanied by a final choral song (*San Franciso News*, 14 November 1939). Ramster (1989) included a 'final tableau of Christopher Sly, stripped and rejected, turning for comfort to the actress who has been playing Kate, inchoately recognising in her a fellow victim of thoughtless and arrogant exploitation' (*G* 26 January 1989). Productions often use *A Shrew*'s final scene as an inspiration for an equivalent but radically different frame (see Introduction pp. 59, 63–4, e.g. Mellor 1989, Edwards 1995).

3b   The scene is often started here, e.g. Devine (1953), Posner (1999).

4   Heap (1985): the Hostess addressed this line as a genuine question to the audience.

7   Devine (1953, 1954): the Hostess tipped water over Sly to wake him and slapped him in the face. Barton (1960), Nunn (1967) started the scene here.

14–15   Posner (1999) gave these lines to Bianca, accompanying fellow ladette Katherina into a rave club.

   For your wife will course you for dreaming here tonight.   15
SLY Will she? I know now how to tame a shrew.
   I dreamt upon it all this night till now,
   And thou hast waked me out of the best dream
   That ever I had in my life.
   But I'll to my wife presently,   20
   And tame her too, and if she anger me.
TAPSTER Nay tarry Sly, for I'll go home with thee
   And hear the rest that thou hast dreamt tonight.

                   Exeunt

FINIS

16 In Dews (1981) on 'Will she?' Sly punched his own hand hard to indicate the kind of thrashing he intended to give his wife.

20 The last line in Watts (1954).

21 After this line in Devine (1953) the players of the inner play were seen heading off to their next performance carrying trunks, bundles, banners, trumpets, baskets and swords. The 'wondering, not yet disillusioned' Sly (*Royal Leamington Spa Courier*, 12 June 1953) turned 'to see the strolling players leaving the Lord's house' as 'the cock crows the awakening of a new day' (*Daily Sketch*, 10 June 1953). Many reviewers were much moved by this, perhaps because reconciliation between Katherina and Petruchio was signalled: the actor who had played Petruchio had his arm around Katherina and gave her some bread to eat. This moment was rather complex if the audience (none of the reviewers mentioned it) remembered that in the Induction the player who assumed the role of Katherina was presented as a boy.

23 Alexander (1992): The Tapster glanced ruefully at his wife as he left with Sly, as if he too wanted to hear about how to tame a wife. Jackson (1971): 'As Sly turned for home to tame his own shrewish wife, he saw the troupe of players leaving town' and did a 'Jack Benny take' (Horobetz 386). Komisarjevsky (1939): Sly, who had led into the interval with a song, now sung his song alone. Brickman (1990) had a Sly who had come to the Sheffield Crucible theatre to see snooker, which the theatre is famous for hosting. After the playing of the Epilogue, Jeffrey Wainwright (*Independent*, 15 November 1990) felt smugly that 'the moral is clear: only people like Christopher Sly, whom we spent the pre-curtain and the interval avoiding in the bar, take the play seriously'. Posner (1999): Sly woke to encounter two ladettes, the actresses who had played Katherina and Bianca, going into a nightclub. They were very unimpressed with his claims that he now knew how to tame a shrew but as they opened the door to the nightclub the music that thumped out loud and clear was Prodigy's 'Smack My Bitch Up', suggesting that it is not only drunken Elizabethan tinkers who fantasise about thumping women.

APPENDIX 1: SLY INTERLUDES
FROM *A SHREW*

INTERLUDE 1

The interlude follows 3.308 and ends scene 3.

Then SLY *speaks*

SLY Sim, when will the fool come again?
LORD He'll come again, my lord, anon.   310
SLY Gi's some more drink here. Souns, where's the tapster?
    Here Sim, eat some of these things.
LORD So I do, my lord.
SLY Here Sim, I drink to thee.
LORD My lord, here comes the players again.   315
SLY O brave, here's two fine gentlewomen.

INTERLUDE 2

The interlude follows scene 11 and begins scene 12.

SLY Sim, must they be married now?
LORD Ay, my lord.

    [Scene 12] *Enter* FERANDO *and* KATE *and* SANDER

SLY Look Sim, the fool is come again now!

INTERLUDE 3

The interlude follows 13.44; scene 13 continues from line 55.

Then SLY *speaks*

SLY I say we'll have no sending to prison!   45
LORD My lord, this is but the play, they're but in jest.
SLY I tell thee Sim, we'll have no sending to prison,
       That's flat!
       Why Sim, am not I Don Christo Vary?
       Therefore I say, they shall not go to prison.   50

LORD No more they shall not my lord, they be run away.

SLY Are they run away, Sim? That's well!

　　　　Then gi's some more drink and let them play again.

LORD Here my lord.

SLY *drinks and then falls asleep*

INTERLUDE 4

The interlude follows 13.126 and ends scene 13.

SLY *sleeps*

LORD Who's within there?

[*Enter* BOY *and servingmen*]

　　　　Come hither sirs, my lord's asleep again.

　　　　Go take him easily up,

　　　　And put him in his own apparel again,　　　　　　　130

　　　　And lay him in the place where we did find him,

　　　　Just underneath the alehouse side below,

　　　　But see you wake him not in any case.

BOY It shall be done, my lord.

　　　　[*To others*] Come, help to bear him hence.　　　135

Exeunt

APPENDIX 2: SPIN-OFFS AND ADAPTATIONS

For Fletcher's *The Woman's Prize*, Lacy's *Sauny the Scot*, Bullock's *Cobler of Preston*, Johnson's *Cobler of Preston*, Worsdale's *Cure for A Scold*, see introduction pp. 5–9. Fragments of *The Shrew* also appeared in *The Mad Wooing* and *The Lady's Advice* in *The Theatre of Ingenuity* (1698).

OPERAS

Operas based on or loosely inspired by *The Shrew* include those by: Carlo Francesco Badini (*Il duca d'Atene*) 1780; Vincente Martin y Soler (*La Capricciosa Coretta*) 1785; John Braham and Thomas Cooke, with some borrowings from Rossini, 14 May 1828, Drury Lane; Hermann Goetz (1874); Spyridon Samaras (1895, lost); Ruperto Chapi (1896); Johan Wagenaar (1909); C. Silver (1922); Renzo Bossi (1923); Alfred Reynolds (1927); M. Persico (1931); Rudolf Karel (1942–4 unfinished); Philip Greeley Clapp (1945–8); Vittorio Giannini (1953); Vissarion Shebalin (1957); Joaquin Gutierrez Herias (1981). Sly-inspired operas include: Ermanno Wolf-Ferrari (*Sly*, 1927), Thomas Eastwood (*Christopher Sly*, 1960) and Dominick Argento (*Christopher Sly*, 1962–3). In 1895 A. Maclean premiered a one-act opera entitled *Petruccio*. John Kendrick Bang wrote *Katharine: A Travesty* (1888), a lively, Gilbert and Sullivan-style parody operetta. The *Boston Journal* (10 October 1897) records a comédie lyrique based on *The Shrew*, libretto by Emile Deshays, music by Frédéric Le Rey (information taken from *Grove*, Dean and Schmidgall).

MUSICAL VERSIONS

These include: a jazz version directed by Edward Massey for the Harvard Dramatic Club in 1927; *I'll Marry You Sunday*, by Irvin Graham, book by Dawn Powell (1944); the extremely popular *Kiss Me, Kate*, music by Cole Porter, book by Bella and Samuel Spewack (1948). The Federal Theatre Negro unit in Seattle, Washington, performed a musical version of *The Taming of the Shrew* in June 1939, adapted by Joseph Staton and Herman Moore, with music by Howard Biggs (Hill 116–18). *Shrew: The Musical*, music and lyrics by J. R. Biggs and Dennis West, was performed at the Georgia Shakespeare Festival in 1993 and 1994.

DANCE VERSIONS

The most famous dance version is that choreographed by John Cranko for the Stuttgart Ballet Company in 1969, music by Kurt-Heinz Stolze. However, others include: Maurice Béjart (1954), music by Scarlatti; John Cranko, Stuttgart Ballet Company in 1969, music by Kurt-Heinz Stolze after Scarlatti. The *International Dictionary of Ballet* also lists ballet versions by Vera Untermullerova (1961) and Louis Falco (1980). Music exists for dance treatments of the play by Mikhail Bronner (1985) and by Aleksi Machavariani (1988). A classical Indian dance version of *The Shrew*, choreographed by Pushkala Gopal (Katherina) and Unnikrishnan (Petruchio), was directed by Hilary Westlake in 1991, and toured the north of England. Harold Collins choreographed a *Shrew* ballet for the Queensland Ballet in 1992. Wolfgang Geisendoerfer, Joachim Lauenroth and Alexander Schneider have also choreographed their own versions of the play.

SPIN-OFF FILMS

Shrew spin-off films held by the National Film and Television Archives in London, listed and described in McKernan and Terris include: *Elstree Calling* (Adrian Brunel GB 1930); *Star Impersonations* (Harry Hughes GB 1930); *You Made Me Love You* (Monty Banks GB 1933); *The Immortal Gentleman* (Widgey R. Newman GB 1935); *Second Best Bed* (Tom Walls GB 1938). McKernan and Terris also suggest *The Quiet Man* (John Ford USA 1952) and *McLintock* (USA 1963) as derivative from *The Shrew*. The script of *The Tamer Tamed* by Elaine Morgan, broadcast by the Welsh Home Service 4 October 1955, is held in Birmingham Central Library.

Silent film spin-offs include *Taming Mrs Shrew*, about taming a nagging wife, and *The Taming of the Shrewd*, about a suffragette who gets her comeuppance, both from 1912 (Ball, 149). The *Animated Tales* broadcast a 27-minute *Shrew* directed by Aida Ziablikova in 1994.

A porn spin-off, *The Taming of the Screw*, is discussed by Richard Burt (93–6). The television series *Moonlighting* devoted an episode to a quirky version of *The Taming of the Shrew*. *Ten Things I Hate About You*, a teen dating movie (1999) directed by Gil Junger, loosely derives from the play. The *Times* (21 April 1994) reported on an Arabic film which relocates the action to a vet's surgery 'where the vet's young wife is broken in like any other animal'. *A Marriage Made in Heaven*, directed by Dicynna Hood, was released on video by Rockhopper Productions (1993).

POST-GARRICK THEATRICAL SPIN-OFFS

These include foreign adaptations such as Paul Delair's (1891) for Constant Coquelin and Jane Hading, inspired by Daly (1887), also used by Cécile Sorel; *La Mégère de Padova*, Marco Micone Théâtre du Monde, Montreal (1995) or Ermete Novelli's adaptation which played in New York in 1907 in Italian. Firmin Gémier played a 1918 adaptation by M. G. de la Fouchardière, which toured internationally. Alexander Ostrovsky's *Easy Money* is also based on *The Shrew*.

DISTINCT SHREW-INSPIRED TEXTS IN ENGLISH

These include: *The Honeymoon*, by John Tobin (1818); *Tantrums*, by Frank Stayton (*Boston Transcript*, 1 November 1912); *The Ladies Shakespeare*, by J. M. Barrie – Katherina feigns being shrewish to get the man she wants – performed by Maude Adams in 1914; *Christopher Sly*, by Giovacchino Forzano, translated by H. B. Cotterill and performed at the New Theatre, London, in 1921 – Sly became a tragic Villon figure; G. J. Nathan, *The Avon Flows* (1937) – *Shrew*, *Romeo and Juliet*, *Othello*; Clement Ramsland's modernised *Shrew* (Northwestern Press, Minn. 1942) has Curtis as a 'Negro mammy' and Grumio plus the four maids in Petruchio's house in black face. *Tinker's Luck*, a musical play by Will Woodhead for the Athenaeum Players, Bury; *The Shrew*, by Charles Marowitz, 1973; *A Shrewd Woman*, by Geoff Bullen (Roundhouse, London 1979); *Showdown* (1976), by Don Evans (action relocated to an African American neighbourhood in Philadelphia); a Chinese/Australian adaptation by Sydney-based Kai Tai Chan, performed at the Portsmouth Festival 1987; *Mussolini: Kate's Part in his Downfall*, by Kathleen McCreery for the Avon Touring Company in 1987.

PROSE VERSIONS

A prose version of *The Shrew* appears in *Lamb's Tales from Shakespeare*. Clemence Dane wrote up the play as a short story, which included Sly, in *Strand Magazine* (March 1934). Miss G. B. Stern published a novel entitled *Petruchio* in 1930.

BIBLIOGRAPHY

PROMPTBOOKS

LOCATION ABBREVIATIONS

BCL: Birmingham Central Library; FL: Folger Library; NYPL: New York Public Library; S: Shattuck reference number; SC: Shakespeare Centre, Stratford-upon-Avon; SO: Stratford Ontario Festival Archive.

1844 Webster s9 FL microfilm; s10 NYPL.

1856 Phelps s16 FL microfilm.

1887 Daly s28, s34 FL microfilm. Most references are to s34. s55 and s56 combine Daly with Sothern and Marlowe and to prevent confusion have been avoided in the commentary. s34 uses the first four-act printed text published in 1887, not the centenary edition of April 1887. References to s29, s30, s31 and s32 (NYPL) are clearly identified as such.

1890 The Bensons s42 SC.

c.1900 Hanford s41 FL microfilm.

1904 Asche s43 SC.

1905 Sothern and Marlowe Folger s47, 48, 49 FL microfilm; s45, 46 NYPL; NYPL + 86-3631 (not listed by Shattuck); s44, s50 City of NY Museum + 305.E-81 (not listed by Shattuck). As with Daly, reference to the conflated pbks s55 and s56 has been avoided.

1908 Anglin s57 NYPL.

1909 Reinhardt, Binghampton, Reinhardt archive.

1913 Harvey, possession of Professor Jan McDonald, Glasgow University.

1913 Harvey, s58, marked up by Poel and Harvey, London Museum.

1915 Jewett s59 FL microfilm.

1915–28? Mrs C. H. Jones, scenario for a silent movie s60 FL microfilm.

1918 Drinkwater, BCL.

1921, 1930? Leiber NYPL (not listed in Shattuck and it is not clear which version of Leiber's production is documented).

1928 Ayliff s62 BCL – all references are to the more legible pbk marked up in blue ink. Another pbk held in the collection is less detailed.

1933 Bridges-Adams s63 SC: s64 SC is also Bridges-Adams but the provenance is not clear.

1935 Gribble s65 NYPL. This consists of two distinct pbks. All references are to the heavily marked stage manager's pbk unless they are designated CS, which refers to the very lightly marked pbk signed 'Carolyn Simonson'.

1935 Payne s66 SC. This pbk covered several of Payne's revivals and is
    catalogued under 1942.

1935 Creswell BCL.

1937 Morgan s68 FL.

1939 Komisarjevsky s69 SC (see also Harvard Theatre collection 371, 372).

1941 Creswell BCL.

1947 Burrell Bristol Old Vic archive.

1947 Burrell radio broadcast (extracts) BCL.

1948 Benthall s71 SC.

1950 Van Gyseghem broadcast (extracts) BCL.

1950 Wolfit broadcast (extracts) BCL.

1952 Davis BCL.

1953 Devine s72 SC.

1954 Watts broadcast BCL.

1954 Devine s73 SC.

1954 Guthrie s74 SO.

1954 Carey s75 Bristol Old Vic archive.

1955 Benthall s76 Bristol Old Vic archive.

1956 Schaefer NYPL – two scripts. One preliminary, one final.

1956 Lloyd NYPL s78.

1959 Dunlop broadcast BCL.

1960 Barton s79. Also pbk for revival directed by Maurice Daniels in 1961 and
    1962.

1962 Langham SO.

1967 Nunn SC.

1973 Gascon SO.

1973 Williams SC.

1973 Cottrell BCL.

1979 Hawthorn SO.

1981 Dews SO.

1982 Kyle SC.

1987 Miller SC.

1988 Monette SO.

1990 Antoon NYPL.

1990 Alexander SC.

1992 Alexander SC.

1993 Kelly West Yorkshire Playhouse Archive.

1995 Edwards SC.

1997 Rose SO.

VIDEO RECORDS OF PERFORMANCE

Notes on the following productions are based on my observations of the
relevant video unless the commentary specifies a reference to the pbk.

1976 Televised revival of Ball (1973).

1978 Leach NYPL.

1981 Dews CBC broadcast SO.

1982 Kyle SC.

1985 Heap, Doomsday project archive, University of Lancaster and St Martin's College.

1987 Miller SC.

1988 Monette SO.

1991 Hodgman, Melbourne Theatre Company archive.

1991 Lynch, Director's rough cut archive video.

1992 Alexander SC.

1994 Rider, Director's rough cut archive video.

1995 Edwards SC.

1997 Rose SO.

PRODUCTION DETAILS BASED ON PERSONAL OBSERVATIONS

Sheard (1998) – viewed 17 July

Unwin (1998) – viewed 4 November

Hamilton (1999) – viewed 25 June

Posner (2000) – viewed 9 March

Kaut-Howson (2001) – viewed 17 March

Quotations from promptbooks have not used capital letters for characters' entire names.

BOOKS AND ARTICLES

Anon., *A Knack to Know a Knave*, ed. G. R. Proudfoot, Malone Society, Oxford University Press, 1964.

Asche, Oscar, *Oscar Asche: His Life*, London: Hurst and Blackett Ltd, 1929.

Babula, William, 'Shakespeare at Lake Tahoe', *Shakespeare Quarterly* 34 (1983): 344–5.

'Shakespeare at Lake Tahoe', *Shakespeare Quarterly* 36 (1985): 359–61.

Ball, Robert Hamilton, *Shakespeare on Silent film: A Strange Eventful History*, London: Allen and Unwin, 1968.

Barrett, Wilson (the younger), *On Stage For Notes: The Story of the Wilson Barrett Company*, Edinburgh and London: Blackwood and Sons, 1954.

Bate, Jonathan and Jackson, Russell (eds.), *Shakespeare: An Illustrated Stage History*, Oxford University Press, 1996.

Bawcutt, N. W., *The Control and Censorship of Caroline Drama: The Records of Sir Henry Herbert, Master of the Revels 1623–73*, Oxford: Clarendon Press, 1996.

Beauman, Sally, *The Royal Shakespeare Company: A History of Ten Decades*, Oxford University Press, 1982.

Beckerman, Bernard, 'The 1965 Season at Stratford, Connecticut', *Shakespeare Quarterly* 16 (1965): 329–33.

Bedford, Arthur, *A Serious Remonstrance in Behalf of the Christian Religion*, 1719, preface by Arthur Freeman. New York: Garland, 1974.

Beerbohm, Max, *More Theatres, 1898–1903*, London: Hart-Davis, 1969.

Benson, Constance, *Mainly Players: Bensonian Memories*, London: Thornton Butterworth Ltd, 1926.

Berry, Ralph, 'Stratford Festival Canada', *Shakespeare Quarterly* 33 (1982): 199–202.

Blumenthal, Eileen, and Taymor, Julie, *Julie Taymor Playing With Fire: Theater Opera Film*, New York: Harry N. Abrams, 1995.

Bullock, Christopher, *The Cobler of Preston and the Adventures of Half an Hour*, London, T. Corbett 1723, reprinted London: Cornmarket Press, 1969.

Burt, Richard, *Unspeakable ShaXXXspeares: Queer Theory and American Kiddie Culture*, Basingstoke: Macmillan, 1998.

Butler, Nicholas, *John Martin-Harvey: The Biography of an Actor-Manager*, Wivenhoe, Essex: published by the author, 1997.

Carlson, Susan, 'The Suffrage Shrew: the Shakespeare Festival, "A Man's Play," and New Women', in *Shakespeare and the Twentieth Century*, the Selected Proceedings of the International Shakespeare Association World Congress Los Angeles, 1996, ed. Jonathan Bate, Jill L. Levenson and Dieter Mehl, London: Associated University Presses, 1998, 85–102.

Carter, Huntly, *The Theatre of Max Reinhardt*, New York: Benjamin Blom, 1914, reissued 1964.

Child, Harold, 'The Stage-History of *The Taming of the Shrew*' in *The Taming of the Shrew*, ed. Arthur Quiller-Couch, Cambridge University Press, 1928.

Clark, Sandra, *The Plays of Beaumont and Fletcher: Sexual Themes and Dramatic Representation*, London: Harvester Wheatsheaf, 1994.

Cochrane, Claire, *Shakespeare and the Birmingham Repertory Theatre 1913–1929*, London: The Society for Theatre Research, 1993.

Cocroft, Thoda, *Great Names and How They Are Made*, Chicago, New York and London: The Dartnell Press, 1941.

Cousin, Geraldine, 'The Touring of the Shrew', *NTQ* 7 (1986): 275–81.

Crosse, Gordon, *Shakespearean Playgoing, 1890–1952*, London: Mowbray, 1953.

Crundell, H. W., '*The Taming of the Shrew* on the XVII Century Stage', *Notes and Queries* 173 (18 September 1937): 207.

Daly, Joseph, *The Life of Augustin Daly*, New York: Macmillan, 1917.

Davies, Robertson, see Guthrie, Tyrone.

Davies, Thomas, *Memoirs of the Life of David Garrick Esq.* London: 2 vols., Longman, Hurst et al., 1808.

Dean, Winton, 'Shakespeare in the Opera House,' *Shakespeare Survey* 18 (1965): 75–93.

Devlin-Glass, Frances, ' "Teasing the Audience with the Play": Feminism and Shakespeare at the Melbourne Theatre Company, 1984–93', *Australasian Drama Studies* 33 (1998): 21–39.

Disher, Maurice Willson, *The Last Romantic: The Authorised Biography of Sir John Martin-Harvey*, London: Hutchinson and Co., 1948.

Dobson, Michael, *The Making of the National Poet: Shakespeare, Adaptation and Authorship, 1660–1769*, Oxford: Clarendon Press, 1992.

Dolan, Frances E., *'The Taming of the Shrew': Texts and Contexts*, Houndmills: Macmillan, 1996.

Dowling, Ellen, 'Christopher Sly on the Stage', *Theatre History Studies* 3 (1983): 87–98.

Durham, Weldon B. (ed.), *American Theatre Companies, 1931–1986*, New York and London: Greenwood Press, 1989.

Elsom, John (ed.), *Is Shakespeare Still Our Contemporary?* London: Routledge, 1989.

Engle, Ron, Londré, Felicia Hardison, and Watermeir, Daniel J., *Shakespeare Companies and Festivals, An International Guide*, Westport, Conn.: Greenwood Press, 1995.

Evans, Maurice, *All This and Evans Too!: A Memoir*, Columbia, S. C.: University of Carolina Press, 1987.

Farjeon, Herbert, *The Shakespearean Scene: Dramatic Criticism*, London: Hutchinson, 194-.

Felheim, Marvin, *The Theater of Augustin Daly: An Account of the Late Nineteenth-Century American Stage*, Cambridge, Mass.: Harvard University Press, 1956.

Fletcher, John, *The Woman's Prize or The Tamer Tamed*, ed. Fredson Bowers in *The Dramatic Works in the Beaumont and Fletcher Canon*, vol. IV, Cambridge University Press, 1979.

Foakes, R. A and Rickert, R. T. (eds.), *Henslowe's Diary*, Cambridge University Press, 1961.

Fowler, J. Beresford, *Shakespearean Talks*, Ilfracombe, Devon: Arthur H. Stockwell, 1975.

Frey, Charles, 'Shakespeare in Seattle', *Shakespeare Quarterly* 32 (1981): 274–77.
'Shakespeare in the Northwest', *Shakespeare Quarterly* 36 (1985): 477–88.

Gaines, Barry, 'Festival Premiere in North Carolina', *Shakespeare Quarterly* 29 (1978): 238–41.

Garner, Shirley Nelson, *'The Taming of the Shrew*: Inside or Outside of the Joke?' in *'Bad' Shakespeare: Revaluations of the Shakespeare Canon*, ed.

Maurice Charney, London and Toronto: Associated University Presses, 1988.

Garrick, David, *Catharine and Petruchio*, in *The Plays of David Garrick*, vol. III, ed. with commentary and notes Harry William Pedicord and Fredrick Louis Bergmann, Carbondale, Ill.: Southern Illinois University Press, 1981.

Gay, Penny, *As She Likes It: Shakespeare's Unruly Women*, London: Routledge, 1994.

'Recent Australian *Shrew*s: the "Larrikin Element"' in *Shakespeare and the Twentieth Century*, the Selected Proceedings of the International Shakespeare Association World Congress Los Angeles, 1996, ed. Jonathan Bate, Jill L. Levenson and Dieter Mehl, London: Associated University Presses, 1998, 168–82.

Genest, John, *Some Account of the English Stage from the Restoration in 1660 to 1830*. 10 vols. Bath: Carrington, 1832.

Gilbey, Liz, 'A New Look at the Shrew', *Plays International*, April 1992: 10–11.

Gsell, Paul, *Gémier, Le Théâtre: entretiens réunis par Paul Gsell*, Paris: Bernard Grasset, 1925.

Guthrie, Tyrone, Davies, Robertson and McDonald, Grant, *Twice Have the Trumpets Sounded: A Record of the Stratford Shakespearean Festival in Canada*, Toronto: Clarke, Irwin, 1954.

Hageman, Elizabeth H., 'Shakespeare in Massachusetts, 1983', *Shakespeare Quarterly* 35 (1984): 222–5.

Hallinan, Tim, 'Interview: Jonathan Miller on the Shakespeare Plays', *Shakespeare Quarterly* 32 (1981): 134–45.

Halstead, William P., *Shakespeare as Spoken: A Collation of 5000 Acting Editions and Promptbooks of Shakespeare*, vol. IV, American Theatre Association, Ann Arbor: University Microfilms International, 1977–c.1983.

Haring-Smith, Tori, *From Farce to Metadrama: A Stage History of 'The Taming of the Shrew', 1594–1983*, Westport, Conn.: Greenwood Press, 1985.

Henderson, Diana E., 'A Shrew for the Times' in *Shakespeare, the Movie: Popularizing the Plays on Film, TV, and Video*, ed. Lynda E. Boose and Richard Burt, London: Routledge, 1997.

Hill, Errol, *Shakespeare in Sable: A History of Black Shakespearean Actors*, Amherst: University of Massachusetts Press, 1984.

Hodgdon, Barbara, *The Shakespeare Trade: Performances and Appropriations*, Philadelphia: University of Pennsylvania Press, 1998.

Holderness, Graham (ed.), *The Shakespeare Myth*, Manchester University Press, 1988.

Holderness, Graham, *Shakespeare in Performance: 'The Taming of the Shrew'*, Manchester University Press, 1989.

Holderness, Graham and Bryan Loughrey (eds.), *A Pleasant Conceited Historie, Called the Taming of a Shrew*, Lanham, Md.: Barnes and Noble, 1992.

Holland, Peter, *English Shakespeares: Shakespeare on the English Stage in the 1990s*, Cambridge University Press, 1997.

Horobetz, Lynn K., 'Shakespeare at the Old Globe, 1971', *Shakespeare Quarterly* 22 (1971): 385–7.

Howard, Pamela, 'Designing the Shrew', *NTQ* 10: (1987), 184–7.

Huesmann, Heinrich, *Welt Theater Reinhardt: Bauten, Spielstätten, Inszenierungen*, Munich: Prestel-Verlag, 1983.

Jackson, Berners, 'Retrospect/ The Stratford Festival 1958–1968' in *The Stratford Scene 1958–1968*, ed. Peter Raby, Toronto: Clarke, Irwin, 1968.

Jackson, Russell, 'Shakespeare's Comedies on Film' in *Shakespeare and the Moving Image: The Plays on Film and Television*, ed. Anthony Davies and Stanley Wells, Cambridge University Press, 1994.

Johnson, Charles, *The Cobler of Preston*, London: W. Wilkins, 1716, reprinted Cornmarket Press, 1969.

Jorgens, Jack, *Shakespeare on Film*, Lanham, Md.: University Press of America, 1991.

Kelly, Judy, 'Shakespeare Festival of Dallas', *Shakespeare Quarterly* 32 (1981): 240–1.

Kemble, John Philip, *Katharine and Petruchio, a comedy; taken by David Garrick from The Taming of the Shrew. Revised by J. P. Kemble and now first published as it is acted at Covent Garden*, London. Printed for the theatre 1810.

Knowles, Richard Paul, 'Neville's Neptune', *Canadian Theatre Review* (Summer 1981): 125–7.

Labriola, Albert C., 'Shakespeare in Pittsburgh', *Shakespeare Quarterly* 32 (1981): 202–6.

Lacy, John, *Sauny the Scot*, in *Shakespeare Made Fit: Restoration Adaptations of Shakespeare*, ed. Sandra Clark, London: J. M. Dent, 1997.

Leiter, Samuel L. (ed.), *Shakespeare Around the Globe. A Guide to Notable Postwar Revivals*, New York: Greenwood Press, 1986.

Macpherson, Rod, in 'Shakespeare on the Saskatchewan', *Canadian Theatre Review*, 54 (1988): 29.

McCullough, Christopher, Review of Barton (1961) in Leiter, *Shakespeare Around the Globe*: 668–9.

McDonald, Jan, '*The Taming of the Shrew* at the Haymarket Theatre, 1844 and 1847' in *Essays on Nineteenth-Century British Theatre*, ed. Kenneth Richards and Peter Thomson, London: Methuen, 1971: 155–70.

Macdonald [usually spelled McDonald], Jan, ' "An Unholy Alliance": William Poel, Martin Harvey and *The Taming of the Shrew*', *Theatre Notebook* 36 (1982): 64–72.

McKernan, Luke and Terris, Olwen (eds.), *Walking Shadows: Shakespeare in the National Film and Television Archives*, London: BFI Publishing, 1994.

McLuskie, Kate, 'Feminist Deconstruction: the example of Shakespeare's *Taming of the Shrew*, *Red Letters* 12 (1982): 33–40.

Marcus, Leah, *Unediting the Renaissance: Shakespeare, Marlowe, Milton*, London: Routledge, 1996.

Margarida, Alice, 'Two "Shrews": Productions by Lunt/Fontanne (1935) and H. K. Ayliff (1927)', *The Drama Review* 25 (2) (Summer 1981): 87–100.

Marlowe, Christopher, *1 Tamburlaine*, ed. J. W. Harper, London: A&C Black, 1971, fifth impression 1992.

Marowitz, Charles, *The Marowitz Shakespeare*, London: Marion Boyars, 1978.

Marshall, Norman, *The Producer and the Play*, London: Macdonald, 1957, 2nd edition 1962.

Martin-Harvey, John (formerly Martin Harvey), *The Autobiography of Sir John Martin-Harvey*, London: Sampson Low, Marston, 1933.

Mazer, Cary, *Shakespeare Refashioned: Elizabethan Plays on Edwardian Stages*, Ann Arbor: UMI Research Press, 1981.

Miller, Stephen Roy, 'A Critical, Old-Spelling Edition of *The Taming of A Shrew*, 1594', PhD thesis, London, 1993.

(ed.), *The Taming of A Shrew: The 1594 Quarto*, Cambridge University Press, 1998.

Moore, William H., 'An Allusion in 1593 to *The Taming of the Shrew*', *Shakespeare Quarterly* 15 (1964): 55–60.

Morrison, Michael A., *John Barrymore, Shakespearean Actor*, Cambridge University Press, 1997.

O'Connor, Garry, *The Secret Woman: A Life of Peggy Ashcroft*, revised and updated, London: Orion Books, 1998.

Odell, G. C. D., *Annals of the New York Stage*, 15 vols., New York: Columbia University Press, 1927–49.

Shakespeare from Betterton to Irving, 2 vols., London: Constable, 1921.

Oldfield, Sybil, *Spinsters of This Parish: The life and times of F. M. Mayor and Mary Sheepshanks*, London: Virago, 1984.

Pepys, Samuel, *The Diary of Samuel Pepys*, ed. Robert Latham and William Matthews, Berkeley: University of California Press, 1970.

Pickford, Mary, *Sunshine and Shadow*, London: William Heinemann, 1956.

Pilkington, Ace G., 'Zeffirelli's Shakespeare' in *Shakespeare and the Moving Image: The Plays on Film and Television*, ed. Anthony Davies and Stanley Wells, Cambridge University Press, 1994.

Planché, J. R., *Recollections and Reflections: A Professional Autobiography*, London: Sampson Low, Marston and Company, 1901

Ranald, Margaret Loftus, 'The Performance of Feminism in *The Taming of the Shrew*', *Theatre Research International* 19 (1994): 214–25.

Rothwell, Kenneth S., *A History of Shakespeare on Screen: A Century of Film and Television*, Cambridge University Press, 1999.

Rothwell, Kenneth S., and Melzer, Annabelle Henkin, *Shakespeare on Screen: An International Filmography and Videography*, London: Mansell, 1990.

Russell, Charles Edward, *Julia Marlowe: Her Life and Art*, New York: D. Appleton, 1926.

Rutter, Carol, *Clamorous Voices: Shakespeare's Women Today*, London: The Women's Press, 1988.

Sadie, Stanley (ed.), *The New Grove Dictionary of Music and Musicians*, 20 vols., London: Macmillan, 1980.

Schafer, Elizabeth, *MsDirecting Shakespeare: Women Direct Shakespeare*, London: The Women's Press, 1998.

Schmidgall, Gary, *Shakespeare and Opera*, Oxford University Press, 1990.

Shakespeare, William, *The Taming of the Shrew*:
  ed. and adapted as a playing edition by Robert Atkins, London: Samuel French, 1925.
  ed. Augustin Daly, arranged to be played in Four Acts, New York: privately printed, 1887.
  ed. Augustin Daly, New York: Centenary edition, privately printed, 13 April 1887.
  ed. Brian Morris, London: Methuen, 1981.
  ed. H. J. Oliver, Oxford: Clarendon Press, 1982.
  ed. John Wilders, London: BBC, 1980.

Shattuck, Charles, *The Shakespeare Promptbooks: A Descriptive Catalogue*, Urbana: University of Illinois Press, 1965.
  Shakespeare on the American Stage: From Booth and Barrett to Sothern and Marlowe, Washington: Folger Shakespeare Library, 1987.
  (ed.), *John Philip Kemble Promptbooks*, Charlottesville: University of Virginia Press, 1974.

Siberry, Michael, 'Petruccio in *The Taming of the Shrew*', *Players of Shakespeare 4*, Cambridge University Press, 1998.

Speaight, Robert, *Shakespeare on the Stage: An Illustrated History of Shakespearian Performance*, London: Collins, 1973.

Spencer, Hazelton, *Shakespeare Improved: The Restoration Versions in Quarto and on the Stage*, Cambridge, Mass.: Harvard University Press, 1927.

Spewack, Bella and Samuel, *Kiss Me, Kate*, *Theatre Arts*, January 1955.

Sprague, A. C., *Shakespeare and the Actors: The Stage Business in His Plays (1660–1905)*, Cambridge, Mass.: Harvard University Press, 1945.

Sprague, A. C. and Trewin, J. C., *Shakespeare's Plays Today: Some Customs and Conventions of the Stage*, London: Sidgwick and Jackson, 1970.

Styan, J. L., *The Shakespeare Revolution: Criticism and Performance in the Twentieth Century*, Cambridge University Press, 1977.

Summers, Montague, *Shakespeare Adaptations*, London: Jonathan Cape, 1922.

Thorn-Drury, G., *Some Seventeenth Century Allusions to Shakespeare and his Works not hitherto collected*, London, 1920.

Trewin, J. C., *Shakespeare on the English Stage 1900–1964, A Survey of Productions*, London: Barrie and Rockliff, 1964.

Van Lennep, W. et al., *The London Stage 1660–1800*, 11 vols., Carbondale: Southern Illinois University Press, 1960–8.

Wearing, J. P., *The London Stage 1890–1899: A Calendar of Plays and Players*, 2 vols., Metuchen, N. J. and London: Scarecrow Press, 1976; *1900–1959*, 6 vols., Metuchen, N. J. and London: Scarecrow Press, 1981–93.

Weiss, Alfred, 'The Edinburgh Festival, 1987', *Shakespeare Quarterly* 39 (1988): 79–89.

Wells, Stanley, 'A prosaic transformation', *TLS* 31 October 1980: 1229.

Wells, Stanley and Taylor, Gary, 'No Shrew, A Shrew, and The Shrew: Internal Revision in *The Taming of the Shrew*' in *Shakespeare: Text, Language, Criticism: Essays in Honour of Marvin Spevack*, ed. Bernhard Fabian and Kurt Tetzeli von Rosador, Hildesheim: Olms-Weidmann, 1987, 351–70.

Williams, Harcourt, *Old Vic Saga*, London: Winchester Publications, 1949.

Williamson, Audrey, *Old Vic Drama: A Twelve Years' Study of Plays and Players*, London: Rockliff, 1948.

Old Vic Drama 2, London: Rockliff, 1957.

Winter, William, *Ada Rehan: A Study*, New York: privately printed for Augustin Daly, 1898.

Shakespeare on the Stage, second series, New York: Yard, 1915.

Worsdale, James, *A Cure for a Scold*, London: Cornmarket Press, 1969.

Zeffirelli, Franco, *Franco Zeffirelli: The Autobiography*, London: Arena Books, 1987.

Zolotow, Maurice, *Stagestruck: The Romance of Alfred Lunt and Lynn Fontanne*, New York: Harcourt, Brace and World, 1964.

VIDEOS

Kiss Me, Petruchio directed by Christopher Dixon, broadcast 1981 (excerpts of Leach 1978).

INDEX